TOP
STOCKS

THIRTY-SECOND EDITION

2026

MARTIN ROTH'S

BEST-SELLING ANNUAL

TOP STOCKS

THIRTY-SECOND EDITION

2026

A SHAREBUYER'S GUIDE TO

LEADING AUSTRALIAN COMPANIES

WILEY

This thirty-second edition first published in 2026 by John Wiley & Sons Australia, Ltd
First edition published as *Top Stocks* by Wrightbooks in 1995
New edition published annually

The right of Martin Roth to be identified as the author of *Top Stocks 2026* has been asserted in accordance
with law.

ISBN: 978-1-394-32876-5

A catalogue record for this
book is available from the
National Library of Australia

Registered Office
John Wiley & Sons Australia, Ltd. Level 4, 600 Bourke Street, Melbourne, VIC 3000, Australia

For details of our global editorial offices, customer services, and more information about Wiley products
visit us at www.wiley.com.

Wiley also publishes its books in a variety of electronic formats and by print-on-demand. Some content that
appears in standard print versions of this book may not be available in other formats.

Cover and part opener image: © Imsuniyah/Adobe Stock
Cover design by Wiley
Charts created using MetaStock

The author and publisher would like to thank Alan Hull (author of *Active Investing*, Revised Edition,
Trade My Way and *Invest My Way*; www.alanhull.com) for generating the five-year share-price charts.

Set in Adobe Garamond Pro 10/12pt by Straive, Chennai, India

Contents

PART I: the companies

PART II: the tables

Preface

In the midst of geopolitical turmoil and economic uncertainty, stock markets in many countries have been setting new records. Investors are excited. Many are also nervous. Can the good times continue? Is a crash looming? (Might it already have occurred by the time this book is published?)

As I have noted in earlier editions, *Top Stocks* is written for times like these, when the future is cloudy (which is most of the time). Because, no matter the direction of the stock market, numerous fine companies continue to emerge in Australia, offering investors great prospects. *Top Stocks 2026* showcases many such companies.

They are often smaller to medium-sized corporations. Some will be unfamiliar to investors. But all meet the stringent *Top Stocks* criteria, including solid profits and moderate debt levels.

Of course, such stocks could not withstand the tidal wave of a substantial market sell-off. They too would be affected. But they should be affected less. And if they are good companies they will continue to thrive and to pay dividends. And they will bounce back faster than many others.

This is the 32nd annual edition of *Top Stocks*, and guiding investors towards value stocks has been one of the paramount aims of the book from the very first edition. Indeed, one of the rationales for the book has always been to highlight the truth that Australia boasts many excellent companies that enjoy high profits — and growing profits — regardless of the direction of the markets. Despite the title, *Top Stocks* is actually a book about companies.

Right from the start it has been an attempt to help investors find the best public companies in Australia, using strict criteria. These criteria are explained fully later. But, in essence, all companies in the book must have been publicly listed for at least five years and must have been making a profit and paying a dividend for each of those five years. They must also meet tough benchmarks of profitability and debt levels. It is completely objective. The author's own personal views count for nothing. In addition, share prices have never been relevant.

Of the 97 companies in *Top Stocks 2026* — 13 more than in last year's edition — fully 66 reported a higher after-tax profit in the latest financial year (June 2025 for most of them), including two that achieved triple-digit profit growth and a further 43 with double-digit growth. In addition, 65 achieved higher earnings per share and 66 paid a higher dividend.

And though, as noted, share prices are not relevant for selection to *Top Stocks*, 74 of the companies in the book have provided investor returns — share price appreciation plus dividends — of an average of at least 10 per cent per year over a five-year period.

Energy transition

Each year I try to identify trends among the companies of *Top Stocks*. Certainly one of the biggest recently has been the rush towards decarbonisation and renewable energy. A growing number of companies are trying to align themselves with this movement.

Some examples from *Top Stocks*:

- AGL Energy is investing heavily in renewable energy assets.
- Australian Ethical Investment invests in companies involved in green energy.
- BHP Group is restructuring its operations in order to gain greater exposure to what it believes are mega-trends of decarbonisation and electrification.
- Downer EDI is a provider of infrastructure for the energy and utilities sectors and expects to benefit from moves towards new energy sources.
- Fortescue Metals is involved in green energy projects in many countries through its Energy division.
- GenusPlus, a supplier of power and communications infrastructure, has been enjoying strong growth from its involvement in a series of renewable energy projects.
- Iluka Resources is a global leader in the mining and processing of a range of rare earth minerals that are key components for a growing number of high-tech industries.
- Lycopodium is involved in two battery recycling schemes and is also working with government and academic bodies on the development of new energy storage technologies.
- Monadelphous Group is involved in large-scale renewable energy projects through its Zenviron joint venture.
- Origin Energy manages a series of wind and solar energy developments and is also involved in battery projects for energy storage.
- PWR Holdings is working with electric car manufacturers for the supply of sophisticated cooling technology. It is also involved in developments in storage batteries for alternative energy systems.
- Rio Tinto is involved in the massive Oyu Tolgoi copper-gold mine development in Mongolia. In Argentina it has acquired the Rincon lithium project and has expressed its interest in acquiring further copper and lithium assets.

- Southern Cross Electrical Engineering expects a growing amount of work from renewable energy projects.
- Wesfarmers holds half the equity in Covalent Lithium, which realised its initial output in July 2025 and will ramp up production during the July 2026 year, with the goal of producing 50 000 tonnes annually of lithium hydroxide for use in lithium batteries.

Cars and trucks

A surprising number — more than 10 per cent — of the companies in *Top Stocks* have some kind of involvement with cars and trucks. The shares of some of these companies have been excellent long-term performers.

- Amotiv, the new name for GUD Holdings, is an important manufacturer of products for the automotive aftermarket and accessories sector.
- ARB is a prominent manufacturer of specialty automotive accessories and an international leader in specialised equipment for four-wheel-drive vehicles.
- CAR Group is the market leader in online automotive advertising.
- Insurance Australia Group is one of Australia's leading vehicle insurers, with brands that include NRMA Insurance and RACV Home and Motor Insurance.
- Lindsay Australia is a prominent trucking company.
- PWR Holdings has a particular specialty in the manufacture of cooling systems for racing car teams and high-performance automobile companies.
- Schaffer manufactures leather goods for the automobile industry through its 83 per cent–owned subsidiary Automotive Leather.
- Smartgroup has important businesses providing vehicle novated leasing and fleet management services.
- Suncorp is another of Australia's leading vehicle insurers, with brands that include AAMI, GIO, Bingle and Shannons, and in New Zealand AA Insurance.
- Super Retail Group manages the Supercheap Auto chain, the largest and most profitable of its four businesses.
- Supply Network is a leading supplier of truck and bus parts.

High-tech companies

For some years in *Top Stocks* I have been talking about the rise and rise of high-tech companies in Australia. They are generally small companies — though large enough to be in the All Ordinaries Index of Australia's 500 largest stocks — and it can sometimes be difficult for outsiders to understand just how they make their money. Thus, many investors avoid them.

But technology has infiltrated just about every facet of our lives, and the best of these companies are set to continue growing. It is worth taking the time to learn more about them.

Profit growth (and share price acceleration) for many of these companies has been outstanding. They are often on high price-earnings ratios, but that reflects the market's belief that high levels of growth will continue. Dividend yields can be low. Nevertheless, they should be on the radar of all serious investors. (To the following table I have added HUB24 and Netwealth, both in the financial services sector, but growing rapidly through employing innovative software for their investment platforms.)

High-tech companies

	5-year share price return (% p.a.)
Codan	24.9
Computershare	26.5
Cosol	1.0
Data#3	10.9
Hansen Technologies	10.3
HUB24	43.5
Netwealth	18.2
Objective	12.7
Technology One	38.8
WiseTech	27.9

Artificial intelligence

Allied with the high-tech theme is artificial intelligence. This has become a huge theme in the US. Many of the companies in this book are working to incorporate AI technology into their operations. But it is probably too early to judge whether such moves will boost profits sufficiently to move the share price. It is perhaps worth noting the comment of Harvey Norman chairman Gerry Harvey, after announcing the June 2025 financial results, that his company is a big player in AI and could be a big, big beneficiary.

Defence

Rising geopolitical tensions and pressure from the US government are motivating many countries, including Australia, to raise defence spending. Several companies in *Top Stocks* could be beneficiaries:

- Bisalloy Steel Group is the only supplier of armour plate to the Australian army for land vehicles and could be a significant beneficiary of AUKUS-related plans for the construction of Australian nuclear submarines.
- Codan has a fast-growing international business providing high-frequency communication equipment for military applications.
- Downer EDI is a provider of infrastructure assets in many sectors. It expects to benefit from growing orders for defence-related projects.
- Duratec provides remediation services for steel and concrete infrastructure assets to help preserve their lives. It has delivered projects at more than 40 defence bases and envisages great potential in government plans to spend $8 billion to expand and upgrade defence infrastructure in Western Australia.

Insurance companies

This edition of *Top Stocks* contains, surprisingly, eight insurance companies (including Helia Group, which is in the financial services sector), double the number of *Top Stocks 2025*.

The others are AUB Group, Insurance Australia Group, Medibank Private, NIB Holdings, QBE Insurance Group, Steadfast Group and Suncorp Group.

In part, this reflects the fact that the insurance sector has been enjoying some good years. Investors must always remember that this is of course a volatile business, and a sudden, sharp rise in claims can wipe out a big chunk of profit.

More protection for investors is offered by the two insurance brokers in the book, AUB and Steadfast, both of whom are making some interesting moves abroad. The two health insurers, NIB and Medibank, are beneficiaries of a growing and ageing population.

Small companies

A particular attraction of *Top Stocks* is the manner in which the book places the spotlight on smaller, emerging companies, many of which have just ascended into the rankings of the top 500 stocks. Some of these companies continue to rise, offering solid gains to astute investors.

A special example is the medical imaging software company Pro Medicus. It entered *Top Stocks 2006* at a share price of $1.15 and a market capitalisation of $108.5 million. It appears in this latest edition of the book at a price of $298.23 and a market capitalisation of $31.2 billion (and a price/earnings ratio of 270.4!).

Another example is Codan, a technology company with a specialty in several niche products. It entered *Top Stocks 2016* at a price of $0.89. In this latest edition it is priced at $30.77.

Supply Network is a provider of truck and bus parts for transport companies, with operations throughout Australia and New Zealand. It entered the book only in *Top Stocks 2020* at a price of $3.99. It appears in *Top Stocks 2026* at a price of $35.48.

Software developer Technology One entered *Top Stocks 2005* at a price of $0.63. In this latest edition it is $38.14.

Here are some of the smaller companies that are appearing in *Top Stocks* for the first time:

- Bisalloy Steel Group is Australia's only manufacturer of the high-performance steel needed for heavy equipment in the mining industry and for defence applications.
- Duratec is a leader in the provision of remediation services aimed especially at extending the life of steel and concrete infrastructure.
- GenusPlus Group is a prominent nationwide supplier of power and communications infrastructure.

- Ive Group is a leading diversified marketing and print communications company serving many of Australia's blue-chip corporations.
- XRF Scientific is a prominent global supplier of precision scientific testing equipment and chemicals for the purpose of preparing samples for analysis.

Who is *Top Stocks* written for?

Top Stocks is written for all those investors wishing to exercise a degree of control over their portfolios. It is for those just starting out, as well as for those with plenty of experience but who still feel the need for some guidance through the thickets of more than 2000 listed stocks.

It is not a how-to book. It does not give step-by-step instructions to 'winning' in the stock market. Rather, it is an independent and objective evaluation of leading companies, based on rigid criteria, with the intention of yielding a large selection of stocks that can become the starting point for investors wishing to do their own research.

A large amount of information is presented on each company, and another key feature of the book is that the data is presented in a common format, to allow readers to make easy comparisons between companies.

It is necessarily a conservative book. All stocks must have been listed for five years even to be considered for inclusion. It is especially suited for those seeking out value stocks for longer-term investment.

Yet, perhaps ironically, the book is also being used by short-term traders seeking a goodly selection of financially sound and reliable companies whose shares they can trade.

In addition, there are many regular readers who buy the book each year, and to them in particular I express my thanks.

What are the entry criteria?

The criteria for inclusion in *Top Stocks* are strict:

- All companies must be included in the All Ordinaries Index, which comprises Australia's 500 largest stocks (out of more than 2000). The reason for excluding smaller companies is that there is often little investor information available on them and some are so thinly traded as to be almost illiquid. In fact, the 500 All Ordinaries companies comprise, by market capitalisation, more than 95 per cent of the entire market.
- It is necessary that all companies be publicly listed since at least the end of 2020, and have a five-year record of profits and dividend payments, each year.
- All companies are required to post a return-on-equity ratio of at least 10 per cent in their latest financial year.
- No company should have a debt-to-equity ratio of more than 70 per cent.

- It must be stressed that share price performance is NOT one of the criteria for inclusion in this book. The purpose is to select companies with good profits and a strong balance sheet. These may not offer the spectacular share-price returns of a high-tech start-up or a promising rare earths miner, but they should also present less risk.
- There are several notable exclusions. Listed managed investments are out, as these mainly buy other shares or investments. Examples are Australian Foundation Investment Company and all the real estate investment trusts.
- A further exclusion are the foreign-registered stocks listed on the ASX. There is sometimes a lack of information available about such companies. In addition, their stock prices tend to move on events and trends in their home countries, making it difficult at times for local investors to follow them.

It is surely a tribute to the strength and resilience of Australian corporations that, once again, despite the volatility of recent years, so many companies have qualified for the book.

Changes to this edition

A total of 10 companies from *Top Stocks 2025* have been omitted from this new edition.

Two were in the process of probably being taken over as this book was published:

- Johns Lyng Group
- Gold Road Resources

Two more saw their debt-to-equity ratio rise above the 70 per cent limit for this book:

- Acrow
- Woolworths Group

The remaining six excluded companies had return-on-equity ratios that fell below the required 10 per cent:

- ANZ Group Holdings
- Elders
- Grange Resources
- Platinum Asset Management
- Reece
- Santos

There are 23 new companies in this book (although 10 of them have appeared in earlier editions of the book, but were not in *Top Stocks 2025*).

The new companies in this book are:

- AUB Group
- Beach Energy
- Bisalloy Steel Group*
- Capral*

- Cedar Woods Properties
- Cosol*
- Downer EDI
- Duratec*
- GenusPlus Group*
- GR Engineering Services*
- Hansen Technologies
- Harvey Norman Holdings
- Helia Group*
- Horizon Oil*
- HUB24*
- Ive Group*
- New Hope
- Northern Star Resources
- QBE Insurance Group
- Shaver Shop Group*
- Suncorp Group
- Universal Store Holdings*
- XRF Scientific*

* Companies that have not appeared in any previous edition of *Top Stocks*.

Appearing in every edition of *Top Stocks*

As I have noted, this is the 32nd edition of *Top Stocks*. Just one company has appeared in every edition — Commonwealth Bank of Australia.

Commonwealth Bank entered the original edition of the book in 1995 at a share price of $9.17 and a market capitalisation of around $11 billion. It is in the latest edition at a share price of $168.14 — having reached $192 — and a market capitalisation of more than $280 billion.

In fact, such has been its growth that it has now become the largest company in the book (and also on the ASX) by market capitalisation, overtaking BHP, which held that title in most previous editions of the book.

Once again it is my hope that *Top Stocks* will serve you well.

Martin Roth
Melbourne
September 2025

Introduction

The 97 companies in this book have been placed as much as possible into a common format for ease of comparison. Please study the following explanations in order to get as much as possible from the large amount of data.

The tables have been made as concise as possible, though they repay careful study, as they contain large amounts of information.

Note that the tables for the banks have been arranged a little differently from the others. Details of these are given later in this Introduction.

Head
At the head of each entry is the company name, with its three-letter ASX code and the website address.

Share-price chart
Under the company name is a long-term share-price chart, to September 2025, provided by Alan Hull (www.alanhull.com), author of *Invest My Way*, *Trade My Way* and *Active Investing*.

Small table
Under the share-price chart is a small table with the following data.

Sector
This is the company's sector as designated by the ASX. These sectors are based on the Global Industry Classification Standard — developed by S&P Dow Jones Indices and Morgan Stanley Capital International — which aim to standardise global industry sectors. You can learn more about these at the ASX website.

Share price
This is the closing price on 5 September 2025. Also included are the 12-month high and low prices, as of the same date.

Market capitalisation

This is the size of the company, as determined by the stock market. It is the share price multiplied by the number of shares in issue. All companies in this book must be in the All Ordinaries Index, which comprises Australia's 500 largest stocks, as measured by market capitalisation.

Price/earnings ratio

The price/earnings ratio (PER) is one of the most popular measures of whether a share is cheap or expensive. It is calculated by dividing the share price — in this case the closing price for 5 September 2025 — by the earnings per share figure. Obviously the share price is continually changing, so the PER figures in this book are for guidance only.

Dividend yield

This is the latest full-year dividend expressed as a percentage of the share price. Like the price/earnings ratio, it changes as the share price moves. It is a useful figure, especially for investors who are buying shares for income, as it allows you to compare this income with alternative investments, such as a bank term deposit or a rental property.

Price-to-NTA-per-share ratio

The NTA-per-share figure expresses the worth of a company's net tangible assets — that is, its assets minus its liabilities and intangible assets — for each share of the company. The price-to-NTA-per-share ratio relates this figure to the share price.

A ratio of one means that the company is valued exactly according to the value of its assets. A ratio below one suggests that the shares are a bargain, though usually there is a good reason for this. Profits are more important than assets.

Some companies in this book have a negative NTA-per-share figure — as a result of having intangible assets valued at more than their net assets — and a price-to-NTA-per-share ratio cannot be calculated.

See Table M, in the second part of this book, for a little more detail on this ratio.

Five-year share price return

The five-year share price return is a single percentage figure that shows how much an investor has earned from a stock over the five years to September 2025. It includes both the change in the share price and all dividends received, and expresses the result as a compounded annual rate of return.

Dividend reinvestment plan

A dividend reinvestment plan (DRP) allows shareholders to receive additional shares in their company in place of the dividend. Usually — though not always — these shares are provided at a small discount to the prevailing price, which can make them quite attractive. And of course no broking fees apply.

Many large companies offer such plans. However, they come and go. When a company needs finance it may introduce a DRP. When its financing requirements become less pressing it may withdraw it. Some companies that have a DRP in place may decide to deactivate it for a time.

The information in this book is based on up-to-date information from the companies. But if you are investing in a particular company in expectations of a DRP be sure to check that it is still on offer. The company's own website will often provide this information.

Company commentary

Each commentary begins with a brief introduction to the company and its activities. Then follow the highlights of its latest business results. For the majority of the companies these are their June 2025 results, which were issued during July and August 2025. Finally, there is a section on the outlook for the company.

Main table

Here is what you can find in the main table.

Revenues

These are the company's revenues from its business activities, generally the sale of products or services. However, it does not usually include additional income from such sources as investments, bank interest or the sale of assets. If the information is available, the revenues figure has been broken down into the major product areas.

As much as possible, the figures are for continuing businesses. When a company sells a part of its operations the financial results for the sold activities are separated from the core results and reported as a separate item. This can mean that the previous year's results are restated — also excluding the sold business — to make year-on-year comparisons more valid.

Earnings before interest and taxation

Earnings before interest and taxation (EBIT) is the firm's profit from its operations before the payment of interest and tax. This figure is often used by analysts examining a company. The reason is that some companies have borrowed extensively to finance their activities, while others have opted for alternative means. By expressing profits before interest payments it is possible to compare the performance of these companies more precisely.

Note that the EBIT figures in this book are calculated by adding together the company's pre-tax profit and its interest payments — both figures that are given in company financial reporting. Some analysts prefer a net interest payments amount — that is, interest payments minus interest receipts. This is not done for this book.

You will also find many companies using a measure called EBITDA, which is earnings before interest, taxation, depreciation and amortisation.

EBIT margin

This is the company's EBIT expressed as a percentage of its revenues. It is a gauge of a company's efficiency. A high EBIT margin suggests that a company is achieving success in keeping its costs low.

Gross margin

The gross margin is the company's gross profit as a percentage of its sales. The gross profit is the amount left over after deducting from a company's sales figure its cost of sales: that is, its manufacturing costs or, for a retailer, the cost of purchasing the goods it sells. The cost of goods sold figure does not usually include marketing or administration costs.

As there are different ways of calculating the cost of goods sold figure, this ratio is better used for year-to-year comparisons of a single company's efficiency, rather than in comparing one company with another.

Many companies do not present a cost of goods sold figure, so a gross margin ratio is not given for every stock in this book.

The revenues for some companies include a mix of sales and services. Where a breakdown is possible, the gross profit figure will relate to sales only.

Profit before tax/profit after tax

The profit before tax figure is simply the EBIT figure minus interest payments. The profit after tax figure is, of course, the company's profit after the payment of tax and also after the deduction of minority interests. Minority interests are that part of a company's profit that is claimed by outside interests, usually the other shareholders in a subsidiary that is not fully owned by the company. Many companies do not have any minority interests, and for those that do it is generally a tiny figure.

As much as possible, I have adjusted the profit figures to exclude non-recurring profits and losses, which are often referred to as significant items. It is for this reason that the profit figures in *Top Stocks* sometimes differ from those in the financial media, where profit figures often include significant items.

Significant items are those that have an abnormal impact on profits, even though they happen in the normal course of the company's operations. Examples are the profit from the sale of a business, the expenses of a business restructuring, the write-down of an asset, an inventory write-down or a bad-debt loss. These are all generally one-off profits or expenses.

Significant items are controversial. It is often a matter of subjective judgement as to what is included and what excluded. After analysing the accounts of hundreds of companies while writing the various editions of this book, it is clear that different companies use varying interpretations of what is significant.

Further, when they do report a significant item there is no consistency as to whether they use pre-tax figures or after-tax figures. Some report both, making it easy to adjust the profit figures in the tables in this book. But difficulties arise when only one figure is given for significant items.

In normal circumstances most companies do not report significant items. But investors should be aware of this issue. It sometimes causes consternation for readers of *Top Stocks* to find that a particular profit figure in this book is substantially different from that given in a media report or by some other source.

It is also worth noting my observation that a growing number of companies present what they call an underlying profit (called a cash profit for the banks), or even a so-called normalised profit, in addition to their reported (statutory) profit. This underlying profit will exclude not only significant items but also discontinued businesses and sometimes other related items. Where all the relevant figures are available, I have generally used these underlying figures for the tables in this book.

As already noted, when a company sells or terminates one of its businesses it will now usually report the profit or loss of that business as a separate item. It will also usually back-date its previous year's accounts, to exclude that business, so that worthwhile comparisons can be made of continuing businesses.

The tables in this book usually refer to continuing businesses only.

Earnings per share

Earnings per share is the after-tax profit divided by the number of shares. Because the profit figure is for a 12-month period the number of shares used is a weighted average of those on issue during the year. This number is provided by the company in its annual report and its results announcements.

Cashflow per share

The cashflow per share ratio tells — in theory — how much actual cash the company has generated from its operations.

In fact, the ratio in this book is not exactly a true measure of cashflow. It is simply the company's depreciation and amortisation figures for the year added to the after-tax profit, and then divided by a weighted average of the number of shares. Depreciation and amortisation are expenses that do not actually utilise cash, so can be added back to after-tax profit to give a kind of indication of the company's cashflow.

By contrast, a true cashflow — including such items as newly raised capital and money received from the sale of assets — would require quite complex calculations based on the company's statement of cashflows.

However, many investors use the ratio as this book presents it, because it is easy to calculate, and it is certainly a useful guide to approximately how much funding the company has available from its operations.

Dividend

The dividend figure is the total for the year, interim and final. It does **not** include special dividends. The level of franking is also provided.

Net tangible assets per share

The NTA per share figure tells the theoretical value of the company — per share — if all assets were sold and then all liabilities paid. It is very much a theoretical figure, as there is no guarantee that corporate assets are really worth the price put on them in the balance sheet. Intangible assets such as goodwill and patent rights are excluded because of the difficulty in putting a sales price on them, and also because they may in fact not have much value if separated from the company.

Note that this book includes right of use assets as intangible assets. Not all analysts do. (A right of use asset is, essentially, a company's contractual right to use a particular asset, such as a lease for a property.)

As already noted, some companies in this book have a negative NTA, due to the fact that their intangible assets are so great, and no figure can be listed for them.

Where a company's most recent financial results are the half-year figures, these are used to calculate this ratio.

Interest cover

The interest cover ratio indicates how many times a company could make its interest payments from its pre-tax profit. A rough rule of thumb says a ratio of at least two to three times is desirable. Below that and fast-rising interest rates could imperil profits. The ratio is derived by dividing the EBIT figure by interest payments. Some companies have no borrowings, and thus no interest payments, and consequently no interest cover figure.

Return on equity

Return on equity is the after-tax profit expressed as a percentage of the shareholders' equity. In theory, it is the amount that the company's managers have made for you — the shareholder — on your money. The shareholders' equity figure used is an average for the year.

Debt-to-equity ratio

This ratio is one of the best-known measures of a company's debt levels. It is total borrowings minus the company's cash holdings, expressed as a percentage of the shareholders' equity. Some companies have no debt at all, or their cash position is greater than their level of debt, which results in a negative ratio, so no figure is listed for them.

Where a company's most recent financial results are the half-year figures, these are used to calculate this ratio.

Current ratio

The current ratio is simply the company's current assets divided by its current liabilities. Current assets are cash or assets that can, in theory, be converted quickly into cash. Current liabilities are normally those payable within a year. Thus, the current ratio measures the ability of a company to repay in a hurry its short-term debt, should the need arise. The surplus of current assets over current liabilities is referred to as the company's working capital.

Where a company's most recent financial results are the half-year figures, these are used to calculate this ratio.

Banks

The tables for the banks are somewhat different from those for most other companies. EBIT and debt-to-equity ratios have little relevance for them, as they have such high interest payments (to their customers). Other differences are examined below.

Operating income

Operating income is used instead of sales revenues. Operating income is the bank's net interest income — that is, its total interest income minus its interest expense — plus other income, such as bank fees, fund management fees and income from activities such as corporate finance and insurance.

Net interest income

Banks borrow money — that is, they accept deposits from savers — and they lend it to businesses, homebuyers and other borrowers. They charge the borrowers more than they pay those who deposit money with them, and the difference is known as net interest income.

Operating expenses

These are all the costs of running the bank. Banks have high operating expenses, and one of the keys to profit growth is cutting these expenses.

Non-interest income to total income

Banks have traditionally made most of their income from savers and from lending out money. But they are also working to diversify into new fields, and this ratio is an indication of their success.

Cost-to-income ratio

As noted, the banks have high costs — numerous branches, expensive computer systems, many staff and so on — and they are all striving to reduce these. The cost-to-income ratio expresses their expenses as a percentage of their operating income, and is one of the ratios most often used as a gauge of efficiency. The lower the ratio drops the better.

Return on assets

Banks have enormous assets, in sharp contrast to, say, a high-tech start-up whose main physical assets may be little more than a set of computers and other technological equipment. So the return on assets — the after-tax profit expressed as a percentage of the year's average total assets — is another measure of efficiency.

PART I
THE COMPANIES

Accent Group Limited

ASX code: AX1   www.accentgr.com.au

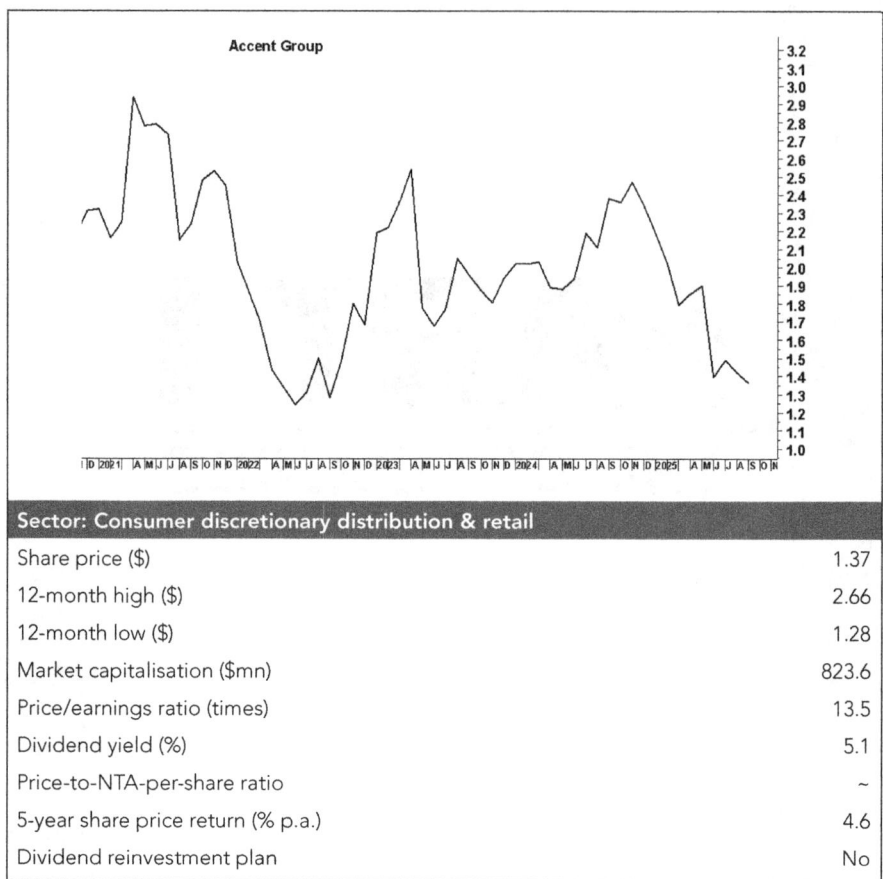

Sector: Consumer discretionary distribution & retail	
Share price ($)	1.37
12-month high ($)	2.66
12-month low ($)	1.28
Market capitalisation ($mn)	823.6
Price/earnings ratio (times)	13.5
Dividend yield (%)	5.1
Price-to-NTA-per-share ratio	~
5-year share price return (% p.a.)	4.6
Dividend reinvestment plan	No

Sydney company Accent Group, which started in 1988 as a small wholesale distributor based in New Zealand, is today a prominent footwear, apparel and accessories wholesaler and retailer. It has grown rapidly through a series of mergers and acquisitions and operates across numerous brands, with exclusive distribution rights in Australia and New Zealand for many of them. Its brands include The Athlete's Foot, Platypus Shoes, Hype DC, Skechers, Merrell, Vans, Dr. Martens, Saucony, Timberland, HOKA, Subtype, Stylerunner, Nude Lucy, Glue Store and UGG. It plans to launch the Sports Direct sporting goods retailing business in Australia.

Latest business results (June 2025, full year)

Sales edged up but profits were down for the second consecutive year. Retail sales rose 2.5 per cent, or 0.7 per cent on a like-for-like basis, with wholesale sales down 5.4 per cent. The company reported record sales and profits for the Nude Lucy brand

and strength for The Athlete's Foot, Hoka, Saucony, Merrell, Hype and Stylerunner. Conversely, slower consumer spending in the broader lifestyle footwear market adversely affected demand for the Vans, Platypus and Skechers brands. New Zealand sales, representing 11 per cent of the total, edged down. During the year the company opened 54 new stores and closed 57. The ending of its relationships with The Trybe and CAT resulted in the closure of 25 stores, and a further 14 underperforming Glue stores were closed. At June 2025 it operated 892 stores, a figure that included its online stores.

Outlook

Accent maintains an ambitious long-term growth strategy and expects profits to continue rising, although it is cautious about the near-term outlook as discretionary consumer spending continues to be hurt by cost of living pressures and economic weakness. In response, it has initiated a program aimed at delivering operational and cost efficiencies over the three years to June 2027. It is achieving particular success with the Nude Lucy and Stylerunner brands. It plans to open at least 30 new stores during the June 2026 year and forecasts high single-digit EBIT growth for the year. It sees great long-term potential in its move into the $5 billion sporting and fitness goods market through a new agreement with UK-based Frasers Group. Frasers, owner of the global Sports Direct retail chain, operates more than 1500 stores in over 30 countries. Accent plans to open 50 Sports Direct stores around Australia over six years, with the first being launched late in 2025. It sees scope for an eventual network of 100 stores.

Year to 29 June*	2024	2025
Revenues ($mn)	1448.1	1476.3
Retail (%)	89	89
Wholesale (%)	11	11
EBIT ($mn)	112.3	112.0
EBIT margin (%)	7.8	7.6
Gross margin (%)	55.8	55.5
Profit before tax ($mn)	84.4	82.0
Profit after tax ($mn)	59.5	57.7
Earnings per share (c)	10.61	10.12
Cash flow per share (c)	40.76	42.61
Dividend (c)	13	7
Percentage franked	100	100
Net tangible assets per share ($)	~	~
Interest cover (times)	4.0	3.7
Return on equity (%)	13.8	12.9
Debt-to-equity ratio (%)	29.2	21.1
Current ratio	1.0	1.1

*30 June 2024

Adairs Limited

ASX code: ADH

investors.adairs.com.au

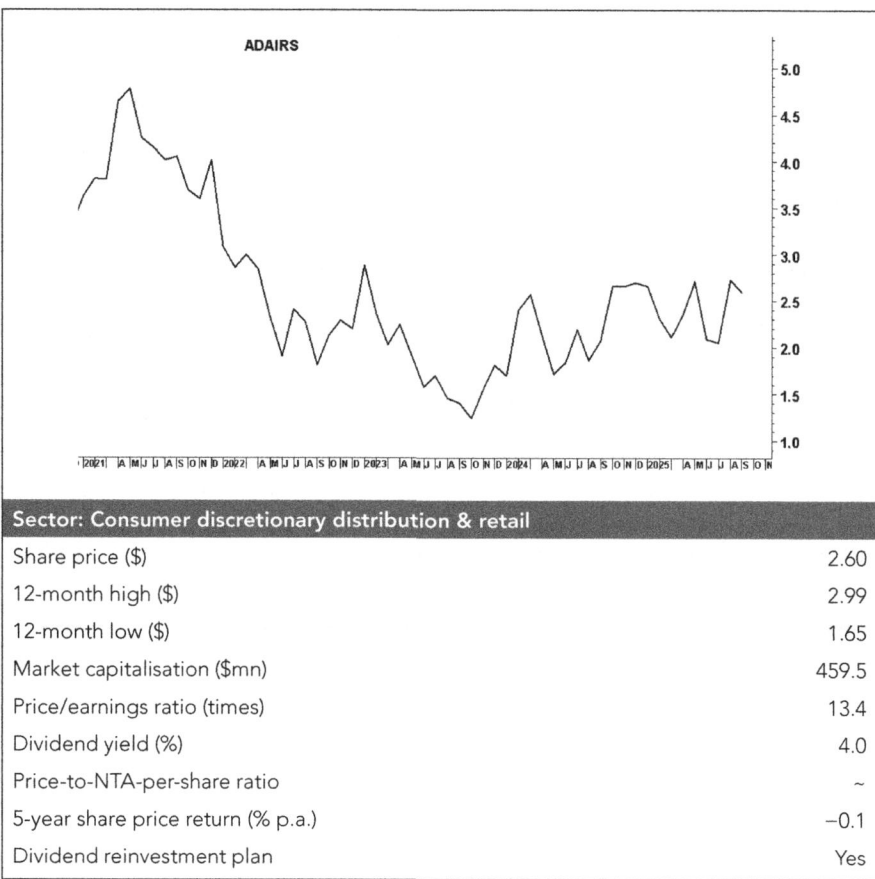

Sector: Consumer discretionary distribution & retail	
Share price ($)	2.60
12-month high ($)	2.99
12-month low ($)	1.65
Market capitalisation ($mn)	459.5
Price/earnings ratio (times)	13.4
Dividend yield (%)	4.0
Price-to-NTA-per-share ratio	~
5-year share price return (% p.a.)	−0.1
Dividend reinvestment plan	Yes

Melbourne-based home furnishings specialist Adairs dates back to 1918 and the opening of a store in Prahran, Melbourne. It has since grown into a nationwide chain of stores specialising in bed linen, bedding, towels, homewares, soft furnishings, children's furnishings and some bedroom furniture. It has also expanded to New Zealand, and it manages a flourishing online business. It operates the Brisbane-based Mocka online furniture and homewares business and the Melbourne-based furniture and bedding retailer Focus on Furniture. At June 2025 it operated 168 Adairs stores and 26 Focus stores.

Latest business results (June 2025, full year)

Revenues edged up but profits were down for the fourth straight year, as Adairs was again hurt by inflationary pressures and a slowdown in consumer spending. Adairs stores rebounded from the previous year, with sales up 9.5 per cent and strong demand for bed linen, home accessories and hard furnishings. Mocka achieved a second year of solid revenues and profit growth under a new leadership team, with sales up 14.7 per cent. A strong Australian performance offset New Zealand weakness. Both Adairs and Mocka recorded double-digit gains in underlying EBIT. However, the Focus on Furniture business saw sales down 6.5 per cent and a sharp decline in profits, with mounting promotional activity insufficient to stimulate sales. A weaker Australian dollar and rising freight costs also pushed profit margins down. Note that the June 2025 year comprised 52 weeks, compared to 53 weeks for June 2024.

Outlook

Adairs manages popular brands with high levels of customer recognition and loyalty. With an addressable Australian home furnishings market of some $12 billion it sees solid scope for expansion. It is launching a new strategic plan, Vision 2030, aimed at generating sustainable growth over the coming five years. It plans a major technology upgrade of all digital systems, costing $25 million to $30 million, to be rolled out over three years to June 2028. It is also working to implement artificial intelligence technology into everyday work practices, aimed at unlocking opportunities for greater productivity. It is effecting a 10 per cent cut in the number of items at Adairs stores. It is also enhancing benefits for the 1 million members of its Linen Lover loyalty scheme, including a partnership with the Qantas Frequent Flyer program. It plans to improve Focus on Furniture by boosting product quality, offering greater choice and opening new stores, including an entry to the Western Australian market. It also plans to open its first Mocka standalone retail store.

Year to 29 June*	2024	2025
Revenues ($mn)	594.4	618.1
Adairs (%)	70	72
Focus (%)	22	19
Mocka (%)	8	9
EBIT ($mn)	66.9	66.7
EBIT margin (%)	11.3	10.8
Gross margin (%)	47.5	46.8
Profit before tax ($mn)	50.7	48.3
Profit after tax ($mn)	35.5	34.0
Earnings per share (c)	20.47	19.34
Cash flow per share (c)	55.25	53.46
Dividend (c)	12	10.5
Percentage franked	100	100
Net tangible assets per share ($)	~	~
Interest cover (times)	4.1	3.6
Return on equity (%)	16.7	15.2
Debt-to-equity ratio (%)	28.7	30.0
Current ratio	0.8	0.8

*30 June 2024

AGL Energy Limited

ASX code: AGL   www.agl.com.au

Sector: Utilities	
Share price ($)	8.23
12-month high ($)	12.20
12-month low ($)	8.03
Market capitalisation ($mn)	5536.7
Price/earnings ratio (times)	8.7
Dividend yield (%)	5.8
Price-to-NTA-per-share ratio	3.7
5-year share price return (% p.a.)	−6.6
Dividend reinvestment plan	No

Sydney-based power generator and supplier AGL Energy is one of Australia's oldest companies, founded in 1837 as Australian Gas Light. Having closed the Liddell black coal power plant in New South Wales in 2023, it now operates three major coal- and gas-fired power stations — the Bayswater black coal power plant in New South Wales, the Loy Yang brown coal mine and power plant in Victoria and the Torrens gas power plant in South Australia. Its fast-growing portfolio of renewable assets includes wind power generation in South Australia, Queensland, New South Wales and Victoria; hydro-electric power generation in Victoria and New South Wales; and solar power in New South Wales. Through its wholesale and retail businesses AGL supplies electricity and gas to more than four million business and residential customers in most states of Australia. It also maintains pool generation sales — electricity sold into the National Electricity Market. In addition, it operates a small telecommunications business.

Latest business results (June 2025, full year)

Lower wholesale electricity prices sent underlying profits down, with the result also affected by higher depreciation charges and the company's decision to limit price increases to its customers. Total electricity customer sales volumes actually fell by 3 per cent from the previous year, with higher residential demand more than offset by declines in business and wholesale volumes. Gas sales volumes edged down 1 per cent. Electricity and gas customer numbers remained stable at 4.1 million, with 380 000 telecommunications customers, up 10 per cent. The company also reported a series of non-cash significant items totalling $596 million, and at the statutory level it recorded a loss.

Outlook

AGL is investing heavily in renewable energy projects as it works towards the closure of the Bayswater power station by 2033 and the Loy Yang A power station by 2035. Its development pipeline of renewable assets has grown to 9.6 gigawatts, with a goal of 12 gigawatts of generating capacity by 2035. It sees great potential in grid-scale battery energy developments, and its target is that these should be generating at least 3 gigawatts of power by 2030. Its 50-megawatt Broken Hill battery project started commercial operations in August 2024, with the 500-megawatt battery project at the former Liddell Power Station site due to begin operations in 2026. The company's early forecast for June 2026 is for underlying EBITDA of $1.92 billion to $2.22 billion — compared to $2.01 billion in June 2025 — and an after-tax profit of $500 million to $700 million.

Year to 30 June	2024	2025
Revenues ($mn)	13 583.0	14 393.0
Electricity (%)	53	49
Generation sales to pool (%)	22	27
Gas (%)	17	16
EBIT ($mn)	1 482.0	1 229.0
EBIT margin (%)	10.9	8.5
Gross margin (%)	29.4	26.3
Profit before tax ($mn)	1 157.0	888.0
Profit after tax ($mn)	812.0	640.0
Earnings per share (c)	120.70	95.13
Cash flow per share (c)	231.74	214.49
Dividend (c)	61	48
Percentage franked	0	100
Net tangible assets per share ($)	3.46	2.22
Interest cover (times)	4.6	3.6
Return on equity (%)	15.4	12.4
Debt-to-equity ratio (%)	33.1	61.5
Current ratio	1.1	0.9

Amotiv Limited

ASX code: AOV amotiv.com

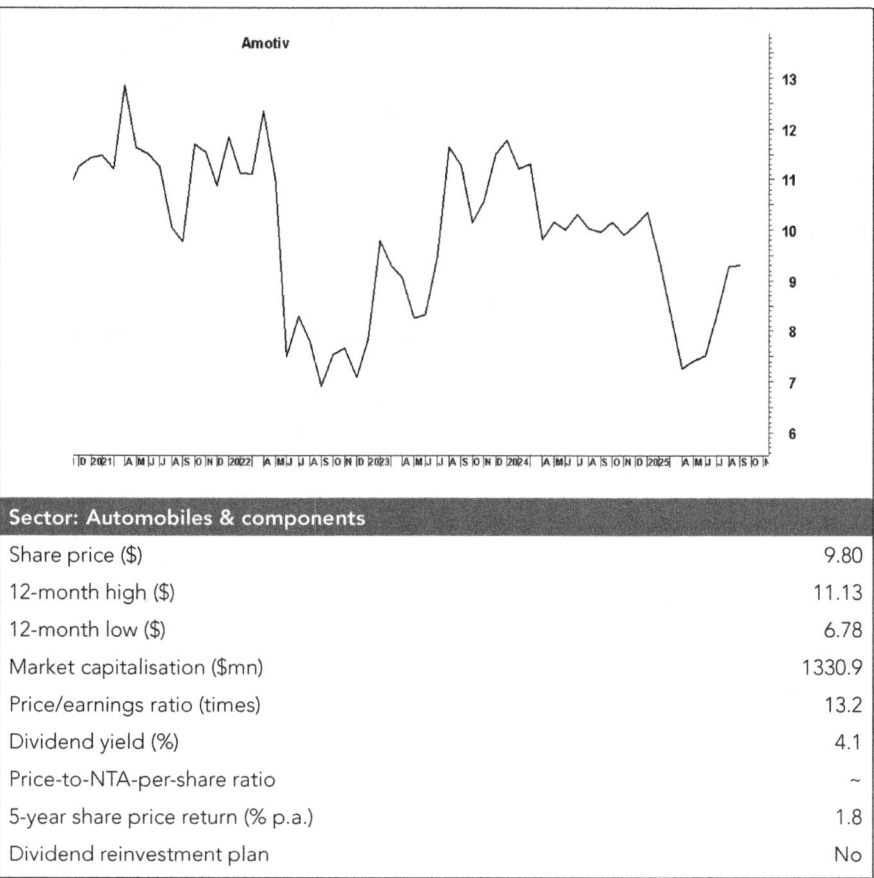

Sector: Automobiles & components	
Share price ($)	9.80
12-month high ($)	11.13
12-month low ($)	6.78
Market capitalisation ($mn)	1330.9
Price/earnings ratio (times)	13.2
Dividend yield (%)	4.1
Price-to-NTA-per-share ratio	~
5-year share price return (% p.a.)	1.8
Dividend reinvestment plan	No

Amotiv, formerly known as GUD Holdings, is based in Melbourne and was founded in 1940. Following the sale of its Davey water pumps and water treatment products business it now solely manufactures and distributes a wide range of specialist products for the automotive aftermarket and accessories sector, with a large portfolio of several dozen brands. It operates primarily in Australia and New Zealand, though with a small but growing exposure to other international markets.

Latest business results (June 2025, full year)

Revenues and profits marked time in a challenging environment for the company. The best result came from the Powertrain & Undercar division, which specialises in a variety of products that include heavy-duty filters, fuel pumps, clutches and brakes. It saw sales up 3 per cent and underlying EBITA up 6 per cent, reflecting organic growth, price increases and operational efficiencies. An acquisition boosted revenues for the

4WD Accessories & Trailering division, but profits were down, in part due to a weak caravan and recreational vehicle market. Revenues and profits were both down for the company's third division, Lighting, Power & Electrical, with a decline in demand from both original equipment manufacturers and domestic resellers. Total international sales — excluding New Zealand — rose 15 per cent to represent 10 per cent of total turnover. The company also announced a non-cash impairment charge of $190 million against its AutoPacific Group subsidiary, a specialist manufacturer of vehicle accessories and trailering equipment, and at the statutory level Amotiv recorded a loss.

Outlook

Amotiv estimates that the total addressable market for its products in Australia and New Zealand is worth some $8.5 billion. With a market share of only around 10 per cent, it sees considerable scope for growth. It also benefits as the number of cars in Australia rises, from around 21 million at present to an estimated 23 million by 2030, and with the average car age also edging up. It has initiated a three-year transformation program with some 25 projects aimed at lowering costs and boosting efficiency. This has already delivered $15 million in cost savings during the June 2025 year, with a further $10 million targeted for June 2026. One of the company's goals is to become a global leader in automotive lighting. It has acquired Swedish lighting specialist Rindab, and plans to use this company as a base for expansion throughout Europe. It has also established manufacturing facilities in South Africa, which it views as a key automotive manufacturing hub for global markets.

Year to 30 June	2024	2025
Revenues ($mn)	987.2	997.4
4WD accessories & trailering (%)	35	36
Lighting, power & electrical (%)	33	32
Powertrain & undercar (%)	32	32
EBIT ($mn)	168.5	170.7
EBIT margin (%)	17.1	17.1
Gross margin (%)	44.1	43.8
Profit before tax ($mn)	141.0	141.5
Profit after tax ($mn)	99.8	103.4
Earnings per share (c)	70.84	74.30
Cash flow per share (c)	107.33	115.18
Dividend (c)	40.5	40.5
Percentage franked	100	100
Net tangible assets per share ($)	~	~
Interest cover (times)	6.1	5.8
Return on equity (%)	10.9	12.5
Debt-to-equity ratio (%)	35.2	52.8
Current ratio	2.0	2.3

ARB Corporation Limited

ASX code: ARB

www.arb.com.au

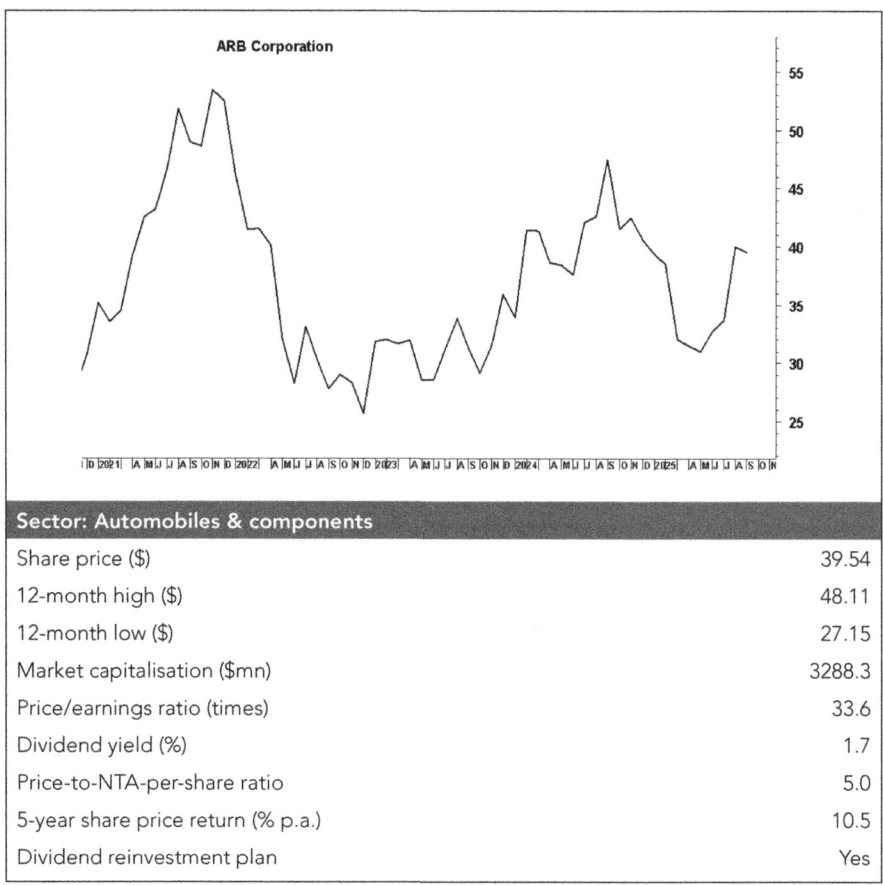

Sector: Automobiles & components	
Share price ($)	39.54
12-month high ($)	48.11
12-month low ($)	27.15
Market capitalisation ($mn)	3288.3
Price/earnings ratio (times)	33.6
Dividend yield (%)	1.7
Price-to-NTA-per-share ratio	5.0
5-year share price return (% p.a.)	10.5
Dividend reinvestment plan	Yes

Melbourne-based ARB, founded in 1975, is a prominent manufacturer of specialty automotive accessories, and an international leader in the design, production and distribution of specialised equipment for four-wheel-drive (4WD) vehicles. These include its Air Locker air-operated locking differential system, as well as a wide range of other products, including bull bars, roof racks, tow bars, canopies and the Old Man Emu range of suspension products. It operates a network of 77 ARB-brand stores throughout Australia. It has established manufacturing facilities in Thailand and it exports to more than 100 countries.

Latest business results (June 2025, full year)

Sales rose, driven by a strong export business, but profits fell. Export revenues of $267 million were up 16 per cent from the previous year, with gains across most regions. American sales were particularly strong, with growth of 21 per cent, thanks especially to new retail partnerships. Australian aftermarket sales of $403 million were slightly down on the previous year, due mainly to a fall in new pickup vehicle sales, which are a key driver of ARB's domestic business. Inflationary pressures constraining consumer spending also hurt demand. Original equipment manufacturer sales to local vehicle manufacturers were flat, having surged 40 per cent in the previous year. Nevertheless, despite the increase in total sales, a combination of rising costs, US tariffs and currency fluctuations all worked to drive down profits.

Outlook

In an environment of global economic and political volatility, ARB believes it can continue to boost sales. Branded ARB stores play a significant role in the company's domestic aftermarket business. It opened three new stores during the June 2025 year and expects to open a further three by June 2026. However, hiring and retaining specialist staff has become a problem. American demand remains strong. In October 2024 ARB acquired a 30 per cent interest in the loss-making 4WD accessories retailer Off Road Warehouse USA, and has since increased its interest to 50 per cent. Following a major restructuring, this business—operating 48 stores in nine US states—has moved into profit, and ARB is now looking to expand the store network. New Zealand has become a buoyant market, with sales rising 22.5 per cent in the June 2025 year, and ARB expects this growth to continue. It has opened a new distribution centre in Dubai, targeting the Middle East market. At June 2025 ARB had no debt and more than $69 million in cash holdings, and it is seeking strategic acquisition opportunities.

Year to 30 June	2024	2025
Revenues ($mn)	693.2	729.9
EBIT ($mn)	143.1	137.3
EBIT margin (%)	20.6	18.8
Gross margin (%)	45.8	45.4
Profit before tax ($mn)	141.4	134.9
Profit after tax ($mn)	102.7	97.5
Earnings per share (c)	124.91	117.74
Cash flow per share (c)	159.50	156.98
Dividend (c)	69	69
Percentage franked	100	100
Net tangible assets per share ($)	6.98	7.83
Interest cover (times)	84.5	58.2
Return on equity (%)	16.2	13.8
Debt-to-equity ratio (%)	~	~
Current ratio	4.1	4.1

Aristocrat Leisure Limited

ASX code: ALL   ir.aristocrat.com

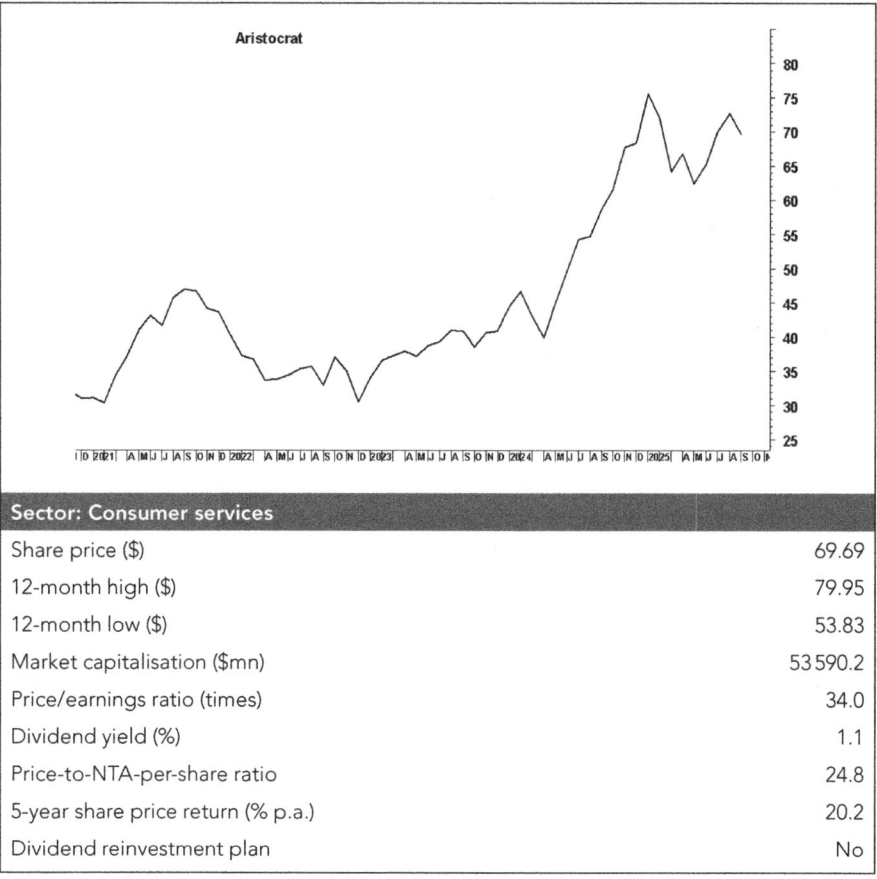

Sector: Consumer services	
Share price ($)	69.69
12-month high ($)	79.95
12-month low ($)	53.83
Market capitalisation ($mn)	53 590.2
Price/earnings ratio (times)	34.0
Dividend yield (%)	1.1
Price-to-NTA-per-share ratio	24.8
5-year share price return (% p.a.)	20.2
Dividend reinvestment plan	No

Sydney-based Aristocrat, founded in 1953, is one of the world's leading developers of hardware and software for the gaming industry. It divides its activities into three operating units. Aristocrat Gaming provides casino games to customers in more than 300 gaming jurisdictions around the world. A second unit, known as Product Madness (formerly Pixel United), is involved in the development of games for electronic mobile devices. The third unit, Aristocrat Interactive, provides customers with online gaming, known as real money gaming (RMG). The company has sold its mobile game business Plarium Global.

Latest business results (March 2025, half year)

Revenues and profits rose by single-digit amounts, with all three divisions reporting gains. Gaming revenues represent more than 60 per cent of total company turnover, and some two-thirds of company profit, and this business benefited from Aristocrat's continuing growth in the important North American market. By contrast, sales and profits in other countries were generally down. The Product Madness business, representing about 30 per cent of company income, saw profits growing at a faster pace than revenues, thanks to a strong focus on operational efficiency and an increase in direct-to-consumer sales. There was particular strength for the Lightning Link and the Heart of Vegas games. The small Aristocrat Interactive division enjoyed a large jump in revenues and profits, with notable strength in the iLottery online lottery business. Note that the results have been adjusted to reflect the sale of the Plarium Global business.

Outlook

Aristocrat enjoys a strong position in the global gaming industry, with high market shares in many regions, notably in North America. With an estimated addressable market of around US$440 billion, it sees substantial potential for growth. It has expressed a particular goal of doubling the value of the company every five years. Nevertheless, this remains a competitive business, and the company is highly dependent on a continuing stream of attractive new and enhanced products. To develop these it must recruit and retain large numbers of highly skilled creative specialists and technology experts, and this has been one of its key challenges. Consequently, its design and development budget remains high at around 11 per cent to 13 per cent of annual revenues. It sees some of the best growth prospects from the RMG sector, and has announced a target of becoming one of the world's leading gaming platforms for global online RMG. It expects its Aristocrat Interactive division to make an increasingly important contribution, with particular potential for the iLottery product.

Year to 30 September	2023	2024
Revenues ($mn)	6295.7	6603.6
EBIT ($mn)	1824.1	1890.8
EBIT margin (%)	29.0	28.6
Profit before tax ($mn)	1670.4	1726.6
Profit after tax ($mn)	1454.1	1303.4
Earnings per share (c)	222.49	204.79
Cash flow per share (c)	280.94	278.84
Dividend (c)	64	78
Percentage franked	100	46
Interest cover (times)	11.9	11.5
Return on equity (%)	22.8	20.0
Half year to 31 March	2024	2025
Revenues ($mn)	2790.9	3034.5
Profit before tax ($mn)	897.1	911.8
Profit after tax ($mn)	664.1	664.9
Earnings per share (c)	103.49	106.09
Dividend (c)	36	44
Percentage franked	100	0
Net tangible assets per share ($)	3.86	2.81
Debt-to-equity ratio (%)	~	5.9
Current ratio	3.1	1.8

ASX Limited

ASX code: ASX www.asx.com.au

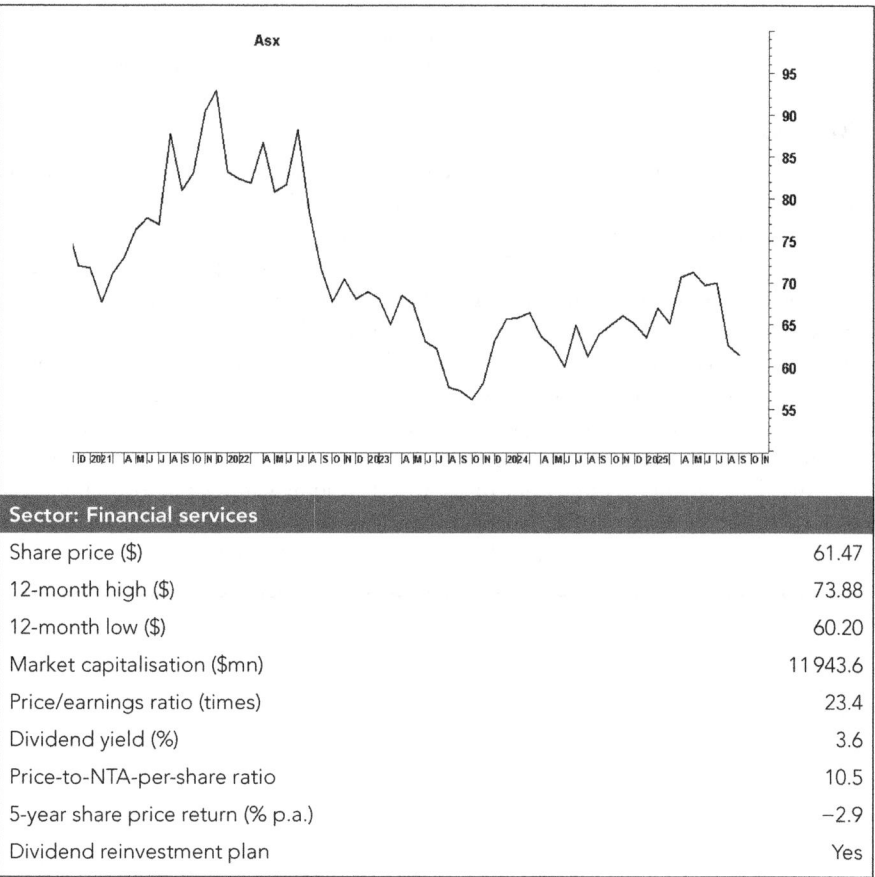

Sector: Financial services	
Share price ($)	61.47
12-month high ($)	73.88
12-month low ($)	60.20
Market capitalisation ($mn)	11 943.6
Price/earnings ratio (times)	23.4
Dividend yield (%)	3.6
Price-to-NTA-per-share ratio	10.5
5-year share price return (% p.a.)	−2.9
Dividend reinvestment plan	Yes

Sydney-based ASX (Australian Securities Exchange) was formed in 1987 through the amalgamation of six independent stock exchanges that formerly operated in the state capital cities. Each of those exchanges had a history of share trading dating back to the 19th century. Though originally a mutual organisation of stockbrokers, in 1998 ASX became a listed company, with its shares traded on its own market. It expanded in 2006 when it merged with the Sydney Futures Exchange. Today it provides primary, secondary and derivative market services, along with clearing, settlement and compliance services. It is also a provider of a range of comprehensive market data and technical services.

Latest business results (June 2025, full year)

Revenues and profits rose, with continuing weakness in the Listings division more than offset by growth in other businesses. The best result came again from the Markets division, with revenues up 10.7 per cent, thanks especially to buoyant activity in futures markets. The Technology and Data division was also strong, with revenues up 8 per cent, reflecting strong demand for equity and derivative market data. The Securities and Payments division benefited from strong debt market activity, with revenues rebounding from the previous year's decline and rising 7.4 per cent. However, the Listings division saw revenues edge down — the second consecutive decline — with reduced income from initial listings and secondary raisings. There were 69 new listings during the year, compared to 56 in the previous year, but with a significant drop in the total market capitalisation of these new companies.

Outlook

ASX's profits are highly geared to levels of market activity. The company also enjoys a degree of protection in its operations, with little effective competition for many of its businesses. Geopolitical volatility is boosting cash market activity and the company plans the launch of a series of new data products. Rising costs have in part resulted from ASX's aborted plans to replace its Clearing House Electronic Subregister System (CHESS), as well as from the necessity to boost staff numbers to meet increasingly stringent regulatory requirements. Following several failures by ASX in its operations, the Australian Securities and Investments Commission announced in June 2025 that it was appointing an expert panel to determine if ASX was effectively managing its businesses. ASX expects that this will increase its operating expenses by between $25 million and $35 million during the June 2026 year, and consequently it expects June 2026 expenses to grow by 14 per cent to 19 per cent from June 2025.

Year to 30 June	2024	2025
Revenues ($mn)	1034.3	1107.2
Markets (%)	30	32
Securities & payments (%)	25	25
Technology & data (%)	25	25
Listings (%)	20	18
EBIT ($mn)	693.8	741.9
EBIT margin (%)	67.1	67.0
Profit before tax ($mn)	681.5	719.2
Profit after tax ($mn)	474.2	510.0
Earnings per share (c)	244.85	262.89
Cash flow per share (c)	265.50	288.31
Dividend (c)	208	223.3
Percentage franked	100	100
Net tangible assets per share ($)	5.73	5.87
Interest cover (times)	56.4	32.7
Return on equity (%)	12.9	13.4
Debt-to-equity ratio (%)	~	~
Current ratio	1.1	1.1

AUB Group Limited

ASX code: AUB   www.aubgroup.com.au

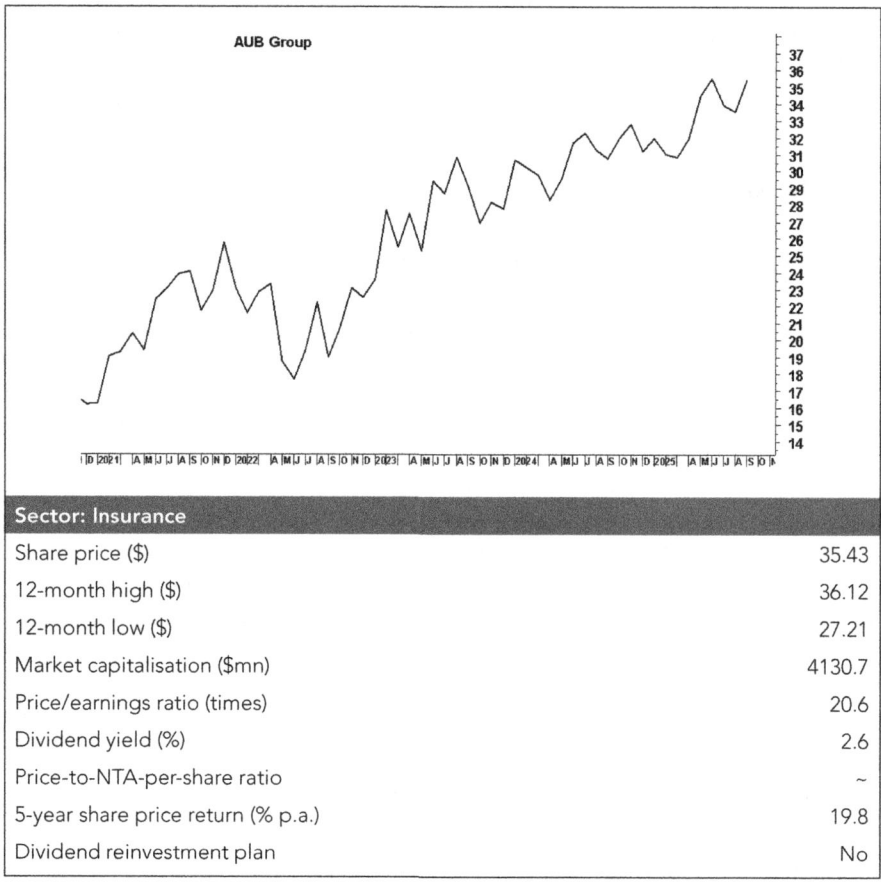

Sector: Insurance	
Share price ($)	35.43
12-month high ($)	36.12
12-month low ($)	27.21
Market capitalisation ($mn)	4130.7
Price/earnings ratio (times)	20.6
Dividend yield (%)	2.6
Price-to-NTA-per-share ratio	~
5-year share price return (% p.a.)	19.8
Dividend reinvestment plan	No

Sydney-based AUB Group, formerly known as Austbrokers Holdings, was established in 1985. It manages a network of retail and wholesale insurance brokers in Australia and New Zealand. It typically holds an equity stake of at least 50 per cent in each business, usually in partnership with the original owners. Its Agencies division creates and manages specialist insurance products. It also maintains a substantial London-based international operation that includes the Lloyd's wholesale broker Tysers.

Latest business results (June 2025, full year)

Revenues and underlying profits rose, in a good result for the company. The International division has become the company's largest, and it enjoyed both organic growth and the benefit of acquisitions. There was a significant rise in British retail premiums to £340 million, from £110 million in the previous year. The Australian Broking division also benefited from a combination of organic growth and some acquisitions, along with continued strong demand for the BizCover online insurance comparison and purchase platform. Australian Broking, though now only 31 per cent of revenues, delivered around 40 per cent of company profit. The Agencies division was particularly strong, with pre-tax profit soaring 30 per cent, in part from the July 2024 acquisition of 70 per cent of the equity of the specialist underwriting agency Pacific Indemnity. NZ revenues grew but a heavy investment in new business initiatives raised costs, and profits just edged up.

Outlook

AUB has achieved success with its model of buying a stake in an insurance broking house but, in most cases, continuing to operate it with the original owners. This has allowed the businesses to preserve their local identity and management, while benefiting from the support of a large group. The company is able to help its members develop their businesses more profitably through the provision of services that include technical support, a centralised data centre, common broking and back-office platforms, human resources and risk compliance. It regards its 2022 acquisition of British broking house Tysers as transformational, providing the foundation for significant expansion in the UK insurance market. AUB has taken equity stakes in two British broking houses, Momentum Broker Solutions and Movo Group, with the aim of replicating its Australian success in the UK. It also continues to seek out further appropriate acquisitions in both Australia and New Zealand. It expects the BizCover digital insurance platform to continue its rapid growth. AUB's early forecast is for underlying after-tax profit in the June 2026 year of $215 million to $227 million.

Year to 30 June	2024	2025
Revenues ($mn)	1009.5	1111.6
International (%)	39	40
Australian broking (%)	34	31
Agencies (%)	17	20
New Zealand broking (%)	8	8
EBIT ($mn)	341.9	375.4
EBIT margin (%)	33.9	33.8
Profit before tax ($mn)	240.0	283.9
Profit after tax ($mn)	171.0	200.2
Earnings per share (c)	156.78	171.75
Cash flow per share (c)	231.14	254.14
Dividend (c)	79	91
Percentage franked	100	100
Net tangible assets per share ($)	~	~
Interest cover (times)	3.4	4.1
Return on equity (%)	12.2	12.5
Debt-to-equity ratio (%)	15.4	28.6
Current ratio	1.2	1.1

Australian Ethical Investment Limited

ASX code: AEF   www.australianethical.com.au

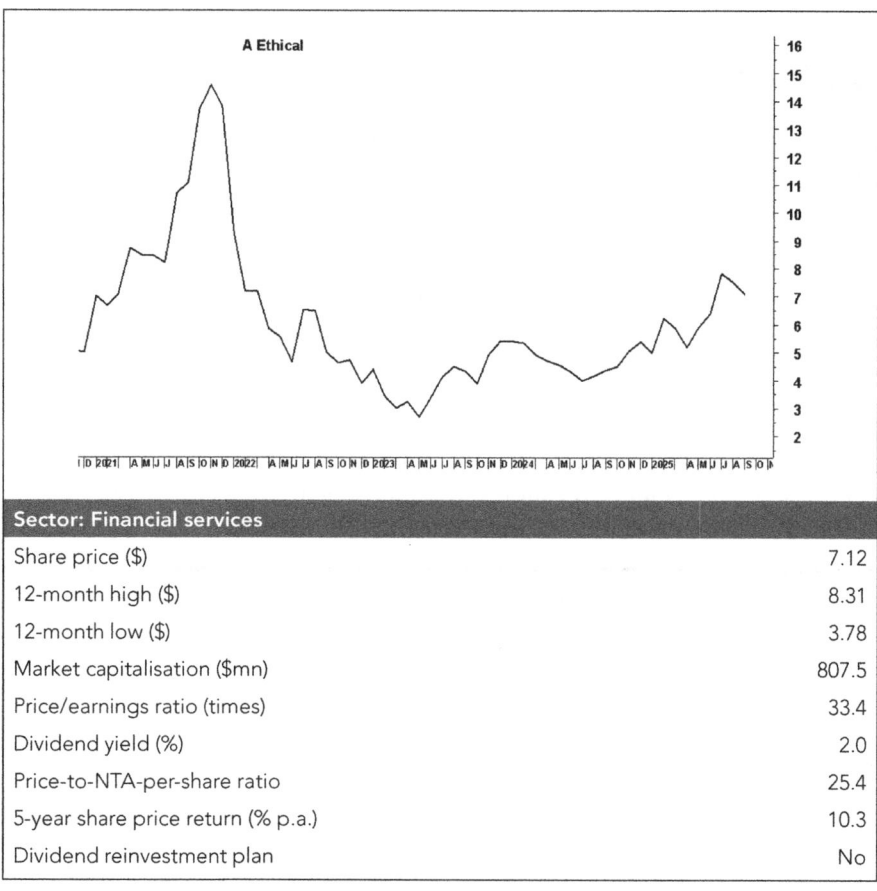

Sector: Financial services	
Share price ($)	7.12
12-month high ($)	8.31
12-month low ($)	3.78
Market capitalisation ($mn)	807.5
Price/earnings ratio (times)	33.4
Dividend yield (%)	2.0
Price-to-NTA-per-share ratio	25.4
5-year share price return (% p.a.)	10.3
Dividend reinvestment plan	No

Australian Ethical, based in Sydney, was founded in 1986. It is a wealth management company that specialises in investments in corporations that meet a set of ethical criteria. It operates a range of wholesale and retail funds — including superannuation — that incorporate Australian and international shares, emerging companies and fixed interest. In 2024 it acquired the fixed income business Altius Asset Management. The company donates up to 10 per cent of its profits to charities and activist groups through its Australian Ethical Foundation.

Latest business results (June 2025, full year)

Buoyant financial markets and the Altius acquisition combined to generate another strong result. An excellent investment performance for the year boosted funds under management by $1.05 billion. In addition, the company achieved net inflows of $0.52 billion, primarily driven by superannuation investments. The Altius acquisition added a further $1.93 billion. Consequently, funds under management at June 2025 of $13.94 billion were up 34 per cent from a year earlier. Careful cost management limited the growth in expenses and, with revenues rising at a faster pace, profit margins expanded.

Outlook

Australian Ethical is a small company but is a leader in the ethical investment movement. In a growing marketplace, with many major financial institutions launching their own similar funds, Australian Ethical has attracted attention because of its perceived independence. The company's pledge is that it seeks out positive investments that support its three pillars of people, planet and animals. Its Ethical Charter gives details of the criteria it uses for its investments, and it provides a public list of the companies in which it is prepared to invest. It is working to achieve growth and is actively seeking diversification opportunities, including appropriate acquisitions. Its $5.5 million acquisition of Altius Asset Management from Australian Unity has strengthened its capabilities in fixed income investing. It created a new operating structure from July 2025 aimed at strengthening its activities, and it has also been upgrading its technology platform and business infrastructure. It has enjoyed success in targeting the retail superannuation market, boosting both brand awareness and fund inflows, at a time where some major funds have been suffering outflows. It is looking to introduce new products, including an international equities fund. Australian Ethical expects further profit growth in the June 2026 year. Nevertheless, it remains heavily exposed to volatile financial markets, and its businesses could be hurt in any sustained downturn. At June 2025 the company had no debt and more than $18 million in cash holdings.

Year to 30 June	2024	2025
Revenues ($mn)	100.5	119.4
EBIT ($mn)	26.3	34.4
EBIT margin (%)	26.2	28.8
Profit before tax ($mn)	26.1	34.3
Profit after tax ($mn)	18.4	23.8
Earnings per share (c)	16.52	21.30
Cash flow per share (c)	17.52	22.54
Dividend (c)	9	14
Percentage franked	100	100
Net tangible assets per share ($)	0.24	0.28
Interest cover (times)	152.1	227.9
Return on equity (%)	64.8	67.4
Debt-to-equity ratio (%)	~	~
Current ratio	2.3	2.0

Beach Energy Limited

ASX code: BPT　　　　　　　　　　　　　　www.beachenergy.com.au

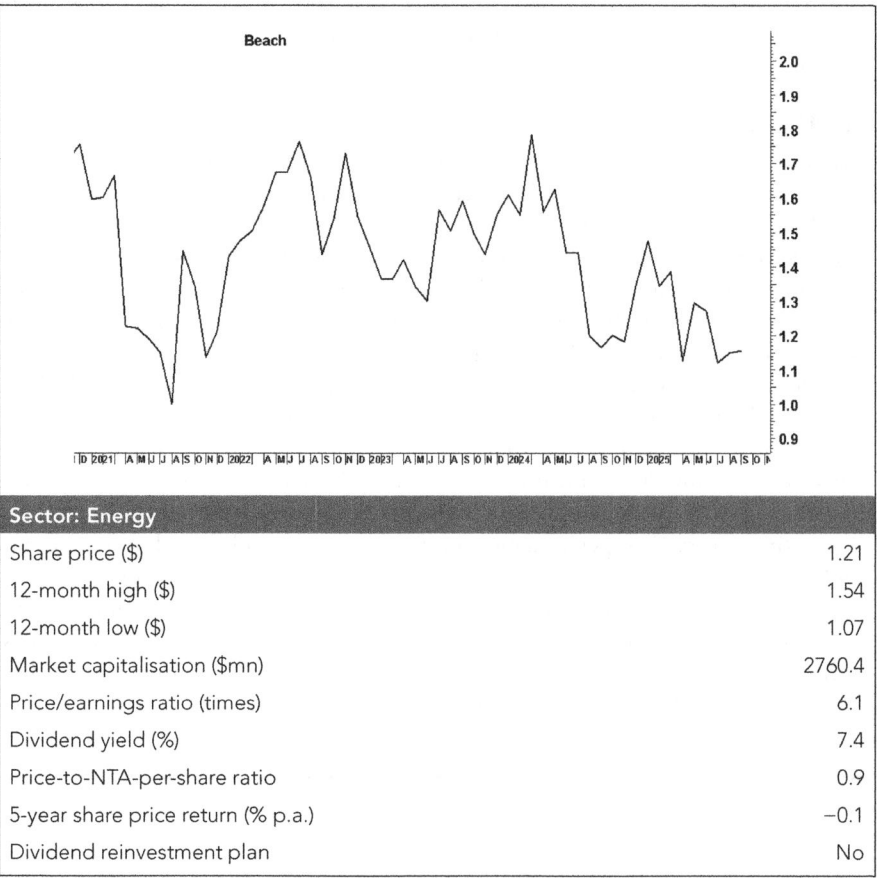

Sector: Energy	
Share price ($)	1.21
12-month high ($)	1.54
12-month low ($)	1.07
Market capitalisation ($mn)	2760.4
Price/earnings ratio (times)	6.1
Dividend yield (%)	7.4
Price-to-NTA-per-share ratio	0.9
5-year share price return (% p.a.)	−0.1
Dividend reinvestment plan	No

Adelaide-based Beach Energy, with a history dating back to 1961, is a major oil and gas producer, and a key supplier of gas to eastern states. Its operations are concentrated on five production hubs — the Cooper/Eromanga Basin region of South Australia and Queensland, the Bass Basin in the Bass Strait, the Otway Basin of Victoria and South Australia, the Perth Basin and the Taranaki Basin in New Zealand. It also maintains an active exploration and development program in other areas of Australia and New Zealand. Seven Group Holdings owns some 30 per cent of Beach's equity.

Latest business results (June 2025, full year)

An increase in sales volumes and higher gas prices boosted revenues and profits, with productivity benefits also helping the result. Total production of 19.7 million barrels of oil equivalent (boe) was up 9 per cent from the previous year, with sales of 24.7 million boe up 16 per cent. The average realised oil price of $124 per barrel fell

13 per cent, but the average realised gas price rose 13 per cent. The result included $352 million in revenues from five LNG cargoes from the new Waitsia Gas Project in Western Australia. The company also recorded a non-cash, after-tax impairment charge of $474 million, due to expectations of lower commodities prices, and at the statutory level the company recorded a loss.

Outlook

Beach is working to boost its output, and for the June 2026 year expects total production of 19.7 million boe to 22 million boe. Following delays and cost overruns at the Waitsia Gas Project, it is now working on the second stage of this development and expects a steady increase in gas output, servicing both West Coast domestic gas customers and global LNG markets. As the supplier of 19 per cent of East Coast gas demand, it maintains an active exploration program at Otway Basin. Its Equinox Rig Campaign in offshore Victoria is targeting new gas supply for the East Coast market from 2028. At its Western Flank oilfields in the Cooper/Eromanga Basin it expects in 2026 to begin a major new oil exploration program. With the Bass Basin and Taranaki Basin sites regarded as non-core assets, it is targeting self-sustaining and self-funding operations, with just minimal new capital investment. It is considering acquisition opportunities. Beach is also believed to be considering further expansion into Queensland.

Year to 30 June	2024	2025
Revenues ($mn)	1859.1	2106.0
Sales gas & ethane (%)	37	43
Crude oil (%)	32	19
Liquefied natural gas (%)	8	17
Condensate (%)	11	8
Liquefied petroleum gas (%)	7	8
EBIT ($mn)	530.0	693.6
EBIT margin (%)	28.5	32.9
Gross margin (%)	27.1	32.6
Profit before tax ($mn)	488.0	645.0
Profit after tax ($mn)	341.3	450.5
Earnings per share (c)	14.97	19.76
Cash flow per share (c)	33.34	39.18
Dividend (c)	4	9
Percentage franked	100	100
Net tangible assets per share ($)	1.42	1.36
Interest cover (times)	12.6	14.3
Return on equity (%)	9.5	13.9
Debt-to-equity ratio (%)	17.5	11.6
Current ratio	1.8	0.7

Beacon Lighting Group Limited

ASX code: BLX   www.beaconlighting.com.au

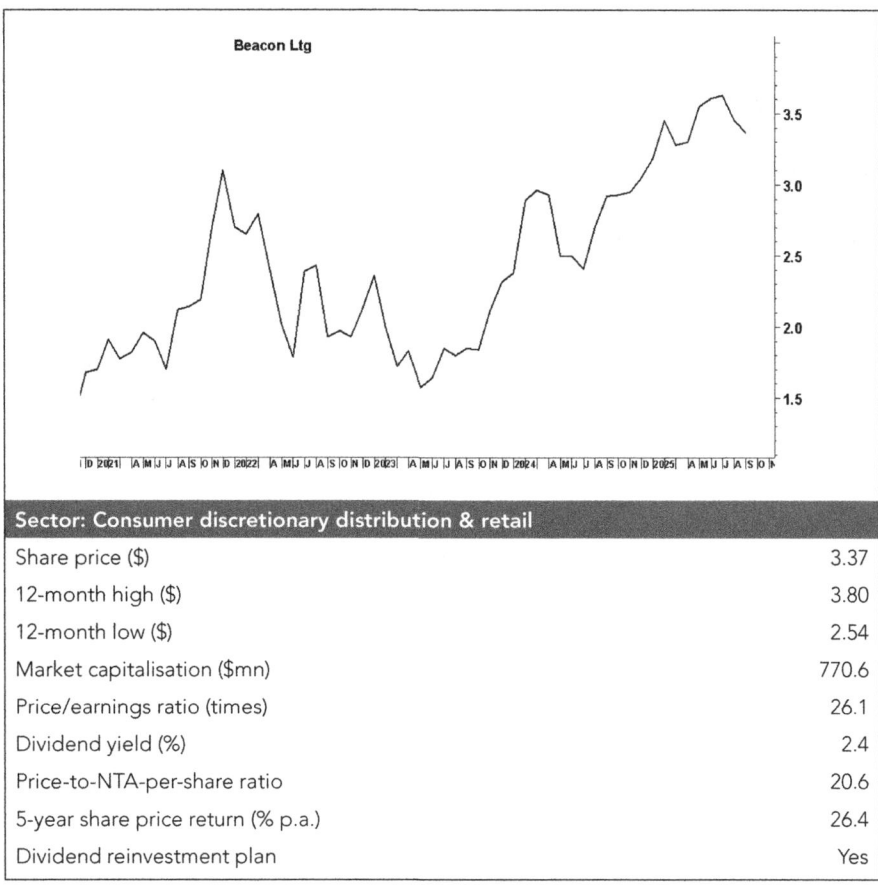

Sector: Consumer discretionary distribution & retail	
Share price ($)	3.37
12-month high ($)	3.80
12-month low ($)	2.54
Market capitalisation ($mn)	770.6
Price/earnings ratio (times)	26.1
Dividend yield (%)	2.4
Price-to-NTA-per-share ratio	20.6
5-year share price return (% p.a.)	26.4
Dividend reinvestment plan	Yes

Melbourne-based lighting specialist Beacon dates back to the launch of the first Beacon Lighting store in 1967. It steadily expanded throughout Australia, and today has 129 stores — two of them franchised — supplying a wide range of lighting fixtures and light globes, as well as ceiling fans. Its Beacon Commercial division supplies many commercial projects, including volume residential developments, apartment complexes, aged care facilities, hotels and retail fit-outs. The Beacon International business operates sales offices in Hong Kong, Germany and the US, with a support office in China.

Latest business results (June 2025, full year)

Sales edged up but profits fell for the second straight year. However, the June 2024 year comprised 53 weeks, compared to 52 weeks for June 2025, and on a like-for-like basis sales rose 4 per cent and profits were in line with the previous year. In an environment of weakened consumer confidence, particularly in the company's home state of Victoria, the continuing focus on trade business proved rewarding, with trade sales in stores rising by 24 per cent, following 27 per cent growth in the previous year. Online trade sales rose 29 per cent. However, Beacon Commercial sales were down. The small Beacon International division continued to grow. During the year the company opened four new stores and closed one.

Outlook

Beacon's business is closely linked to trends in the housing market, although it is also affected by the state of the economy and levels of consumer confidence. Much of its product range is imported, so it is also vulnerable to currency fluctuations and supply chain disruptions. In response, Beacon has a variety of strategies for growth. It expects to continue opening new stores, with a long-term aspirational target of around 195 stores nationwide. It will continue its successful focus on boosting services to trade customers, estimating the trade market in Australia for its products as worth $2.1 billion annually. Initiatives include the roll-out of further trade-specific products, dedicated trade rooms at its stores, trade seminars, a trade training program and enhanced internet platforms to facilitate online business. Trade revenues have risen strongly to represent around 40 per cent of relevant sales, and the company hopes to raise this to 50 per cent by June 2028. It is also achieving success with its online sales channels, which now represent 12 per cent of company income. It has initiated what it calls its Beacon Lighting 2030 Stores Network Strategy, a five-year plan to enhance the appeal of its stores.

Year to 29 June*	2024	2025
Revenues ($mn)	323.1	328.9
EBIT ($mn)	51.8	51.0
EBIT margin (%)	16.0	15.5
Gross margin (%)	69.0	69.1
Profit before tax ($mn)	43.3	42.2
Profit after tax ($mn)	30.1	29.4
Earnings per share (c)	13.35	12.91
Cash flow per share (c)	28.75	28.78
Dividend (c)	7.9	8
Percentage franked	100	100
Net tangible assets per share ($)	0.17	0.16
Interest cover (times)	6.1	5.8
Return on equity (%)	19.1	16.9
Debt-to-equity ratio (%)	~	~
Current ratio	1.7	1.7

*30 June 2024

BHP Group Limited

ASX code: BHP   www.bhp.com

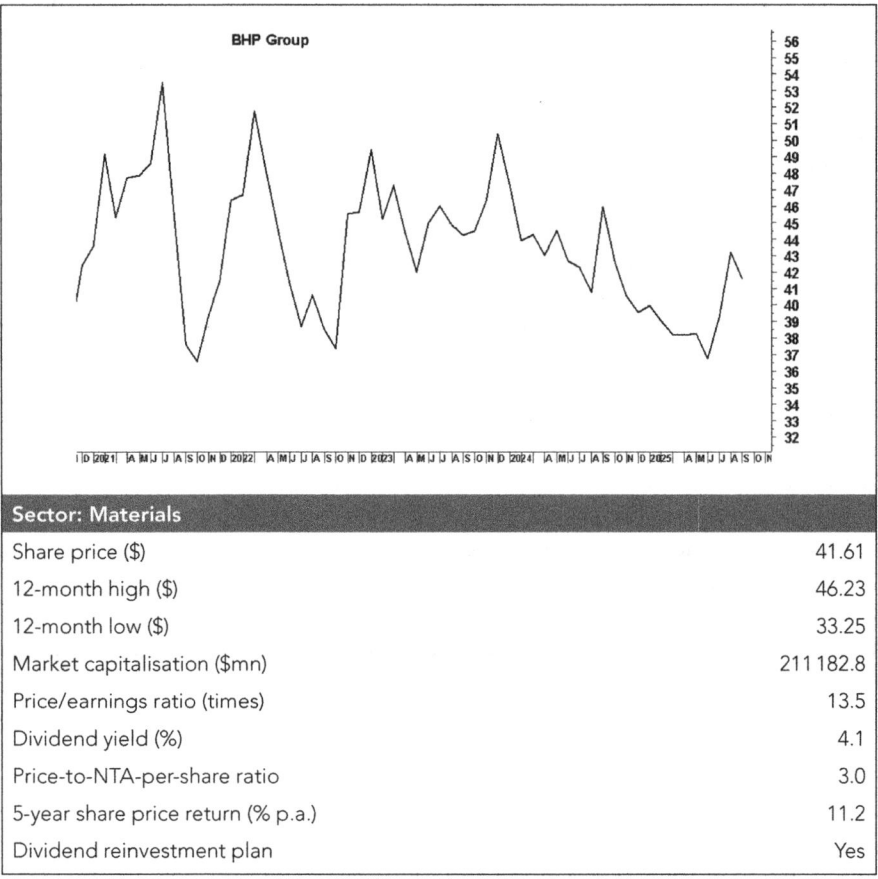

Sector: Materials	
Share price ($)	41.61
12-month high ($)	46.23
12-month low ($)	33.25
Market capitalisation ($mn)	211 182.8
Price/earnings ratio (times)	13.5
Dividend yield (%)	4.1
Price-to-NTA-per-share ratio	3.0
5-year share price return (% p.a.)	11.2
Dividend reinvestment plan	Yes

Melbourne-based resources giant BHP was founded as Broken Hill Proprietary in 1885. In 2001 it merged with another resources major, Billiton, which dated back to 1851. Today it segments its operations into five broad product areas—iron ore, copper, coal, nickel and potash—with activities in many countries.

Latest business results (June 2025, full year)

Weaker iron ore and coal prices sent profits down, only partly offset by stronger copper prices. The mainstay iron ore business saw revenues down 18 per cent, despite a small increase in production, with EBIT falling 28 per cent. This resulted from a 19 per cent decline in average prices for the year. Nevertheless, such is the company's strength in iron ore, including its low production costs, that it contributed around 55 per cent of total EBIT. Copper revenues rose 21 per cent, with EBIT jumping

53 per cent supported by higher production levels and a rising copper price. BHP's copper business now generates revenues nearly equal to those from iron ore. However, coal operations were hit by reduced output and falling prices, with revenues down 34 per cent, and this business fell into the red. During the year the company announced the temporary suspension of its loss-making nickel operations. Note that BHP reports its results in US dollars. The figures in this book are based on prevailing exchange rates.

Outlook

BHP is restructuring its operations in order to gain greater exposure to what it believes are mega-trends of decarbonisation and electrification. It spent nearly US$10 billion on growth projects in the June 2025 year, and plans to raise this to around US$11 billion annually in each of the next two years. It is placing a particular emphasis on copper developments, expecting demand to grow steadily over the longer term, and it is already one of the world's leading producers. It has formed a joint venture company with Canada's Lundin Mining to develop copper mines in the Vicuña region of Chile and Argentina, one of the largest copper discoveries in 30 years. It also has a 45 per cent interest in the major Resolution copper project in the US. It maintains a strong investment program at Port Hedland with the aim of boosting iron ore production. It is facing rising costs and delays at its huge Jansen potash project in Canada, and does not now expect production to begin until 2027. With nickel prices remaining weak, it has sold its stake in the Kabanga nickel project in Tanzania.

Year to 30 June	2024	2025
Revenues ($mn)	84 330.3	78 864.6
Iron ore (%)	50	45
Copper (%)	33	44
Coal (%)	14	10
EBIT ($mn)	37 645.5	32 858.5
EBIT margin (%)	44.6	41.7
Profit before tax ($mn)	34 315.2	30 133.8
Profit after tax ($mn)	20 697.0	15 626.2
Earnings per share (c)	408.39	308.03
Cash flow per share (c)	566.69	468.60
Dividend (c)	219.61	171.02
Percentage franked	100	100
Net tangible assets per share ($)	12.88	13.66
Interest cover (times)	11.3	12.1
Return on equity (%)	30.6	22.3
Debt-to-equity ratio (%)	16.7	24.1
Current ratio	1.7	1.5

Bisalloy Steel Group Limited

ASX code: BIS   www.bisalloy.com

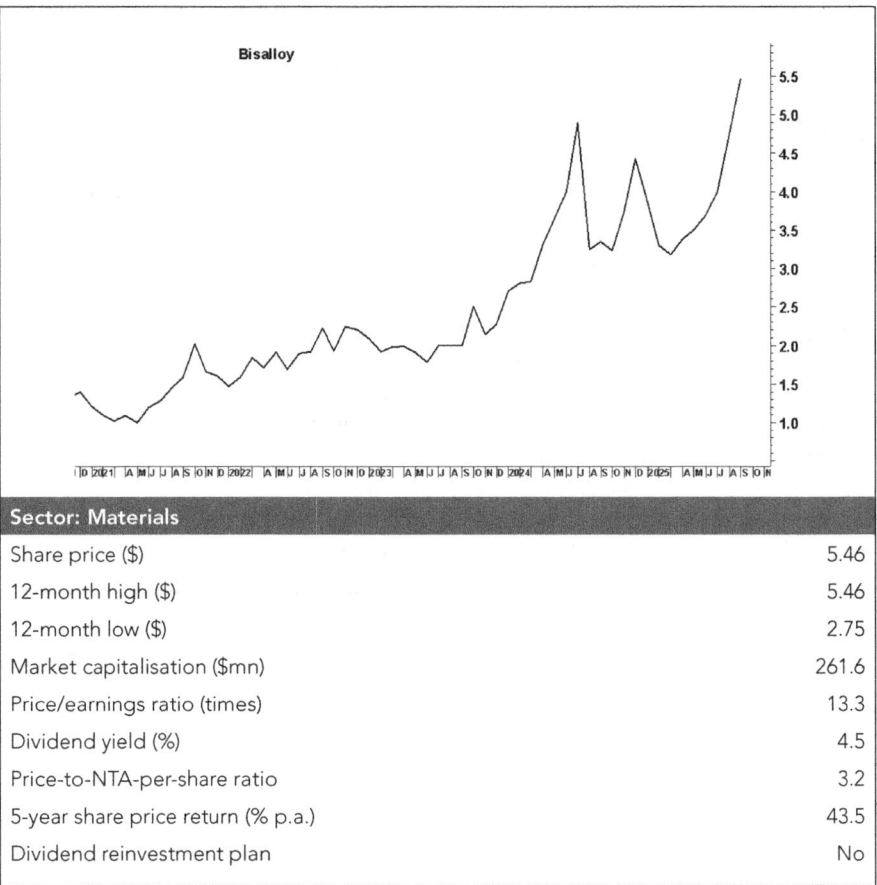

Sector: Materials	
Share price ($)	5.46
12-month high ($)	5.46
12-month low ($)	2.75
Market capitalisation ($mn)	261.6
Price/earnings ratio (times)	13.3
Dividend yield (%)	4.5
Price-to-NTA-per-share ratio	3.2
5-year share price return (% p.a.)	43.5
Dividend reinvestment plan	No

Wollongong-based Bisalloy was established in 1980 and is today Australia's only manufacturer of high-performance quenched and tempered steel plate. It exports to many countries and operates a joint venture company in China with Shandong Steel, as well as distribution centres in Thailand and Indonesia.

Latest business results (June 2025, full year)

Sales revenues were little changed from the previous year, but a favourable product mix delivered higher average prices, and profits rose. Some lower energy and transportation costs also helped the result. Australian production and sales actually fell 3 per cent to $108.9 million, due mainly to reduced demand from resources companies in Western Australia as iron ore prices weakened and BHP suspended nickel operations. This was partially offset by rising demand from the gold sector and increased defence-related business. There was a one-off boost from the company's participation in the AUKUS Hull Steel qualification contract. Exports rose as the company enhanced its regional collaboration efforts, with Indonesian sales of $27.6 million a 13 per cent increase from the previous year. The Chinese joint venture contributed $2.8 million to Bisalloy's profit, up from $2.4 million in the previous year.

Outlook

Bisalloy's high-performance quenched and tempered steel plate finds its primary application in the mining sector, where it is needed for truck trays, especially for the transportation of iron ore. It is also vital for the mining buckets used in material loaders. It is estimated that truck trays need replacing every four years in the iron ore industry and approximately every seven years for trucks carrying coal. Buckets need replacing even more frequently. The company's armour and protection plate business represents just a small proportion of total income, but makes the company a beneficiary of any rise in Australian military spending. It is the only supplier of armour plate to the Australian army for land vehicles and could be a significant beneficiary of AUKUS-related plans for the construction of Australian nuclear submarines. In an era of rising global tensions Bisalloy believes it is well positioned to benefit from rising defence spending in many countries. It also sees considerable scope to expand its Chinese joint venture, which produces steel plate at two Chinese facilities, with South-East Asian nations presenting further growth opportunities. Bisalloy sees great potential in its new OptiWear monitoring system for the mining and mineral processing industries, using digital sensors to help gauge exact wear levels in real time for truck trays, crushers, chutes, pipes, buckets and other items of equipment.

Year to 30 June	2024	2025
Revenues ($mn)	152.9	152.8
EBIT ($mn)	23.8	28.8
EBIT margin (%)	15.6	18.8
Gross margin (%)	25.3	28.8
Profit before tax ($mn)	23.1	28.0
Profit after tax ($mn)	15.7	19.6
Earnings per share (c)	33.04	40.91
Cash flow per share (c)	37.64	45.29
Dividend (c)	19.5	24.5
Percentage franked	100	100
Net tangible assets per share ($)	1.52	1.68
Interest cover (times)	32.6	35.1
Return on equity (%)	22.4	25.5
Debt-to-equity ratio (%)	~	~
Current ratio	2.3	2.2

Brambles Limited

ASX code: BXB   www.brambles.com

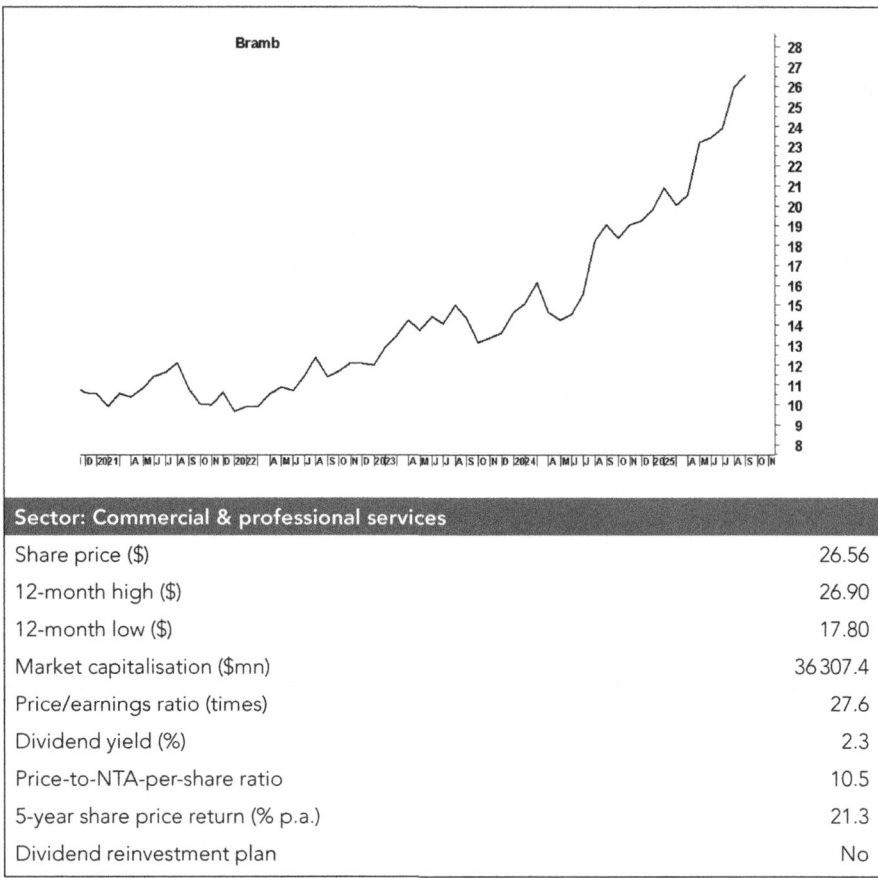

Sector: Commercial & professional services	
Share price ($)	26.56
12-month high ($)	26.90
12-month low ($)	17.80
Market capitalisation ($mn)	36 307.4
Price/earnings ratio (times)	27.6
Dividend yield (%)	2.3
Price-to-NTA-per-share ratio	10.5
5-year share price return (% p.a.)	21.3
Dividend reinvestment plan	No

Sydney-based Brambles has a history that dates back to 1875, when Walter Bramble opened a butcher's business, later expanding into transportation and logistics. Today, following a long series of acquisitions, it is the global leader in pallets, crates and container pooling services under the brand name CHEP (Commonwealth Handling Equipment Pool, a term used by the Australian government to designate pallets and other assets left in Australia by the United States Army after World War II). It owns approximately 348 million pallets, crates and containers and operates through a network of more than 750 service centres in 60 countries.

Latest business results (June 2025, full year)

In a volatile environment for global trade Brambles enjoyed further solid gains in revenues and profits. An increase in new business offset a small decline in demand from existing customers. Coupled with modest price rises, sales revenues rose 3 per cent on a constant currency basis. Underlying profits rose 10 per cent on a constant currency basis, thanks to asset efficiency initiatives and work by Brambles to improve supply chain productivity. The company saw growth in all regions. More than half of all business is with the Americas, where sales and profits realised moderate growth. There were significant productivity gains but with the benefits partly offset by inflationary pressures. The best result came from the Europe/Middle East/Africa segment, where underlying profits rose 14 per cent on a small increase in revenues, thanks especially to productivity gains. CHEP Asia Pacific achieved moderate rises in revenues and profits, with this business also a beneficiary of productivity gains. Note that Brambles reports its results in US dollars. The figures in this book are based on prevailing exchange rates.

Outlook

Brambles is heavily influenced by trends in global trade and, more generally, by the global economy, and it is concerned about the near-term outlook. It is hurt by the high expenses of its American operations, with profit margins below those prevailing elsewhere, and it is working to drive down costs. It has initiated a five-year program with the goal of stimulating growth and boosting productivity. It wishes to improve organisational efficiency through process simplification and automation, and it is introducing updated digital tools, advanced analytics and automated supply networks. It is also working to expand its regions of operation. The company's early forecast is for sales growth of 3 per cent to 5 per cent in the June 2026 year, with profits rising by 8 per cent to 11 per cent.

Year to 30 June	2024	2025
Revenues ($mn)	9917.3	10 261.1
CHEP Americas (%)	55	55
CHEP EMEA (%)	37	37
CHEP Asia-Pacific (%)	8	8
EBIT ($mn)	1915.5	2 110.3
EBIT margin (%)	19.3	20.6
Profit before tax ($mn)	1697.7	1 898.6
Profit after tax ($mn)	1172.9	1 329.5
Earnings per share (c)	84.29	96.13
Cash flow per share (c)	171.21	186.30
Dividend (c)	51.99	62.23
Percentage franked	35	30
Net tangible assets per share ($)	2.41	2.52
Interest cover (times)	8.8	10.0
Return on equity (%)	25.4	26.7
Debt-to-equity ratio (%)	51.4	50.3
Current ratio	0.6	0.7

Breville Group Limited

ASX code: BRG   www.brevillegroup.com

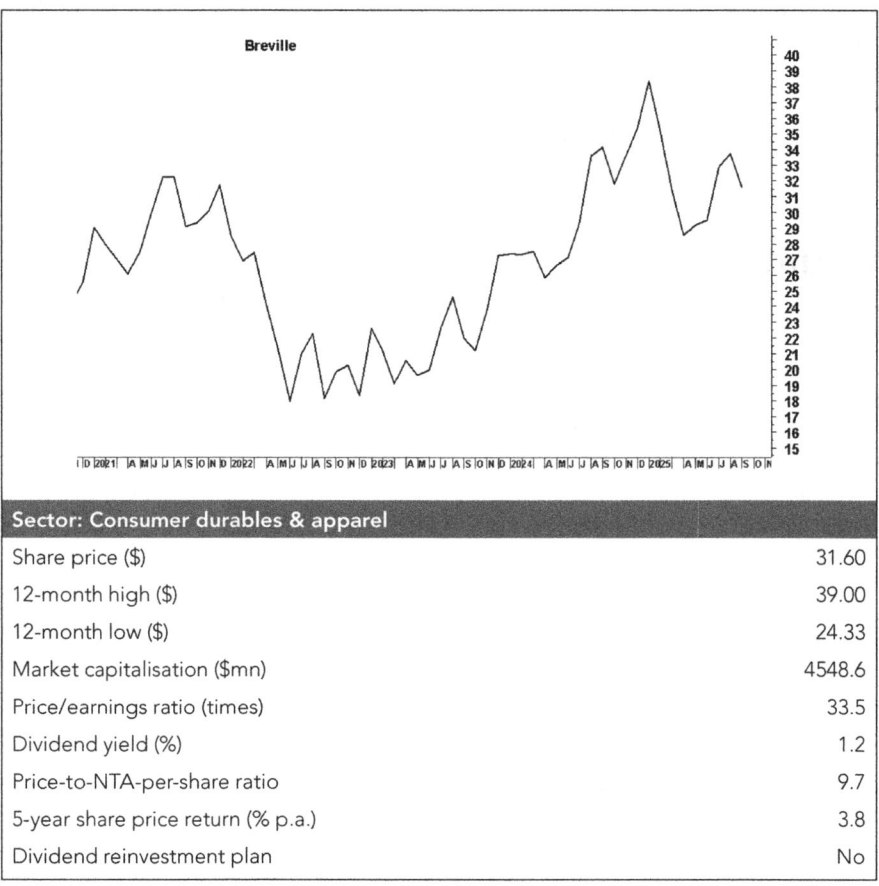

Sector: Consumer durables & apparel	
Share price ($)	31.60
12-month high ($)	39.00
12-month low ($)	24.33
Market capitalisation ($mn)	4548.6
Price/earnings ratio (times)	33.5
Dividend yield (%)	1.2
Price-to-NTA-per-share ratio	9.7
5-year share price return (% p.a.)	3.8
Dividend reinvestment plan	No

Sydney-based Breville Group traces its origins to the production of the first Breville radio in 1932. It later moved into the home appliance business and was subsequently acquired by Housewares International. In 2008 Housewares changed its name to Breville Group, and today the company is a leading designer and distributor of electrical kitchen home appliances under various brands, including Breville, Sage, Lelit, Baratza, ChefSteps and Kambrook. Breville sells its products in some 80 countries, and international business is responsible for around 80 per cent of company turnover. Premier Investments holds about 25 per cent of Breville's equity.

Latest business results (June 2025, full year)

New products, new markets and its strengths in coffee-making equipment combined to generate a strong result. All regions delivered growth, with strong demand for coffee equipment leading to 12 per cent revenues growth in constant currency—15.1 per cent in Australian dollars—in the Europe/Middle East/Africa segment. Sales were up 11.5 per cent in the Americas, led by both coffee and cooking equipment. The Asia/Pacific segment recorded 10.7 per cent growth, with particularly strong performances from Australia, New Zealand and South Korea. The company enjoyed good demand for new products that included the Oracle Jet espresso machine, the Luxe coffee brewer and the Smart Oven air fryer. Breville's Distribution division sells products designed and developed by third parties, and represents about 12 per cent of total turnover. It recorded a second consecutive double-digit rise in profits on just a 1 per cent increase in sales.

Outlook

Breville has been achieving great success with its strategy of developing premium home appliances for the American, European and Asia-Pacific markets. North America alone now represents half of company revenues and Europe has passed the Asia-Pacific region as the second-largest market. The company regards coffee in particular as offering great potential. Its 2022 acquisition of premium Italian coffee equipment manufacturer Lelit and the 2020 purchase of coffee grinder manufacturer Baratza have made Breville a force in the international specialty coffee equipment sector. However, with much of its product range manufactured in China, the company faces significant disruption to its sales in the US, its largest single market, due to the imposition of tariffs. It boosted shipments to the US in advance of the tariffs and is now working on a range of strategies, including moving some production to Mexico and South-East Asia. Following its successful entry into China and Middle East markets during the June 2025 year the company plans further geographic expansion.

Year to 30 June	2024	2025
Revenues ($mn)	1530.0	1696.6
EBIT ($mn)	188.1	206.4
EBIT margin (%)	12.3	12.2
Gross margin (%)	36.4	36.6
Profit before tax ($mn)	165.7	189.9
Profit after tax ($mn)	118.5	135.9
Earnings per share (c)	82.69	94.45
Cash flow per share (c)	124.41	141.26
Dividend (c)	33	37
Percentage franked	100	100
Net tangible assets per share ($)	2.60	3.25
Interest cover (times)	8.4	12.5
Return on equity (%)	14.6	14.9
Debt-to-equity ratio (%)	~	~
Current ratio	2.3	2.2

Capral Limited

ASX code: CAA   www.capral.com.au

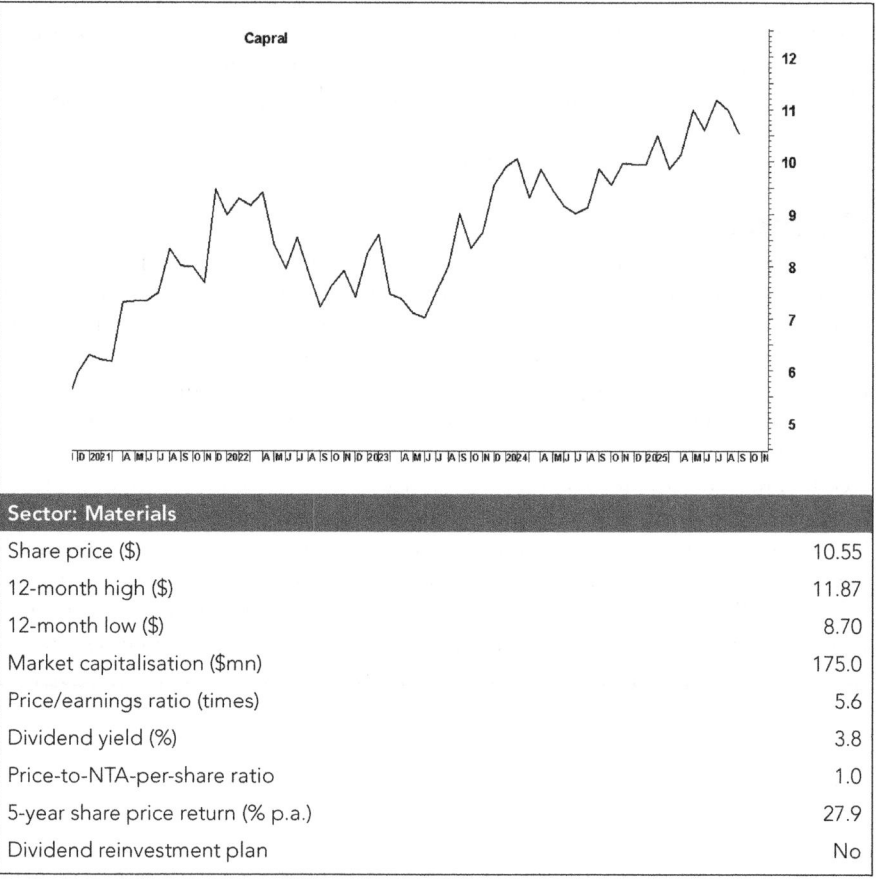

Sector: Materials	
Share price ($)	10.55
12-month high ($)	11.87
12-month low ($)	8.70
Market capitalisation ($mn)	175.0
Price/earnings ratio (times)	5.6
Dividend yield (%)	3.8
Price-to-NTA-per-share ratio	1.0
5-year share price return (% p.a.)	27.9
Dividend reinvestment plan	No

Established in 1936 as British Aluminium Australia, Ipswich-based Capral has evolved through several ownership structures and name changes, and is today a leading manufacturer and supplier of aluminium products. These include a wide range of products for industrial and construction applications, and the company is a prominent supplier to the transport, marine, defence and general fabrication sectors. In August 2025 it acquired Perth-based aluminium systems and hardware business Comsupply.

Latest business results (June 2025, half year)

Revenues rose but profits fell, although a $2.5 million tax benefit meant that the after-tax and EPS figures rose. Volume sales of 31 100 tonnes fell 7 per cent from the June 2024 half due to reduced demand in the industrial sector and continued weakness in residential construction. However, higher prices meant that sales revenues were up. Competition from imports remained a challenge. The company reported that it was able to maintain market share gains with direct customers, but sales volumes to resellers declined.

Outlook

Industrial applications comprise nearly half of Capral's sales and the company has noted that demand has softened for the first time since 2020, with transportation-related demand falling from historic highs and many infrastructure projects coming to an end. However, it sees opportunities in the marine sector, where ferry building and defence shipbuilding activity remains solid. It also views government solar initiatives as offering potential. Residential construction represents 41 per cent of Capral sales and the company expects housing starts to increase, due to possible further interest rate cuts and a rising population. Consequently, Capral expects December 2025 full-year profit to be roughly in line with 2024. However, its finances are influenced by global aluminium prices and currency rates, which can be volatile, and it notes that uncertainty around US tariff policies has led to increased uncertainty. It is also concerned about continuing inflationary cost pressures, and has been investing in new technology to boost productivity and reduce its cost base. It is working to enhance its presence in architectural markets. It also wishes to expand its direct distribution channels. It views its Comsupply acquisition as providing a significant boost to its presence in the Western Australian market. Comsupply has more than 350 customer accounts with a diverse product offering and some $15 million in annual revenues. At June 2025 Capral had no debt and nearly $53 million in cash holdings, and it continues to seek out acquisitions that strengthen its national distribution network and complement its servicing and technical capabilities.

Year to 31 December	2023	2024
Revenues ($mn)	656.9	649.7
EBIT ($mn)	38.5	34.4
EBIT margin (%)	5.9	5.3
Profit before tax ($mn)	31.8	28.9
Profit after tax ($mn)	31.8	32.5
Earnings per share (c)	177.47	187.95
Cash flow per share (c)	305.73	325.82
Dividend (c)	55	40
Percentage franked	100	0
Interest cover (times)	5.8	6.2
Return on equity (%)	16.1	15.1
Half year to 30 June	2024	2025
Revenues ($mn)	313.4	327.2
Profit before tax ($mn)	14.7	12.8
Profit after tax ($mn)	14.7	15.3
Earnings per share (c)	84.30	90.83
Dividend (c)	0	0
Percentage franked	~	~
Net tangible assets per share ($)	8.20	10.18
Debt-to-equity ratio (%)	~	~
Current ratio	1.8	1.9

CAR Group Limited

ASX code: CAR

cargroup.com

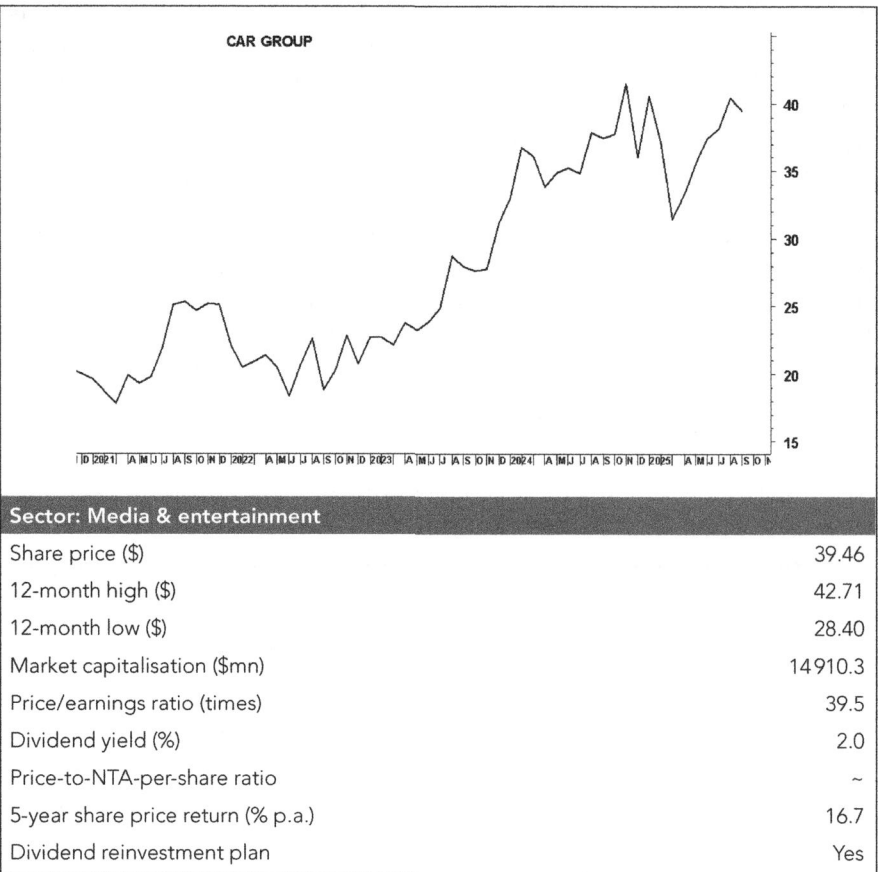

Sector: Media & entertainment	
Share price ($)	39.46
12-month high ($)	42.71
12-month low ($)	28.40
Market capitalisation ($mn)	14910.3
Price/earnings ratio (times)	39.5
Dividend yield (%)	2.0
Price-to-NTA-per-share ratio	~
5-year share price return (% p.a.)	16.7
Dividend reinvestment plan	Yes

CAR Group was founded in Melbourne in 1997 and has grown to become the market leader in online automotive advertising. It also operates specialist websites for the sale of other goods that include boats, motorcycles, trucks, construction equipment, farm machinery and caravans. It has expanded abroad, with interests in automotive businesses in the US, Asia and Latin America, and these operations now generate more than half of company turnover. A smaller division provides a diverse range of data services for customers, including research and reporting, valuations, appraisals, website development and photography services.

Latest business results (June 2025, full year)

CAR Group reported another good result, with strength across most businesses. In a strong automotive market, Australian businesses achieved 8 per cent growth in revenues. However, the best performances came from abroad, with double-digit revenue increases in all three markets. Latin America was especially strong, with revenues surging 26 per cent, thanks to new products and expansion to new markets. North America benefited from new products, offsetting a decline in the recreational vehicle market. Asian revenues rose 16 per cent, with continuing strong progress in the South Korean Encar business.

Outlook

CAR Group calculates that it does business in four countries—Australia, the US, Brazil and South Korea—with a total addressable market of some $16.4 billion annually, including $9.4 billion in the North American non-auto market alone, and it sees significant scope for long-term growth. However, with Australia viewed as a largely mature market, the best future expansion could come from abroad. The company's early June 2026 forecast is for continuing double-digit revenue growth in its overseas businesses and high single-digit growth in Australia, with the after-tax profit up between 9 per cent and 13 per cent. It is introducing new systems and technology to Webmotors, which is the leading automotive digital marketplace in Brazil, and is realising significant expansion in dealer numbers. It also expects continuing strong progress in its Korean Encar operation—which is that country's leader in automotive classifieds—thanks especially to increased uptake of the company's Guarantee vehicle inspection service. In the US its Trader Interactive business is a leader in the operation of specialist websites for the sale of items that include motorcycles, aeroplanes, snowmobiles, heavy equipment and recreational vehicles. It views Trader Interactive's Boatmart site for personal watercraft as offering particularly strong potential. CAR Group is making strong moves into artificial intelligence, which it expects to enhance its products and boost operational efficiency.

Year to 30 June	2024	2025
Revenues ($mn)	1098.7	1183.9
Australia—online advertising (%)	36	37
North America (%)	25	26
Latin America (%)	17	17
Asia (%)	11	11
Australia—data, research and services (%)	5	4
EBIT ($mn)	524.0	573.8
EBIT margin (%)	47.7	48.5
Profit before tax ($mn)	438.0	485.0
Profit after tax ($mn)	344.0	377.0
Earnings per share (c)	91.25	99.84
Cash flow per share (c)	132.32	145.21
Dividend (c)	73	80
Percentage franked	50	45
Net tangible assets per share ($)	~	~
Interest cover (times)	6.1	6.5
Return on equity (%)	11.6	12.9
Debt-to-equity ratio (%)	33.7	35.4
Current ratio	2.0	1.8

Cedar Woods Properties Limited

ASX code: CWP   www.cedarwoods.com.au

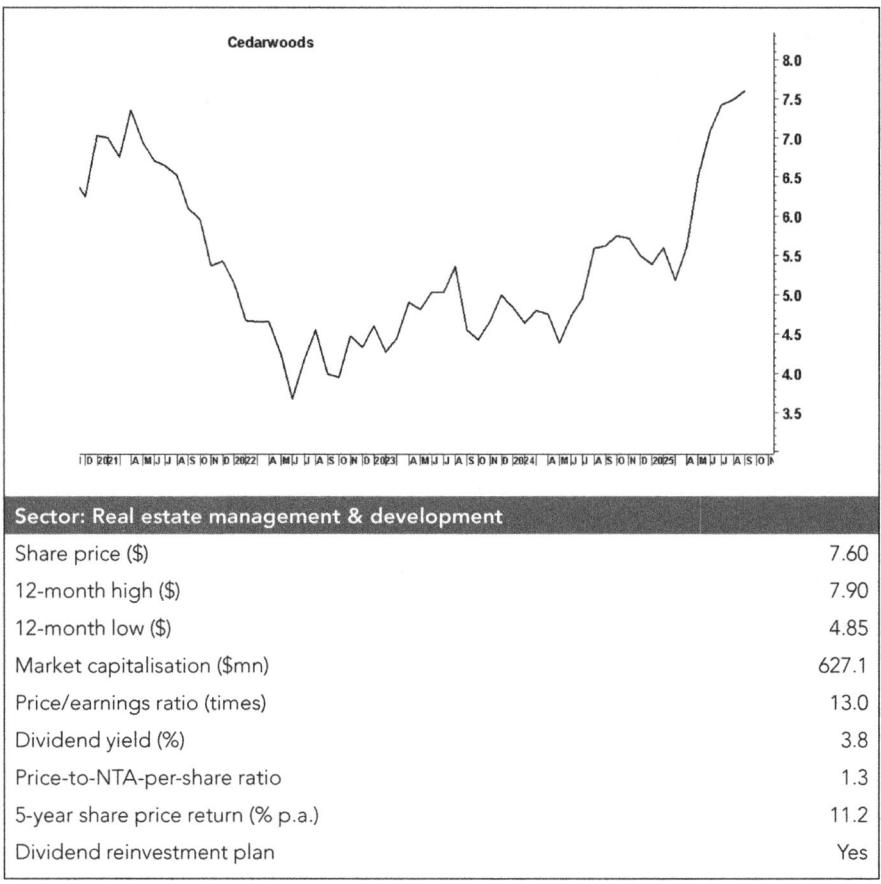

Cedarwoods

Sector: Real estate management & development	
Share price ($)	7.60
12-month high ($)	7.90
12-month low ($)	4.85
Market capitalisation ($mn)	627.1
Price/earnings ratio (times)	13.0
Dividend yield (%)	3.8
Price-to-NTA-per-share ratio	1.3
5-year share price return (% p.a.)	11.2
Dividend reinvestment plan	Yes

Perth-based Cedar Woods, founded in 1987, is a prominent property developer. Its main interests are in urban land subdivision for residential, commercial and industrial purposes. Its work includes apartment projects, integrated housing developments, business parks, mixed-use developments, large-scale master-planned communities and commercial projects. Its original focus was on its home state, but it has also become very active in Melbourne, Brisbane and Adelaide.

Latest business results (June 2025, full year)

In an environment of rising housing demand, Cedar Woods achieved excellent growth in sales and profits. In particular, the Western Australian and Queensland markets remained strong, though Victoria was more subdued. Net sales of 1264 units were a 5 per cent increase from the previous year, with settlements of 1125 units similar to June 2024.

Presales of $660 million were 18 per cent higher than the previous year. The company said that rising prices over the past two years have boosted profit margins. During the year the company completed its Greville town house development in Brisbane and its Glenside apartment development in Brisbane. It commenced work on the Incontro apartments development in Perth and the Vera apartments development in Brisbane.

Outlook

Cedar Woods has a strategy of targeting high-growth urban corridors in close proximity to transport infrastructure for its developments, and it continues to build up its land bank. It is a beneficiary of a national housing shortage that seems likely to take years to resolve. The company notes that, with just 938 000 homes expected to be built by 2029, against the government's 1.2 million target, Australia is on track to fall short by more than 260 000 homes, at a time when the population continues to expand. It has successfully initiated strategic partnerships with the Queensland Investment Corporation and Tokyo Gas Real Estate for joint developments and is seeking further similar arrangements. Its work has at times been held back by rising prices of materials, along with labour shortages and long approval processes, and some of these problems persist. Cedar Woods anticipates continuing strength in Brisbane, Perth and Adelaide projects, but relative weakness in Melbourne, due to generally greater supply and a subdued economy. Of its presales of $660 million, it expects some 60 per cent to settle in the June 2026 year. Consequently, it is forecasting 10 per cent after-tax profit growth for the year. Thanks to a pipeline of 35 projects comprising more than 9400 units across four states, along with a growing land bank, it is optimistic about the medium-term outlook.

Year to 30 June	2024	2025
Revenues ($mn)	386.3	465.9
EBIT ($mn)	68.2	84.1
EBIT margin (%)	17.6	18.0
Gross margin (%)	24.8	28.4
Profit before tax ($mn)	57.1	68.8
Profit after tax ($mn)	40.5	48.1
Earnings per share (c)	49.15	58.36
Cash flow per share (c)	51.77	61.04
Dividend (c)	25	29
Percentage franked	100	100
Net tangible assets per share ($)	5.56	5.91
Interest cover (times)	6.1	5.5
Return on equity (%)	9.1	10.1
Debt-to-equity ratio (%)	26.1	25.7
Current ratio	2.3	1.6

Clinuvel Pharmaceuticals Limited

ASX code: CUV   www.clinuvel.com

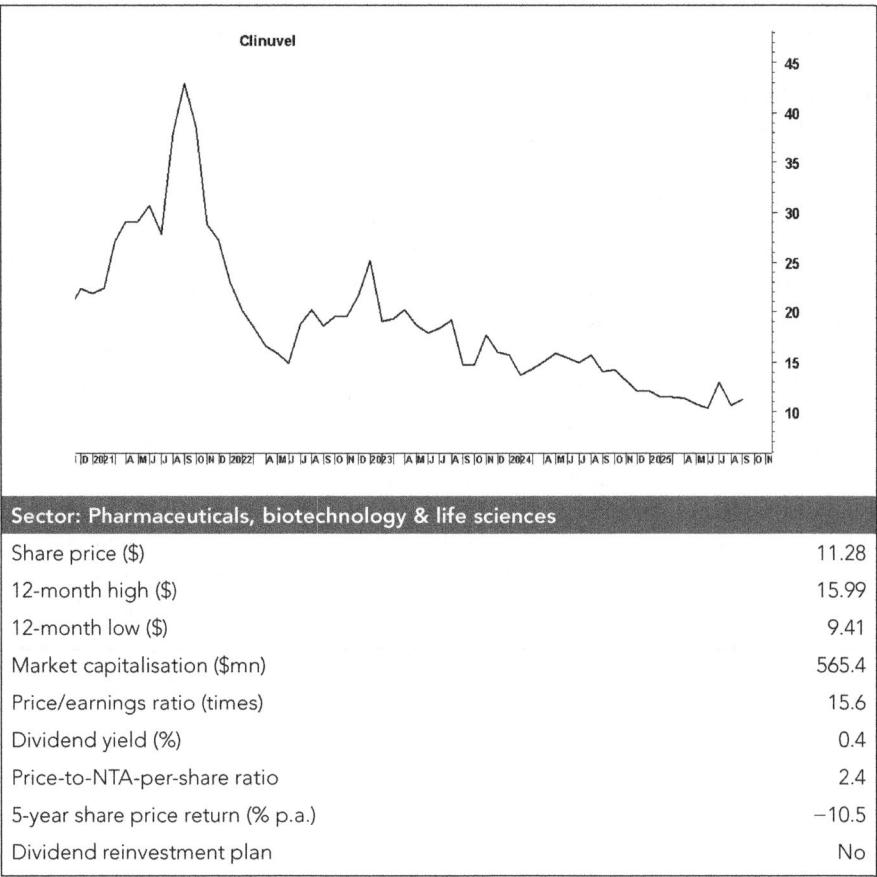

Sector: Pharmaceuticals, biotechnology & life sciences	
Share price ($)	11.28
12-month high ($)	15.99
12-month low ($)	9.41
Market capitalisation ($mn)	565.4
Price/earnings ratio (times)	15.6
Dividend yield (%)	0.4
Price-to-NTA-per-share ratio	2.4
5-year share price return (% p.a.)	−10.5
Dividend reinvestment plan	No

Melbourne-based biopharmaceutical company Clinuvel dates back to 1987, when scientists devised technologies for the protection of skin using human hormones. Today it is a global company with a focus on developing drugs for the treatment of various skin disorders. Its lead therapy afamelanotide — known as Scenesse — has been shown to be effective in treating severe phototoxicity (intolerance of light) in many badly affected patients. It has been approved by regulators for commercial distribution in many countries. The company is also developing other drugs.

Latest business results (June 2025, full year)

Clinuvel reported further increases in revenues and profits as Scenesse demand continued to rise, with a growing number of patients, prescribing doctors and centres administering treatment. In North America the number of specialty treatment centres rose from 85 to 104, with 120 expected by the end of 2025. A 20 per cent jump in expenses reduced profit margins. Staffing costs were up 31 per cent, the communication, branding and marketing budget doubled, and clinical and non-clinical development costs more than trebled.

Outlook

Scenesse reduces the severity of phototoxic skin reactions in patients with a rare light intolerance condition known as erythropoietic protoporphyria. Such patients can experience severe pain from sun exposure, as well as swelling and scarring of exposed areas of the body such as the face and hands, with hospitalisation and powerful pain killers sometimes necessary. Scenesse is the first drug developed for this condition. It was launched in Europe in 2016 and in the US in 2020, and the company is actively seeking to have it approved in other countries. In addition, Clinuvel is involved in a series of drug trials. It has launched highly promising tests in the US to determine whether Scenesse can be used to treat vitiligo, a skin disorder where patches of skin become pale or white. Clinuvel has stated that if Scenesse were approved for treating vitiligo it could transform the company, with expected revenues of up to $570 million in the first two years of distribution. It is also working on the development of a range of over-the-counter skin protection products, based on Scenesse. It has developed a new drug, Prénumbra, a liquid formulation of Scenesse, and has begun studies on using this drug in the treatment of arterial ischaemic stroke. It is developing a third drug, Neuracthel, which it believes could have applications in the treatment of neurological, endocrinological and degenerative diseases. At June 2025 Clinuvel had no debt and cash holdings of more than $224 million.

Year to 30 June	2024	2025
Revenues ($mn)	88.2	95.0
EBIT ($mn)	50.7	51.6
EBIT margin (%)	57.5	54.3
Profit before tax ($mn)	50.7	51.6
Profit after tax ($mn)	35.6	36.2
Earnings per share (c)	71.51	72.23
Cash flow per share (c)	73.80	74.59
Dividend (c)	5	5
Percentage franked	100	100
Net tangible assets per share ($)	4.04	4.79
Interest cover (times)	1237.0	1322.8
Return on equity (%)	19.4	16.3
Debt-to-equity ratio (%)	~	~
Current ratio	8.8	9.7

Cochlear Limited

ASX code: COH   www.cochlear.com

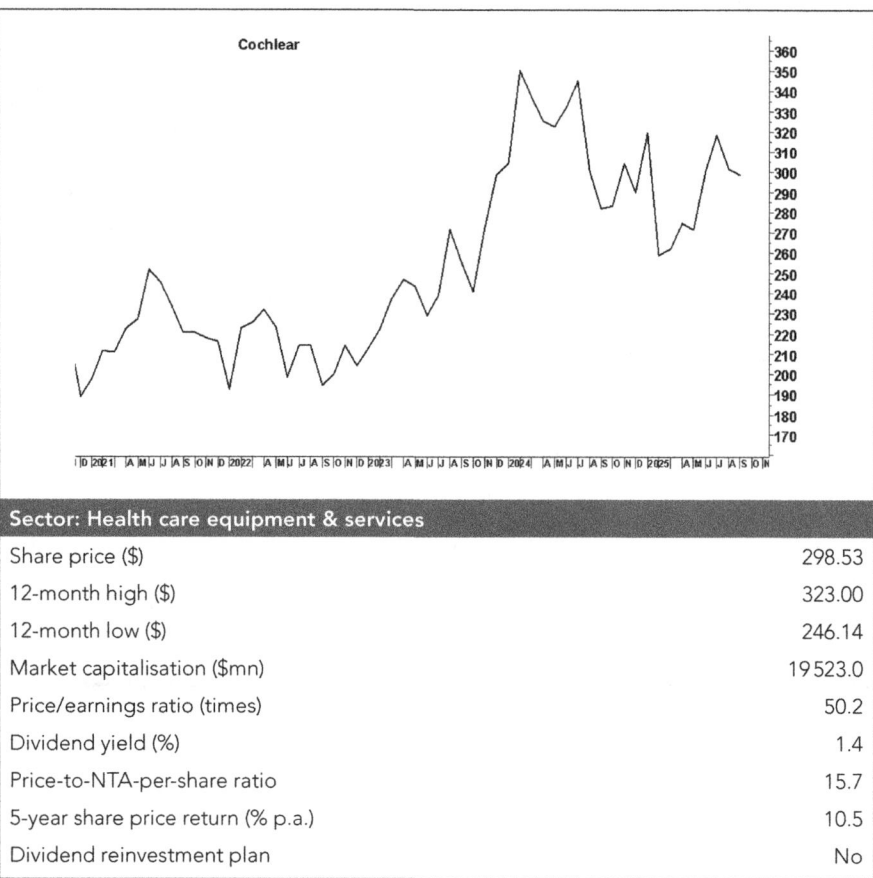

Sector: Health care equipment & services	
Share price ($)	298.53
12-month high ($)	323.00
12-month low ($)	246.14
Market capitalisation ($mn)	19523.0
Price/earnings ratio (times)	50.2
Dividend yield (%)	1.4
Price-to-NTA-per-share ratio	15.7
5-year share price return (% p.a.)	10.5
Dividend reinvestment plan	No

Sydney-based Cochlear, founded in 1981, has around 60 per cent of the world market for cochlear bionic-ear implants, which are intended to assist the communication ability of people suffering from severe hearing impediments. It also sells the Baha bone-anchored hearing implant, as well as a range of acoustic products. With manufacturing facilities and technology centres in Australia, Europe, Asia and North America, it has sales in over 180 countries, and overseas business accounts for more than 90 per cent of revenues and profits.

Latest business results (June 2025, full year)

Sales and profits rose again, with strength in implants and acoustics more than offsetting weakness in the services business. Cochlear implant sales rose 12 per cent to 53 968 units, with revenues up 11 per cent. There was particular strength in emerging markets, with unit growth of more than 20 per cent. Acoustics revenues rose 8 per cent, driven by strong demand for the Osia implant as the company introduced it to new markets. However, services revenues fell 9 per cent. The company attributed this in part to a tapering in demand for the new Nucleus 8 sound processor, due to high levels of satisfaction with the older Nucleus 7 model along with cost-of-living pressures.

Outlook

Cochlear continues to launch new products at an impressive rate, with a high level of research and development spending, and this is helping it maintain its market leadership. It expects strong growth in the June 2026 year, thanks to its new Nucleus Nexa implant, which it claims is the world's only smart cochlear implant system with upgradeable firmware. Launched in Australia and Germany in June 2025, it has already achieved strong sales. US Food and Drug Administration approval was achieved in July 2025. However, Cochlear has conceded that delays in bringing this product to market generated a modest loss of market share for its products in several countries. The company forecasts double-digit growth for acoustics revenues as it introduces the Osia system to new markets, along with the launch of the Baha 7 sound processor. It also expects a rebound in services revenues as its customer base expands, together with a contribution from the launch of the Kanso 3 sound processor. It believes its products will be exempt from US tariffs under a special waiver for certain medical devices. At June 2025 Cochlear had no debt and cash holdings of more than $275 million. Its early June 2026 forecast is for an after-tax profit of $435 million to $460 million.

Year to 30 June	2024	2025
Revenues ($mn)	2235.6	2343.1
Cochlear implants (%)	59	62
Services (%)	30	26
Acoustics (%)	11	12
EBIT ($mn)	494.0	529.5
EBIT margin (%)	22.1	22.6
Gross margin (%)	74.5	73.3
Profit before tax ($mn)	484.8	518.5
Profit after tax ($mn)	356.8	388.9
Earnings per share (c)	544.43	594.30
Cash flow per share (c)	673.97	732.45
Dividend (c)	410	430
Percentage franked	75	83
Net tangible assets per share ($)	17.97	19.05
Interest cover (times)	53.7	48.1
Return on equity (%)	19.9	20.5
Debt-to-equity ratio (%)	~	~
Current ratio	2.3	2.4

Codan Limited

ASX code: CDA   www.codan.com.au

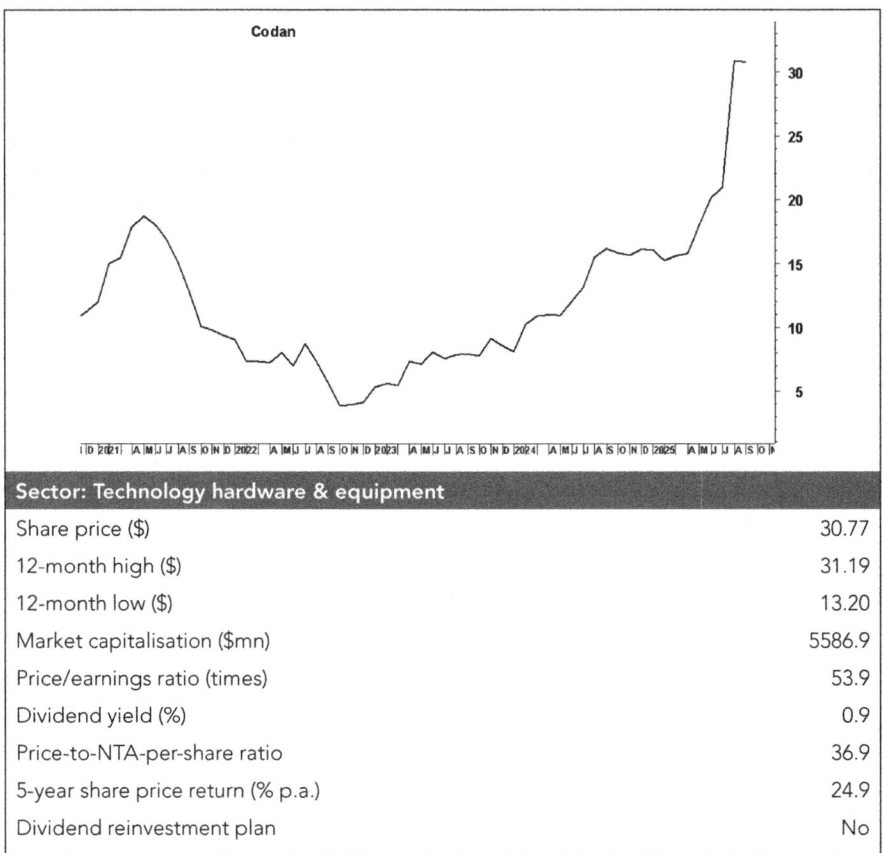

Sector: Technology hardware & equipment	
Share price ($)	30.77
12-month high ($)	31.19
12-month low ($)	13.20
Market capitalisation ($mn)	5586.9
Price/earnings ratio (times)	53.9
Dividend yield (%)	0.9
Price-to-NTA-per-share ratio	36.9
5-year share price return (% p.a.)	24.9
Dividend reinvestment plan	No

Adelaide electronics company Codan was founded in 1959. Its fast-growing Communications division produces high-frequency communication equipment for military and public safety use. The Metal Detection division is a leading world manufacturer of metal-detecting products, including Minelab detectors for hobbyists, gold detectors for small-scale miners and landmine detectors for humanitarian applications. Codan sells to more than 150 countries, and overseas sales represent around 90 per cent of company revenues. It has manufacturing sites and sales offices in many countries. In December 2024 it acquired the American operator-worn communications equipment maker Kägwerks.

Latest business results (June 2025, full year)

Sales and profits rose strongly in an excellent result. The Communications division achieved a 26 per cent increase in revenues, with profits up 34 per cent. Its DTC business, which supplies specialised communications equipment to military forces, law enforcement, first responders and others, enjoyed a particularly strong year underpinned by surging global defence expenditure. The Zetron business, which supplies emergency and mission-critical communications equipment, was also strong. The Kägwerks acquisition made a seven-month contribution. Metal detector revenues rose 16 per cent — following a 25 per cent rise in the previous year — with profits ahead 26 per cent. A strong gold price was a particular incentive for rising demand in Africa. However, mine detection sales fell as the US government cut back on humanitarian aid initiatives. Two countries — the US and the UAE — were responsible for more than half of total company sales.

Outlook

Codan is a significant force in two niche high-tech product areas. In particular, its DTC business has become a significant beneficiary of growing military spending around the world, and revenues from defence customers have grown to represent 38 per cent of total Communications division sales. There is particularly strong demand for DTC's defence-related unmanned systems, with June 2025 sales of $100 million more than double the figure for the previous year. The Kägwerks acquisition provides Codan with inclusion in the US Army's Nett Warrior Program for communications equipment. At June 2025 the Communications division held an order book of $253 million, up 28 per cent from a year earlier, and the company believes revenues for this division could grow by as much as 20 per cent in June 2026. The Metal Detection division is releasing a new gold detector, Gold Monster 2000, retailing at approximately twice the price of the Gold Monster 1000, and Codan expects this and a series of other new releases to contribute to growth in the June 2026 year.

Year to 30 June	2024	2025
Revenues ($mn)	550.5	674.2
Communications (%)	59	61
Metal detection (%)	40	38
EBIT ($mn)	114.0	146.3
EBIT margin (%)	20.7	21.7
Gross margin (%)	55.4	56.2
Profit before tax ($mn)	104.5	133.9
Profit after tax ($mn)	81.4	103.5
Earnings per share (c)	44.95	57.09
Cash flow per share (c)	63.23	77.90
Dividend (c)	22.5	28.5
Percentage franked	100	100
Net tangible assets per share ($)	0.60	0.83
Interest cover (times)	12.0	11.8
Return on equity (%)	19.1	21.3
Debt-to-equity ratio (%)	16.9	14.9
Current ratio	1.7	1.7

Coles Group Limited

ASX code: COL   www.colesgroup.com.au

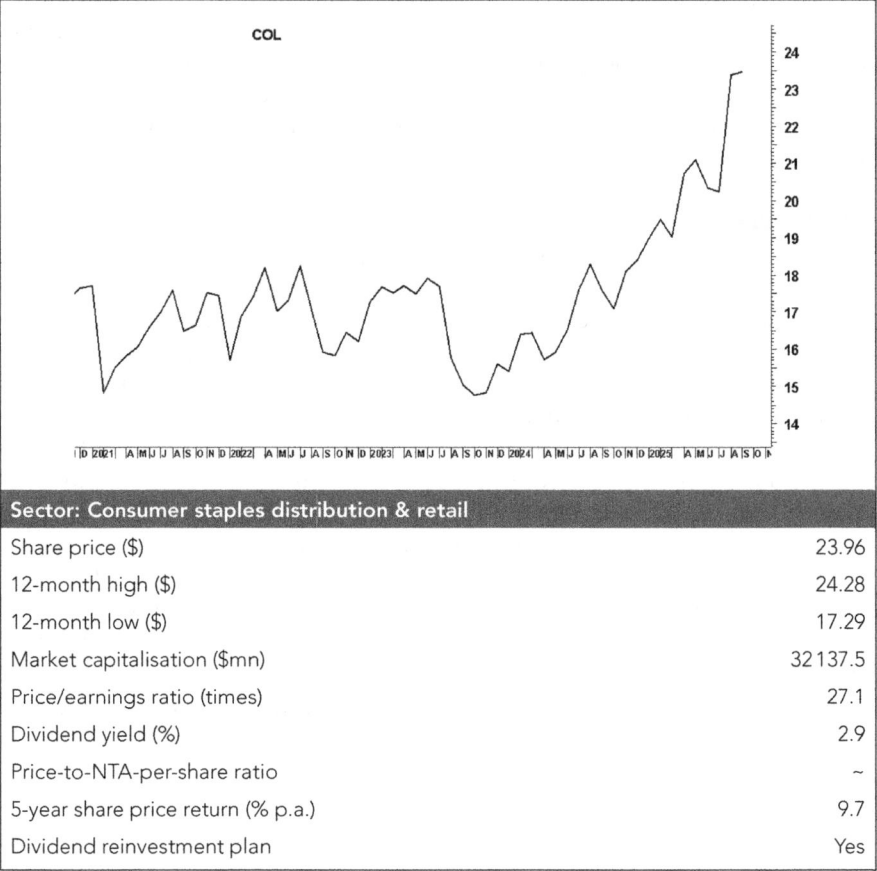

Sector: Consumer staples distribution & retail	
Share price ($)	23.96
12-month high ($)	24.28
12-month low ($)	17.29
Market capitalisation ($mn)	32 137.5
Price/earnings ratio (times)	27.1
Dividend yield (%)	2.9
Price-to-NTA-per-share ratio	~
5-year share price return (% p.a.)	9.7
Dividend reinvestment plan	Yes

Melbourne-based Coles Group dates back to 1914 and the opening of the first Coles store in the Melbourne suburb of Collingwood. Over many years it evolved from a single variety store to a chain of supermarkets, then expanded further with the acquisition of the Myer department store business. In 2006 the company sold Myer and in 2007 Coles was acquired by Wesfarmers. In 2018 it was demerged from Wesfarmers as, once again, an independent company. At June 2025 it operated 860 supermarkets nationwide and 998 liquor stores, the latter under the Liquorland, Vintage Cellars and First Choice banners. It is a 50 per cent shareholder of the Flybuys loyalty program.

Latest business results (June 2025, full year)

In another difficult year, with Australian households facing rising cost of living pressures, Coles saw revenues up but underlying profits down. However, the June 2024 year comprised 53 weeks, compared to 52 weeks for June 2025, and on a normalised basis the after-tax profit edged up 3.1 per cent. The Supermarkets division achieved sales growth of 4.3 per cent on a normalised basis, exactly the same as in the previous year. The company's eCommerce sales were particularly strong, up by a normalised 24.4 per cent, following 30.1 per cent growth in the previous year. Coles exclusive products showed 5.7 per cent growth. Supermarkets EBIT rose a normalised 8.3 per cent. Liquor division sales rose 1.1 per cent in a subdued consumer environment, but for the second straight year EBIT recorded a double-digit decline. During the year Coles opened eight new supermarkets and 16 new liquor stores.

Outlook

The big supermarket chains are generally immune to declines in discretionary consumer spending, apart from liquor sales. However, it is noteworthy that consumers are trading down to cheaper home brands. Coles has made a substantial investment in these products over many years and has become a beneficiary of this move. It expects that the steady expansion of Australia's population will underpin its long-term growth, although it has faced political pressures over pricing policies and its treatment of suppliers and smaller competitors. An investment of more than $1 billion in new automated distribution centres is helping to boost margins, and the company continues to work at reducing its cost base. Consequently, it believes it will be able to cut hundreds of prices while maintaining profit margins. It has been investing in technology aimed at reducing stock loss, particularly from a rising wave of shoplifting. It is restructuring its underperforming liquor business.

Year to 29 June*	2024	2025
Revenues ($mn)	43 571.0	44 352.0
Supermarkets (%)	90	91
Liquor (%)	8	8
EBIT ($mn)	2 139.0	2 189.0
EBIT margin (%)	4.9	4.9
Gross margin (%)	24.3	26.4
Profit before tax ($mn)	1 697.0	1 648.0
Profit after tax ($mn)	1 210.0	1 181.0
Earnings per share (c)	90.70	88.40
Cash flow per share (c)	210.79	225.30
Dividend (c)	68	69
Percentage franked	100	100
Net tangible assets per share ($)	~	~
Interest cover (times)	4.8	4.0
Return on equity (%)	34.7	31.8
Debt-to-equity ratio (%)	27.0	33.6
Current ratio	0.6	0.6

*30 June 2024

Collins Foods Limited

ASX code: CKF   www.collinsfoods.com

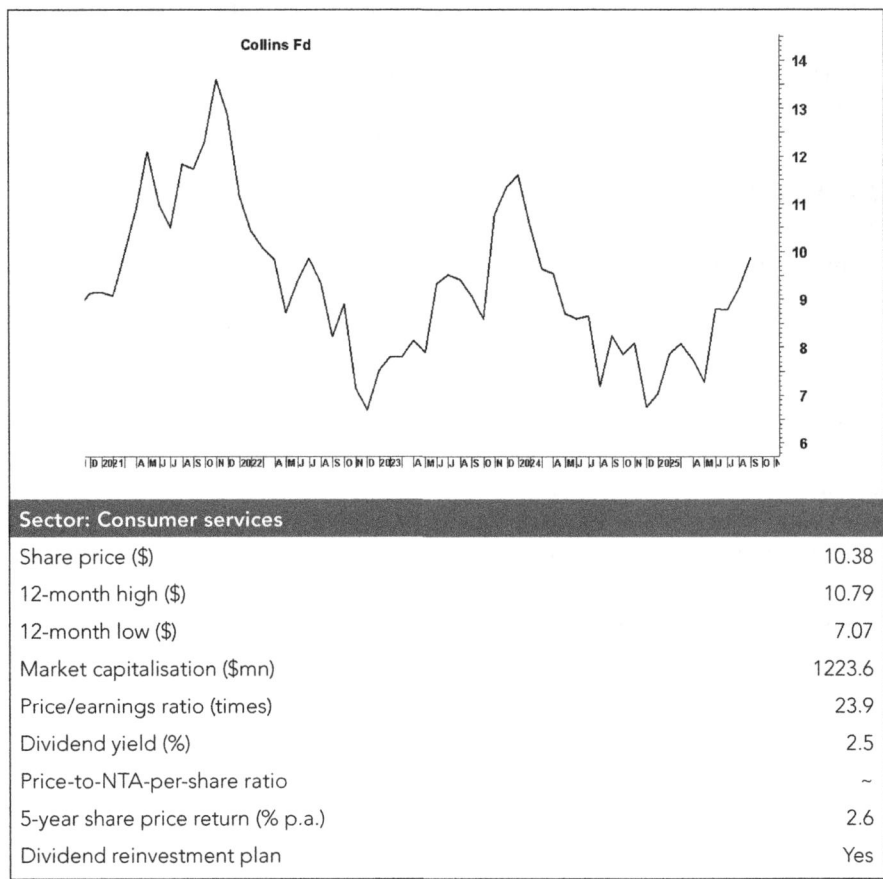

Collins Fd

Sector: Consumer services	
Share price ($)	10.38
12-month high ($)	10.79
12-month low ($)	7.07
Market capitalisation ($mn)	1223.6
Price/earnings ratio (times)	23.9
Dividend yield (%)	2.5
Price-to-NTA-per-share ratio	~
5-year share price return (% p.a.)	2.6
Dividend reinvestment plan	Yes

Collins Foods, based in Brisbane, dates back to 1968 when it obtained the KFC fried chicken franchise for Queensland. Today it operates KFC outlets across Australia and is the country's largest KFC franchisee. It also manages the Taco Bell Mexican restaurant brand in Australia. It operates KFC stores in Germany and the Netherlands.

Latest business results (April 2025, full year)

Revenues rose but profits fell as higher costs and weaker consumer sentiment, particularly in Europe, hurt margins. A second-half recovery was insufficient to offset first-half weakness. Domestic KFC operations achieved a 3 per cent increase in sales, with the opening of a net nine new stores and same-store growth of 0.3 per cent. European revenues fell slightly, despite the opening of three new stores. Same-store sales fell by 2.5 per cent in the Netherlands and 3.3 per cent in Germany. Significant labour inflation in the Netherlands hurt profitability there, and the company also reported that war in the Middle East adversely affected consumer sentiment towards

American brands. Taco Bell recorded a fall in revenues and this business remained in the red. The result also included a $35 million non-cash impairment of 16 Netherlands restaurants, and at the statutory level the company's after-tax profit was just $8.8 million. At the end of the period the company operated 288 franchised KFC restaurants in Australia, up from 279 a year earlier, with a further 62 in the Netherlands, up from 59, and 16 in Germany, unchanged from the previous year. It also ran 27 Taco Bell restaurants in Australia.

Outlook

KFC has a strong image in Australia and continues to grow. In the quick-service restaurant category it is the second-largest brand, after McDonald's. It plans further expansion of its domestic network, with 28 to 30 new restaurants expected by 2028. It benefits from the fast-growing adoption of digital apps by its customers, with digital channels now responsible for more than a third of domestic sales. A new agreement with the KFC master franchisor Yum! Brands will allow Collins to accelerate restaurant development in Germany, which it regards as an under-penetrated market and potentially a new strategic growth pillar for the company. Its initial target is for 40 to 70 new KFC restaurants in Germany over the coming five years. By contrast, it has scaled back ambitious growth plans for the Netherlands in order to boost operational performance and productivity in that country. It has expressed a desire to sell its underperforming Taco Bell business.

Year to 27 April*	2024	2025
Revenues ($mn)	1488.9	1519.5
KFC Australia (%)	75	76
KFC Europe (%)	21	21
Taco Bell Australia (%)	4	3
EBIT ($mn)	122.2	114.5
EBIT margin (%)	8.2	7.5
Gross margin (%)	50.4	51.1
Profit before tax ($mn)	81.3	70.9
Profit after tax ($mn)	55.6	51.1
Earnings per share (c)	47.35	43.38
Cash flow per share (c)	137.30	137.97
Dividend (c)	28	26
Percentage franked	100	100
Net tangible assets per share ($)	~	~
Interest cover (times)	3.0	2.6
Return on equity (%)	13.7	12.3
Debt-to-equity ratio (%)	38.7	34.1
Current ratio	0.5	0.6

*28 April 2024

Commonwealth Bank of Australia

ASX code: CBA   www.commbank.com.au

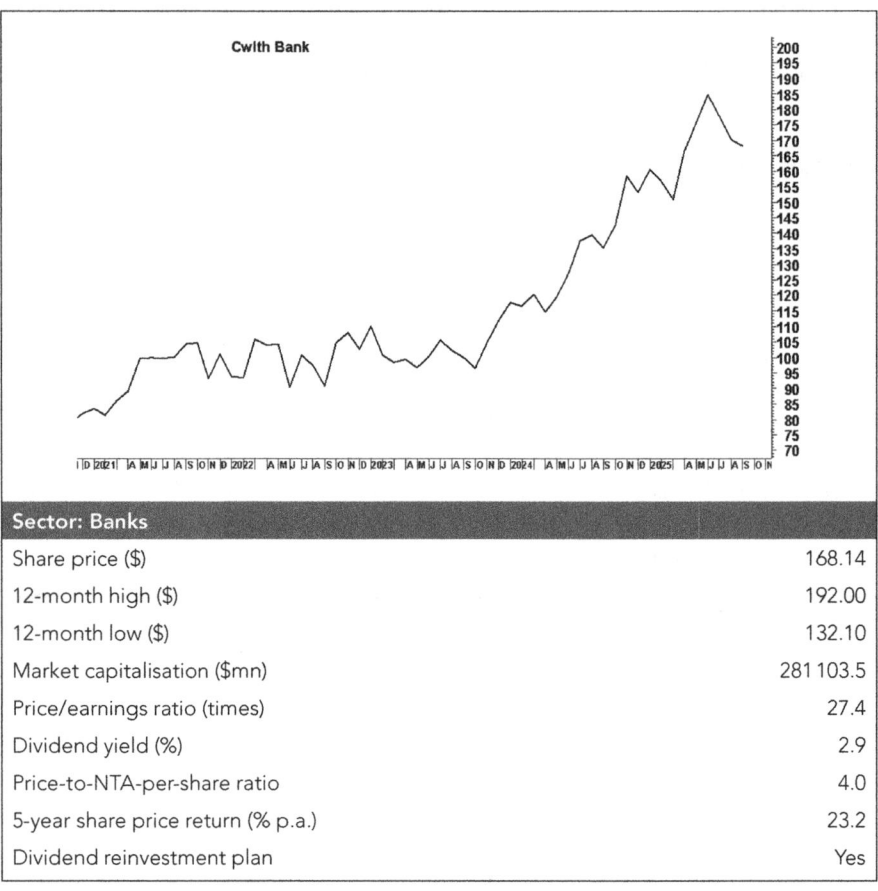

Sector: Banks	
Share price ($)	168.14
12-month high ($)	192.00
12-month low ($)	132.10
Market capitalisation ($mn)	281 103.5
Price/earnings ratio (times)	27.4
Dividend yield (%)	2.9
Price-to-NTA-per-share ratio	4.0
5-year share price return (% p.a.)	23.2
Dividend reinvestment plan	Yes

The Commonwealth Bank, based in Sydney, was founded in 1911 as a state-owned institution. Privatised during the 1990s, it is today Australia's largest bank, and one of the country's top providers of home loans, personal loans and credit cards, as well as the largest holder of deposits, while its Commonwealth Securities business is a prominent online stockbroker. It has significant interests in New Zealand through ASB Bank. It owns Bankwest in Western Australia.

Latest business results (June 2025, full year)

Profits bounced back after the decline of the previous year, driven by lending volume growth and a stable net interest margin. This was partly offset by a 6 per cent increase in operating expenses, due to both inflation and an acceleration of the bank's capital investment program for new technology. The core Retail Banking Services division achieved a 2 per cent rise in profits, reflecting deposit and lending balance growth. Profits for the Business Banking division were up 8 per cent, thanks to solid lending growth and higher equities trading volumes. The smaller Institutional Banking and Markets division benefited from higher earnings on deposits and equity, along with increased capital markets activity, and profits rose 9 per cent. Strong lending and deposit growth in New Zealand was offset by inflationary pressures, and profits were in line with the previous year.

Outlook

Commonwealth Bank occupies a powerful position in the domestic economy as well as in the local banking industry, and it is optimistic about the medium-term outlook. It views the Australian economy as generally resilient but is wary of rising geopolitical tensions and technological challenges. Thanks to a large branch network, offering many cross-selling opportunities, it has pricing power that has generally enabled it to maintain a cost advantage over some of its rivals. In recent years it has been boosting market share, and now claims more than a third of the retail banking market and a quarter share in business banking. Nevertheless, it faces rising competition, not only from other banks but also from large global technology firms that are increasingly expanding their presence, especially in the payments and small business segments. In response to continuing high levels of cyber-crime and financial fraud it has accelerated its technology modernisation program, including more than $900 million invested during the June 2025 year to help protect customers. With customers increasingly moving to digital channels for their banking, it has signed an agreement with artificial intelligence giant OpenAI to develop new personalised services.

Year to 30 June	2024	2025
Operating income ($mn)	26 921.0	28 290.0
Net interest income ($mn)	22 824.0	24 023.0
Operating expenses ($mn)	12 337.0	13 015.0
Profit before tax ($mn)	14 154.0	14 743.0
Profit after tax ($mn)	9 836.0	10 252.0
Earnings per share (c)	587.93	613.16
Dividend (c)	465	485
Percentage franked	100	100
Non-interest income to total income (%)	15.2	15.1
Net tangible assets per share ($)	39.17	42.29
Cost-to-income ratio (%)	45.8	46.0
Return on equity (%)	13.6	13.5
Return on assets (%)	0.8	0.8

Computershare Limited

ASX code: CPU   www.computershare.com

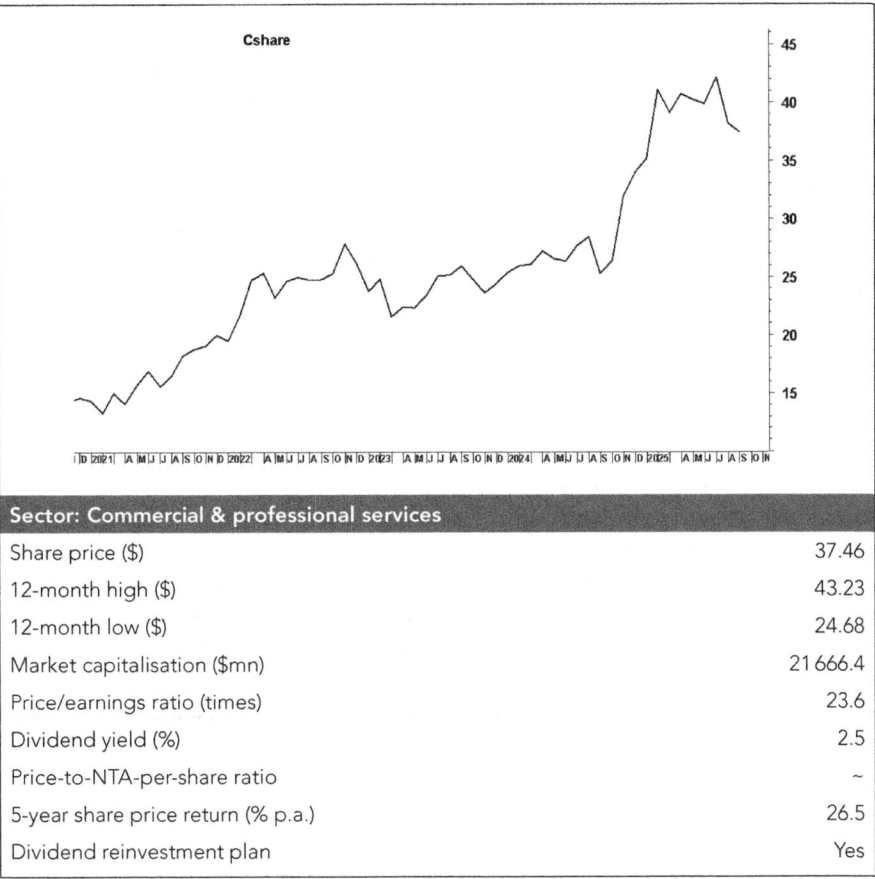

Sector: Commercial & professional services	
Share price ($)	37.46
12-month high ($)	43.23
12-month low ($)	24.68
Market capitalisation ($mn)	21 666.4
Price/earnings ratio (times)	23.6
Dividend yield (%)	2.5
Price-to-NTA-per-share ratio	~
5-year share price return (% p.a.)	26.5
Dividend reinvestment plan	Yes

Melbourne-based Computershare, established in 1978, is one of the world's leading financial services and technology providers for the global securities industry, offering services to listed companies, investors, employees, exchanges and other financial institutions. These offerings include share registration, employee equity plans, corporate governance, class action administration and other specialised financial, governance and stakeholder communication services. Its global corporate trust business helps administer debt securities in the US. The company manages more than 75 million customer records for more than 25 000 clients across all major financial markets, with significant market shares in many countries. More than 90 per cent of revenues come from abroad, including more than half from the US.

Latest business results (June 2025, full year)

Revenues and profits rose again, with strength across most businesses, although slightly dampened by falling interest rates. The core Issuer Services division, which includes register maintenance, stakeholder relationship management and corporate governance services, recorded growth in all product lines. The Employee Share Plans division achieved double-digit profit growth, thanks to new client fees and higher participant trading activity. Corporate Trust division revenues and profits also rose, reflecting stronger market activity driving new business. Margin income—the interest that the company earns on the cash it holds on behalf of clients—fell 9 per cent to US$761 million. Note that Computershare reports its results in US dollars. The Australian dollar figures in this book have been converted at prevailing exchange rates.

Outlook

Computershare is a beneficiary of robust worldwide equity markets, and can suffer in periods of volatility. It is also hurt by rising inflation. Nevertheless, it continues to gain market share in its issuer services operation, and it is actively working on many new technological innovations. It notes that companies are increasingly using employee share plans to attract and reward staff. Thanks to the continuing roll-out of its EquatePlus technology, Computershare is achieving success in drawing new clients to its employee share plan business. It expects its issuer services business to benefit from an increase in merger and acquisition activity during the June 2026 year. Two acquisitions have helped it expand its investor relations product offerings. Its corporate trust business is seeing a pleasing recovery in debt issuance volumes. It holds a considerable amount of clients' funds in various forms, which means that its financial results benefit from rising interest rates, but can be hurt when they fall. The company's early forecast is for June 2026 EPS growth of around 4 per cent.

Year to 30 June	2024	2025
Revenues ($mn)	4421.0	4715.7
Issuer services ($)	41	40
Corporate trust (%)	32	31
Employee share plans & voucher services (%)	15	16
EBIT ($mn)	1256.2	1395.1
EBIT margin (%)	28.4	29.6
Profit before tax ($mn)	1052.2	1216.5
Profit after tax ($mn)	747.2	931.7
Earnings per share (c)	124.82	158.78
Cash flow per share (c)	171.16	201.26
Dividend (c)	82	93
Percentage franked	10	0
Net tangible assets per share ($)	~	~
Interest cover (times)	6.2	7.8
Return on equity (%)	24.1	30.0
Debt-to-equity ratio (%)	23.7	24.5
Current ratio	2.9	2.2

Cosol Limited

ASX code: COS

cosol.global

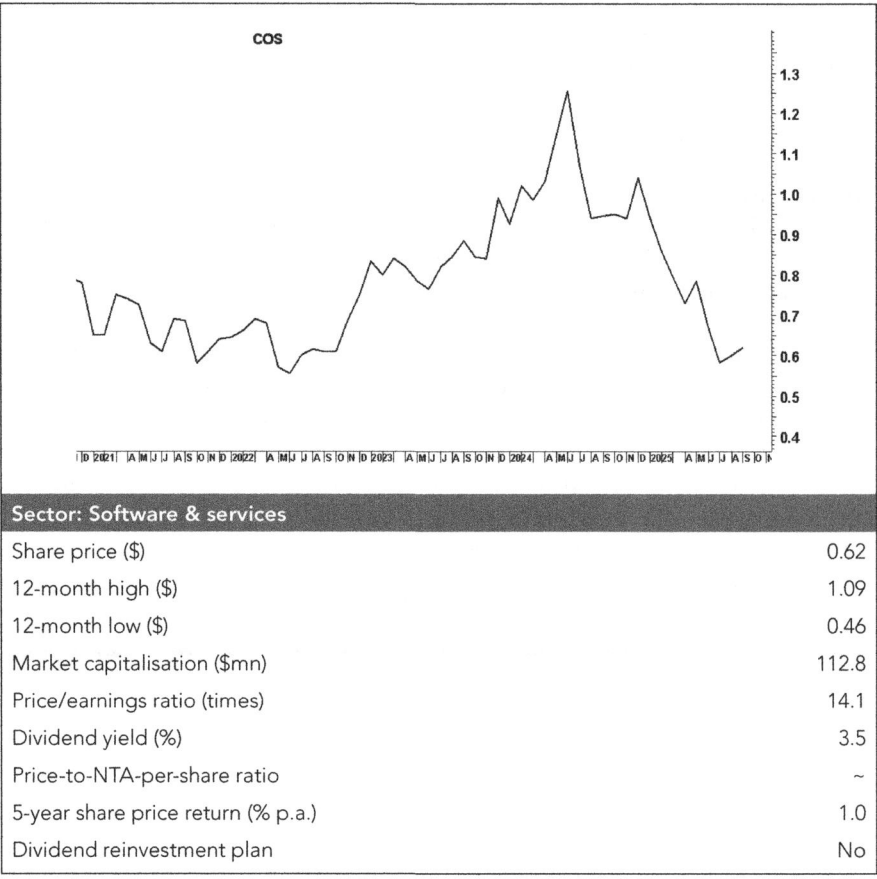

Sector: Software & services	
Share price ($)	0.62
12-month high ($)	1.09
12-month low ($)	0.46
Market capitalisation ($mn)	112.8
Price/earnings ratio (times)	14.1
Dividend yield (%)	3.5
Price-to-NTA-per-share ratio	~
5-year share price return (% p.a.)	1.0
Dividend reinvestment plan	No

Digital services specialist Cosol, founded in 2000, is based in Brisbane and specialises in the provision of software platforms and data management systems for the enterprise asset management sector. Through its products, customers in asset-intensive industries such as natural resources, infrastructure, defence and utilities can more efficiently optimise and enhance their operations. It functions from offices in Australia and the US, and more than 10 per cent of its income derives from abroad, principally North America. In December 2024 it acquired the data analytics specialist Toustone.

Latest business results (June 2025, full year)

Revenues rose, with organic growth augmented by the Toustone acquisition, but profits fell. At the underlying EBITDA level profits actually rose, but rising depreciation and amortisation charges led to declines in EBIT and pre- and after-tax profits, with operating margins also down. Organic revenues were up by more than 10 per cent, with a full-year contribution from several important multi-year contracts secured in the previous year, including with QBuild, Horizon Power and CleanCo. During the year the company boosted customer numbers by 13 per cent. The natural resources sector was responsible for 54 per cent of company revenues, with 15 per cent from infrastructure and transport companies and 13 per cent from energy and water businesses.

Outlook

Asset management involves the operation and maintenance of physical assets in a cost-effective manner. In some industries asset management costs can account for up to half of operating expenses, and efficient asset management is essential for profitability and growth. Cosol has developed a series of digital products, based on what it terms its Asset Management as a Service model, that permit clients to solve complex operational challenges. Its latest product, Con-AI, uses artificial intelligence to allow clients to extract maximum value from their asset base quickly and easily by providing answers in a clear and conversational manner, and making unnecessary the need for technical proficiency or the navigation of multiple screens. It believes that Con-AI will lead to a significant reduction in management time spent on business analysis. Cosol has grown rapidly, both organically and through acquisitions. It expects its Toustone acquisition to provide a significant boost to its intellectual property and proprietary software products. However, the company has expressed concerns that its rapid expansion has placed bigger-than-expected pressure on profit margins, which were lower than anticipated in the June 2025 year. Consequently, ensuring that all growth is strongly profitable has become a primary focus, with solid double-digit profit growth forecast for June 2026.

Year to 30 June	2024	2025
Revenues ($mn)	101.9	116.8
EBIT ($mn)	13.4	12.8
EBIT margin (%)	13.2	11.0
Gross margin (%)	33.6	31.8
Profit before tax ($mn)	12.0	11.0
Profit after tax ($mn)	8.5	7.9
Earnings per share (c)	4.98	4.38
Cash flow per share (c)	5.93	6.04
Dividend (c)	2.39	2.17
Percentage franked	100	100
Net tangible assets per share ($)	~	~
Interest cover (times)	9.6	7.1
Return on equity (%)	15.2	10.8
Debt-to-equity ratio (%)	17.3	25.7
Current ratio	1.4	1.5

Credit Corp Group Limited

ASX code: CCP   www.creditcorpgroup.com.au

Sector: Financial services	
Share price ($)	16.40
12-month high ($)	18.51
12-month low ($)	11.28
Market capitalisation ($mn)	1116.3
Price/earnings ratio (times)	11.9
Dividend yield (%)	4.1
Price-to-NTA-per-share ratio	1.3
5-year share price return (% p.a.)	0.7
Dividend reinvestment plan	No

Sydney-based Credit Corp was formed in 1992, although it has its origins in companies that started in the early 1970s. It engages in debt collection activity, through the acquisition of defaulted consumer debt for companies in numerous industries, notably the banking, finance, telecommunications and utilities sectors. It has operations in Australia, New Zealand and the United States, as well as a large call centre in the Philippines. It maintains an agency collection service, under the brands National Credit Management, Baycorp and Collection House, for clients who wish to outsource debt collections without actually selling the debt. It also operates a consumer lending business with brands that include CarStart, Wallet Wizard and Wizit.

Latest business results (June 2025, full year)

A strong US performance and further growth in the company's high-margin consumer lending operation helped deliver a solid result, reversing two years of profit decline.

Favourable market conditions and some impressive productivity gains powered the US division to a large jump in revenues and profits, and it now represents nearly a quarter of company turnover, with profit margins higher than those prevailing domestically. By contrast, the debt-buying business in Australia and New Zealand was hit by rising competition and sluggish growth, and revenues and profits were down. The consumer lending business continued to expand, and at June 2025 the company's loan book stood at $466 million, up 5 per cent from a year earlier. Consumer lending represented 37 per cent of turnover but around half of company profit.

Outlook

Credit Corp's main business effectively involves buying consumer debt at a discount to its face value, and then seeking to recover an amount in excess of the purchase price. Often this recovery takes the form of phased payments over an extended period, and Credit Corp thus has substantial recurring income. Setting an appropriate price for the acquisition of parcels of debt is one of the keys to success, and Credit Corp has acquired considerable expertise in this. Nevertheless, it is wary about the near-term outlook for its domestic debt-buying operations, though it expects its US business to continue to grow. It is working to expand its consumer lending business, and sees great potential in its planned new Wizit digital credit card, aimed at the credit-impaired consumer segment. In addition, the company has announced plans to enter the British lending market. Credit Corp's early forecast is for an after-tax profit in the June 2026 year of between $100 million and $110 million.

Year to 30 June	2024	2025
Revenues ($mn)	519.6	545.6
Debt ledger purchasing Australia/NZ (%)	48	40
Consumer lending Australia/NZ (%)	34	37
Debt ledger purchasing US (%)	17	23
EBIT ($mn)	142.1	169.9
EBIT margin (%)	27.4	31.1
Profit before tax ($mn)	116.2	133.6
Profit after tax ($mn)	81.2	94.1
Earnings per share (c)	119.29	138.24
Cash flow per share (c)	133.70	150.78
Dividend (c)	38	68
Percentage franked	100	100
Net tangible assets per share ($)	11.55	12.55
Interest cover (times)	5.5	4.7
Return on equity (%)	10.0	11.0
Debt-to-equity ratio (%)	42.4	38.7
Current ratio	6.1	6.9

CSL Limited

ASX code: CSL

investors.csl.com

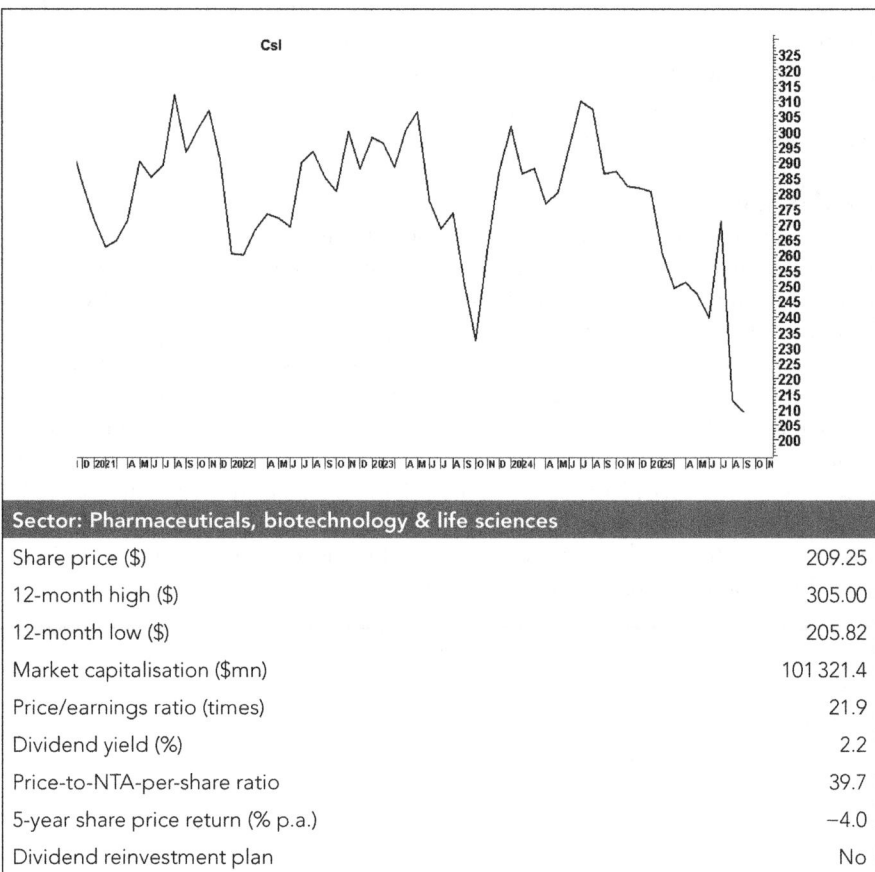

Sector: Pharmaceuticals, biotechnology & life sciences	
Share price ($)	209.25
12-month high ($)	305.00
12-month low ($)	205.82
Market capitalisation ($mn)	101 321.4
Price/earnings ratio (times)	21.9
Dividend yield (%)	2.2
Price-to-NTA-per-share ratio	39.7
5-year share price return (% p.a.)	−4.0
Dividend reinvestment plan	No

Melbourne-based CSL, formerly the state-owned Commonwealth Serum Laboratories, was founded in 1916. It has grown organically and through acquisition to become a major global biotechnology company, with operations in numerous countries—with particular strength in the US, Australia, Germany, the UK, China and Switzerland—and more than 90 per cent of revenues derive from outside Australia. Its principal business, through its CSL Behring division, is the provision of plasma-derived coagulation therapies for the treatment of a range of medical conditions. The CSL Seqirus division is one of the world's largest influenza vaccine companies and a producer of other prescription medicines and pharmaceutical products. The CSL Vifor division, based on the 2022 acquisition of Swiss biotech company Vifor Pharma, makes products for renal therapy and iron deficiency. CSL is Australia's largest healthcare company and enjoys high margins and high market shares for many of its products.

Latest business results (June 2025, full year)

Revenues and profits continued their upward trajectory, led by the core CSL Behring division. Revenues for this business rose 6 per cent, with profits up nearly 8 per cent, and particularly strong demand for haemophilia products. The company also achieved further success in reducing plasma collection costs. CSL Vifor reported revenue growth of 8 per cent, with profits up nearly 15 per cent, thanks especially to growing demand for the company's range of drugs for kidney disease. CSL Seqirus saw revenues up 2 per cent, but profits down 8 per cent, hurt by a decline in US vaccination rates. Note that CSL reports its results in US dollars. The figures in this book are based on prevailing exchange rates.

Outlook

CSL remains a powerhouse biotechnology company, with an impressive research and development capability and a solid pipeline of potential new products. It plans a major restructuring of its operations, costing up to $770 million during the June 2026 year and aimed at delivering annualised cost savings to the company of up to $550 million. A key strategy is the demerger of CSL Seqirus by mid-2026, creating a global vaccine leader listed on the ASX, and with the expectation of making the business more agile and efficient to manage. The company also plans to consolidate its many research and development hubs, as well as merging the medical and commercial operations of its CSL Behring and CSL Vifor businesses. It has closed 22 underperforming plasma collection centres, and it expects to reduce total employee numbers by up to 15 per cent.

Year to 30 June	2024	2025
Revenues ($mn)	22 424.2	23 935.4
CSL Behring (%)	72	72
CSL Seqirus (%)	14	14
CSL Vifor (%)	14	14
EBIT ($mn)	5 834.8	6 418.5
EBIT margin (%)	26.0	26.8
Gross margin (%)	51.8	51.9
Profit before tax ($mn)	5 113.6	5 729.2
Profit after tax ($mn)	4 003.0	4 618.5
Earnings per share (c)	828.77	954.15
Cash flow per share (c)	1 123.01	1 277.39
Dividend (c)	397.35	452.19
Percentage franked	0	0
Net tangible assets per share ($)	~	5.28
Interest cover (times)	8.1	9.3
Return on equity (%)	15.9	16.6
Debt-to-equity ratio (%)	54.3	43.6
Current ratio	2.2	2.5

Data#3 Limited

ASX code: DTL   investor.data3.com

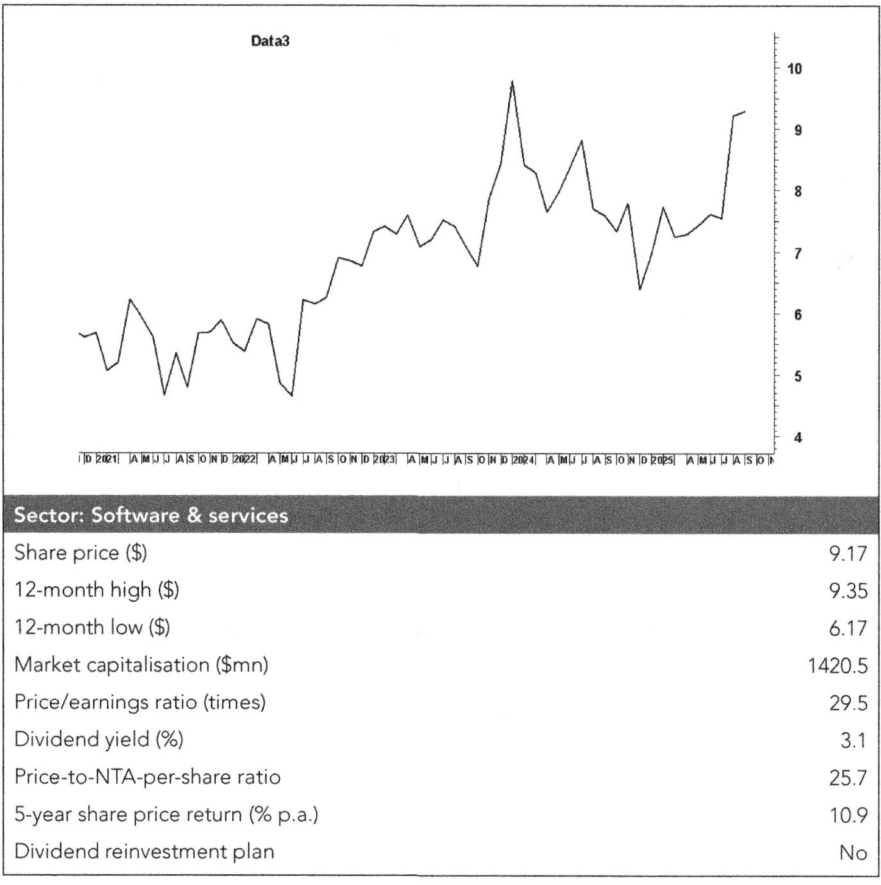

Sector: Software & services	
Share price ($)	9.17
12-month high ($)	9.35
12-month low ($)	6.17
Market capitalisation ($mn)	1420.5
Price/earnings ratio (times)	29.5
Dividend yield (%)	3.1
Price-to-NTA-per-share ratio	25.7
5-year share price return (% p.a.)	10.9
Dividend reinvestment plan	No

Brisbane-based IT consultant Data#3 was formed in 1984 from the merger of computer software consultancy Powell, Clark and Associates with IBM typewriter dealer Albrand Typewriters and Office Machines. Today it operates from offices around Australia and in Fiji, providing information and communication technology services to a wide range of sectors that include banking and finance, mining, tourism and leisure, legal, health care, manufacturing, distribution, government and utilities.

Latest business results (June 2025, full year)

Revenues rose and the company achieved its seventh straight year of higher profits, with growth across most of its businesses. The largest division, Infrastructure Solutions, supplies hardware such as servers, storage devices and network systems. A strong second half offset first-half weakness, and sales rose, with a series of operational efficiencies boosting profit margins. The Services division, comprising a variety of service-related businesses, also achieved growth, driven by a 25 per cent surge in sales for the Managed Services business, thanks to some large contracts in the mining industry. Continued strength in the government and education sectors boosted the Software Solutions division. Recurring revenue rose from 67 per cent to 69 per cent of total company income.

Outlook

Technology investment continues to grow in Australia, and Data#3 expects IT, and particularly digital transformation, to play a leading role in the country's economic future. A key competitive advantage is the strength of its partnerships with major vendors, notably Microsoft, Cisco and Hewlett Packard, with each of whom it is the leading Australian partner. It sees particular potential in the evolution of artificial intelligence, which it is embedding in all its products. Thanks to its partnership with Microsoft it is experiencing strong demand for Microsoft Copilot AI workshops. The company's internal adoption of AI is boosting its own operational efficiency by improving its systems and processes. Another key growth sector is cybersecurity, which has become the leading priority for many customers. In 2024 Data#3 opened its own Security Operations Centre to help protect customers, and it has launched a series of new Microsoft data security software products. A new incentive program from Microsoft is expected to put pressure on the Software Solutions division in the June 2026 year. However, the company is optimistic of continuing growth from its two other divisions. Thanks to its expertise in the design and implementation of networking projects at large sites, the company expects to benefit from a series of major infrastructure developments in advance of the 2032 Brisbane Olympics.

Year to 30 June	2024	2025
Revenues ($mn)	805.7	852.7
Infrastructure solutions (%)	60	59
Services (%)	31	32
Software solutions (%)	9	9
EBIT ($mn)	63.2	70.2
EBIT margin (%)	7.8	8.2
Gross margin (%)	33.5	33.9
Profit before tax ($mn)	62.1	69.1
Profit after tax ($mn)	43.3	48.2
Earnings per share (c)	28.00	31.12
Cash flow per share (c)	32.56	35.31
Dividend (c)	25.5	28.1
Percentage franked	100	100
Net tangible assets per share ($)	0.29	0.36
Interest cover (times)	56.7	67.5
Return on equity (%)	60.5	60.6
Debt-to-equity ratio (%)	~	~
Current ratio	1.1	1.1

Downer EDI Limited

ASX code: DOW   www.downergroup.com

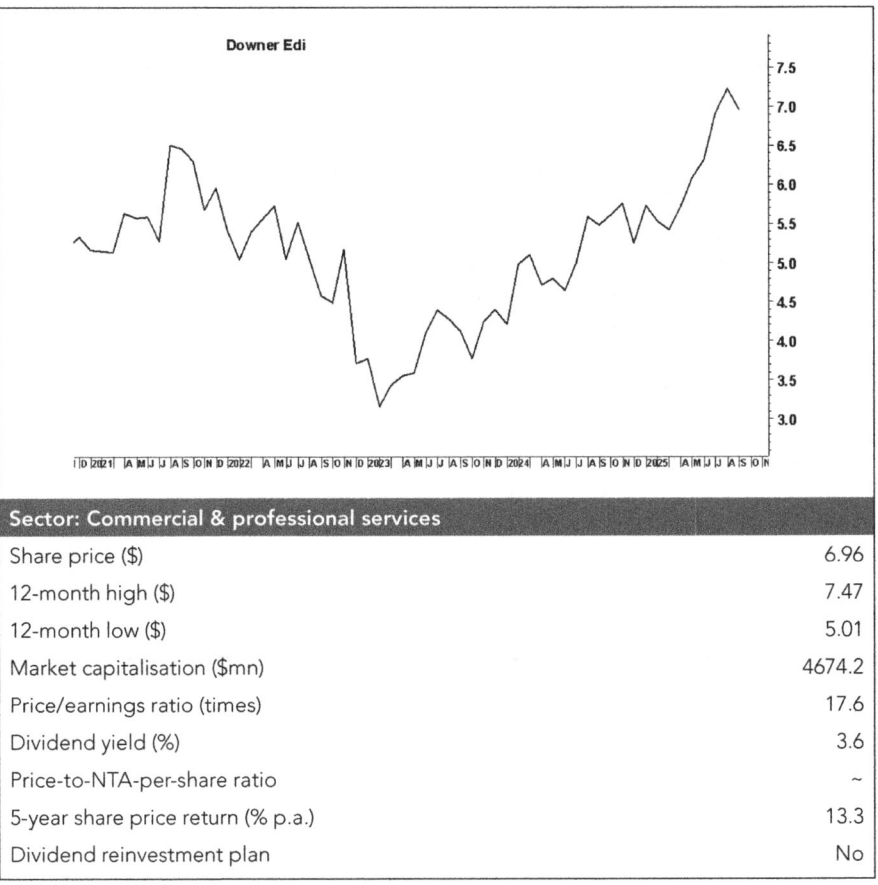

Sector: Commercial & professional services	
Share price ($)	6.96
12-month high ($)	7.47
12-month low ($)	5.01
Market capitalisation ($mn)	4674.2
Price/earnings ratio (times)	17.6
Dividend yield (%)	3.6
Price-to-NTA-per-share ratio	~
5-year share price return (% p.a.)	13.3
Dividend reinvestment plan	No

Sydney-based integrated services provider Downer EDI was established in New Zealand in the 1930s. It later expanded to Australia, and has grown substantially through a long series of mergers and acquisitions. It designs, builds and maintains a wide variety of infrastructure assets, with a focus on transportation, utilities, social infrastructure and citizen services, defence, telecommunications and energy. Nearly 30 per cent of its income derives from abroad, principally from its operations in New Zealand.

Latest business results (June 2025, full year)

Revenues edged down but underlying profits showed healthy gains, with strength across most areas of business, as Downer realised the benefits of a major restructuring program aimed at simplifying its operations and improving margins. The company classifies its activities into three broad divisions. The largest of these, Transport, saw revenues largely unchanged from the previous year, but with profits up 11 per cent as the company improved contract delivery and cut costs. NZ roadworks activity remained strong. Weakness in Australian roadworks was offset by growth in airport runway projects. Revenues fell for the Energy and Utilities division, but profits jumped 44 per cent as the company exited some low-margin work and effected a turnaround in this business. The Facilities division — the most profitable of the three divisions — saw revenues flat for the year but with profits edging up and some notable growth in government and defence estate maintenance businesses.

Outlook

Downer is a major force in the construction and maintenance of infrastructure facilities in Australia and NZ. It has been undertaking a major restructuring of its operations over several years. It has divested itself of some large non-core activities, including its cleaning businesses in Australia and NZ, its Australian laundries business and its NZ catering operation. It is also selling its 49 per cent interest in transportation company Keolis Downer and it continues to exit low-margin work. The next phase of its transformation includes investment in modernising its work practices, with further digitisation and the adoption of artificial intelligence technology to drive productivity. Consequently, it expects a further profit rise in the June 2026 year, even with little revenue advance. It sees great long-term growth potential from its exposure to several key themes. Among these is the transition away from coal towards a variety of energy sources, including renewable energy. It also expects to benefit from the likely expansion of defence spending in Australia, and in September 2025 it announced a new $3.05 billion contract to provide property and asset services for 36 Department of Defence sites.

Year to 30 June	2024	2025
Revenues ($mn)	10 979.5	10 481.5
Transport (%)	52	51
Energy & utilities (%)	27	28
Facilities (%)	19	21
EBIT ($mn)	369.3	470.4
EBIT margin (%)	3.4	4.5
Profit before tax ($mn)	269.0	371.1
Profit after tax ($mn)	193.9	264.7
Earnings per share (c)	28.92	39.46
Cash flow per share (c)	80.53	90.52
Dividend (c)	17	24.9
Percentage franked	32	89
Net tangible assets per share ($)	~	~
Interest cover (times)	3.7	4.7
Return on equity (%)	9.3	12.8
Debt-to-equity ratio (%)	20.2	11.2
Current ratio	1.1	0.9

Duratec Limited

ASX code: DUR   www.duratec.com.au

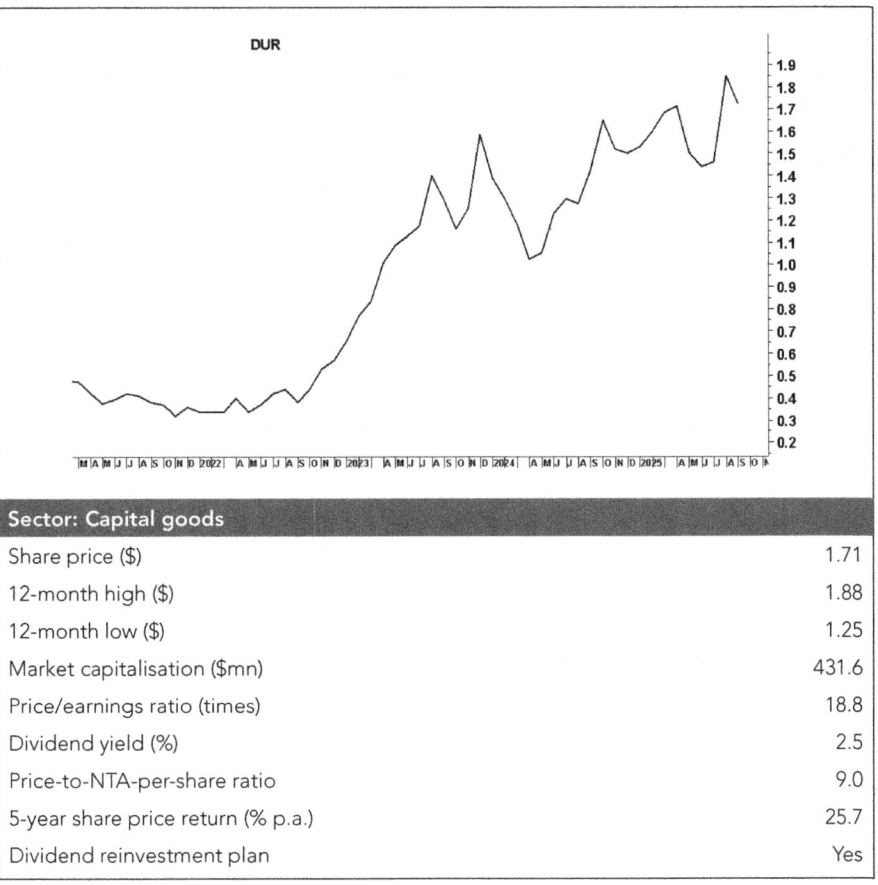

Sector: Capital goods	
Share price ($)	1.71
12-month high ($)	1.88
12-month low ($)	1.25
Market capitalisation ($mn)	431.6
Price/earnings ratio (times)	18.8
Dividend yield (%)	2.5
Price-to-NTA-per-share ratio	9.0
5-year share price return (% p.a.)	25.7
Dividend reinvestment plan	Yes

Perth engineering company Duratec was founded in 2010. It has grown rapidly, and is today a leader in the provision of remediation services aimed especially at extending the life of steel and concrete infrastructure. It operates from 19 locations throughout Australia. It owns MEnD, a boutique engineering consultancy, and WPF, a provider of specialist engineering services to the energy sector. It holds a 49 per cent stake in DDR Australia, a majority Aboriginal-owned contracting and project management company. In August 2025 it acquired electrical infrastructure provider EIG Australia.

Latest business results (June 2025, full year)

Revenues and profits rose modestly in a mixed year. The company's largest division, Defence, saw its revenues fall 18 per cent to $181.4 million due to timing delays in project awards. The Mining and Industrial division was also weak, with revenues down 12 per cent to $136.6 million following the completion of a large BHP contract and some project award delays. By contrast, the small Energy division enjoyed an excellent year, with revenues jumping 77 per cent to $82.5 million, thanks to several high-value contracts, including with Santos and Woodside Energy. The Building and Facade division saw revenues and profits flat for the year.

Outlook

Duratec's core activity involves the repair and remediation of ageing structures. For many owners of decaying large infrastructure assets, repair can be a cheaper option than replacement, and the company has gained a high reputation for its work, with a substantial amount of repeat business. It has a significant exposure to defence-related activity. It has delivered projects at more than 40 defence bases and stands to be a beneficiary of rising Australian military spending. In particular, it envisages great potential in government plans to spend $8 billion to expand and upgrade defence infrastructure in Western Australia. It sees the mining and industrial sectors as entering a new phase of asset life-cycle management, and estimates a total annual addressable market for the iron ore industry alone of $1.2 billion for its work. It is also optimistic about the energy sector, where it estimates the total addressable market for maintenance work at some $5 billion per year. It expects the 2032 Brisbane Olympics to drive demand for asset rejuvenation and remediation. It believes the $9 million acquisition of EIG Australia will allow it to enter new markets and diversify its revenue streams. At August 2025 Duratec had an order book worth $390 million and it was tendering for a further $1.65 billion worth of business.

Year to 30 June	2024	2025
Revenues ($mn)	555.8	573.0
Defence (%)	40	32
Mining & industrial (%)	28	24
Building & façade (%)	20	20
Energy (%)	8	14
EBIT ($mn)	31.5	32.6
EBIT margin (%)	5.7	5.7
Gross margin (%)	17.3	18.6
Profit before tax ($mn)	29.1	29.5
Profit after tax ($mn)	21.4	22.8
Earnings per share (c)	8.66	9.10
Cash flow per share (c)	14.60	15.56
Dividend (c)	4	4.25
Percentage franked	100	100
Net tangible assets per share ($)	0.16	0.19
Interest cover (times)	13.3	10.4
Return on equity (%)	40.7	34.2
Debt-to-equity ratio (%)	~	~
Current ratio	1.1	1.2

Evolution Mining Limited

ASX code: EVN   www.evolutionmining.com.au

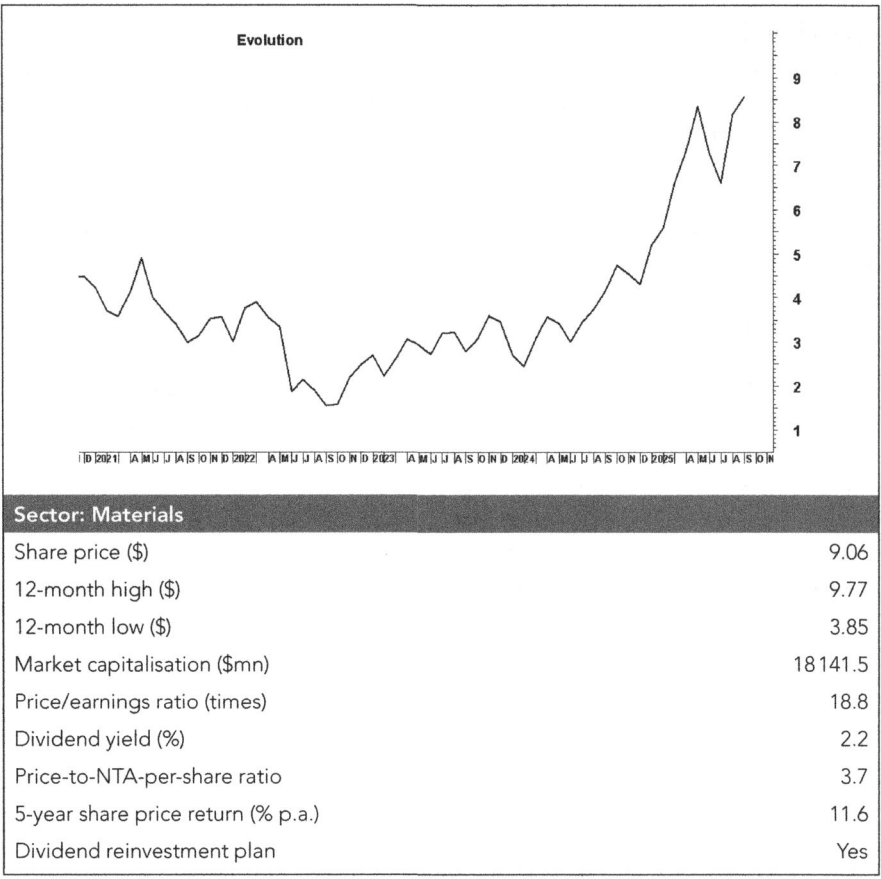

Sector: Materials	
Share price ($)	9.06
12-month high ($)	9.77
12-month low ($)	3.85
Market capitalisation ($mn)	18 141.5
Price/earnings ratio (times)	18.8
Dividend yield (%)	2.2
Price-to-NTA-per-share ratio	3.7
5-year share price return (% p.a.)	11.6
Dividend reinvestment plan	Yes

Gold and copper mining company Evolution Mining, based in Sydney, was formed in 2011 from the merger of Catalpa Resources and Conquest Mining and the acquisition of two mines from Newcrest Mining. It now operates five fully owned mines — Cowal in New South Wales, Ernest Henry and Mt Rawdon in Queensland, Mungari in Western Australia and Red Lake in Ontario, Canada — as well as an 80 per cent holding in the Northparkes mine in New South Wales. In addition, it maintains an active exploration program.

Latest business results (June 2025, full year)

Increased production and a surging gold price sent profits rocketing. Total gold production for the year of 750 512 ounces was up 5 per cent from the previous year, with copper production of 76 261 tonnes up 12 per cent. The average all-in sustaining production cost of $1653 per ounce was 12 per cent higher than the previous year, driven especially by inflationary pressures. The average gold price received by the company of $4300 per ounce was up 35 per cent from the previous year, with the average copper price of $14 470 per tonne up 6 per cent.

Outlook

Evolution's strategy is to build its gold reserves through developing or acquiring new assets, while also improving the quality of its portfolio and driving down expenses in order to remain a low-cost producer. In particular, it has aimed at delivering operational stability and predictability through the ownership of a number of similar-sized mines, rather than holding just a single mine or a dominant mine. It plans capital spending of up to $980 million in the June 2026 year. At its largest mine, Cowral, it has initiated a major project aimed at extending operations to 2042. The completion of a mine extension feasibility study for Ernest Henry will lead to prolonging mine life to 2040. A major expansion project, completed in April, has led to increased production at Mungari. With the cessation of mining activities at Mt Rawdon, Evolution is looking to transform the mine site into a hydro-electric power station and energy storage facility. It is also actively seeking new gold and copper deposits at its existing operations as well as at sites in Australia, the US and Canada. The company has set a gold production target of 710 000 ounces to 780 000 ounces for the June 2026 year, with copper production of 70 000 to 80 000 tonnes. It expects an average all-in sustaining cost in the range of $1720 to $1880 per ounce.

Year to 30 June	2024	2025
Revenues ($mn)	3215.8	4351.5
Cowal (%)	31	33
Ernest Henry (%)	28	23
Red Lake (%)	11	13
Mungari (%)	12	12
Northparkes (%)	9	12
EBIT ($mn)	853.3	1481.8
EBIT margin (%)	26.5	34.1
Gross margin (%)	28.7	35.8
Profit before tax ($mn)	704.8	1321.4
Profit after tax ($mn)	481.8	958.2
Earnings per share (c)	25.12	48.10
Cash flow per share (c)	59.80	85.40
Dividend (c)	7	20
Percentage franked	100	100
Net tangible assets per share ($)	2.04	2.45
Interest cover (times)	5.7	9.2
Return on equity (%)	13.0	21.1
Debt-to-equity ratio (%)	36.7	19.4
Current ratio	1.1	1.5

Fiducian Group Limited

ASX code: FID   www.fiducian.com.au

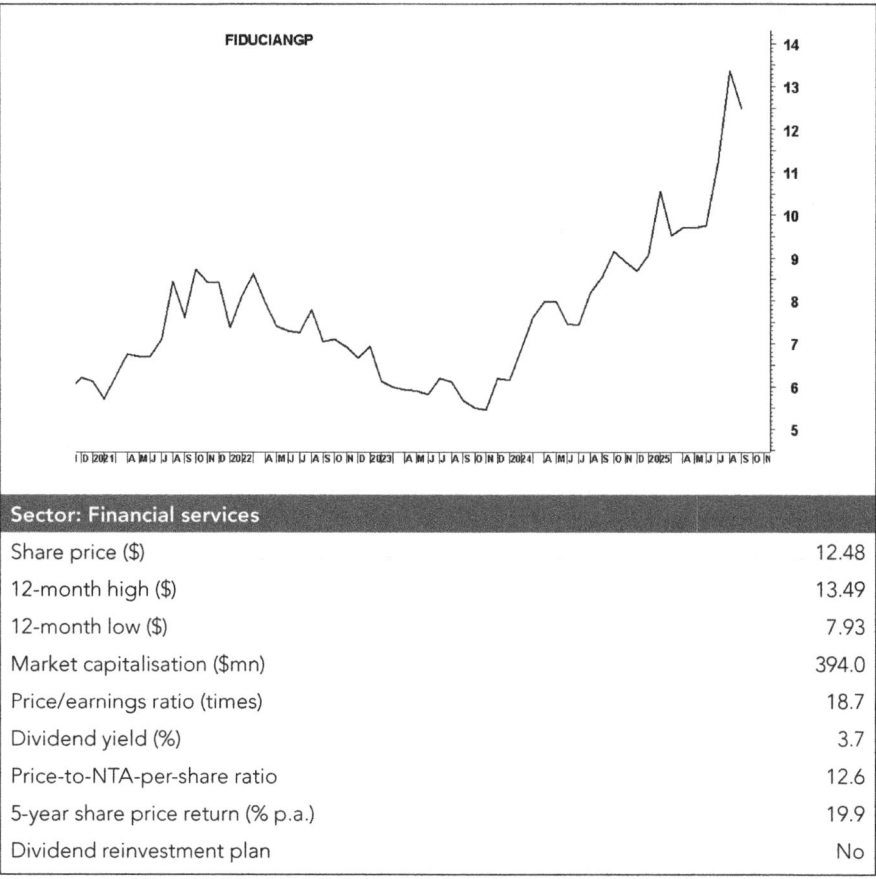

Sector: Financial services	
Share price ($)	12.48
12-month high ($)	13.49
12-month low ($)	7.93
Market capitalisation ($mn)	394.0
Price/earnings ratio (times)	18.7
Dividend yield (%)	3.7
Price-to-NTA-per-share ratio	12.6
5-year share price return (% p.a.)	19.9
Dividend reinvestment plan	No

Sydney financial services company Fiducian Group was founded in 1996 by executive chairman Indy Singh, who owns more than a third of the company equity. Initially it specialised in the provision of masterfund, client administration and financial planning services to financial advisory groups. It has since expanded and is now a holding company with five divisions—Fiducian Portfolio Services is in charge of trustee and superannuation services; Fiducian Investment Management Services operates the company's managed funds; Fiducian Services is the administration service provider for all the company's products; Fiducian Financial Services manages the company's financial planning businesses; and Fiducian Business Services provides accounting and business services.

Latest business results (June 2025, full year)

Underlying revenues and profits rose for the second consecutive year in a good result. For reporting purposes the company divides its operations into broad segments. The largest of these is the funds management business, which again enjoyed solid growth in a buoyant market environment. Financial planning operations also achieved gains in revenues and profits as the company opened one new office and continued to work at expanding this business. However, profit margins for financial planning remained substantially below those for other activities. The third key segment, platform administration, which offers portfolio wrap administration services to financial planners, reported higher revenues, thanks to continuing inflows from the company's advisers, but with profits edging down. At June 2025 the total funds under management, advice and administration of $14.8 billion was up from $13.5 billion a year earlier.

Outlook

Fiducian managed 46 financial planning offices across Australia at June 2025, both company-owned and franchised, with a total of 77 financial advisers. It is continually seeking new offices to join the group, and it has also been achieving solid organic growth. At the same time, Fiducian itself has been named as a possible takeover target for a larger financial institution. The funds management business offers a suite of funds from various asset managers, and the company believes that its method of choosing managers with differing investment styles offers the ability to deliver above-average returns with greater diversification and reduced risk. As fund volumes increase the company's profit margins expand. It is paying around $2.4 million to acquire a new client base for its financial planning operations, and it expects this to provide a boost to future business. However, Fiducian is vulnerable to any major downturn in financial markets. At June 2025 it had no debt and cash holdings of nearly $35 million.

Year to 30 June	2024	2025
Revenues ($mn)	79.3	87.6
Funds management (%)	37	38
Financial planning (%)	36	36
Platform administration (%)	27	26
EBIT ($mn)	24.1	29.0
EBIT margin (%)	30.4	33.1
Profit before tax ($mn)	24.1	29.0
Profit after tax ($mn)	17.7	21.0
Earnings per share (c)	56.33	66.80
Cash flow per share (c)	71.00	80.74
Dividend (c)	39.3	46.6
Percentage franked	100	100
Net tangible assets per share ($)	0.84	0.99
Interest cover (times)	~	~
Return on equity (%)	33.6	36.6
Debt-to-equity ratio (%)	~	~
Current ratio	2.7	3.2

Fortescue Limited

ASX code: FMG   www.fortescue.com

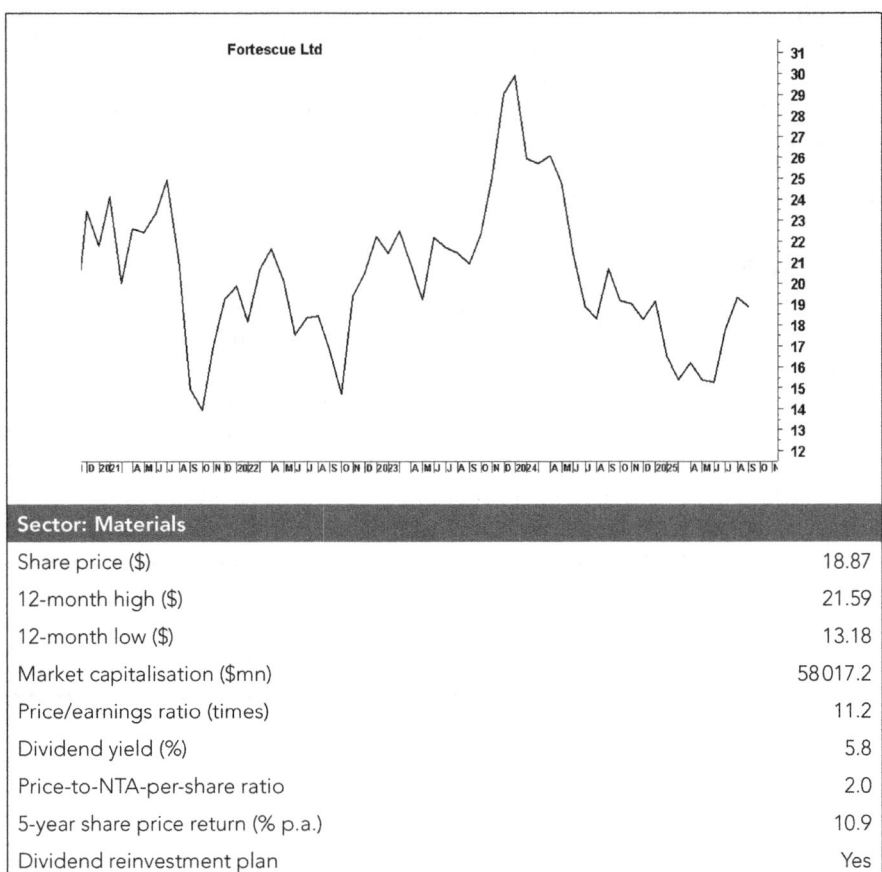

Sector: Materials	
Share price ($)	18.87
12-month high ($)	21.59
12-month low ($)	13.18
Market capitalisation ($mn)	58 017.2
Price/earnings ratio (times)	11.2
Dividend yield (%)	5.8
Price-to-NTA-per-share ratio	2.0
5-year share price return (% p.a.)	10.9
Dividend reinvestment plan	Yes

Perth-based Fortescue was founded in 2003. It has been responsible for discovering and developing some of the largest iron ore mines in the world and is today one of the world's largest iron ore producers. Its Australian operations are in the Pilbara region, at the Chichester Hub, comprising the Cloudbreak and Christmas Creek mines; at the Western Hub, comprising the Solomon and Eliwana mines; and at Iron Bridge. It operates its own heavy-haul railway between the mines and port facilities at Port Hedland. In addition, it is involved in the Belinga Iron Ore Project in Gabon. It is engaged in exploration work at sites in Australia and abroad. It is also involved in a variety of green energy projects. Some 85 per cent to 90 per cent of its iron ore sales are to China. In 2025 it acquired Red Hawk Mining.

Latest business results (June 2025, full year)

Weakness in the iron ore price sent revenues and profits down. Sales of 198.4 million tonnes were up from 191.3 million tonnes in the previous year, but the average price received of US$85 per tonne was down from US$103. Average production costs also fell, from US$18.24 per tonne to US$17.99. The company's tiny Energy division contributed US$81 million in revenues, down from US$91 million in the previous year, and remained in the red. Note that Fortescue reports its results in US dollars. The figures in this book are based on prevailing exchange rates.

Outlook

Fortescue is responsible for major iron ore developments in Western Australia. Its primary production hubs of Chichester and Western have sufficient proven reserves for 10 to 12 more years of production, and the company is actively working to extend the lives of its mines. Iron Bridge, a joint venture with Formosa Steel, marked Fortescue's entry into the high-grade segment of the iron ore market. Initial shipments from Iron Bridge were in 2023, with 7.1 million tonnes in the June 2025 year. The company has also shipped its first ore from Belinga in Gabon, and has reported that the project has the potential to be of significant scale. The $254 million acquisition of Red Hawk Mining enhances Fortescue's growth potential by giving it ownership of the large Blacksmith iron ore deposit, just 30 kilometres west of Fortescue's own Solomon mine. Thanks to Blacksmith's close proximity to Fortescue's established infrastructure, the acquisition offers significant synergy benefits. Fortescue expects to ship 195 million tonnes to 205 million tonnes of ore in the June 2026 year.

Year to 30 June	2024	2025
Revenues ($mn)	27 606.1	23 909.2
EBIT ($mn)	13 160.6	8 247.7
EBIT margin (%)	47.7	34.5
Gross margin (%)	52.4	41.4
Profit before tax ($mn)	12 575.8	7 676.9
Profit after tax ($mn)	8 610.6	5 189.2
Earnings per share (c)	279.93	168.77
Cash flow per share (c)	385.54	294.15
Dividend (c)	197	110
Percentage franked	100	100
Net tangible assets per share ($)	9.44	9.59
Interest cover (times)	22.5	14.5
Return on equity (%)	30.3	17.3
Debt-to-equity ratio (%)	2.5	5.6
Current ratio	2.7	2.4

GenusPlus Group Limited

ASX code: GNP   www.genus.com.au

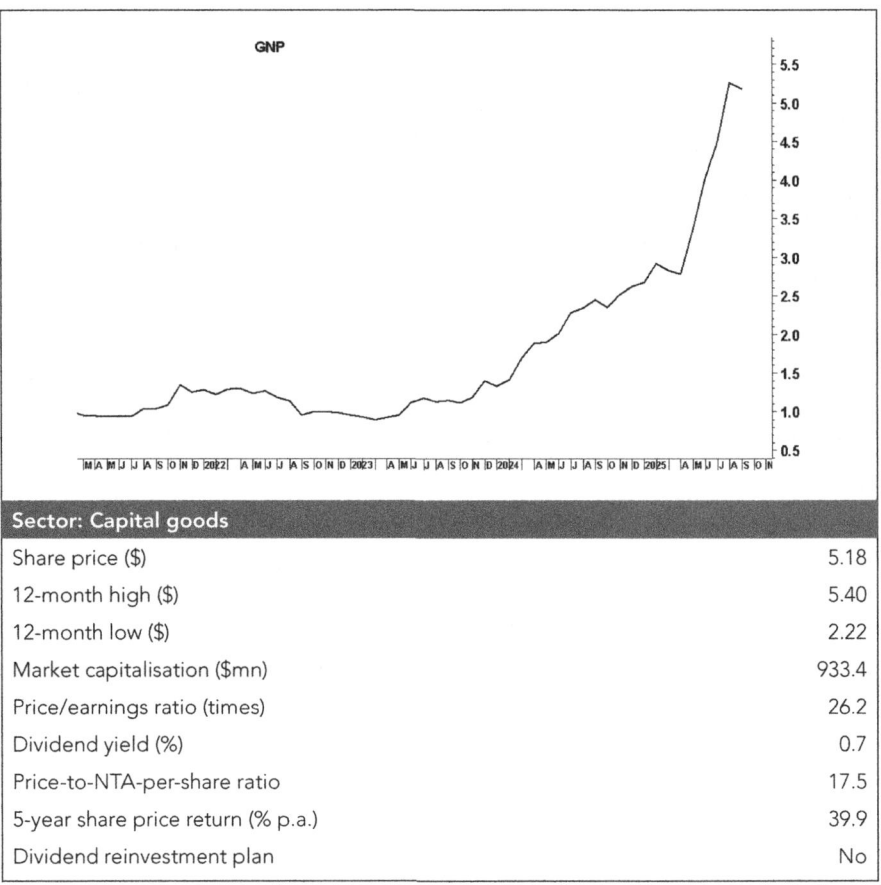

Sector: Capital goods	
Share price ($)	5.18
12-month high ($)	5.40
12-month low ($)	2.22
Market capitalisation ($mn)	933.4
Price/earnings ratio (times)	26.2
Dividend yield (%)	0.7
Price-to-NTA-per-share ratio	17.5
5-year share price return (% p.a.)	39.9
Dividend reinvestment plan	No

Perth-based engineer GenusPlus, founded in 2017, grew out of the communications infrastructure contractor Powerlines Plus, which had been established in 2009. It has grown rapidly to become a prominent nationwide supplier of power and communications infrastructure. It designs and builds electrical transmission and distribution networks, substations and battery systems. It also designs and constructs communications network systems and wireless infrastructure.

Latest business results (June 2025, full year)

Strong organic growth and the contribution of a series of acquisitions generated a surge in sales and profits, with strength across all businesses. The largest division, Infrastructure, saw revenues up 30 per cent, with some major new contracts, but with profits edging just a little higher as costs rose. The Energy and Engineering division achieved an excellent 54 per cent increase in revenues thanks in part to its exposure to large-scale battery energy storage system projects. Profits for this division rocketed nearly two and a half times. The Services division realised a 38 per cent increase in revenues, with a significant contribution from high-value communications-related contracts, and a substantial rise in profits. Recurring revenues rose from $224 million to $311 million. During the year GenusPlus made five acquisitions.

Outlook

GenusPlus has developed a strong reputation for its work in power and communications infrastructure. As transmission networks around Australia go through a major transition from traditional energy sources to new and renewable energy the company expects significant opportunities for its activities over the coming 10 to 20 years. A particular strategy has been to invest heavily in diversifying from its Western Australian home into the East Coast infrastructure market, where it sees great potential. East Coast revenues represented 42 per cent of total company income in the June 2025 year, up from 35 per cent a year earlier. Among its successes are the $140 million contract from Ausgrid to perform sub-transmission line works for the Hunter–Central Coast Renewable Energy Zone in New South Wales and stage one of the North West Transmission Developments in Tasmania, a massive $1 billion project. Its Services division is benefiting from continued growth in 5G wireless construction, with 6G development under way. At June 2025 GenusPlus had net cash holdings of more than $84 million and it continues to seek out further acquisitions. It held an order book worth $2 billion, up from just $500 million a year before, and was tendering for a further $2.4 billion of business. It expected EBITDA to grow 20 per cent to 25 per cent in June 2026.

Year to 30 June	2024	2025
Revenues ($mn)	551.2	751.3
Infrastructure (%)	56	54
Energy & engineering (%)	28	30
Services (%)	16	16
EBIT ($mn)	29.6	54.8
EBIT margin (%)	5.4	7.3
Profit before tax ($mn)	27.7	52.6
Profit after tax ($mn)	19.3	35.4
Earnings per share (c)	10.84	19.75
Cash flow per share (c)	19.20	27.50
Dividend (c)	2.5	3.6
Percentage franked	100	100
Net tangible assets per share ($)	0.35	0.30
Interest cover (times)	15.9	24.8
Return on equity (%)	17.0	25.2
Debt-to-equity ratio (%)	~	~
Current ratio	1.5	1.2

GR Engineering Services Limited

ASX code: GNG   www.gres.com.au

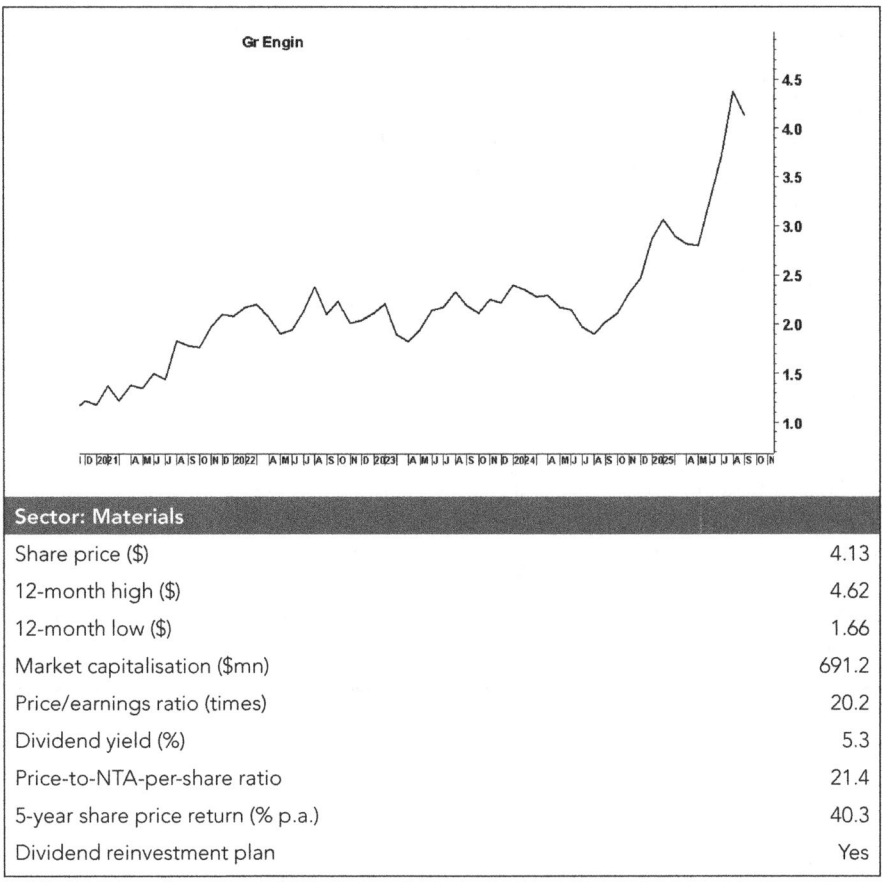

Gr Engin

Sector: Materials	
Share price ($)	4.13
12-month high ($)	4.62
12-month low ($)	1.66
Market capitalisation ($mn)	691.2
Price/earnings ratio (times)	20.2
Dividend yield (%)	5.3
Price-to-NTA-per-share ratio	21.4
5-year share price return (% p.a.)	40.3
Dividend reinvestment plan	Yes

Perth-based GR Engineering, founded in 1986, is an engineering consulting and contracting company that provides engineering design and construction services to the mining and mineral processing industries. Its GR Production Services subsidiary operates and maintains energy and resource production assets for the oil and gas industry. Its Mipac and Paradigm Engineers subsidiaries provide control systems, operational technology and engineering services for the mineral processing, iron ore and energy sectors. GR Engineering has offices and operations in several countries, and overseas work represents nearly 20 per cent of total company income.

Latest business results (June 2025, full year)

Revenues and profits rose in a good result, with the completion during the year of many major and minor projects. Among these were Evolution Mining's $155 million Mungari Future Growth Project at Kalgoorlie, LRL Australia's $71 million Kathleen Valley

Lithium Backfill Project at Leinster, Western Australia, and Develop Global's $26 million Woodlawn Copper-Zinc Mine Restart Project in New South Wales. The GR Production Services subsidiary enjoyed higher revenues and profits with work for the energy sector around Australia. However, Mipac and Paradigm Engineers were hurt by the suspension of BHP's nickel activities.

Outlook

GR has a high reputation for its services and it works for many major resources and energy companies. With a solid order book at June 2025 it was optimistic about the outlook, noting that it was engaged in 30 studies across a broad range of commodities in Australia and overseas. Major projects under way included the $155 million upgrade to Vault Minerals' King of the Hills mining operations in Western Australia, the $78 million Eloise Copper Mine Expansion Project for AIC Mines in Queensland and the US$81 million Kainantu Gold Mine Process Plant Project for K92 Mining in Papua New Guinea. Its GR Production Services business generates longer-term operations and maintenance (O&M) services revenues, typically with contract terms that vary between one year and five years. Among its major work is an O&M contract worth $26 million annually for QPM Energy at the Moranbah gas plant in Queensland and contracts for Santos worth $27 million per year for work in the Surat Basin and the Cooper Basin. The Mipac and Paradigm Engineers businesses perform services for many of the world's largest resource companies, and expect revenues and profits to rebound in the June 2026 year. At June 2025 GR had no debt and more than $70 million in cash holdings, and is seeking acquisitions that provide scale, diversity and technical expertise to its businesses.

Year to 30 June	2024	2025
Revenues ($mn)	424.1	479.0
Mineral processing ($)	82	80
Oil & gas (%)	18	20
EBIT ($mn)	46.7	52.5
EBIT margin (%)	11.0	11.0
Profit before tax ($mn)	46.1	51.1
Profit after tax ($mn)	31.2	34.2
Earnings per share (c)	18.92	20.46
Cash flow per share (c)	23.04	25.20
Dividend (c)	19	22
Percentage franked	100	100
Net tangible assets per share ($)	0.17	0.19
Interest cover (times)	79.9	38.9
Return on equity (%)	49.5	50.6
Debt-to-equity ratio (%)	~	~
Current ratio	1.1	1.2

GWA Group Limited

ASX code: GWA   www.gwagroup.com.au

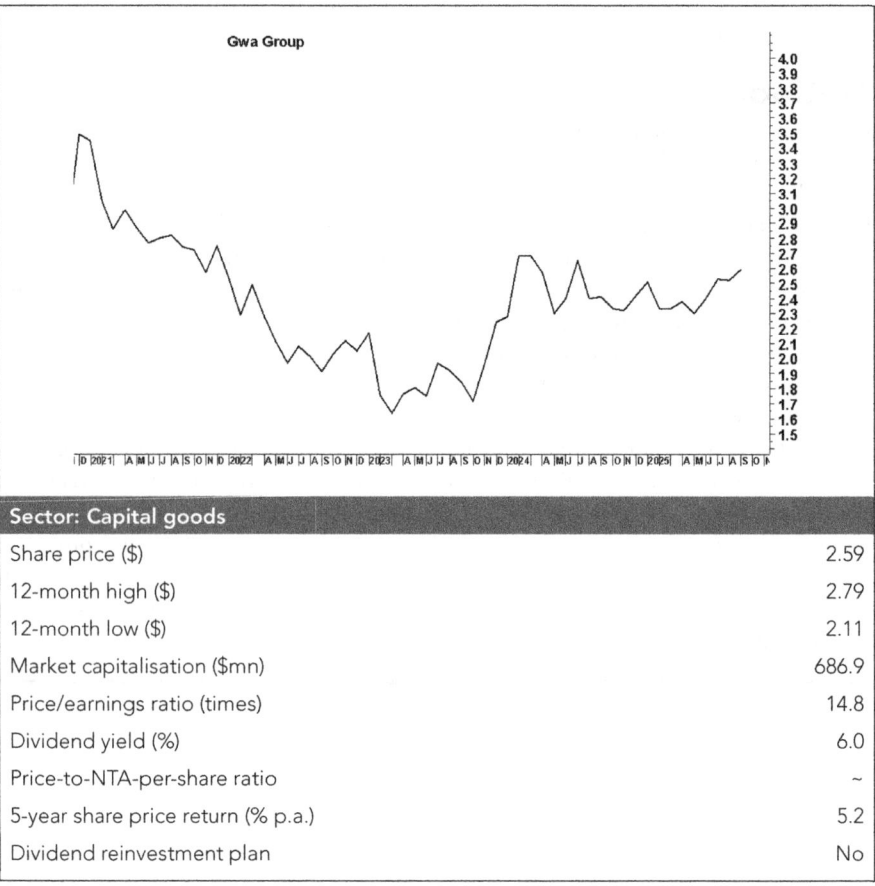

Sector: Capital goods	
Share price ($)	2.59
12-month high ($)	2.79
12-month low ($)	2.11
Market capitalisation ($mn)	686.9
Price/earnings ratio (times)	14.8
Dividend yield (%)	6.0
Price-to-NTA-per-share ratio	~
5-year share price return (% p.a.)	5.2
Dividend reinvestment plan	No

Brisbane-based GWA is a prominent designer, importer and distributor of residential and commercial bathroom, laundry and kitchen products, marketed under brands that include Caroma, Dorf, Methven and Clark. About 16 per cent of its sales are to the United Kingdom and New Zealand.

Latest business results (June 2025, full year)

Sales and profits rose again modestly in a subdued housing market. Australian revenues rose 2.4 per cent, with solid demand from plumbers and from volume home builders. The company also achieved major project wins in the care sector, with particular strength in Victoria. British sales rose by nearly 6 per cent, with growth in social housing and a particularly strong contribution from three new contracts that were signed at the end of the previous year. However, continued weakness in the

New Zealand construction sector led to a further decline in sales in that market. Thanks to disciplined cost management, the company's cost of sales figure edged down for the second straight year, even as sales rose.

Outlook

GWA is almost completely exposed to a bathroom, laundry and kitchen fixtures market that in Australia is worth more than $2 billion annually. It claims market shares as high as 50 per cent for some of its products. In an uncertain economic environment, it has a variety of tactics for growth. It is achieving success with its strategy of targeting plumbers with a variety of dedicated products and training initiatives, and it has embedded plumbing specialists at all its markets in Australia and New Zealand. It is also giving priority to sectors where it has a competitive advantage, including volume home builders, commercial aged care and healthcare, multi-residential projects, and social and affordable housing. Around 57 per cent of its Australian sales go to the residential repair and renovation market, and demand is expected to remain flat as households cut back on discretionary spending. The commercial segment represents a further 25 per cent of Australian sales, and the company sees flat demand for the June 2026 year, though it believes it can continue to achieve solid sales to the care sector. Residential detached housing is around 16 per cent of Australian sales, with demand not expected to grow until late in the June 2026 year. The company is working to develop new products. It has launched a new range of entry-level sanitaryware for the affordable housing market and it also has products aimed at the aged care and healthcare markets.

Year to 30 June	2024	2025
Revenues ($mn)	413.5	418.5
EBIT ($mn)	72.8	76.3
EBIT margin (%)	17.6	18.2
Gross margin (%)	39.3	40.5
Profit before tax ($mn)	63.7	66.9
Profit after tax ($mn)	45.6	46.5
Earnings per share (c)	17.20	17.52
Cash flow per share (c)	24.53	23.48
Dividend (c)	15	15.5
Percentage franked	100	100
Net tangible assets per share ($)	~	~
Interest cover (times)	8.0	8.1
Return on equity (%)	15.0	15.3
Debt-to-equity ratio (%)	31.4	27.7
Current ratio	1.6	1.6

Hansen Technologies Limited

ASX code: HSN   www.hansencx.com

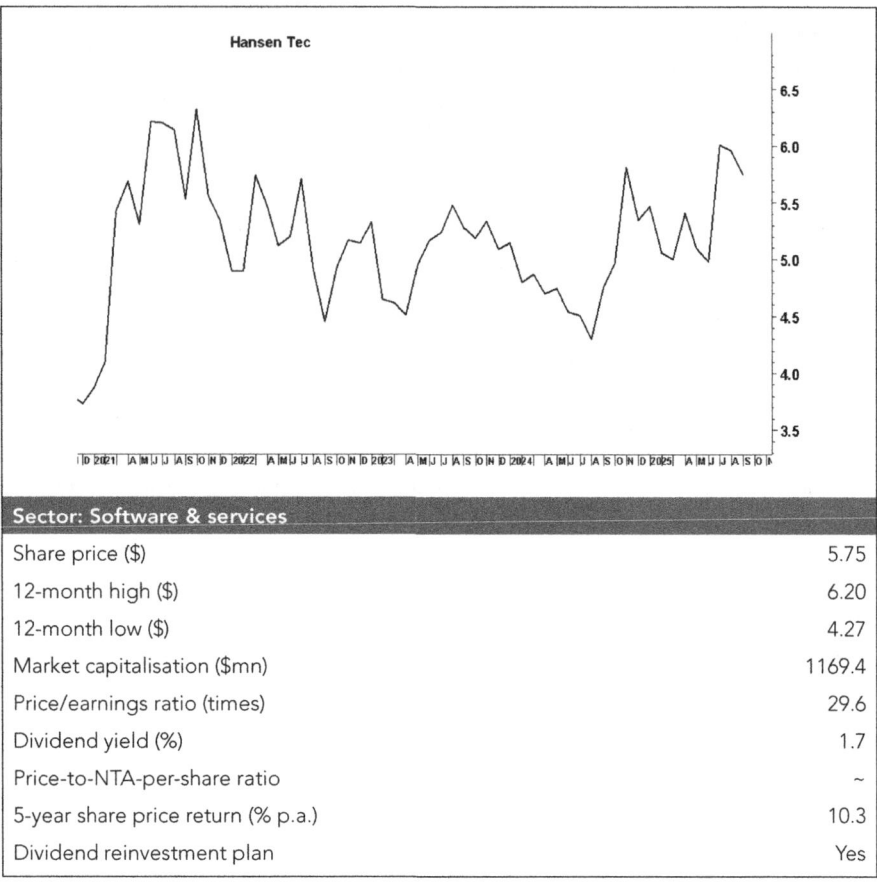

Sector: Software & services

Share price ($)	5.75
12-month high ($)	6.20
12-month low ($)	4.27
Market capitalisation ($mn)	1169.4
Price/earnings ratio (times)	29.6
Dividend yield (%)	1.7
Price-to-NTA-per-share ratio	~
5-year share price return (% p.a.)	10.3
Dividend reinvestment plan	Yes

Melbourne company Hansen Technologies dates back to an IT business launched in 1971. It later moved into the development of billing software systems and is today a significant global provider of these services, specialising in the electricity, gas, water, pay television and telecommunications sectors. Hansen has 26 offices around the world and services customers in over 80 countries.

Latest business results (June 2025, full year)

In a good result, revenues and underlying profits rose solidly, thanks to a contribution from German utilities billing software provider powercloud, acquired in 2024, along with new business wins and renewals. A significant new contract was a five-year master agreement worth $50 million with British internet, television and phone provider VMO2. Hansen now classifies its operations into two segments. The larger of these, Energy & Utilities, saw revenue growth of 8 per cent, much of this from powercloud.

However, profits actually fell for this division, hurt by lower gross margins from powercloud, along with restructuring costs related to the acquisition. The Communications & Media division enjoyed an excellent year, with profits rising 29 per cent on a 15 per cent increase in revenues, and with Hansen a clear beneficiary of a rise in capital spending by media companies on high-speed digital infrastructure. More than two-thirds of total revenues came from the Europe/Middle East/Africa segment, with 20 per cent from the Americas.

Outlook

Though a small company, Hansen has developed a high reputation for its services. Its billing software enables its customers to create, sell and deliver new products and services, as well as manage and analyse customer data and control critical revenue management and customer support processes. Once it does business with a customer it stands to benefit further from a long-term stream of recurring revenue. Hansen's particular strategy is growth by acquisition, and with the billing services industry still fragmented and largely regionalised, it expects further attractive acquisition opportunities to present themselves. In April 2025 it strengthened its presence in Germany with the acquisition of key software applications from CONUTI, a long-standing partner of powercloud. Hansen is a significant beneficiary of European Union moves to have 80 per cent of electricity customers using smart meters by 2029. It spends heavily on research and development initiatives. It views artificial intelligence applications as offering particular potential, and has been integrating AI capabilities into its products. Hansen has expressed interest in leveraging its billing technology through moves into new industries such as financial services, healthcare or education.

Year to 30 June	2024	2025
Revenues ($mn)	353.1	392.5
Energy & utilities (%)	58	56
Communications & media (%)	42	44
EBIT ($mn)	40.4	55.5
EBIT margin (%)	11.4	14.1
Profit before tax ($mn)	35.6	50.2
Profit after tax ($mn)	26.0	39.6
Earnings per share (c)	12.79	19.44
Cash flow per share (c)	37.14	45.19
Dividend (c)	10	10
Percentage franked	44	58
Net tangible assets per share ($)	~	~
Interest cover (times)	8.4	10.5
Return on equity (%)	7.7	11.0
Debt-to-equity ratio (%)	7.2	4.5
Current ratio	1.4	1.6

Harvey Norman Holdings Limited

ASX code: HVN   www.harveynormanholdings.com.au

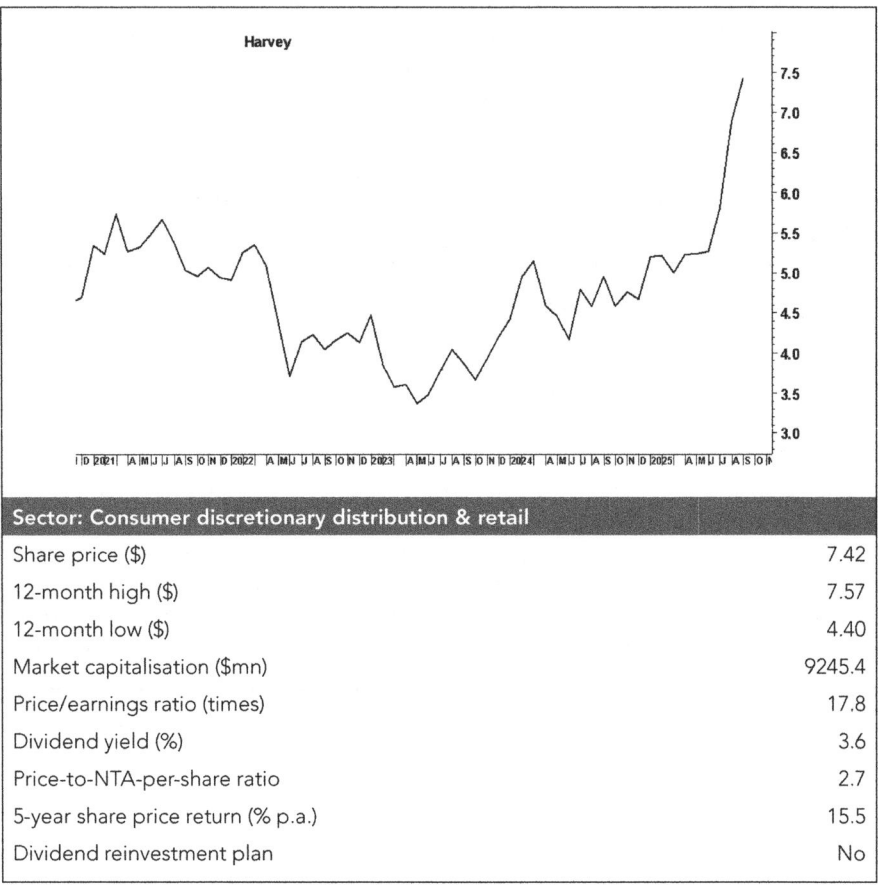

Sector: Consumer discretionary distribution & retail	
Share price ($)	7.42
12-month high ($)	7.57
12-month low ($)	4.40
Market capitalisation ($mn)	9245.4
Price/earnings ratio (times)	17.8
Dividend yield (%)	3.6
Price-to-NTA-per-share ratio	2.7
5-year share price return (% p.a.)	15.5
Dividend reinvestment plan	No

Sydney-based Harvey Norman, established in 1982, operates a chain of 316 retail stores specialising in electrical and electronic goods, home appliances, furniture, flooring, carpets and manchester items throughout Australia, New Zealand, Ireland, the United Kingdom, Singapore, Malaysia, Slovenia and Croatia, under the Harvey Norman, Domayne and Joyce Mayne banners. The 195 Australian stores are independently held as part of a franchise operation, from which Harvey Norman receives income for advisory and advertising services. It also receives a considerable amount of income from its own stores, from its $4.5 billion property portfolio and from the provision of finance to franchisees and customers.

Latest business results (June 2025, full year)

Sales and profits bounced back, with strength across most areas of operation. After declining for three straight years, total store sales — franchise and company-owned — rose 5.5 per cent to $9.35 billion. Revenues from the company's overseas stores of

$2.76 billion was up 4.9 per cent. However, total overseas profits fell, with a large loss from the company's entry to the English market more than offsetting rises in most other countries. Franchise income received by Harvey Norman rose 7.4 per cent to $1.04 billion. Though less than a quarter of company turnover, franchise revenue represents more than half of total profit, if property revaluations are excluded. Property revenue of $504.2 million was up 53.9 per cent. The company said that, when excluding the impact of property revaluations, its pre-tax profit was $590.4 million, 9.3 per cent higher than the previous year.

Outlook

Harvey Norman has high fixed costs, so even a modest rise in sales can translate to a larger increase in earnings. The company has pointed to a low jobless rate and rising immigration levels as reasons for optimism about future demand. In addition, it benefits from continuing technological innovation that induces customers to upgrade to the latest mobile phones and other electronic devices. It also expects to be a significant beneficiary of growing consumer demand for AI-enabled technologies. It is experiencing high start-up costs as it enters the British West Midlands region, with a second store planned there during the June 2026 year, but is optimistic about the long-term outlook for its moves into England. It is seeing a rebound in New Zealand, its largest overseas market, where the recent performance has been sluggish. It is also optimistic about Malaysia, with four new stores set to open during the June 2026 year. With home building activity increasing it expects growing demand for furniture and bedding.

Year to 30 June	2024	2025
Revenues ($mn)	4110.0	4465.3
Retail (%)	68	66
Franchising operations (%)	23	23
Property (%)	8	11
EBIT ($mn)	652.7	871.0
EBIT margin (%)	15.9	19.5
Gross margin (%)	31.1	30.8
Profit before tax ($mn)	541.7	753.1
Profit after tax ($mn)	352.5	518.0
Earnings per share (c)	28.29	41.57
Cash flow per share (c)	35.80	49.98
Dividend (c)	22	26.5
Percentage franked	100	100
Net tangible assets per share ($)	2.54	2.73
Interest cover (times)	5.9	7.4
Return on equity (%)	7.9	11.1
Debt-to-equity ratio (%)	14.8	13.6
Current ratio	2.3	1.4

Helia Group Limited

ASX code: HLI   www.helia.com.au

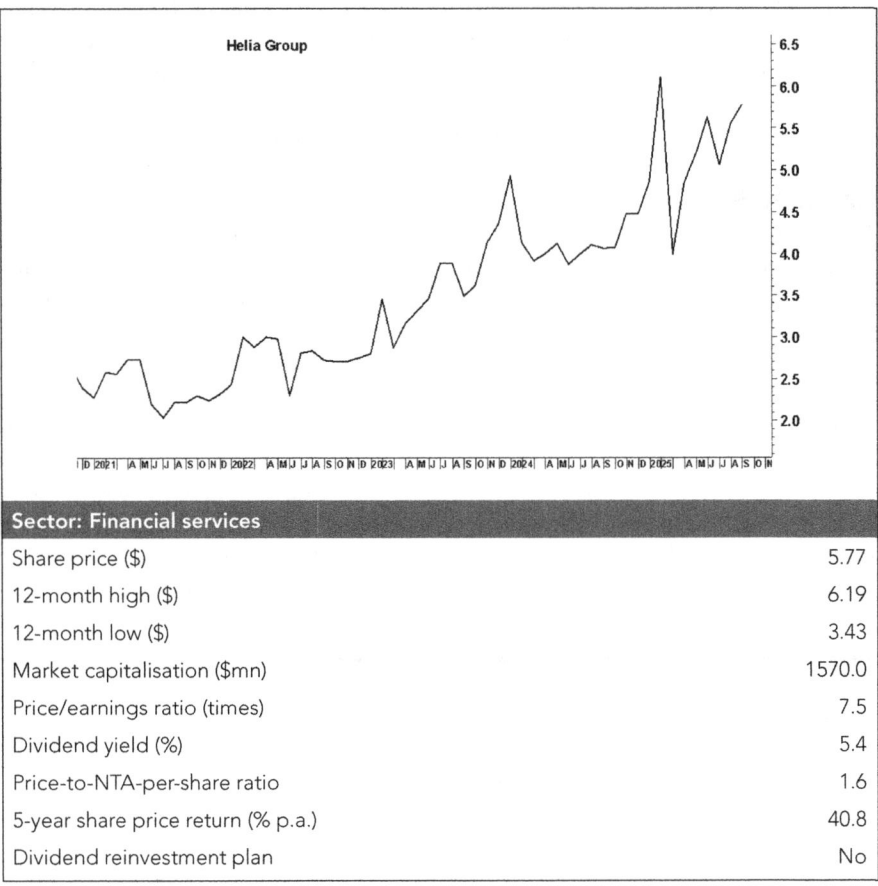

Sector: Financial services	
Share price ($)	5.77
12-month high ($)	6.19
12-month low ($)	3.43
Market capitalisation ($mn)	1570.0
Price/earnings ratio (times)	7.5
Dividend yield (%)	5.4
Price-to-NTA-per-share ratio	1.6
5-year share price return (% p.a.)	40.8
Dividend reinvestment plan	No

Sydney financial services company Helia, founded in 1965, specialises in the provision of lenders mortgage insurance for homebuyers. It was formerly known as Genworth Mortgage Insurance and was part of the US-based Genworth Financial group.

Latest business results (June 2025, half year)

A significant increase in investment income and a continuing low claims environment combined to generate a strong rise in revenues and profits. A strong labour market, relatively low levels of unemployment and rising house prices meant that fewer people defaulted on their mortgages. The company's insurance revenue fell 6 per cent to $182.2 million due to lower levels of gross written premium in recent years. Insurance service expenses were also down as a result of the lower levels of mortgage default. The company's net realised and unrealised investment income soared from $41.3 million in June 2024 to $103 million.

Outlook

Lenders mortgage insurance provides protection to home loan lenders when the homebuyer can manage only a small deposit, protecting the lender against the risk of loss if the homebuyer defaults on the mortgage and the lender is unable to recover the loan amount from a sale of the property. Helia is one of the leaders in this business. However, it faces some significant challenges to its operations. Commonwealth Bank of Australia, responsible for 40 per cent of Helia's premium income, has announced that from 2026 it is moving its business to a rival lender. Further, ING Bank Australia, responsible for an additional 21 per cent of premium income, has initiated negotiations with a new lender, with a view to moving its business. ING's contract with Helia expires in June 2026. The company also faces the prospect of losing income from changes to the government's Home Guarantee Scheme for first home buyers. Under these changes, first home buyers are able to buy a home with a deposit as low as 5 per cent of the value of the mortgage and avoid the necessity for lenders mortgage insurance. At present, insurance is normally needed if the deposit represents less than 20 per cent of the value. In response to these concerns, Helia has begun a comprehensive business review, with a view to creating a simpler and more efficient business. With the housing market remaining firm, it is also actively seeking new business opportunities. The company's December 2025 full-year forecast is for insurance revenue of $350 million to $390 million, compared to $389 million in December 2024, with claims remaining low.

Year to 31 December	2023	2024
Revenues ($mn)	600.7	532.7
EBIT ($mn)	412.5	348.6
EBIT margin (%)	68.7	65.4
Profit before tax ($mn)	394.9	329.8
Profit after tax ($mn)	247.7	220.9
Earnings per share (c)	76.53	76.47
Cash flow per share (c)	76.75	76.90
Dividend (c)	29	31
Percentage franked	100	100
Interest cover (times)	23.5	18.5
Return on equity (%)	21.1	19.9
Half year to 30 June	2024	2025
Revenues ($mn)	237.2	286.6
Profit before tax ($mn)	138.3	192.3
Profit after tax ($mn)	97.0	133.7
Earnings per share (c)	32.80	49.10
Dividend (c)	15	16
Percentage franked	100	100
Net tangible assets per share ($)	3.63	3.72
Debt-to-equity ratio (%)	14.6	~

Horizon Oil Limited

ASX code: HZN   www.horizonoil.com.au

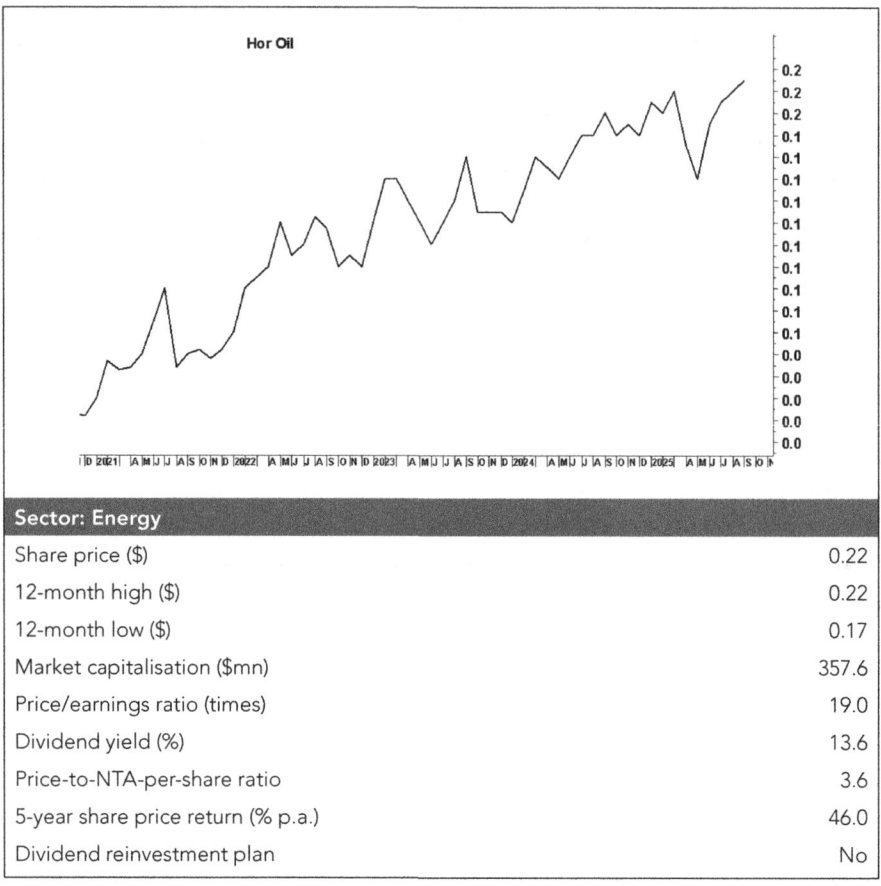

Sector: Energy	
Share price ($)	0.22
12-month high ($)	0.22
12-month low ($)	0.17
Market capitalisation ($mn)	357.6
Price/earnings ratio (times)	19.0
Dividend yield (%)	13.6
Price-to-NTA-per-share ratio	3.6
5-year share price return (% p.a.)	46.0
Dividend reinvestment plan	No

Sydney company Horizon, established in 1969, is a small oil and gas producer. Its key resource is in the Beibu Gulf in southern China, where it holds a 27 per cent holding, and works with the China National Offshore Oil Company as operator, and with two other partners, Roc Oil and Oil Australia. Its other main project is a 26 per cent holding in the Maari oil field off the south Taranaki coast in New Zealand, where Horizon is working with Austrian oil and gas company OMV as operator and with Cue Energy as a partner. A smaller project is at the Mereenie oil and gas field in the Northern Territory, where it has a 25 per cent holding, in partnership with operator Central Petroleum, New Zealand's Echelon Resources and Cue Energy. In 2025 it acquired gas assets in Thailand.

Latest business results (June 2025, full year)

Production and sales volumes rose, with oil and gas from the 2024 Mereenie acquisition helping offset natural field decline at the company's other producing assets. However, lower oil prices sent revenues down, with profits also sharply lower. The company's share of production of 1.62 million barrels of oil equivalent (boc) was up from 1.43 million boe in the previous year. Sales volumes of 1.62 million boe was up from 1.3 million boe. The average realised price of US$65.1 per boe was down from US$85.7. Operating costs of US$76.8 million were up from US62.9 million, in part reflecting increased expenses associated with the Mereenie acquisition. Profit margins were also hurt by higher depreciation and finance charges. Note that Horizon reports its results in US dollars. The figures in this book are based on prevailing exchange rates.

Outlook

The company has stated that its strategy is to maximise free cashflow, focus on shareholder returns and invest in organic growth, while also seeking out high-quality new business opportunities. It sees continuing demand for its products, especially natural gas. A 10-year extension of its permit at Maari, to 2037, has provided certainty about the outlook for New Zealand operations. In 2025 it acquired a 7.5 per cent share in the Sinphuhorm gas field and a 60 per cent share in the Nam Phong gas field, both in Thailand, for around US$37.5 million. Having expanded its operations through entering Australia and Thailand it has significantly de-risked its portfolio, with no single asset now delivering more than 30 per cent of company income. At June 2025 Horizon had net cash holdings of more than US$14 million.

Year to 30 June	2024	2025
Revenues ($mn)	168.9	162.0
China development (%)	69	45
New Zealand development (%)	31	41
Australia development (%)	0	14
EBIT ($mn)	63.8	34.9
EBIT margin (%)	37.8	21.5
Gross margin (%)	43.6	27.1
Profit before tax ($mn)	59.4	25.6
Profit after tax ($mn)	39.2	18.8
Earnings per share (c)	2.43	1.16
Cash flow per share (c)	5.27	4.29
Dividend (c)	3	3
Percentage franked	0	0
Net tangible assets per share ($)	0.08	0.06
Interest cover (times)	14.4	3.8
Return on equity (%)	28.9	16.7
Debt-to-equity ratio (%)	~	~
Current ratio	2.3	2.3

HUB24 Limited

ASX code: HUB   www.hub24.com.au

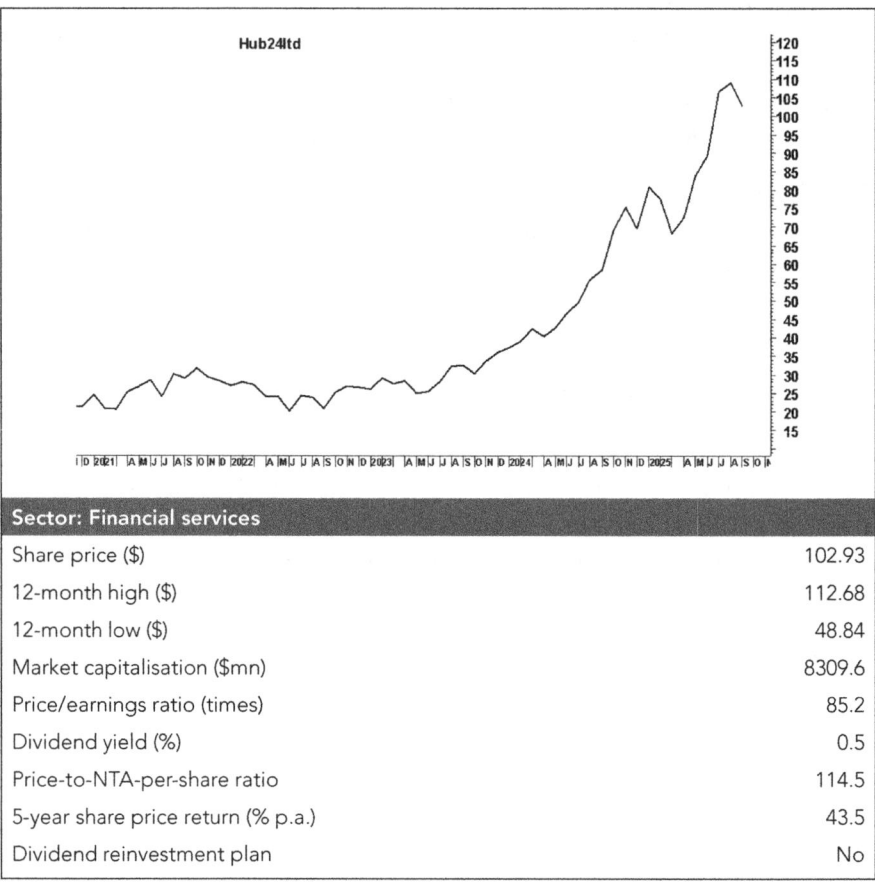

Sector: Financial services	
Share price ($)	102.93
12-month high ($)	112.68
12-month low ($)	48.84
Market capitalisation ($mn)	8309.6
Price/earnings ratio (times)	85.2
Dividend yield (%)	0.5
Price-to-NTA-per-share ratio	114.5
5-year share price return (% p.a.)	43.5
Dividend reinvestment plan	No

Financial services provider HUB24, based in Sydney, was established in 2007 and specialises in integrated platform technology for the wealth management industry. Its flagship HUB24 platform enables financial advisers and others to manage client portfolios, offering portfolio administration, investment execution and reporting tools. The company also offers PARS—Portfolio Administration and Reporting Service—which is a non-custody portfolio tool providing a range of services for financial professionals and their clients. In its Tech Solutions division the company provides financial tools, including self-managed superannuation fund administration software, along with technology and data services for the wealth industry.

Latest business results (June 2025, full year)

Revenues and underlying profits rose strongly as the company achieved success in attracting a wave of new business. The core Platform division recorded revenues of

$323 million, up 28 per cent from the previous year, thanks to net fund inflows of $19.8 billion. At June 2025 funds under administration of $112.7 billion were 34 per cent higher than a year before. During the year the company signed 143 new distribution agreements, with 572 new advisers using the platform. The much smaller Tech Solutions division saw revenues up 9 per cent to $77 million. With revenues growing at a faster pace than costs, the company achieved excellent profit growth at both divisions.

Outlook

HUB24 is a beneficiary of moves by financial advisers and clients away from the large legacy superannuation platform providers and towards more agile providers like HUB24. It also benefits from the continuing strong growth in superannuation funds in Australia. As a result of its heavy investment in technology, HUB24 has been recognised as offering one of the most versatile platforms. Thanks to its rapid growth it has reported that at June 2025 more than 5000 financial advisers were using its platform, representing a third of all advisers in Australia. It has launched HUB24 Private Invest, aimed especially at high-net-worth investors, providing easier access to a broad range of wholesale investments, and has linked this with its advanced new Engage reporting tool. It has also taken a minority equity holding in the investment portal Reach Alternative Investments, with a view to offering clients access to a range of private equity funds. With a current market share of only around 9 per cent for its platform — up from 4 per cent just four years earlier — HUB24 believes it can continue to grow strongly. Its target is for funds under administration of $148 billion to $162 billion by June 2027.

Year to 30 June	2024	2025
Revenues ($mn)	323.5	400.4
Platform (%)	78	81
Tech solutions (%)	22	19
EBIT ($mn)	90.6	129.1
EBIT margin (%)	28.0	32.2
Profit before tax ($mn)	88.3	125.2
Profit after tax ($mn)	67.8	97.8
Earnings per share (c)	83.60	120.78
Cash flow per share (c)	129.01	176.91
Dividend (c)	38	56
Percentage franked	100	100
Net tangible assets per share ($)	0.69	0.90
Interest cover (times)	38.9	33.5
Return on equity (%)	13.2	18.6
Debt-to-equity ratio (%)	~	~
Current ratio	3.0	1.9

IDP Education Limited

ASX code: IEL

investors.idp.com

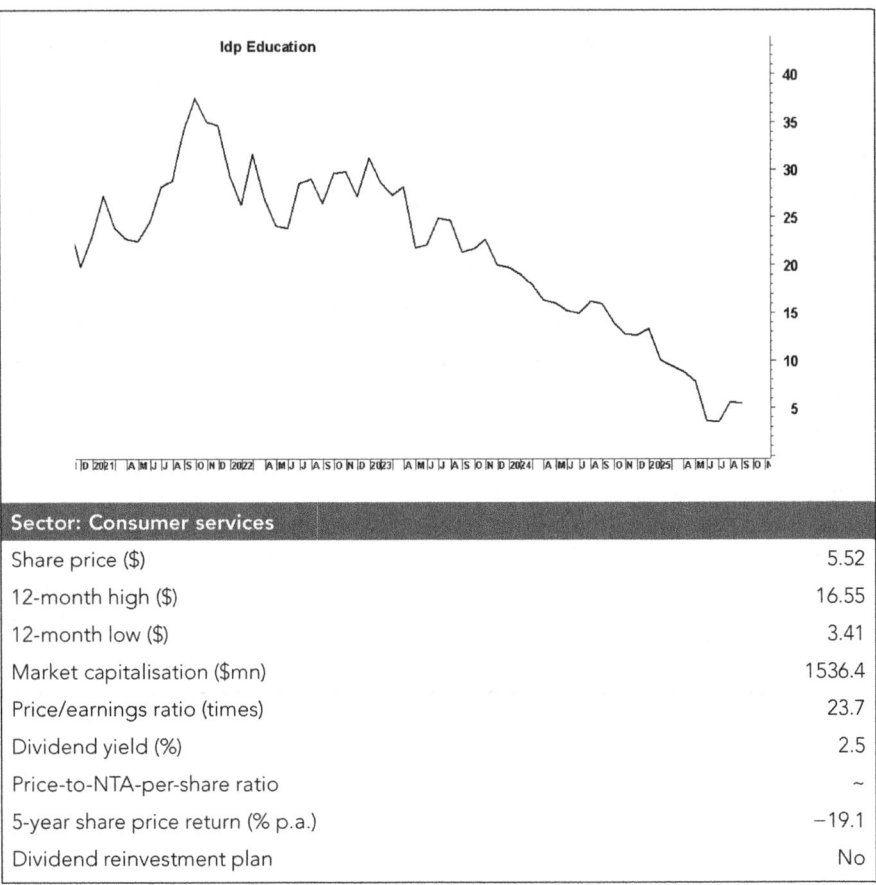

Sector: Consumer services	
Share price ($)	5.52
12-month high ($)	16.55
12-month low ($)	3.41
Market capitalisation ($mn)	1536.4
Price/earnings ratio (times)	23.7
Dividend yield (%)	2.5
Price-to-NTA-per-share ratio	~
5-year share price return (% p.a.)	−19.1
Dividend reinvestment plan	No

Melbourne-based IDP Education dates back to 1969 and the launch of the Australian Asian Universities Cooperation Scheme, aimed at helping Asian students study in Australia. In 1981 it changed its name to the International Development Program (IDP) and opened a series of offices throughout Asia. It has since expanded through acquisition and organic growth, and today helps students from around the world find placements in higher education programs in English-speaking countries. It also works with University of Cambridge ESOL Examinations and the British Council to administer worldwide testing for the International English Language Testing System.

Latest business results (June 2025, full year)

A big decline in international student numbers slugged IDP, which reported a sharp drop in revenues and underlying profits. This resulted especially from moves by governments in Australia, Canada and the UK to limit the numbers of international students they accept into their countries. Student placement numbers for IDP fell 29 per cent. However, thanks to fee rises during the year, revenues for this business were down only 16 per cent. The company's other main source of income, English language testing, saw volumes down 18 per cent and revenues falling 15 per cent. The key Indian market was directly responsible, with a 49 per cent plunge in revenues. Language testing income from all other countries actually rose 11 per cent. IDP operates a small English language teaching business, mainly in Cambodia, representing less than 5 per cent of total company turnover, and this reported a small increase in revenues and profits.

Outlook

IDP has been hit hard by all the new limitations on its operations. It does not expect any near-term amelioration, forecasting that student placement numbers could fall a further 20 per cent to 30 per cent in the June 2026 year. In response it has announced a multi-year transformation program aimed at generating profitable growth. In the initial phase it will incur one-off restructuring costs of up to $45 million in order to reduce its annual cost base by $25 million through simplifying its operations, placing a greater focus on high-value activities and leveraging its global purchasing power to effect spending cuts. It also plans to accelerate the adoption of digital and artificial intelligence technologies in order to boost automation and productivity. It expects to raise prices again and is seeking new revenue streams, including English language testing opportunities in China. Consequently, despite declining business, it believes it can hold June 2026 profits to roughly the same level as June 2025.

Year to 30 June	2024	2025
Revenues ($mn)	1037.2	882.2
Asia (%)	72	65
Rest of World (%)	23	28
Australasia (%)	5	7
EBIT ($mn)	242.8	121.9
EBIT margin (%)	23.4	13.8
Profit before tax ($mn)	217.9	93.7
Profit after tax ($mn)	154.3	64.7
Earnings per share (c)	55.44	23.25
Cash flow per share (c)	75.36	45.23
Dividend (c)	34	14
Percentage franked	73	50
Net tangible assets per share ($)	~	~
Interest cover (times)	9.7	4.3
Return on equity (%)	29.7	12.3
Debt-to-equity ratio (%)	32.5	30.9
Current ratio	1.6	1.4

Iluka Resources Limited

ASX code: ILU   www.iluka.com

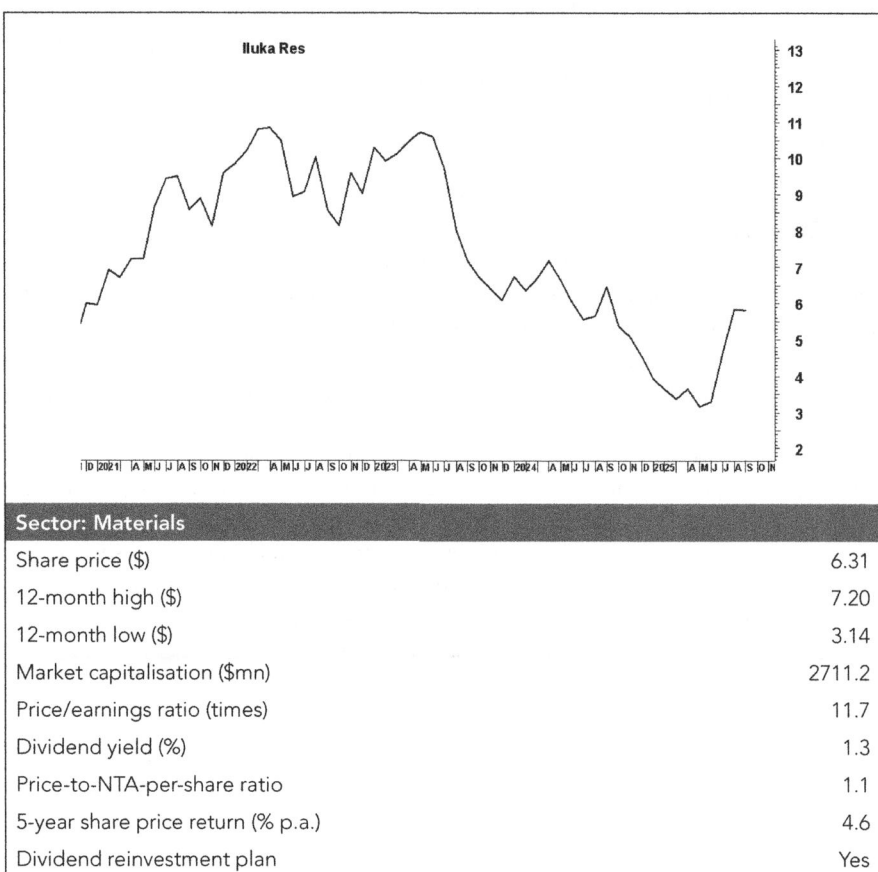

Iluka Res

Sector: Materials	
Share price ($)	6.31
12-month high ($)	7.20
12-month low ($)	3.14
Market capitalisation ($mn)	2711.2
Price/earnings ratio (times)	11.7
Dividend yield (%)	1.3
Price-to-NTA-per-share ratio	1.1
5-year share price return (% p.a.)	4.6
Dividend reinvestment plan	Yes

Perth resources company Iluka started in 1954 as Westralian Sands, before merging in 1998 with the titanium mineral business of RGC and subsequently taking its present name. It is today a global leader in the mining and processing of mineral sands and rare earths. It has significant operations in Western Australia: it manages the Cataby mine, a large ilmenite deposit with associated zircon and rutile; its Eneabba development involves the reclaiming and processing of a strategic stockpile high in monazite; its Narngulu mineral separation plant produces zircon, rutile and ilmenite products; and the Capel operation incorporates two synthetic rutile kilns. In South Australia it operates the world's largest zircon mine, Jacinth-Ambrosia, and it is involved in exploration and development work in other states. It holds a 20 per cent interest in ASX-listed Deterra Royalties, a company that receives royalties from certain BHP iron ore tenements.

Latest business results (June 2025, half year)

Lower realised prices across key products drove revenues and profits down, despite higher zircon sales volumes and improved unit production costs. The company arranges its sales profile into four products. Zircon volume sales rose 19 per cent from the June 2024 half, but with average prices down about 10 per cent. Synthetic rutile sales fell 18 per cent, with average prices a little lower. Ilmenite sales dropped 58 per cent, with rutile sales down 13 per cent. Profits would have fallen further but for a series of cost control measures, with a 19 per cent reduction in unit cash costs. In addition, exploration and corporate spending was down.

Outlook

Rare earth minerals are a key component for a growing number of high-tech industries. They are essential for the creation of powerful magnets for wind turbines and electric vehicles. They are also needed for industrial robots and in modern rechargeable batteries, as well as for many defence industry applications, including jet engines and drones. Consequently, they are in growing demand globally. However, with some 80 per cent of the world's supply now coming from China, countries in the West have been urging Australia, which has large-scale reserves of rare earths, to boost output. Iluka is building Australia's first rare earth refinery at its Eneabba operation, with initial output expected from 2027. Its rutile-rich critical minerals development at Balranald in New South Wales is on track for commissioning late in 2025. It is investigating a possible new rare earths and zircon development at Wimmera in western Victoria.

Year to 31 December	2023	2024
Revenues ($mn)	1291.0	1170.3
EBIT ($mn)	479.3	334.8
EBIT margin (%)	37.1	28.6
Profit before tax ($mn)	471.5	325.3
Profit after tax ($mn)	342.6	231.3
Earnings per share (c)	80.50	54.14
Cash flow per share (c)	119.22	98.39
Dividend (c)	7	8
Percentage franked	100	100
Interest cover (times)	61.4	35.2
Return on equity (%)	16.9	10.2
Half year to 30 June	2024	2025
Revenues ($mn)	629.7	577.8
Profit before tax ($mn)	187.0	125.2
Profit after tax ($mn)	133.7	92.0
Earnings per share (c)	31.30	21.50
Dividend (c)	4	2
Percentage franked	100	100
Net tangible assets per share ($)	5.30	5.64
Debt-to-equity ratio (%)	~	20.5
Current ratio	4.9	3.8

Insurance Australia Group Limited

ASX code: IAG   www.iag.com.au

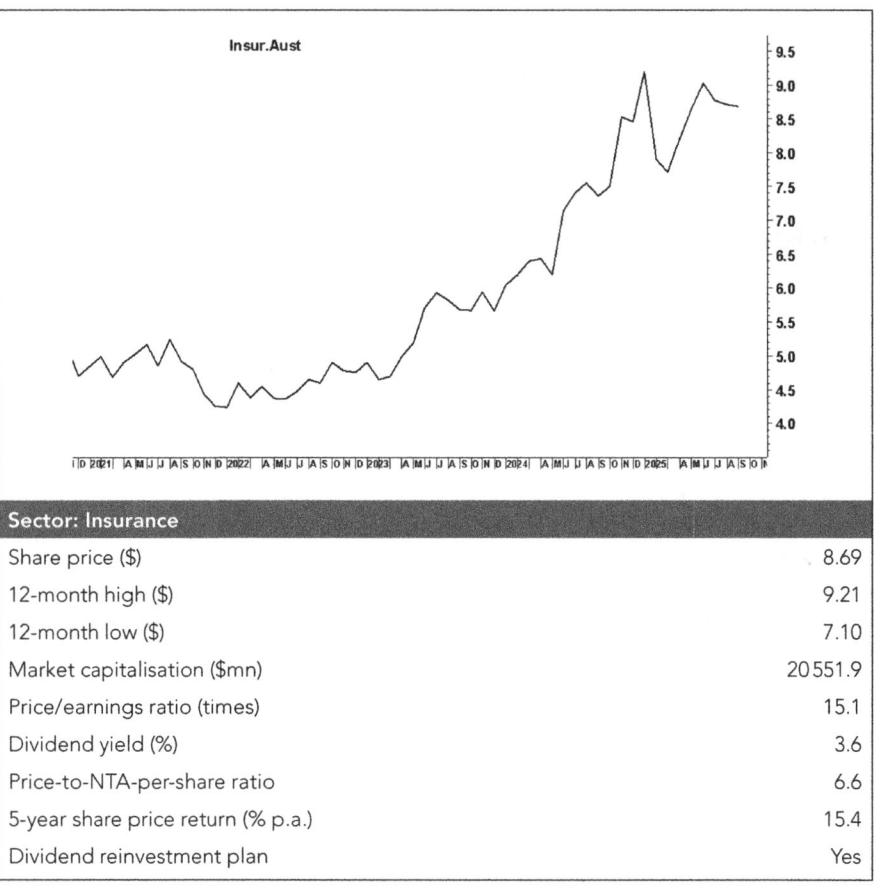

Sector: Insurance	
Share price ($)	8.69
12-month high ($)	9.21
12-month low ($)	7.10
Market capitalisation ($mn)	20 551.9
Price/earnings ratio (times)	15.1
Dividend yield (%)	3.6
Price-to-NTA-per-share ratio	6.6
5-year share price return (% p.a.)	15.4
Dividend reinvestment plan	Yes

Sydney-based Insurance Australia Group (IAG), formerly NRMA Insurance, dates back to 1925, when the National Roads and Motorists' Association began providing insurance to its members in New South Wales and the Australian Capital Territory. It subsequently demutualised and listed on the ASX. It has grown through acquisition, and is now the largest general insurance group in Australia and New Zealand. Its brands include NRMA Insurance, CGU, WFI, ROLLiN' and Swann Insurance, all in Australia, as well as NZI, State, AMI and Lumley Insurance in New Zealand. In Victoria it provides general insurance products under the RACV brand through a distribution and underwriting relationship with RACV. It operates a reinsurance partnership with Berkshire Hathaway, the American company associated with famed investor Warren Buffett.

Latest business results (June 2025, full year)

Rising premiums, new customers and a good investment performance helped deliver further strong growth in revenues and profits. Gross written premium of $17.1 billion was up 4.3 per cent from the previous year as the company boosted vehicle and home insurance premiums. Buoyant markets meant the company's investment portfolio added $403 million to income, up from $286 million a year earlier. The pre-tax insurance profit of $1.7 billion generated an insurance margin — insurance and investment profits as a percentage of premiums, a key measure of profitability — of 17.5 per cent, up from 15.6 per cent in the previous year and up from just 9.6 per cent two years earlier. New Zealand business benefited from a significant reduction in disaster claims, along with modest gross written premium growth.

Outlook

IAG occupies a strong position in the Australian and New Zealand general insurance business, giving it considerable pricing power. But the insurance business is inherently volatile, and any unforeseen major natural disaster has the capacity to take a big chunk from company earnings. It continues to benefit from moves made in 2021 to reset its business, with a simpler operating model and a greater focus on its core activities. It expects to continue raising its insurance premiums in order to meet rising costs involved in house and car repairs. It has entered into an agreement to buy the insurance business of RACQ in Queensland and is seeking Australian Competition and Consumer Commission approval to buy the insurance business of RACWA in Western Australia. IAG believes it can achieve gross written premium growth in the low-to-mid-single digits in the June 2026 year, with an insurance profit of $1.45 billion to $1.65 billion and an insurance margin of 14 per cent to 16 per cent.

Year to 30 June	2024	2025
Revenues ($mn)	16 127.0	17 221.0
EBIT ($mn)	1 676.0	2 405.0
EBIT margin (%)	10.4	14.0
Profit before tax ($mn)	1 491.0	2213.0
Profit after tax ($mn)	898.0	1359.0
Earnings per share (c)	37.31	57.49
Cash flow per share (c)	45.45	66.79
Dividend (c)	27	31
Percentage franked	46	48
Net tangible assets per share ($)	1.09	1.33
Interest cover (times)	9.1	12.5
Return on equity (%)	13.5	19.4
Debt-to-equity ratio (%)	26.2	23.8

IPH Limited

ASX code: IPH   www.iphltd.com.au

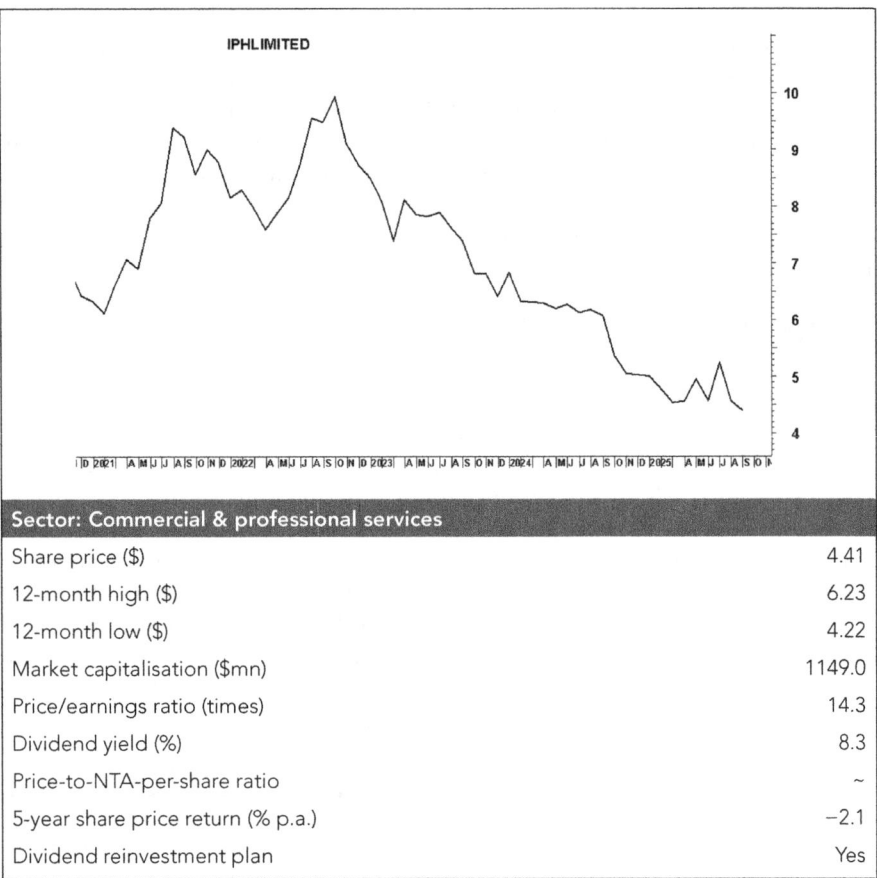

Sector: Commercial & professional services	
Share price ($)	4.41
12-month high ($)	6.23
12-month low ($)	4.22
Market capitalisation ($mn)	1149.0
Price/earnings ratio (times)	14.3
Dividend yield (%)	8.3
Price-to-NTA-per-share ratio	~
5-year share price return (% p.a.)	−2.1
Dividend reinvestment plan	Yes

Sydney-based IPH, formed in 2014 but with roots that stretch back to 1887, is a holding company for a group of businesses offering a wide range of intellectual property services and products. These include the filing, prosecution, enforcement and management of patents, designs, trademarks and other intellectual property. IPH incorporates seven brands: AJ Park, Griffith Hack, Smart & Biggar, Spruson & Ferguson, Pizzeys, ROBIC and Applied Marks. It operates in more than 25 countries, with offices in Australia, Canada, China, Hong Kong, Indonesia, Malaysia, New Zealand, the Philippines, Singapore and Thailand. In 2024 it acquired the Canadian intellectual property firm Bereskin & Parr.

Latest business results (June 2025, full year)

Revenues and profits continued to grow, though profit margins were down. However, most of the growth came from Canada, thanks to acquisitions, including a nine-month contribution from Bereskin & Parr. On a like-for-like, currency-adjusted basis, revenues were flat and profits edged down. Australian and New Zealand businesses achieved a second consecutive single-digit rise in revenues and profits, despite fewer patent filings. Asian operations saw revenues flat for the year with profits marginally down, although the company reported market share gains in Singapore. The integration of Bereskin & Parr into the group and its merger with Smart & Biggar were completed successfully, realising significant synergies and a continued increase in new Canadian business.

Outlook

IPH has established itself as one of the leaders in Australia, New Zealand, Canada and South-East Asia in the intellectual property business. It has expanded steadily, through organic growth and acquisition. As it grows it achieves economies of scale that boost margins. It is achieving success with its strategy of leveraging its network of companies, with a growing number of referrals between member companies in different regions. It has targeted Canada as a market with great potential and is rapidly expanding operations there, with four acquisitions since 2022. It has restructured its leadership team and is now working to optimise its network of member companies with the goal of boosting organic growth and operational efficiencies. Having realigned its cost base, it expects to deliver annual cost savings of $8 million to $10 million from the June 2026 year. It sees an increase in IPH Group filings across the Asian region as providing a platform for growth. Canadian revenues are set to grow as significant backlogs are cleared at the Canadian Intellectual Property Office. IPH is initiating work to upgrade its technology and embed artificial intelligence into all its core activities.

Year to 30 June	2024	2025
Revenues ($mn)	605.6	706.2
Australia & New Zealand (%)	48	42
Canada (%)	32	41
Asia (%)	20	17
EBIT ($mn)	136.5	138.5
EBIT margin (%)	22.5	19.6
Profit before tax ($mn)	101.7	110.4
Profit after tax ($mn)	77.9	82.0
Earnings per share (c)	32.13	30.81
Cash flow per share (c)	58.95	57.90
Dividend (c)	35	36.5
Percentage franked	32	25
Net tangible assets per share ($)	~	~
Interest cover (times)	3.9	4.9
Return on equity (%)	12.9	12.3
Debt-to-equity ratio (%)	56.5	50.7
Current ratio	2.8	2.7

Ive Group Limited

ASX code: IGL   www.ivegroup.com.au

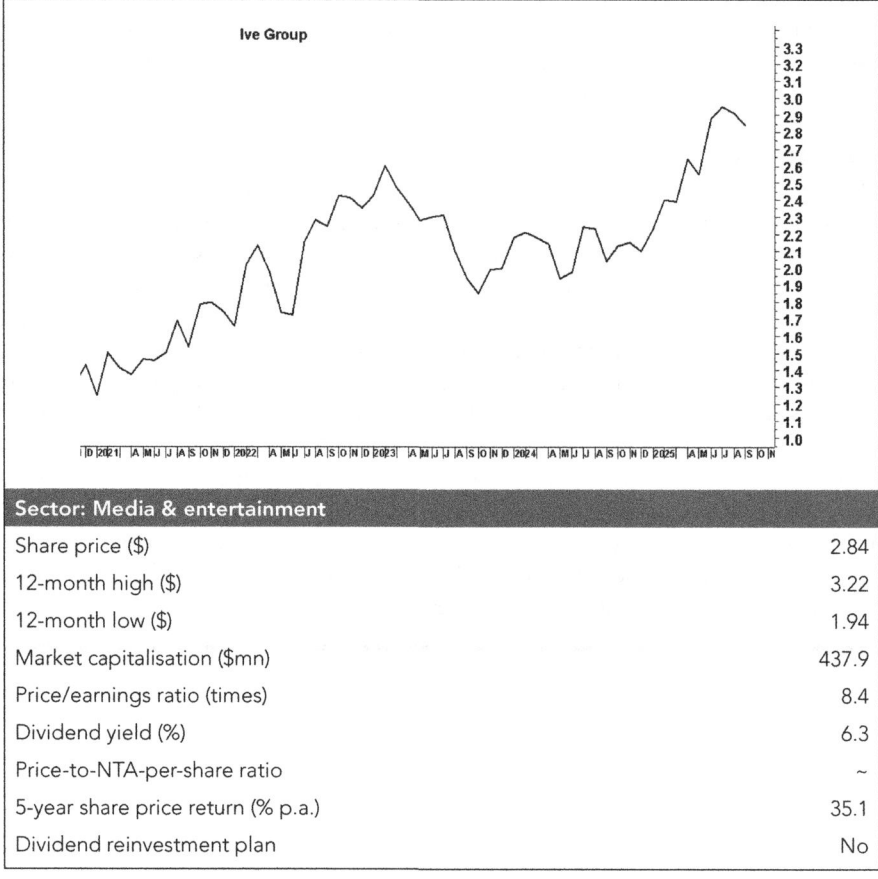

Sector: Media & entertainment	
Share price ($)	2.84
12-month high ($)	3.22
12-month low ($)	1.94
Market capitalisation ($mn)	437.9
Price/earnings ratio (times)	8.4
Dividend yield (%)	6.3
Price-to-NTA-per-share ratio	~
5-year share price return (% p.a.)	35.1
Dividend reinvestment plan	No

Marketing and communications specialist Ive Group, based in Sydney, traces its roots back to the 1921 launch of a local newspaper in Balmain, which later developed into a printing business. Subsequently the company evolved steadily into one of Australia's leading diversified marketing and print communications companies, with services that include direct marketing mail, letterbox distribution, creative services, logistics, uniforms and apparel, digital catalogues, retail display, general commercial printing, packaging and integrated marketing. It has about 2800 customers spanning most industry sectors, including many of Australia's largest corporations.

Latest business results (June 2025, full year)

Revenues fell, despite a small contribution from recent acquisitions, reflecting economic weakness and softer demand in the second half, particularly due to uncertainty surrounding the federal election. However, underlying profits enjoyed solid growth as the company succeeded in cutting expenses through a series of cost efficiencies. The company also realised significant synergy benefits from its 2022 acquisition of the assets of printing company Ovato and its 2023 acquisition of packaging company JacPak. Its third-party logistics (3PL), brand activations and packaging businesses all enjoyed important new business wins.

Outlook

Ive has grown to become a prominent integrated marketing communications business with leading market positions across many of the sectors in which it operates. More than half its income derives from the retail sector, with the financial, corporate services and publishing sectors also important. It enjoys strong connections with its clients and reports an average relationship among its top 20 customers of more than 10 years. Much of its growth in recent years has come by acquisition. Its $16 million Ovato acquisition made Ive Australia's only large-scale heatset web offset printer for high-quality colour printing. The $35 million JacPak acquisition strengthened Ive's presence in the packaging business. The company is enjoying particularly strong demand for its 3PL operations, which provide clients with warehousing and inventory management for their products, together with packaging and shipping. In late 2025 it moved to a new 33 000 square metre site in Melbourne in order to cater for burgeoning demand for 3PL services. In 2026 it will consolidate some of its Sydney businesses, including commercial printing and packaging, brand activations and paper storage to what it calls a new 42 000 square metre supersite. The company has stated that diversification into new service areas is a core element of its growth strategy and that it is actively seeking strategically attractive and accretive acquisitions. Ive's early forecast is for an underlying June 2026 after-tax profit of $50 million to $54 million.

Year to 30 June	2024	2025
Revenues ($mn)	972.8	959.2
EBIT ($mn)	81.0	93.6
EBIT margin (%)	8.3	9.8
Gross margin (%)	46.7	49.4
Profit before tax ($mn)	62.7	76.5
Profit after tax ($mn)	43.0	52.1
Earnings per share (c)	27.98	33.71
Cash flow per share (c)	60.42	63.41
Dividend (c)	18	18
Percentage franked	100	100
Net tangible assets per share ($)	~	~
Interest cover (times)	4.4	5.5
Return on equity (%)	22.2	25.6
Debt-to-equity ratio (%)	64.2	51.7
Current ratio	1.4	1.4

JB Hi-Fi Limited

ASX code: JBH

investors.jbhifi.com.au

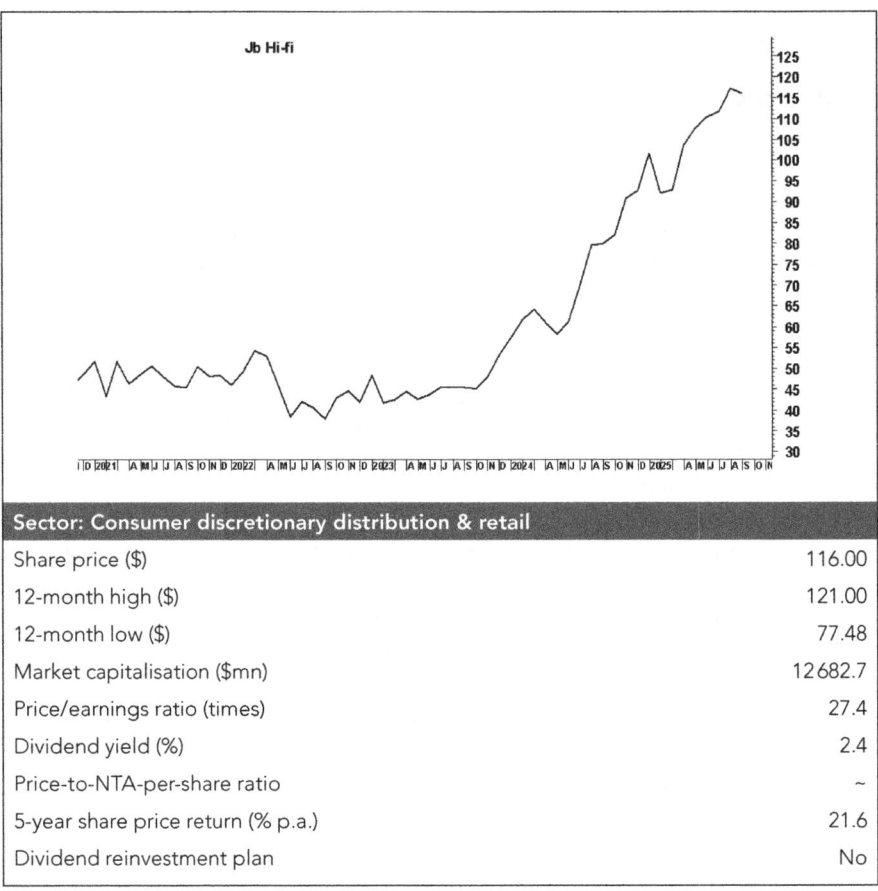

Jb Hi-fi

Sector: Consumer discretionary distribution & retail	
Share price ($)	116.00
12-month high ($)	121.00
12-month low ($)	77.48
Market capitalisation ($mn)	12682.7
Price/earnings ratio (times)	27.4
Dividend yield (%)	2.4
Price-to-NTA-per-share ratio	~
5-year share price return (% p.a.)	21.6
Dividend reinvestment plan	No

Melbourne-based JB Hi-Fi dates back to the opening in 1974 of a single recorded music store in the Melbourne suburb of East Keilor. It has since grown into a nationwide chain of home electronic and home appliance products outlets, and it has also expanded to New Zealand. In Australia it operates The Good Guys chain of home appliance stores, as well as specialised divisions that sell to the commercial and educational sectors. The company also maintains an online presence. In 2024 it acquired a 75 per cent stake in premium home appliance retailer E&S Trading. At June 2025 it operated in Australia 206 JB Hi-Fi and JB Hi-Fi Home stores, 107 The Good Guys stores and 12 E&S stores. In New Zealand it operated 23 JB Hi-Fi stores.

Latest business results (June 2025, full year)

Profits rebounded after two years of decline in a good result, with growth across all businesses. The company's JB Hi-Fi stores in Australia benefited from continuing demand for mobile phones, small appliances, computers and games hardware, including a particular boost from the fourth-quarter launch of the Nintendo Switch 2 game console. Key growth categories for The Good Guys were floorcare, portable appliances, cooking and computers. New store openings contributed to a 21 per cent jump in New Zealand sales with profits at the EBITDA level more than doubling. There was a 10-month contribution from the E&S acquisition. Online sales continued their steady growth.

Outlook

JB Hi-Fi has a strong brand image throughout Australia and great customer loyalty. It has shown an impressive ability to contain costs. It continues to open new stores, though at a slower pace than in previous years. It is boosting floor space at its stores for growth categories such as mobile phones, gaming and connected technology. It is also working to strengthen its membership program and its online activities. It plans to open a further six new stores in Australia during the June 2026 year and three in New Zealand. It is developing strategies to streamline its supply chain, with enhanced stock availability during peak trade periods and improved flow of bulky products. It is also expanding its customer base for the commercial sector. The E&S Trading acquisition has boosted the company's exposure to the premium home appliance and bathroom categories as well as to important new commercial construction customers. Continued investment in new stores and a program of strategic initiatives are aimed at boosting the underperforming New Zealand business.

Year to 30 June	2024	2025
Revenues ($mn)	9592.4	10 554.8
JB Australia (%)	69	67
The Good Guys (%)	28	27
JB New Zealand (%)	3	3
E&S (%)	0	2
EBIT ($mn)	658.4	705.7
EBIT margin (%)	6.9	6.7
Gross margin (%)	22.3	22.4
Profit before tax ($mn)	627.4	668.0
Profit after tax ($mn)	438.8	462.4
Earnings per share (c)	401.46	423.06
Cash flow per share (c)	616.65	659.84
Dividend (c)	261	275
Percentage franked	100	100
Net tangible assets per share ($)	~	~
Interest cover (times)	21.2	18.7
Return on equity (%)	29.5	29.1
Debt-to-equity ratio (%)	~	~
Current ratio	1.2	1.2

Jumbo Interactive Limited

ASX code: JIN www.jumbointeractive.com

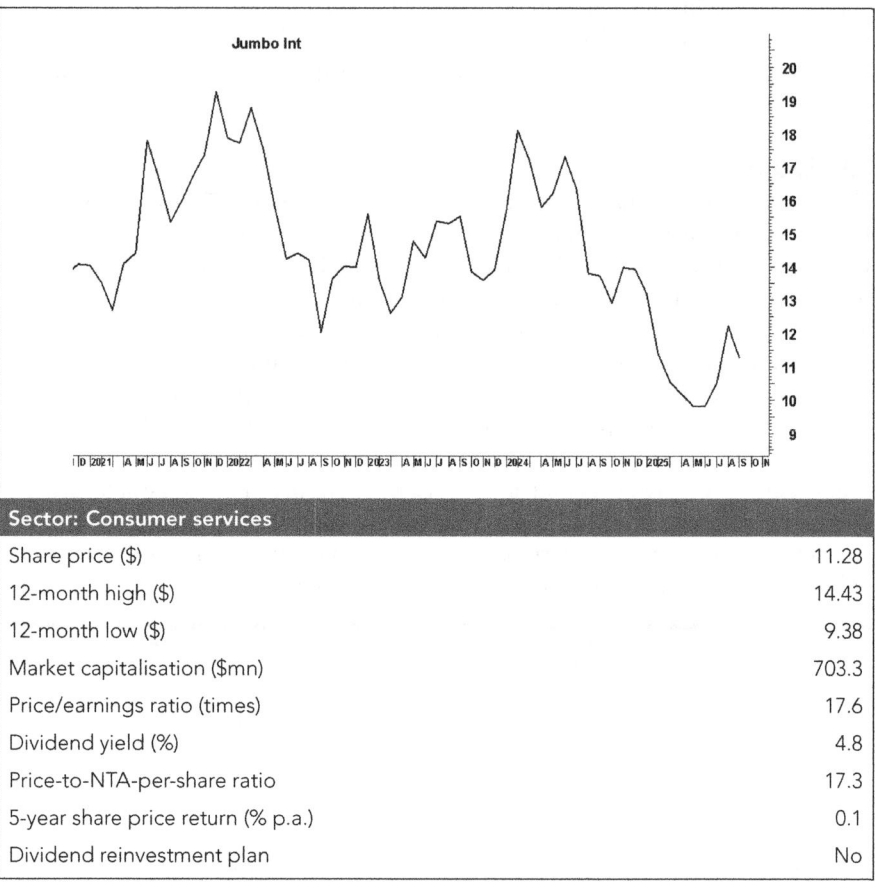

Sector: Consumer services	
Share price ($)	11.28
12-month high ($)	14.43
12-month low ($)	9.38
Market capitalisation ($mn)	703.3
Price/earnings ratio (times)	17.6
Dividend yield (%)	4.8
Price-to-NTA-per-share ratio	17.3
5-year share price return (% p.a.)	0.1
Dividend reinvestment plan	No

Jumbo Interactive was founded in Brisbane in 1995 as an internet service provider, but has since evolved into a major operator of internet services for lotteries. Its core business, Oz Lotteries, involves the provision of lottery services for The Lottery Corporation at its ozlotteries.com website. These lotteries include OzLotto, Powerball, TattsLotto and Lucky Lotteries. Its Jumbo Lottery Platform manages lotteries for charitable organisations and other institutions. It also runs a Managed Services division to provide lottery management services to charities and other organisations, with operations in the United Kingdom and Canada. About 18 per cent of revenues derive from overseas activities.

Latest business results (June 2025, full year)

Revenues and profits fell for the first time in 10 years. The previous year had seen a surge in business based on some large Powerball jackpots, including one record

$200 million jackpot in February 2024. In the June 2025 year there were 56 large jackpots — defined as any Division 1 jackpot worth more than $15 million — compared to 55 in the previous year. However, the total Division 1 prize pool fell from $2.4 billion to $2 billion, and there were no jackpots greater than $100 million, compared to three in the June 2024 year. Total lottery transaction value for the company fell 15.9 per cent to $457.2 million. In the previous year it had jumped 21.1 per cent. The number of active players fell 21 per cent to 858 000, although the average spend per active player rose 7 per cent to $533. The Managed Services division, now representing 18 per cent of total company turnover, achieved a total transaction value of $288 million and saw revenues and profits rise modestly. The small Software-as-a-Service division — its Jumbo Lottery Platform business — is now 7 per cent of company turnover, and it enjoyed good growth, with more than $250 million in total transaction value, up 17 per cent.

Outlook

Jumbo is a significant beneficiary of the Australian love of gambling. However, as its latest results indicate, its business can be greatly influenced by lottery jackpot levels. It regards active player numbers as the foundation for future expansion and spends heavily on promotional activities aimed at attracting new customers. Its Jumbo Lottery Platform business continues to achieve solid organic growth, working with 10 active partner charities, up from seven in the June 2024 year. The Managed Services division, which manages lotteries in Canada and the UK, shows steady growth and the company is seeking new markets. In September 2025 Jumbo announced a new contract with RSL Queensland to move the Dream Home Art Union lottery—which generates around $200 million in annual ticket sales—onto the Jumbo Lottery Platform.

Year to 30 June	2024	2025
Revenues ($mn)	159.3	145.3
EBIT ($mn)	64.2	57.9
EBIT margin (%)	40.3	39.8
Profit before tax ($mn)	63.7	57.3
Profit after tax ($mn)	43.3	40.2
Earnings per share (c)	68.86	64.15
Cash flow per share (c)	88.49	85.22
Dividend (c)	54.5	54.5
Percentage franked	100	100
Net tangible assets per share ($)	0.71	0.65
Interest cover (times)	138.7	96.6
Return on equity (%)	40.3	33.9
Debt-to-equity ratio (%)	~	~
Current ratio	1.9	2.4

Lindsay Australia Limited

ASX code: LAU   www.lindsayaustralia.com.au

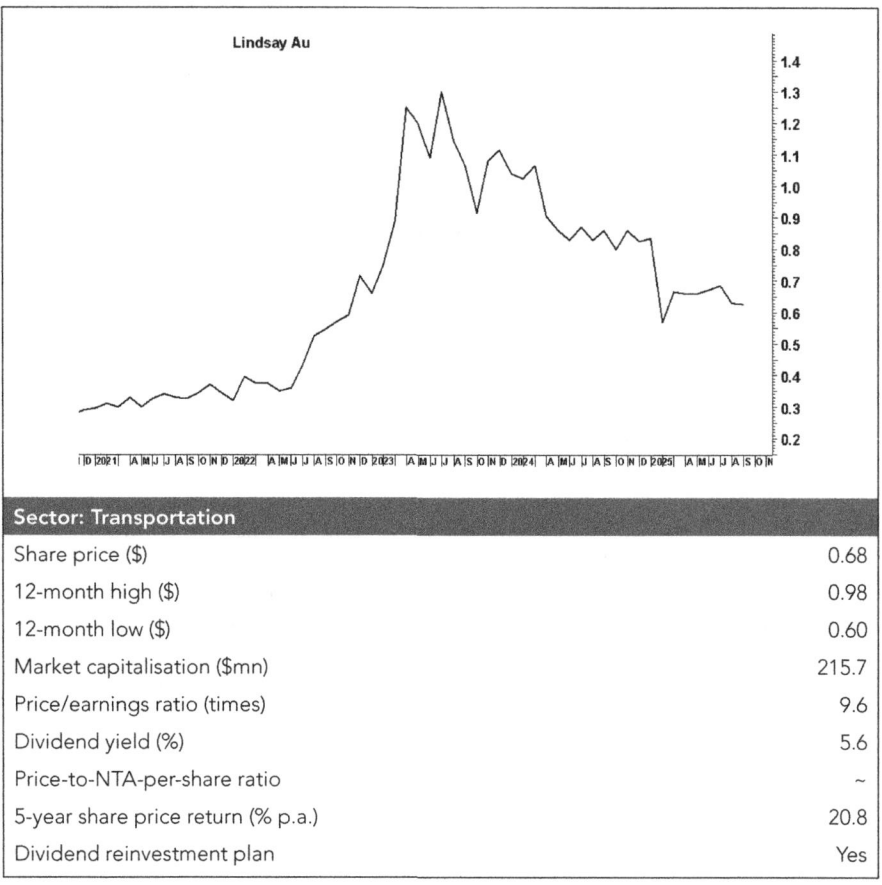

Sector: Transportation	
Share price ($)	0.68
12-month high ($)	0.98
12-month low ($)	0.60
Market capitalisation ($mn)	215.7
Price/earnings ratio (times)	9.6
Dividend yield (%)	5.6
Price-to-NTA-per-share ratio	~
5-year share price return (% p.a.)	20.8
Dividend reinvestment plan	Yes

Brisbane-based trucking company Lindsay Australia was established as Lindsay Brothers in 1953. It quickly developed a specialty in the transportation of fruit and vegetables and became a pioneer in the use of refrigerated trailers. It is today a fully integrated transport, logistics and rural supply company, servicing customers in the food-processing, food services, rural and horticultural sectors, with particular strength in the eastern states. It operates from branches around the country, with a fleet of more than 1000 vehicles. Its Lindsay Rural and Hunter retail businesses operate a network of regional stores supplying farmers with an extensive range of agricultural services and products. In February 2025 it acquired Western Australian logistics and packaging business GJ Freight and in July 2025 it acquired Tasmanian transportation company SRT Logistics.

Latest business results (June 2025, full year)

Revenues rose but profits fell for a second consecutive year in a challenging environment. Transport division revenues edged up nearly 2 per cent, thanks to some organic growth, as well as selective targeting by the company of new food categories. Lindsay also received a small contribution from the GJ Freight acquisition. However, inflationary pressures and rising competition, along with reduced demand for horticultural-related business, hurt underlying profits, which fell 12 per cent. The much smaller rural supplies operation enjoyed a relatively strong result, with sales up 9 per cent and underlying profits up 11 per cent. The Hunter business also achieved growth in its first full year under Lindsay ownership, although profit margins were hurt by higher operating costs.

Outlook

Lindsay occupies a strong position in the transportation and rural supplies sectors within its regions of operation. It has a particular strength in sectors that include refrigerated transportation, horticulture and the delivery of fresh fruit and vegetables. It has benefited from consolidation within the industry. It continues to invest in the growth of its road fleet, including the acquisition of larger new trailer combinations that will boost operational performance. Its rail business also continues to grow. However, the transportation industry is greatly influenced by the state of the national economy, and, at a time of economic weakness in Australia, excess transport capacity is leading to heightened competition and placing pressure on profit margins. With its horticulture business sometimes affected by seasonal or weather issues Lindsay is working to boost its exposure to other sectors that include meat and dairy. Its $108 million acquisition of SRT Logistics provides Lindsay with a strong foothold in the Tasmanian transport and logistics sector.

Year to 30 June	2024	2025
Revenues ($mn)	804.4	849.8
Transport — freight services (%)	70	68
Rural — sale of goods (%)	19	19
Hunter — sale of goods (%)	11	13
EBIT ($mn)	58.0	46.5
EBIT margin (%)	7.2	5.5
Profit before tax ($mn)	44.2	31.9
Profit after tax ($mn)	30.4	22.3
Earnings per share (c)	9.74	7.09
Cash flow per share (c)	27.54	25.47
Dividend (c)	4.9	3.8
Percentage franked	100	100
Net tangible assets per share ($)	~	~
Interest cover (times)	4.2	3.2
Return on equity (%)	21.9	14.6
Debt-to-equity ratio (%)	~	3.2
Current ratio	1.0	1.6

Lovisa Holdings Limited

ASX code: LOV   www.lovisa.com.au

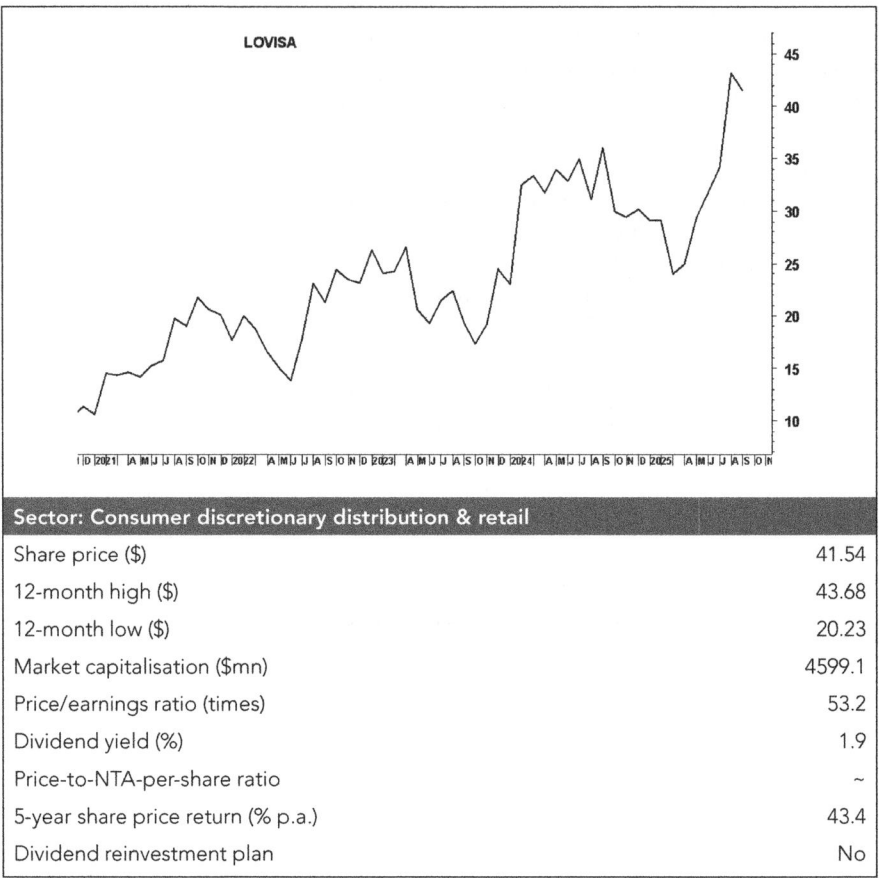

Sector: Consumer discretionary distribution & retail	
Share price ($)	41.54
12-month high ($)	43.68
12-month low ($)	20.23
Market capitalisation ($mn)	4599.1
Price/earnings ratio (times)	53.2
Dividend yield (%)	1.9
Price-to-NTA-per-share ratio	~
5-year share price return (% p.a.)	43.4
Dividend reinvestment plan	No

Melbourne-based jewellery and accessories retailer Lovisa Holdings was established in 2010. It specialises in lower-cost but up-to-date fashion pieces. It has grown significantly since its launch, and at June 2025 operated 1031 stores globally, including 229 in the US, its largest single market, and 182 in Australia. The store numbers also included 38 franchised businesses in 16 countries of the Middle East, Africa and South America.

Latest business results (June 2025, full year)

Revenues and profits rose again, though not at the rapid pace of previous years. Revenue growth of 14.2 per cent mainly reflected new store openings. On a like-for-like basis, sales edged up 1.7 per cent. Tight cost control led to a rise in the gross margin. Once again the strongest growth came from abroad. European sales rose 22 per cent to $281 million. American sales, up 20 per cent to $213 million, overtook Australia/New Zealand, where sales rose just 2 per cent to $205 million. During the year the company opened 162 new stores, including 86 in Europe and 42 in the

Americas, and closed 21. It opened its first store in Zambia and entered new franchise relationships in Panama, Ivory Coast and Republic of Congo.

Outlook

Lovisa says that the key driver for future growth is its continued global store roll-out, and it remains optimistic about the outlook, despite a slowdown in discretionary consumer spending in many countries. It locates its stores within high-foot-traffic areas of high-performing shopping centres, and aims to develop some 100 new fashion jewellery lines every week for a younger demographic. It views digital media as an important part of its marketing strategy, and operates dedicated e-commerce sites across all its key markets. It also maintains a presence on popular online marketplaces, including WeChat and others in China, which it regards as a highly promising growth market, and it is increasing its social media engagement. Product innovation is a key component of what Lovisa believes to be its competitive advantage, and the company employs large product development teams in Melbourne, London and Los Angeles to ensure it identifies new trends in a speedy fashion in order to meet market demand. It is working to streamline and optimise its supply base in Asia while also ensuring it can speedily deliver new products to its stores. In support of its stores it operates warehouses in Australia, China, Poland and the US. With its business largely transacted in US dollars, it is affected by currency rate trends.

Year to 29 June*	2024	2025
Revenues ($mn)	698.7	798.1
Europe (%)	33	35
Americas (%)	25	27
Australia/New Zealand (%)	29	26
Africa/Middle East (%)	8	7
Asia (%)	5	5
EBIT ($mn)	128.4	139.1
EBIT margin (%)	18.4	17.4
Profit before tax ($mn)	110.6	118.2
Profit after tax ($mn)	82.4	86.3
Earnings per share (c)	75.38	78.08
Cash flow per share (c)	160.56	176.28
Dividend (c)	87	77
Percentage franked	17	0
Net tangible assets per share ($)	~	~
Interest cover (times)	7.2	6.6
Return on equity (%)	102.8	108.7
Debt-to-equity ratio (%)	29.2	43.8
Current ratio	0.9	0.8

*30 June 2024

Lycopodium Limited

ASX code: LYL   www.lycopodium.com

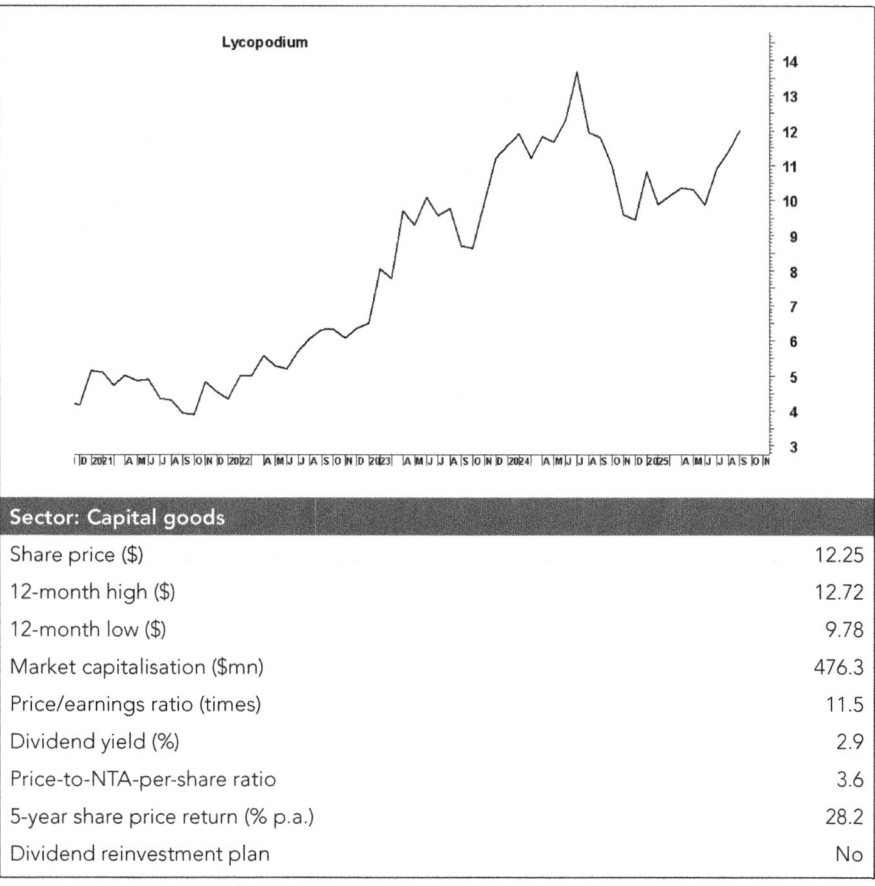

Sector: Capital goods	
Share price ($)	12.25
12-month high ($)	12.72
12-month low ($)	9.78
Market capitalisation ($mn)	476.3
Price/earnings ratio (times)	11.5
Dividend yield (%)	2.9
Price-to-NTA-per-share ratio	3.6
5-year share price return (% p.a.)	28.2
Dividend reinvestment plan	No

Founded in 1992, Perth-based Lycopodium is an engineering and project management company. Its particular specialty is the provision of engineering and project delivery services in the resources, rail infrastructure and industrial processes sectors, with numerous blue-chip customers. It has operations in many countries and 18 offices in Australia, Canada, the US, Argentina, Brazil, Peru, South Africa, Namibia, Botswana, Ghana and the Philippines.

Latest business results (June 2025, full year)

Rising costs, notably for labour, and project delays were among the factors generating a fall in revenues and profits. In addition, revenues were predominantly driven by Engineering, Procurement and Construction Management (EPCM) projects, rather than by more profitable Engineering, Procurement and Construction (EPC) projects. Work in the resources sector is responsible for more than 90 per cent of company income, with revenues down 4 per cent and profits falling 13 per cent. A bright spot was the Rail Infrastructure division, which achieved an 8 per cent rise in sales and a 46 per cent surge in profits. By contrast, the Industrial Processes division experienced another bad year, with revenues down 10 per cent and profits crashing by more than 80 per cent. Overseas operations were responsible for more than 60 per cent of total turnover.

Outlook

Despite economic weakness around the world, Lycopodium expects a significant level of investment to continue in the resources sector, related especially to the global energy transition, which is boosting demand for low-emission technologies. Thanks to many new development projects, especially for lithium, copper, graphite, cobalt, nickel and rare earths, it forecasts solid demand for its services. Many of the major development projects for these minerals are in Latin America, and Lycopodium has been working to expand its presence there. In December 2023 it opened an office in Peru and in July 2025 it acquired a majority stake in SAXUM, a multi-disciplinary engineering and project management services company based in Argentina. In April 2025 it opened an office in Vancouver, Canada, with the aim of pursuing contracts with the many resources companies based in that city. As a leader in the provision of gold mining infrastructure, Lycopodium is optimistic about the outlook for this business as gold demand continues to rise, in part due to central bank purchases in response to global geopolitical and economic tensions. The company also sees great potential for its rail work as the Australian government continues to invest heavily in rail infrastructure across both passenger and freight networks.

Year to 30 June	2024	2025
Revenues ($mn)	344.5	333.9
EBIT ($mn)	70.5	61.7
EBIT margin (%)	20.5	18.5
Profit before tax ($mn)	69.7	60.5
Profit after tax ($mn)	50.7	42.2
Earnings per share (c)	127.61	106.23
Cash flow per share (c)	144.15	123.71
Dividend (c)	77	35
Percentage franked	100	100
Net tangible assets per share ($)	2.85	3.41
Interest cover (times)	92.8	51.3
Return on equity (%)	41.8	30.2
Debt-to-equity ratio (%)	~	~
Current ratio	2.3	2.6

Macmahon Holdings Limited

ASX code: MAH   www.macmahon.com.au

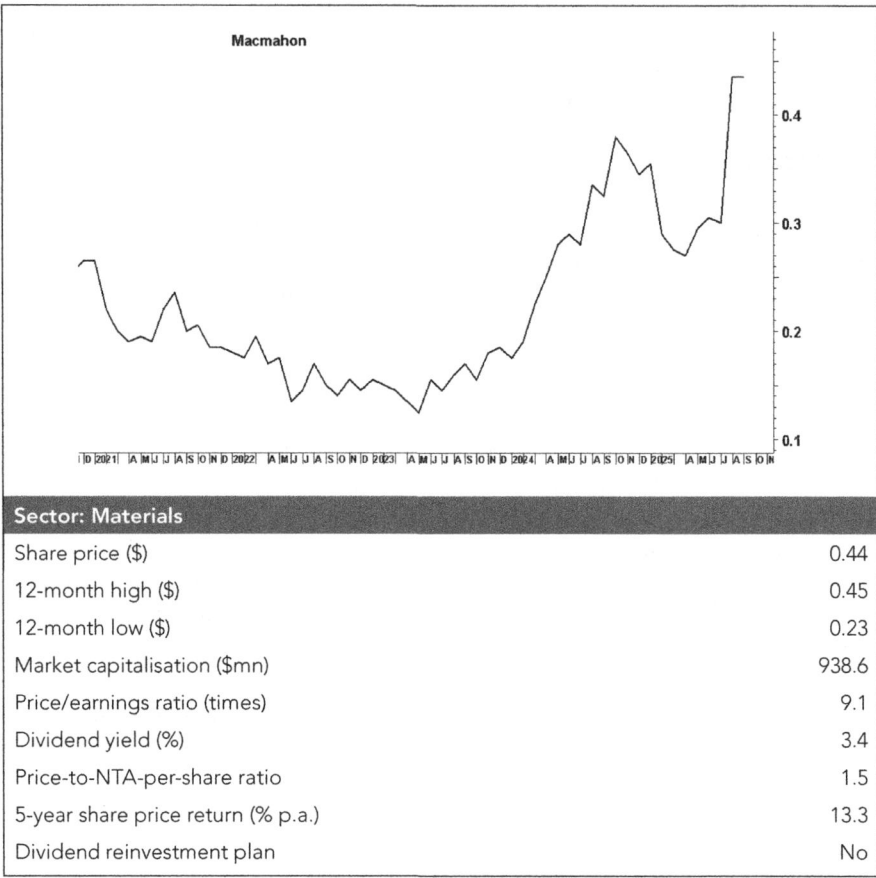

Sector: Materials	
Share price ($)	0.44
12-month high ($)	0.45
12-month low ($)	0.23
Market capitalisation ($mn)	938.6
Price/earnings ratio (times)	9.1
Dividend yield (%)	3.4
Price-to-NTA-per-share ratio	1.5
5-year share price return (% p.a.)	13.3
Dividend reinvestment plan	No

Perth-based contracting group Macmahon Holdings, established in 1963, has a specialty in the provision of mining services. In surface mining it offers a broad array of services, including mine planning, drill and blast, crushing and screening, water management and equipment operation and maintenance, with operations in Australia and Asia. In underground mining it provides development and production services as well as services to facilitate ventilation and access to underground mines, including shaft sinking, raise drilling and shaft lining. Other activities include civil engineering, and in August 2024 it acquired civil engineer Decmil Group.

Latest business results (June 2025, full year)

A 10-month contribution from Decmil and strong organic growth helped generate another solid rise in revenues and underlying profits. The surface mining business performed well, with significant contract extensions and new wins that included over $500 million of new work in Indonesia and a $900 million contract extension for the Byerwen coal mine in Queensland. The underground mining operation won business that included a $317 million contract for the Poboya gold project in Indonesia. The company's civil infrastructure business also performed well, with the Decmil acquisition adding $400 million of new work. Altogether, gold projects contributed 53 per cent of total company turnover for the year, with coal a further 19 per cent. Overseas work, mainly in Indonesia, was responsible for 8 per cent of revenues. At June 2025 the company held a $5.4 billion order backlog, which was up from $4.6 billion a year earlier.

Outlook

Macmahon has a solid reputation and provides contracting services to many of Australia's mining companies. Levels of activity in the mining sector remain strong and the company sees ahead a tender pipeline of some $24.2 billion of projects. With its strength in gold mining operations, it has benefited from the surging gold price. It is working to reduce capital intensity in its operations, with a particular aim of a further expansion in civil infrastructure and underground mining operations. It has a goal of boosting underground mining and civil infrastructure revenues by 50 per cent over the coming two to three years. It is also working to expand its Indonesian presence. It sees great potential in its Decmil acquisition, which allows Macmahon to diversify its operations and provides a natural hedge to the cyclicality of contract mining. Macmahon's early forecast is for revenues of $2.6 billion to $2.8 billion in the June 2026 year, with underlying EBITA of $180 million to $195 million, up from $171.4 million in June 2025.

Year to 30 June	2024	2025
Revenues ($mn)	2031.3	2427.5
EBIT ($mn)	142.0	173.8
EBIT margin (%)	7.0	7.2
Profit before tax ($mn)	113.5	137.7
Profit after tax ($mn)	91.9	102.4
Earnings per share (c)	4.36	4.81
Cash flow per share (c)	14.41	15.23
Dividend (c)	1.05	1.5
Percentage franked	57	100
Net tangible assets per share ($)	0.30	0.30
Interest cover (times)	5.0	4.8
Return on equity (%)	14.8	15.4
Debt-to-equity ratio (%)	23.1	23.5
Current ratio	1.3	1.2

Macquarie Group Limited

ASX code: MQG   www.macquarie.com

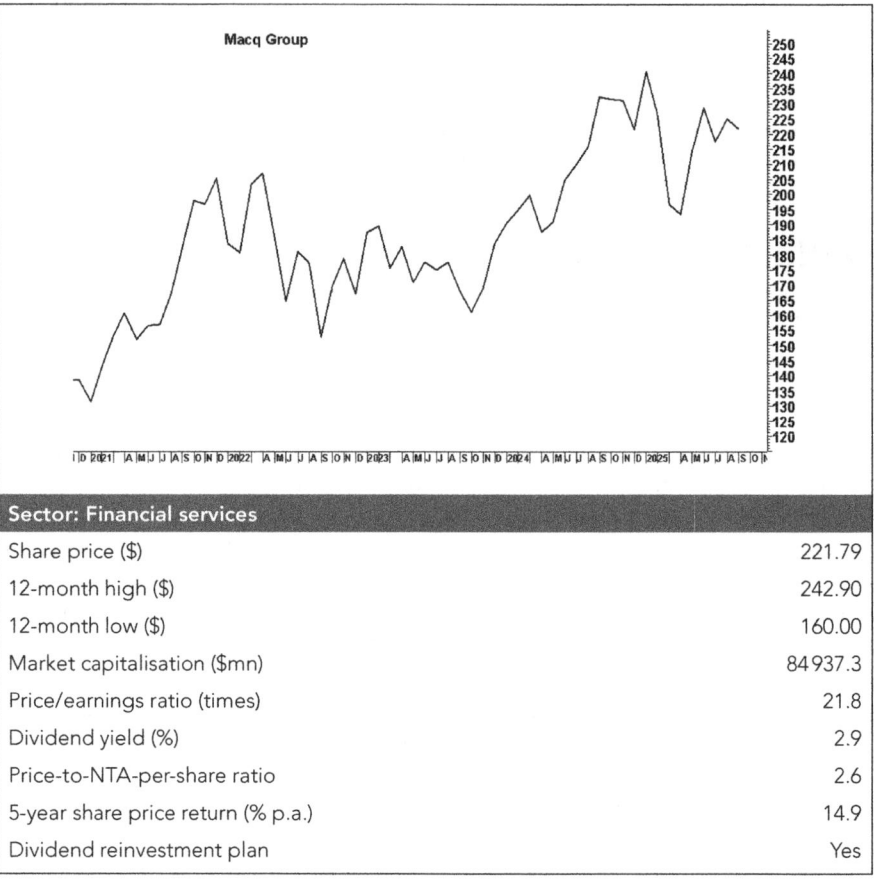

Sector: Financial services	
Share price ($)	221.79
12-month high ($)	242.90
12-month low ($)	160.00
Market capitalisation ($mn)	84 937.3
Price/earnings ratio (times)	21.8
Dividend yield (%)	2.9
Price-to-NTA-per-share ratio	2.6
5-year share price return (% p.a.)	14.9
Dividend reinvestment plan	Yes

Sydney-based Macquarie Group was established in 1969 as Hill Samuel Australia, a subsidiary of a British merchant bank. It is now Australia's leading locally owned investment bank, with a wide spread of activities and boasting special expertise in specific industries that include finance, resources and commodities, energy, infrastructure and real estate. It operates in 31 markets around the world, and international business accounts for around two-thirds of total company revenue.

Latest business results (March 2025, full year)

Revenues and profits rebounded after the decline of the previous year, driven by two of the bank's four broad operating segments. Macquarie Asset Management, which saw earnings plummet by 48 per cent in March 2024, this time achieved a 33 per cent jump, thanks especially to higher performance fees and profits from the sale of the helicopter leasing business Macquarie Rotorcraft. The Banking and

Financial Services division, which provides banking and wealth management services to Australian customers, achieved an 11 per cent rise in profits. During the year the home loan portfolio rose 19 per cent to $141.7 billion. By contrast, the largest business segment, Commodities and Global Markets, saw profits down 12 per cent, as more subdued market conditions reduced client hedging activity, particularly in energy sectors. The fourth company division, Macquarie Capital, recorded profits that were roughly in line with the previous year, with higher advisory and brokerage fee income offset by lower investment-related income.

Outlook

At a time of global political and economic volatility, Macquarie is again cautious about the near-term outlook. However, it continues to believe that it is well-placed to deliver a superior medium-term performance as it builds on its existing businesses and steadily moves into new products and new markets. It has been placing a strong emphasis on building a portfolio of decarbonisation assets, and Macquarie Asset Management's Green Investments team is managing some $19 billion in assets, up fourfold in just three years. The Commodities and Global Markets division too is active in renewable energy, thanks to its expertise in carbon markets, enabling it to structure specialised financial products for its clients. The bank is also active in the digital network sector, with a growing investment in data centres around the world, along with a significant involvement in the expansion of global fibre networks and telecommunications infrastructure. The Banking and Financial Services division continues to grow steadily, thanks in part to a portfolio of technology-driven products and services, including a rapidly expanding home loans book, and Macquarie sees opportunities for further expansion.

Year to 31 March	2024	2025
Operating income ($mn)	16 887.0	17 208.0
Net interest income ($mn)	3 459.0	3 507.0
Operating expenses ($mn)	1 2061.0	12 140.0
Profit before tax ($mn)	4 826.0	5 068.0
Profit after tax ($mn)	3 522.0	3 715.0
Earnings per share (c)	953.66	1 015.44
Dividend (c)	640	650
Percentage franked	40	35
Non-interest income to total income (%)	79.5	79.6
Net tangible assets per share ($)	74.15	86.01
Cost-to-income ratio (%)	71.4	70.5
Return on equity (%)	10.6	10.8
Return on assets (%)	0.9	0.9

Mader Group Limited

ASX code: MAD   www.madergroup.com.au

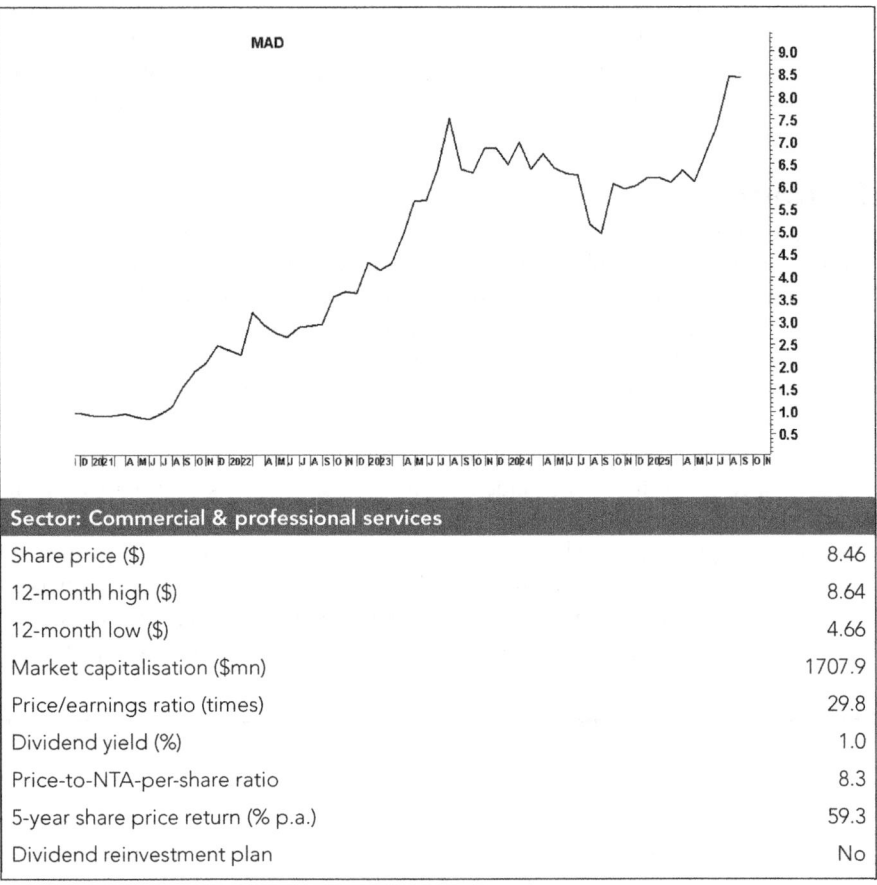

Sector: Commercial & professional services	
Share price ($)	8.46
12-month high ($)	8.64
12-month low ($)	4.66
Market capitalisation ($mn)	1707.9
Price/earnings ratio (times)	29.8
Dividend yield (%)	1.0
Price-to-NTA-per-share ratio	8.3
5-year share price return (% p.a.)	59.3
Dividend reinvestment plan	No

Perth-based contractor Mader was founded in 2005 and is a specialist in mobile and fixed plant equipment maintenance and support. Its key business is the supply of tradespeople for the maintenance of heavy mobile equipment in the resources and energy sectors. However, it has grown rapidly to provide support services of many kinds to a wide range of industries. It works throughout Australia and has also expanded abroad, with 19 per cent of revenues derived from North America. It is also moving into Africa and the Asia-Pacific region.

Latest business results (June 2025, full year)

Mader once again recorded double-digit growth in sales and profits, with strength across most businesses. Australian revenues rose 17 per cent to $686.2 million, with particularly strong demand for the Infrastructure Maintenance and the Rail Services divisions. A new division, Road Transport Maintenance, achieved 65 per cent growth in sales. However

North American revenues, which jumped by 34 per cent in the previous year, this time fell 7 per cent to $166.1 million, with US weakness offsetting another strong performance in Canada. Revenues from Asia and Africa of $19.9 million were up 81 per cent, thanks to strong demand for specialist mining maintenance services and Mader's moves into new markets. At June 2025 the company was servicing some 490 customers at more than 640 locations in nine countries.

Outlook

Mader is a beneficiary of the continuing strength of the Australian and North American resources and energy sectors. It maintains an ambitious growth program, based on service, geographical expansion and sector diversification. In Australia it has moved from its resources base to the provision of services to a range of sectors that include infrastructure, rail, road transport, power generation and marine, and it continues to seek out new growth opportunities. However, it sees its best near-term prospects in the large North American market. In the US it has operations in multiple commodities across 37 states, and despite recent weakness believes the growth potential remains excellent. It entered the Canadian market in 2022 and continues to grow strongly, with services now extended to nine provinces and territories. Its Mader Energy business unit is targeting field maintenance support service opportunities for customers in the natural gas compression industry. Mader is also working to extend its services to customers in other countries. The company's early forecast for June 2026 is for continuing growth, delivering revenues of at least $1 billion and an after-tax profit of more than $65 million.

Year to 30 June	2024	2025
Revenues ($mn)	774.5	872.2
Australia (%)	76	79
North America (%)	23	19
EBIT ($mn)	74.7	84.0
EBIT margin (%)	9.6	9.6
Gross margin (%)	20.9	19.3
Profit before tax ($mn)	70.5	80.1
Profit after tax ($mn)	50.4	57.1
Earnings per share (c)	25.21	28.36
Cash flow per share (c)	37.47	41.02
Dividend (c)	7.8	8.8
Percentage franked	100	100
Net tangible assets per share ($)	0.76	1.01
Interest cover (times)	17.7	21.6
Return on equity (%)	36.0	30.7
Debt-to-equity ratio (%)	19.4	3.9
Current ratio	1.7	1.9

Magellan Financial Group Limited

ASX code: MFG   magellanfinancialgroup.com

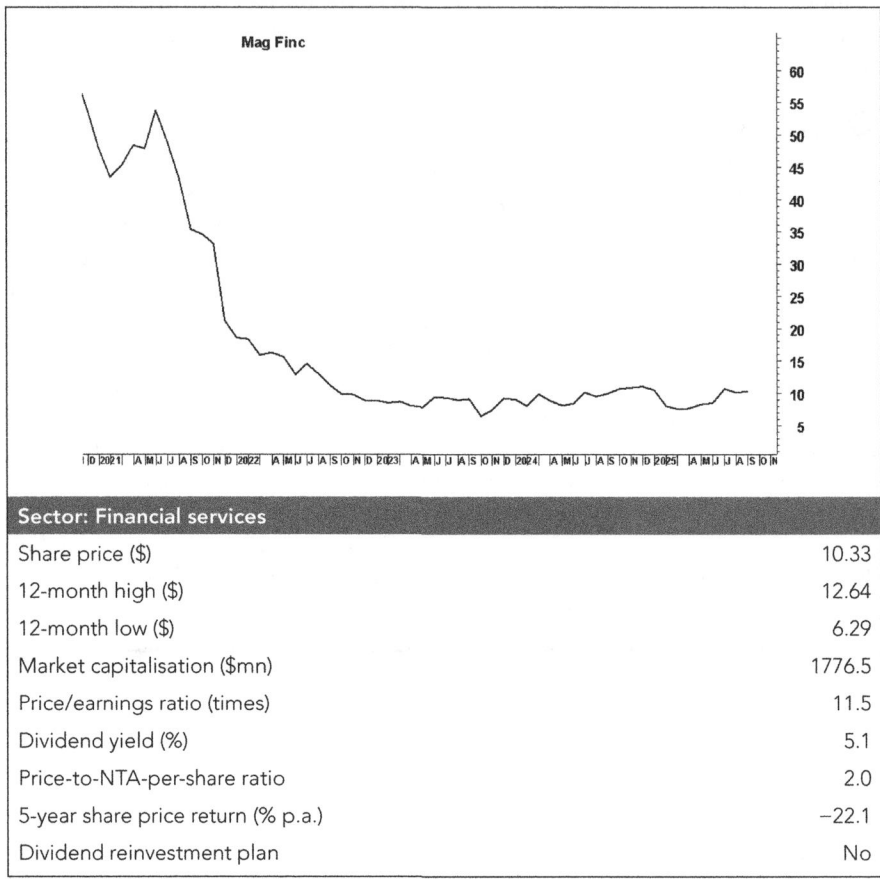

Mag Finc

Sector: Financial services	
Share price ($)	10.33
12-month high ($)	12.64
12-month low ($)	6.29
Market capitalisation ($mn)	1776.5
Price/earnings ratio (times)	11.5
Dividend yield (%)	5.1
Price-to-NTA-per-share ratio	2.0
5-year share price return (% p.a.)	−22.1
Dividend reinvestment plan	No

Sydney-based Magellan is a specialist investment management company that evolved in 2006 from the ASX-listed Pengana Hedgefunds Limited. Its main business is Magellan Asset Management, which offers managed funds to retail and institutional investors, with particular specialties in global equities, global listed infrastructure and, through Airlie Funds Management, in Australian equities. In 2024 it acquired a 29.5 per cent equity stake in global funds management firm Vinva Investment Management.

Latest business results (June 2025, full year)

Revenues fell again as the company reduced its fees, but profits bounced back, due especially to a boost in partnership income. Management and services fee income was down by 9 per cent to $235.8 million, which followed a 22 per cent drop in the previous year. Performance fee income, which soared 67 per cent in the previous year, this time slumped 42 per cent to $11.1 million. Employee expenses, which fell 20 per cent in the previous year as the company worked to cut costs, this time edged up 2 per cent. Total assets under management rose 8 per cent to $39.6 billion, supported by favourable market conditions and growing client interest in new products. Magellan has entered into a series of partnerships with companies in which it holds an equity stake, and its share of these companies' profits tripled to $31 million, boosting Magellan's own profits.

Outlook

Magellan is working to rebuild after a difficult period when the continuing underperformance of its main global funds sparked a chain of client withdrawals and management departures. It believes it is now on a path to recovery, thanks in particular to a solid performance from its funds. It has added key executives to its team as well as introducing several new equity funds and enhancing its global distribution network. The company has stated that its strategy is to evolve from a traditional asset manager to a financial services group active in two fields, investment management and specialist financial services. It views its investments in high-quality businesses as a key part of this strategy. Its 36 per cent holding in the financial services firm Barrenjoey Capital Partners has proven very successful, as this business continues to grow. The $138.5 million acquisition of a stake in Vinva Investment Management is also seen as part of this strategy. Vinva runs a series of funds that have delivered excellent returns since 2010, and it boasts a strong distribution team, providing a boost to Magellan's own investment capabilities and its distribution channels.

Year to 30 June	2024	2025
Revenues ($mn)	278.3	247.3
EBIT ($mn)	212.1	218.7
EBIT margin (%)	76.2	88.4
Profit before tax ($mn)	211.1	218.4
Profit after tax ($mn)	151.5	159.7
Earnings per share (c)	83.66	89.75
Cash flow per share (c)	85.85	92.07
Dividend (c)	65.1	52.3
Percentage franked	50	92
Net tangible assets per share ($)	5.02	5.19
Interest cover (times)	205.0	806.9
Return on equity (%)	15.3	15.8
Debt-to-equity ratio (%)	~	~
Current ratio	7.2	3.0

Medibank Private Limited

ASX code: MPL   www.medibank.com.au

Sector: Insurance	
Share price ($)	5.08
12-month high ($)	5.31
12-month low ($)	3.53
Market capitalisation ($mn)	13 990.3
Price/earnings ratio (times)	27.9
Dividend yield (%)	3.5
Price-to-NTA-per-share ratio	7.6
5-year share price return (% p.a.)	17.7
Dividend reinvestment plan	No

Melbourne-based Medibank Private was established by the Australian government in 1976 as a not-for-profit private health insurer. It was privatised and listed on the ASX in 2014. Today it is Australia's largest private health insurer, with a market share of around 26 per cent, operating under the Medibank and ahm brands. It has also branched into other areas, including travel insurance, pet insurance, life insurance, income protection and funeral insurance. Its Medibank Health division specialises in the provision of a diverse mix of healthcare services.

Latest business results (June 2025, full year)

Rising policyholder numbers helped generate small rises in revenues and profits, bolstered by a $17.9 million increase in net investment income to $207.8 million. The company reported that its underlying after-tax profit — adjusted for movement in the Covid equity reserve and for the normalisation of investment returns — rose 8.5 per cent to $618.7 million. Policyholder numbers grew by 1.4 per cent, double the rate of the previous year, with 4.3 per cent growth for the budget ahm health insurance brand, which is aimed at younger customers, and 0.3 per cent growth for the Medibank brand. Total premium revenue rose 3.6 per cent, outstripping the net claims expense, which was up 3.2 per cent. The very small Medibank Health division — representing less than 5 per cent of company turnover — achieved further double-digit increases in revenues and profits. Medibank Health is now generating approximately 9 per cent of total company profit.

Outlook

Medibank occupies a central role in the national health sector. It should benefit from a growing and ageing population. It has achieved success — ahead of many rivals — in retaining customers and reducing churn. Nevertheless, its business is heavily regulated, and it is difficult to achieve significant growth. It is under pressure from the private hospital sector for help in meeting fast-rising costs and declining patient numbers. In addition, with many households facing cost of living pressures, private health insurance growth rates could start to decline. It is experiencing growth for its non-resident health insurance operations. It expects continuing strong growth for its Medibank Health division, which provides online and telehealth services, home care support, and a variety of prevention and health management services. It is targeting acquisitions to further strengthen this business, with the corporate health and wellbeing sectors a particular focus. It is integrating artificial intelligence technology across its operations. It forecasts moderate health insurance industry growth in the June 2026 year, and it aims to boost its market share.

Year to 30 June	2024	2025
Revenues ($mn)	8175.8	8604.0
EBIT ($mn)	715.5	737.7
EBIT margin (%)	8.8	8.6
Profit before tax ($mn)	711.7	728.8
Profit after tax ($mn)	492.5	500.8
Earnings per share (c)	17.88	18.18
Cash flow per share (c)	20.99	21.59
Dividend (c)	16.6	18
Percentage franked	100	100
Net tangible assets per share ($)	0.67	0.67
Interest cover (times)	188.3	82.9
Return on equity (%)	21.7	21.6
Debt-to-equity ratio (%)	~	~
Current ratio	1.9	1.9

Metcash Limited

ASX code: MTS   www.metcash.com

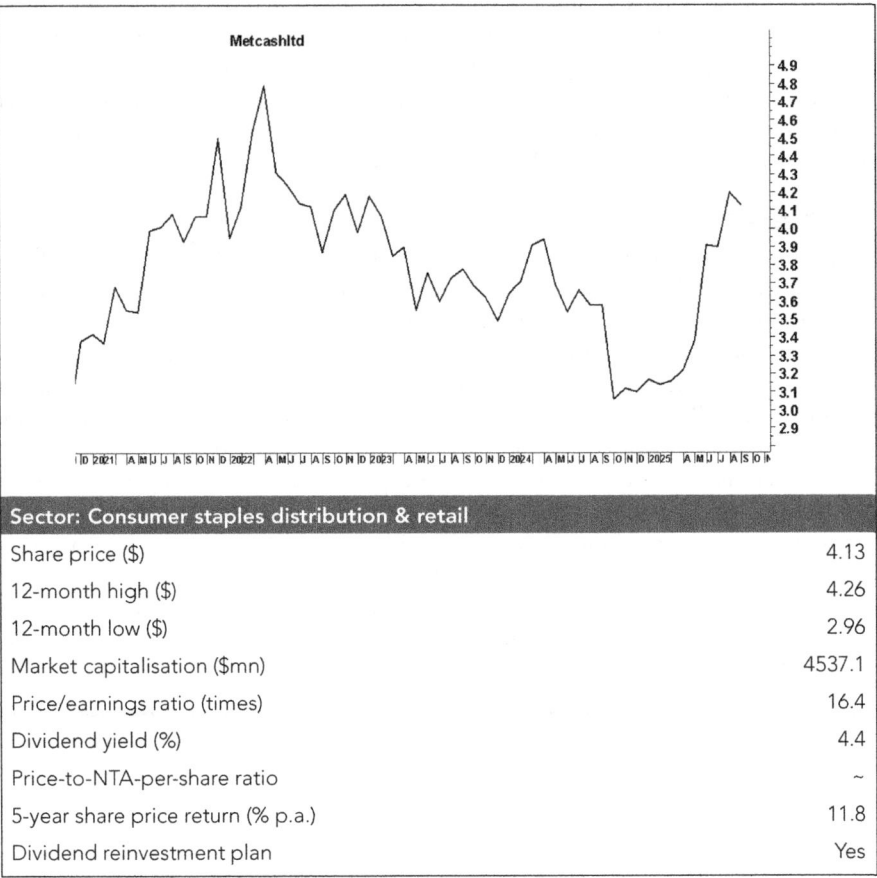

Sector: Consumer staples distribution & retail	
Share price ($)	4.13
12-month high ($)	4.26
12-month low ($)	2.96
Market capitalisation ($mn)	4537.1
Price/earnings ratio (times)	16.4
Dividend yield (%)	4.4
Price-to-NTA-per-share ratio	~
5-year share price return (% p.a.)	11.8
Dividend reinvestment plan	Yes

Sydney-based Metcash, with a history dating back to 1927, is a leading food and liquor wholesaler. Its Food division supports a network of more than 2400 independently owned grocery stores and supermarkets, with more than half of these under the IGA brand. This division also incorporates the foodservice distribution business Superior Foods, acquired in June 2024. The Liquor division is Australia's largest supplier of liquor to independently owned liquor retailers, with more than 12 000 customers. These include the Independent Brands Australia network of Cellarbrations, The Bottle-O, IGA Liquor and Porters Liquor. The Hardware division operates the Independent Hardware Group, which supplies more than 700 stores, including the Mitre 10, Home Hardware, Total Tools and Hardings Hardware chains.

Latest business results (April 2025, full year)

Revenues rose, in part reflecting the acquisition of Superior Foods, but weakness in the Liquor and Hardware divisions pushed down pre-tax and after-tax profits.

Food sales and profits were up strongly, with growing demand at supermarkets. Tobacco sales slumped by nearly 20 per cent, following a decline of nearly 14 per cent in the previous year, which Metcash attributed to an acceleration in illicit trade and a move to alternatives. Superior Foods contributed revenues of $1.26 billion. Liquor division sales rose, with notable strength in the second half, and the company claimed market share gains. However, the impact of lower wholesale price inflation led to a small decline in profits. Hardware division revenues were also stronger, thanks especially to an expansion of the store network, though a combination of subdued trading activity, some intense competition and an increase in depreciation charges led to a decline in profits. Nevertheless, though just 15 per cent of total turnover, the Hardware division contributed around 35 per cent of company EBIT.

Outlook

Metcash maintains its $300 million Program Horizon efficiency drive aimed at reducing costs and boosting productivity, with an emphasis on technological innovation. It sees particular potential in its $412 million acquisition of Superior Foods, a leading food service company that supplies some 20 000 cafes, restaurants, hotels and canteens from 23 branches across Australia. The acquisition is generating annual cost synergies as well as providing Metcash with significant further consolidation opportunities in the fragmented $21 billion food service market, and it has established a new business unit, Foodservice and Convenience. It believes the sharp decline in tobacco sales is slowing. It also sees an easing of pricing pressures in the hardware business, and expects margins to improve.

Year to 30 April	2024	2025
Revenues ($mn)	15 912.4	17 323.0
Food (%)	52	54
Liquor (%)	32	31
Hardware (%)	16	15
EBIT ($mn)	482.6	495.6
EBIT margin (%)	3.0	2.9
Gross margin (%)	12.2	12.9
Profit before tax ($mn)	403.7	385.4
Profit after tax ($mn)	282.3	275.5
Earnings per share (c)	28.31	25.14
Cash flow per share (c)	47.57	47.04
Dividend (c)	19.5	18
Percentage franked	100	100
Net tangible assets per share ($)	~	~
Interest cover (times)	6.1	4.5
Return on equity (%)	21.8	17.5
Debt-to-equity ratio (%)	16.5	35.3
Current ratio	1.1	1.0

Monadelphous Group Limited

ASX code: MND   www.monadelphous.com.au

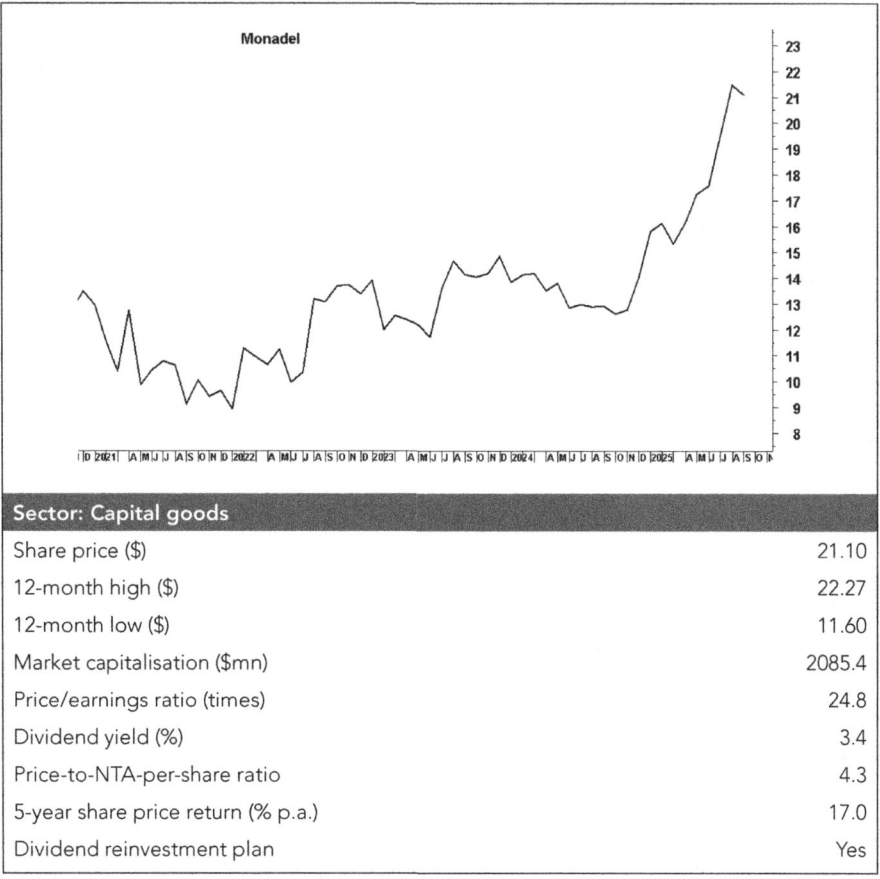

Sector: Capital goods	
Share price ($)	21.10
12-month high ($)	22.27
12-month low ($)	11.60
Market capitalisation ($mn)	2085.4
Price/earnings ratio (times)	24.8
Dividend yield (%)	3.4
Price-to-NTA-per-share ratio	4.3
5-year share price return (% p.a.)	17.0
Dividend reinvestment plan	Yes

Perth-based Monadelphous, established in 1972, is an engineering company that provides a wide range of construction, maintenance, project management and support services to the minerals, energy and infrastructure industries. It operates from branches throughout Australia, with a client base that includes most of the country's resource majors. It has also established a presence in overseas markets that include China, Mongolia, Papua New Guinea and the Philippines. Its Zenviron joint venture is involved in large-scale renewable energy projects and its Mondium joint venture is involved in minerals processing.

Latest business results (June 2025, full year)

Revenues and profits rose again in another good year for the company. Monadelphous classifies its activities into two broad segments. The best result came from the Engineering Construction division, with a 30 per cent rise in revenues, following a 32 per cent jump in the previous year, and strong demand across the iron ore, energy, copper, lithium and renewable energy sectors. The Maintenance and Industrial Services division recorded a modest increase in revenues, with maintenance services and sustaining capital works in the energy sector providing a boost. Altogether, the energy and iron ore sectors provided nearly 60 per cent of total revenues.

Outlook

Monadelphous is a key participant in the Australian minerals, energy and infrastructure industries and is a beneficiary of the continuing strength of these businesses, even in a period of political and economic volatility. With a robust order book, it expects further growth in the June 2026 year. Since July 2025 it has received some $1.1 billion in major orders in the energy sector, including a significant seven-year contract for Shell's Prelude Floating Liquefied Natural Gas facility in Western Australia. A $200 million contract with Woodside will enable the processing of gas from that company's Scarborough Energy Project. The iron ore sector remains buoyant, despite lower prices, and Monadelphous continues to experience strong demand for construction and maintenance work from long-term customers Rio Tinto, BHP and Fortescue. It is increasing its exposure to decarbonisation projects, and hopes to benefit from the significant capital investment it believes will be needed to meet expected growing demand for copper and critical minerals. Its Zenviron joint venture is a beneficiary of a growing number of renewable energy projects. In Victoria it has received a contract from EnergyAustralia for the construction of the 350 MW Wooreen battery energy storage system. Monadelphous is working to address skills shortages, which are driving labour costs higher and leading to delays in completing projects.

Year to 30 June	2024	2025
Revenues ($mn)	2015.9	2162.6
Maintenance & industrial services (%)	66	59
Engineering construction (%)	34	41
EBIT ($mn)	95.7	122.9
EBIT margin (%)	4.7	5.7
Gross margin (%)	7.1	7.5
Profit before tax ($mn)	91.9	119.1
Profit after tax ($mn)	62.2	83.7
Earnings per share (c)	64.08	85.01
Cash flow per share (c)	103.71	128.83
Dividend (c)	58	72
Percentage franked	100	100
Net tangible assets per share ($)	4.59	4.86
Interest cover (times)	25.3	32.4
Return on equity (%)	13.8	17.4
Debt-to-equity ratio (%)	~	~
Current ratio	1.6	1.6

Monash IVF Group Limited

ASX code: MVF   www.monashivfgroup.com.au

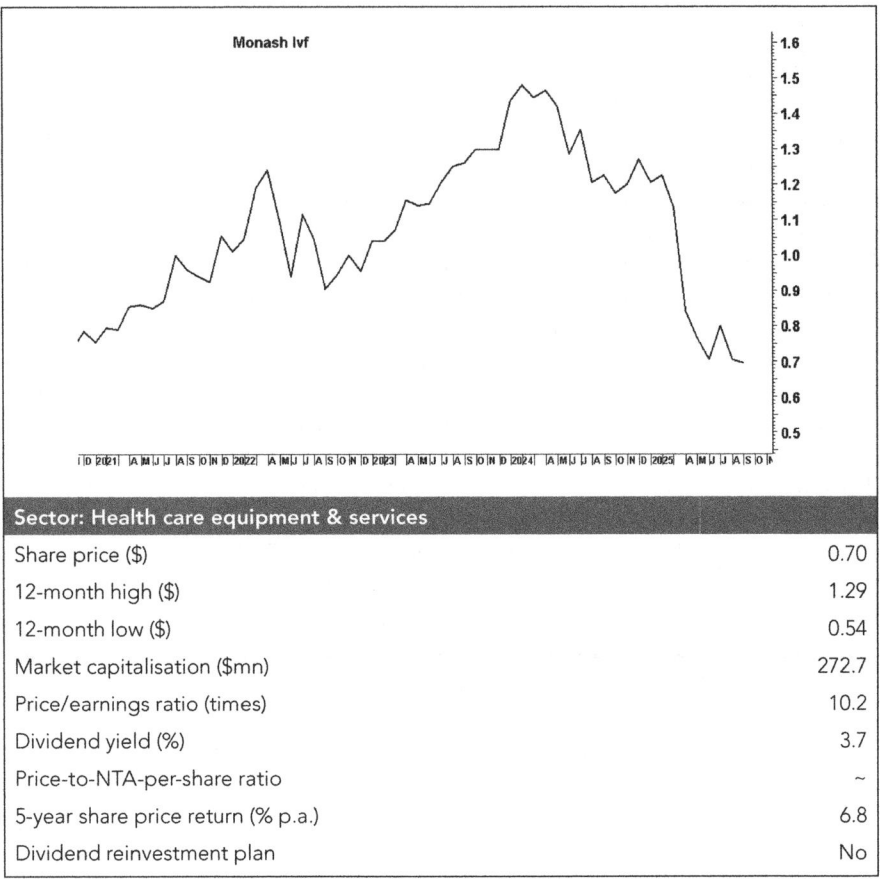

Sector: Health care equipment & services	
Share price ($)	0.70
12-month high ($)	1.29
12-month low ($)	0.54
Market capitalisation ($mn)	272.7
Price/earnings ratio (times)	10.2
Dividend yield (%)	3.7
Price-to-NTA-per-share ratio	~
5-year share price return (% p.a.)	6.8
Dividend reinvestment plan	No

Melbourne-based Monash IVF traces its origins to the start of in vitro fertilisation research at Monash University in 1971, and it has become a global pioneer in a wide range of assisted reproductive technology services. These include frozen embryo births, birth from donor eggs, surgically removed sperm, sperm micro-injection technology, surrogate births and vitrified egg pregnancy. The company is also a provider of specialised women's imaging services. It operates clinics throughout Australia and has expanded to Malaysia, Singapore and Indonesia.

Latest business results (June 2025, full year)

Revenues rose but underlying profits were down in a mixed year for the company. Australian operations saw revenues up 6 per cent but the underlying after-tax profit down 8 per cent. Price rises helped boost revenues, along with a full-year contribution from the Fertility North acquisition in Western Australia and the new Gold Coast and Cremorne day surgery units. Offsetting these were a 1.7 per cent decline in the Australian IVF industry and weakness for the company in the Victorian and Queensland markets. The results were also adversely affected by a 10 per cent rise in staffing costs and an 18 per cent jump in depreciation and amortisation. International operations, representing 7 per cent of total turnover, enjoyed a 13 per cent increase in revenues, which followed a 28 per cent rise in the previous year, but with the underlying after-tax profit down 8 per cent.

Outlook

It is estimated that one in six Australian couples experience infertility issues, with the fertility clinic market worth some $765 million in 2024. Demand continues to grow, driven by several factors, including the fact that more women wish to have children later in life, along with a growing success rate for fertility treatments. In addition, Australia offers substantial government funding, more than many other countries, for fertility treatments. Monash occupies a leading position in the provision of these services. It is optimistic about the long-term outlook for its activities, and continues to seek out new acquisition opportunities, as well as recruiting additional fertility specialists. However, it was hit during the June 2025 year with news of two separate incidents, in Brisbane and Melbourne, in which human error led to embryos being wrongly transferred. Consequently, the company suffered some loss of demand for its services, particularly in Queensland and Victoria, and it has reported that the near-term outlook for its business remains weakened. Its early forecast is for underlying after-tax profit of $20 million to $23 million in the June 2026 year.

Year to 30 June	2024	2025
Revenues ($mn)	255.0	271.9
EBIT ($mn)	43.4	45.2
EBIT margin (%)	17.0	16.6
Profit before tax ($mn)	38.0	37.8
Profit after tax ($mn)	29.9	26.7
Earnings per share (c)	7.67	6.86
Cash flow per share (c)	12.44	12.51
Dividend (c)	5	2.6
Percentage franked	100	100
Net tangible assets per share ($)	~	~
Interest cover (times)	8.1	6.1
Return on equity (%)	11.6	11.0
Debt-to-equity ratio (%)	19.6	35.6
Current ratio	0.5	0.7

National Australia Bank Limited

ASX code: NAB   www.nab.com.au

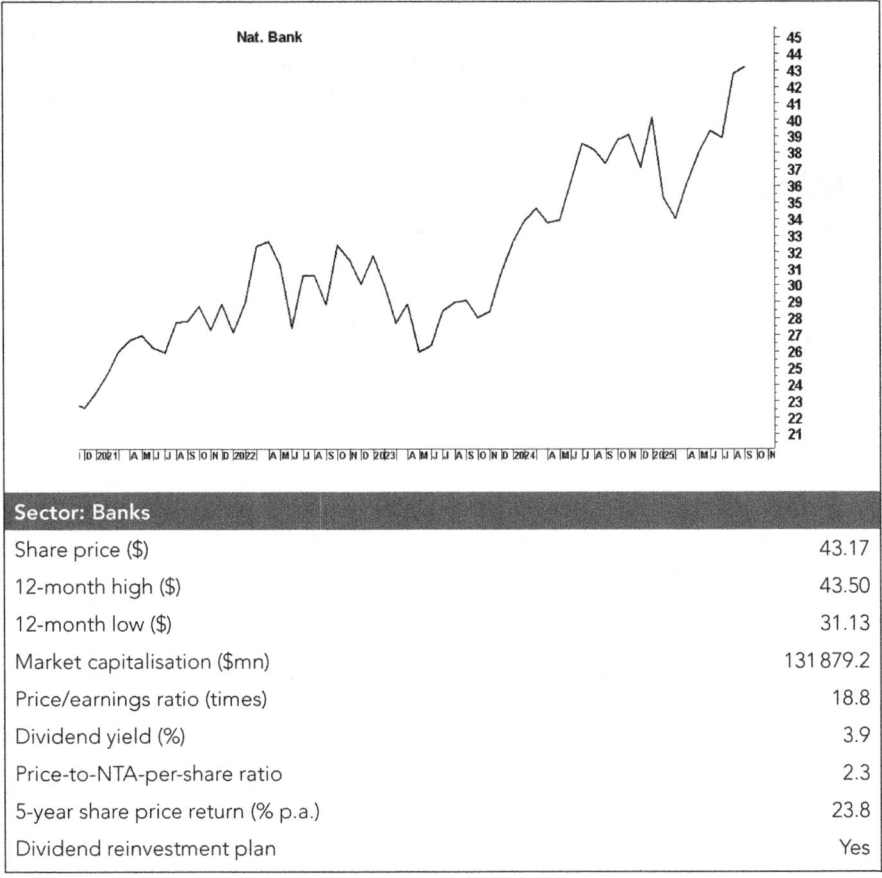

Sector: Banks	
Share price ($)	43.17
12-month high ($)	43.50
12-month low ($)	31.13
Market capitalisation ($mn)	131 879.2
Price/earnings ratio (times)	18.8
Dividend yield (%)	3.9
Price-to-NTA-per-share ratio	2.3
5-year share price return (% p.a.)	23.8
Dividend reinvestment plan	Yes

National Australia Bank, based in Melbourne, has a history dating back to the establishment of the National Bank of Australasia in 1858. It is one of Australia's largest banks, with a wide spread of financial activities and particular strength in business banking. It owns the Bank of New Zealand and also operates offices in several countries in Asia. It is involved in financial planning and wealth management, including through its long-established JBWere advisory service. Other activities include the nabtrade online broking service and the ubank online bank.

Latest business results (March 2025, half year)

Profits edged up, a pleasing result in a competitive environment for much of the bank's business. Costs rose by 3 per cent from the March 2024 half, reflecting higher personnel and financial crime-related costs, together with the bank's continuing investment in technology initiatives. The net interest margin of 1.70 per cent was down from 1.72 per cent, and the bank reported that it would have fallen further but for a solid trading income performance. Of NAB's four divisions, the Business and Private Banking arm, representing more than 40 per cent of bank profit, saw cash earnings slightly lower, owing to rising costs and reduced margins. The bank also reported a drop in agricultural loans, although it also experienced a rise in its market share for small and medium-sized business lending. New Zealand profits rose 4.1 per cent, thanks to volume growth and higher markets and treasury income. The Personal Banking division achieved a 3.6 per cent gain in profits, with the Corporate and Institutional Banking division also managing a small earnings increase.

Outlook

The bank has expressed concerns about escalating global trade tensions, but nevertheless remains optimistic about the underlying growth outlook for both the Australian and New Zealand economies. It is facing growing competition in business lending, where it is market leader, and where profit margins are higher than for home loans. In response it continues to roll out its digital business lending platform, along with continuing innovations for business transaction accounts. In its Personal Banking division it is moving to enhance margins by sourcing a greater percentage of its home loans business inhouse, rather than relying on external mortgage brokers. Continuing investment in NAB's branch network has boosted its retail deposit performance. The Corporate and Institutional Banking division is benefiting from a focus on long-term relationships with key clients, along with a technology-enabled drive to simplify banking processes.

Year to 30 September	2023	2024
Operating income ($mn)	20 654.0	20 646.0
Net interest income ($mn)	16 807.0	16 757.0
Operating expenses ($mn)	9 023.0	10 026.0
Profit before tax ($mn)	10 829.0	10 095.0
Profit after tax ($mn)	7 731.0	7 102.0
Earnings per share (c)	246.52	229.17
Dividend (c)	167	169
Percentage franked	100	100
Non-interest income to total income (%)	18.6	18.8
Cost-to-income ratio (%)	43.7	48.6
Return on equity (%)	12.9	11.6
Return on assets (%)	0.7	0.7
Half year to 31 March	2024	2025
Operating income ($mn)	10 138.0	10 281.0
Profit before tax ($mn)	5 098.0	5 115.0
Profit after tax ($mn)	3 548.0	3 583.0
Earnings per share (c)	114.00	116.90
Dividend (c)	84	85
Percentage franked	100	100
Net tangible assets per share ($)	18.16	18.55

Netwealth Group Limited

ASX code: NWL www.netwealth.com.au

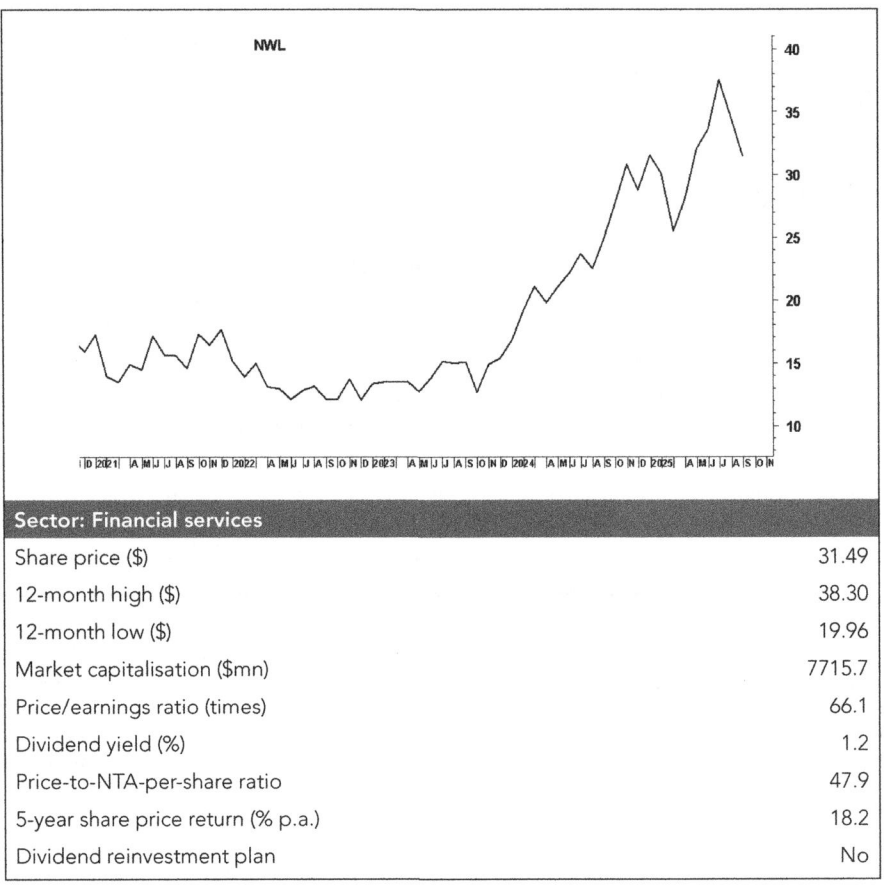

Sector: Financial services	
Share price ($)	31.49
12-month high ($)	38.30
12-month low ($)	19.96
Market capitalisation ($mn)	7715.7
Price/earnings ratio (times)	66.1
Dividend yield (%)	1.2
Price-to-NTA-per-share ratio	47.9
5-year share price return (% p.a.)	18.2
Dividend reinvestment plan	No

Melbourne-based financial services business Netwealth was founded in 1999. Through its wealth management platform it specialises in superannuation products, investor-directed portfolio services for self-managed superannuation, managed accounts and managed funds. The founding Heine family own more than half the company equity.

Latest business results (June 2025, full year)

Netwealth enjoyed another good year, with revenues and profits again up strongly. During the year the company recorded net inflows to its funds of $15.8 billion, up 40 per cent from the previous year. Total funds under administration at June 2025 of $112.8 billion were up 28 per cent. The number of client accounts was up 13 per cent to 162 234 and adviser numbers grew 6 per cent to 3971. Effective cost control during the year meant that company revenues grew at a faster pace than expenses, and margins rose.

Outlook

Netwealth runs a wealth management platform, which is a comprehensive software system that is designed to help financial advisers and others to track their investment portfolios, perform research on new investments and execute trades. It is estimated that more than $1 trillion in investor assets are currently being managed on such platforms in Australia and it is a highly competitive business. The leaders, with around 70 per cent of the market, are major financial institutions such as Insignia Financial, BT Panorama, AMP, Colonial First State and Macquarie Group. These are mostly losing market share, and catching up on them are several smaller and fast-growing firms like Netwealth, which have a particular strength in the development of user-friendly technology. Netwealth says that, based on industry analysis, it was again one of Australia's fastest-growing platform providers — exceeded only by HUB24 — in the 12 months to March 2025, boosting its market share by 1.1 per cent to 8.7 per cent. It is working to increase its exposure to high-net-worth individuals as well as to what it terms the affluent adviser market — advisers looking after clients with account balances of $500 000 to $750 000. Its August 2024 full acquisition of data management software house Xeppo means Netwealth can provide financial advisers with a specialist service that gives them the ability to connect and unify all their client data and systems. It expects its October 2024 acquisition of digital content creator Flux Group to broaden its range of products and services, and enable its advisers to better connect with younger clients. At June 2025 Netwealth had no debt and more than $148 million in cash holdings.

Year to 30 June	2024	2025
Revenues ($mn)	249.5	316.4
EBIT ($mn)	121.0	157.7
EBIT margin (%)	48.5	49.8
Profit before tax ($mn)	120.4	157.1
Profit after tax ($mn)	83.4	116.5
Earnings per share (c)	34.16	47.63
Cash flow per share (c)	35.66	49.98
Dividend (c)	28	38.5
Percentage franked	100	100
Net tangible assets per share ($)	0.50	0.66
Interest cover (times)	211.6	262.4
Return on equity (%)	62.3	67.8
Debt-to-equity ratio (%)	~	~
Current ratio	5.1	4.8

New Hope Corporation Limited

ASX code: NHC   www.newhopegroup.com.au

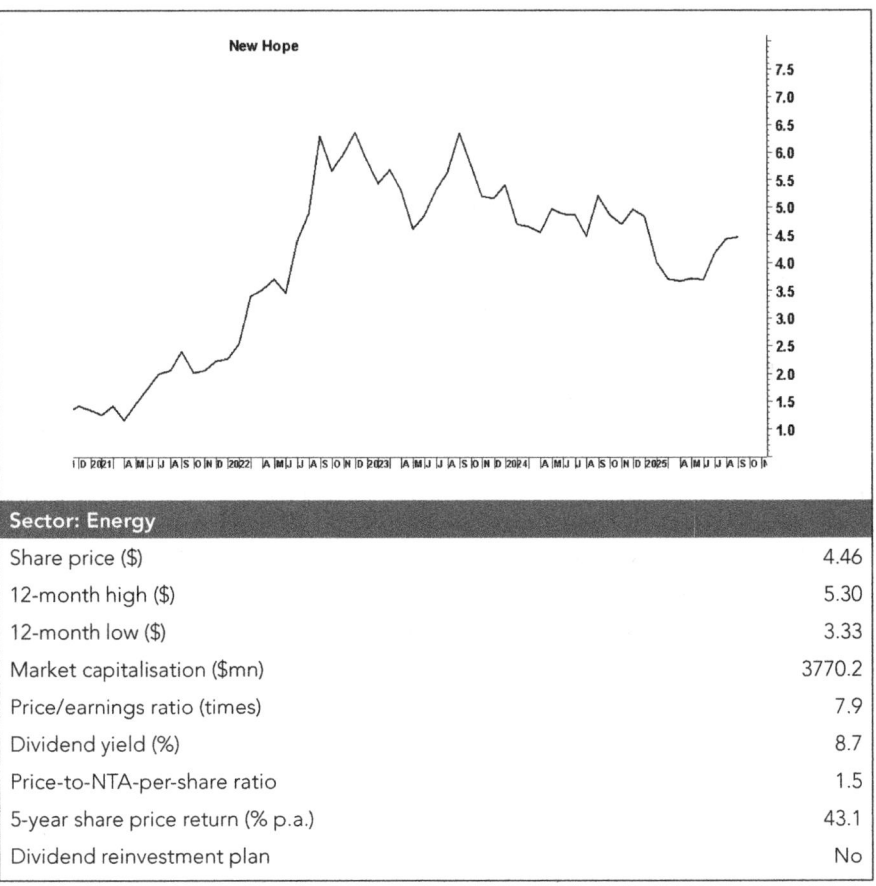

Sector: Energy	
Share price ($)	4.46
12-month high ($)	5.30
12-month low ($)	3.33
Market capitalisation ($mn)	3770.2
Price/earnings ratio (times)	7.9
Dividend yield (%)	8.7
Price-to-NTA-per-share ratio	1.5
5-year share price return (% p.a.)	43.1
Dividend reinvestment plan	No

Brisbane-based coal miner New Hope was founded in 1952. It operates the 80-per-cent-owned Bengalla thermal coal mine in New South Wales and the New Acland thermal coal mine in Queensland. Its subsidiary Queensland Bulk Handling manages a coal export facility at the port of Brisbane. Another business, Bridgeport Energy, holds interests in exploration tenements and petroleum leases in Queensland, South Australia and Victoria. The company complements its coal mining operations with agricultural enterprises on land surrounding its coal mines. Washington H. Soul Pattinson owns 39 per cent of New Hope's equity.

Latest business results (January 2025, half year)

A substantial increase in coal production offset falling prices to deliver higher revenues and profits. Output from the company's two mines jumped 56 per cent from the January 2024 half to 8.3 million tonnes, while actual coal sales of 5.4 million tonnes were up 44 per cent. However, the average price received fell from $197 per tonne to $173.

New Hope reported that its Bengalla mine continued to experience logistical challenges due to higher-than-expected losses from rail haulage and infrastructure providers. Nevertheless, thanks to disciplined cost control and increased production volumes the company was able to reduce unit costs. In addition to its coal business, the company reported other revenues of $30 million, which included pastoral and oil income.

Outlook

New Hope is a significant producer of thermal coal, which is used for the generation of electricity. Most sales are to customers in Asia, including 44 per cent of sales to Japan. Following a major upgrade, it has succeeded in boosting production at its Bengalla mine, and it is also actively working to expand the New Acland mine, along with the construction of access roads and other infrastructure. It holds a 23 per cent equity stake in Malabar Resources, which has initiated production at the Maxwell mine in NSW. New Hope sees this investment as helping it diversify its portfolio by providing exposure to metallurgical coal. In addition, it holds further coal assets in NSW and Queensland, offering the potential for future development. The company's fortunes are heavily reliant on global coal prices, which recently have weakened significantly. This follows what has been referred to as a coal super-cycle, between 2021 and 2024, when prices soared thanks to rising demand and some supply constraints, notably from Russian mines. In addition, the company's sales have been hit by rail network problems at the Cross River Rail Project in Brisbane, forcing it to secure alternative rail haulage capacity.

Year to 31 July	2023	2024
Revenues ($mn)	2754.5	1802.2
EBIT ($mn)	1559.2	710.3
EBIT margin (%)	56.6	39.4
Profit before tax ($mn)	1545.0	697.2
Profit after tax ($mn)	1087.4	475.9
Earnings per share (c)	125.97	56.31
Cash flow per share (c)	142.37	76.20
Dividend (c)	51	39
Percentage franked	100	100
Interest cover (times)	109.8	54.1
Return on equity (%)	45.0	18.8
Half year to 31 January	2024	2025
Revenues ($mn)	856.6	1019.4
Profit before tax ($mn)	364.1	463.5
Profit after tax ($mn)	251.7	340.3
Earnings per share (c)	29.80	40.30
Dividend (c)	17	19
Percentage franked	100	100
Net tangible assets per share ($)	2.88	3.07
Debt-to-equity ratio (%)	~	~
Current ratio	4.1	2.3

NIB Holdings Limited

ASX code: NHF   www.nib.com.au

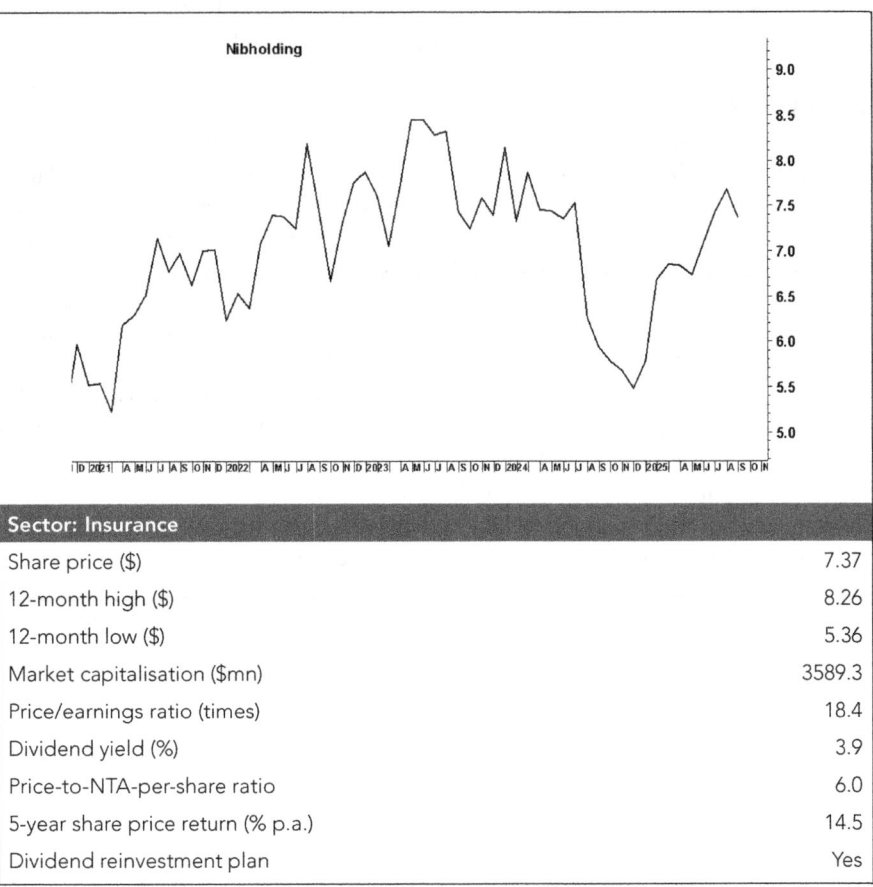

Sector: Insurance	
Share price ($)	7.37
12-month high ($)	8.26
12-month low ($)	5.36
Market capitalisation ($mn)	3589.3
Price/earnings ratio (times)	18.4
Dividend yield (%)	3.9
Price-to-NTA-per-share ratio	6.0
5-year share price return (% p.a.)	14.5
Dividend reinvestment plan	Yes

Newcastle private health insurer NIB Holdings was established as the Newcastle Industrial Benefits Hospital Fund in 1952 by workers at the BHP steelworks. It subsequently demutualised and became the first private health insurer to list on the ASX. It is also active in New Zealand. Other businesses are travel insurance and the provision of specialist insurance services to international students and workers in Australia. Through its new nib Thrive business it has entered the National Disability Insurance Scheme (NDIS) plan management sector.

Latest business results (June 2025, full year)

Revenues and profits rose, with continuing growth in the company's flagship Australian Residents Health Insurance and a strong investment performance. The Australian health insurance business represents around 80 per cent of total company income, with revenue growth of 7.3 per cent driven by an increase in policyholder numbers and price increases. New Zealand health insurance represents a further 11 per cent of company turnover, with higher prices driving an 8.1 per cent rise in revenues. However, a substantial increase in claims led to this business falling into the red. The company's health insurance program for international students and workers in Australia enjoyed further double-digit gains in premium revenues and profits. The small nib Thrive business also achieved increases in revenues and profits. Note that a reduced taxation bill led to a substantial increase in NIB's after-tax profit.

Outlook

NIB believes a growing and ageing population in Australia will help deliver continued growth in policyholder numbers for its health insurance operations. However, this is a highly regulated business, with restrictions on health insurance premium price rises. At the same time the company faces twin problems of rising claims expenses and increased pricing demands from private hospitals, which are seeking to restore profitability after a period of low activity during the Covid pandemic. This is all occurring at a time when many households are facing severe cost of living pressures. NIB benefits from its New Zealand exposure, where it is the country's second-largest health insurer, and it expects this business to move back into profitability in the June 2026 year. It is working to branch into new areas of activity, and sees particularly strong prospects for its moves into the NDIS plan management sector. Its new nib Health Services division incorporates healthcare support providers Midnight Health and Honeysuckle Health, offering health consulting and telehealth medical services. NIB is undertaking a strategic review of its travel insurance business, where profits declined in the June 2025 year.

Year to 30 June	2024	2025
Premium revenues ($mn)	3369.3	3631.3
EBIT ($mn)	276.6	277.8
EBIT margin (%)	8.2	7.7
Profit before tax ($mn)	259.0	259.2
Profit after tax ($mn)	176.4	194.3
Earnings per share (c)	36.43	39.97
Cash flow per share (c)	44.94	49.60
Dividend (c)	29	29
Percentage franked	100	100
Net tangible assets per share ($)	0.97	1.23
Interest cover (times)	15.7	14.9
Return on equity (%)	17.6	18.3
Debt-to-equity ratio (%)	~	4.3
Current ratio	2.1	2.2

Nick Scali Limited

ASX code: NCK

www.nickscali.com.au

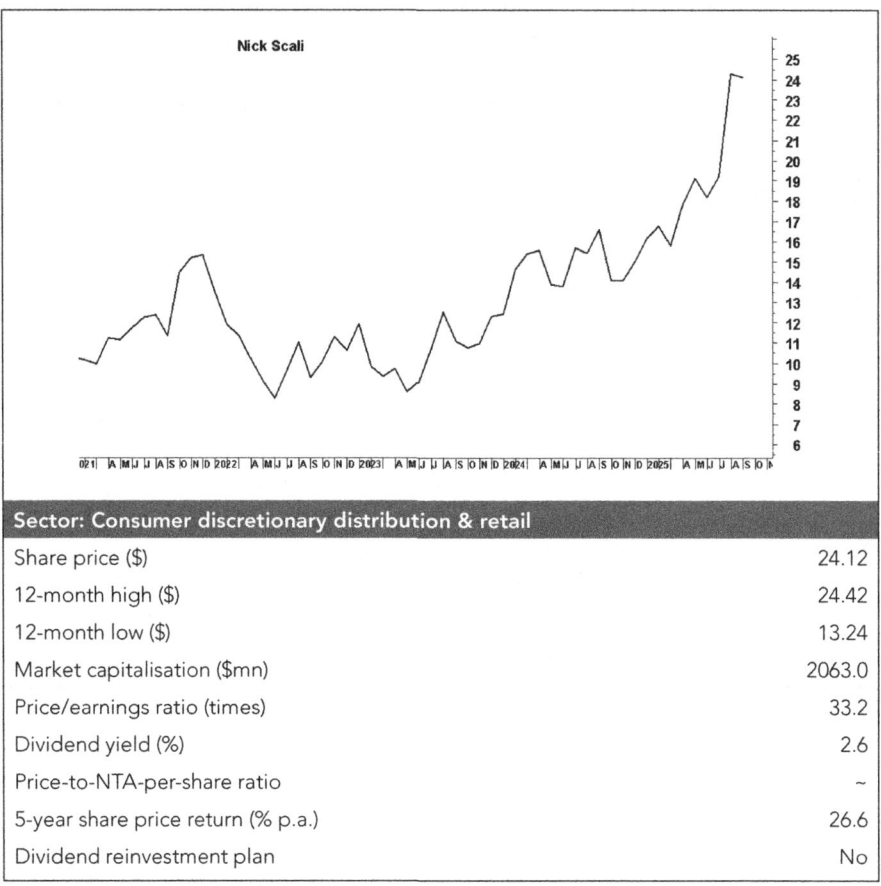

Sector: Consumer discretionary distribution & retail	
Share price ($)	24.12
12-month high ($)	24.42
12-month low ($)	13.24
Market capitalisation ($mn)	2063.0
Price/earnings ratio (times)	33.2
Dividend yield (%)	2.6
Price-to-NTA-per-share ratio	~
5-year share price return (% p.a.)	26.6
Dividend reinvestment plan	No

Sydney-based Nick Scali, founded in 1962, is one of Australia's largest furniture importers and retailers. It specialises in leather and fabric lounge suites along with dining room and bedroom furniture. It also owns Plush Sofas. In 2024 it entered the British market with the acquisition of Anglia Home Furnishings.

Latest business results (June 2025, full year)

Profits fell for the second consecutive year, hit by losses at the company's new UK operations and rising costs domestically. Total Australia and New Zealand written sales orders of $459.9 million represented a 2.8 per cent increase from the previous year, but actual sales revenues dipped 1.4 per cent to $453.5 million. Continuing enhancements to the company's digital marketing platforms drove a 21.8 per cent jump in online written sales orders to $42.4 million. But higher costs, particularly employment expenses, sent the underlying Australia/New Zealand after-tax profit down from $83.5 million in the June 2024 year to $73.2 million. The new British business, acquired in May 2024, made a full-year contribution, with sales of $41.8 million but an underlying after-tax loss of $11.2 million. During the year the company opened one new Nick Scali store in New South Wales and one new Plush store in Victoria. At June 2025 it operated 60 Nick Scali Furniture stores in Australia, and five in New Zealand, along with 45 Plush stores in Australia. It also managed 20 stores in the UK.

Outlook

Nick Scali is directly affected by trends in consumer spending, interest rates, currency movements, housing sales, renovation activity and the general economy. Despite short-term volatility it is optimistic about the longer-term outlook. It has achieved success in boosting profit margins with its Plush acquisition of 2021, and its long-term target is for at least 86 Nick Scali stores and up to 100 Plush stores across Australia and New Zealand. During the June 2026 year it expects to open at least five new stores. It sees great potential in its acquisition of Anglia Home Furnishings, which operated large-scale stores in out-of-town retail parks across the UK under the name Fabb Furniture. It has initiated major renovations, transitioning the stores to the existing Nick Scali lounge and dining product range, with a marketing campaign aimed at establishing the Nick Scali brand. Consequently, British stores achieved a gross profit margin of 51.8 per cent in the June 2025 second half, compared to just 41 per cent before the acquisition. Nick Scali is also looking to expand the British store network.

Year to 30 June	2024	2025
Revenues ($mn)	468.2	495.3
EBIT ($mn)	132.9	109.5
EBIT margin (%)	28.4	22.1
Gross margin (%)	65.5	63.5
Profit before tax ($mn)	117.8	92.5
Profit after tax ($mn)	82.0	62.0
Earnings per share (c)	100.43	72.57
Cash flow per share (c)	156.05	134.91
Dividend (c)	68	63
Percentage franked	100	100
Net tangible assets per share ($)	~	~
Interest cover (times)	8.8	6.4
Return on equity (%)	37.5	23.6
Debt-to-equity ratio (%)	~	~
Current ratio	1.1	1.0

Nine Entertainment Company Holdings Limited

ASX code: NEC   www.nineforbrands.com.au

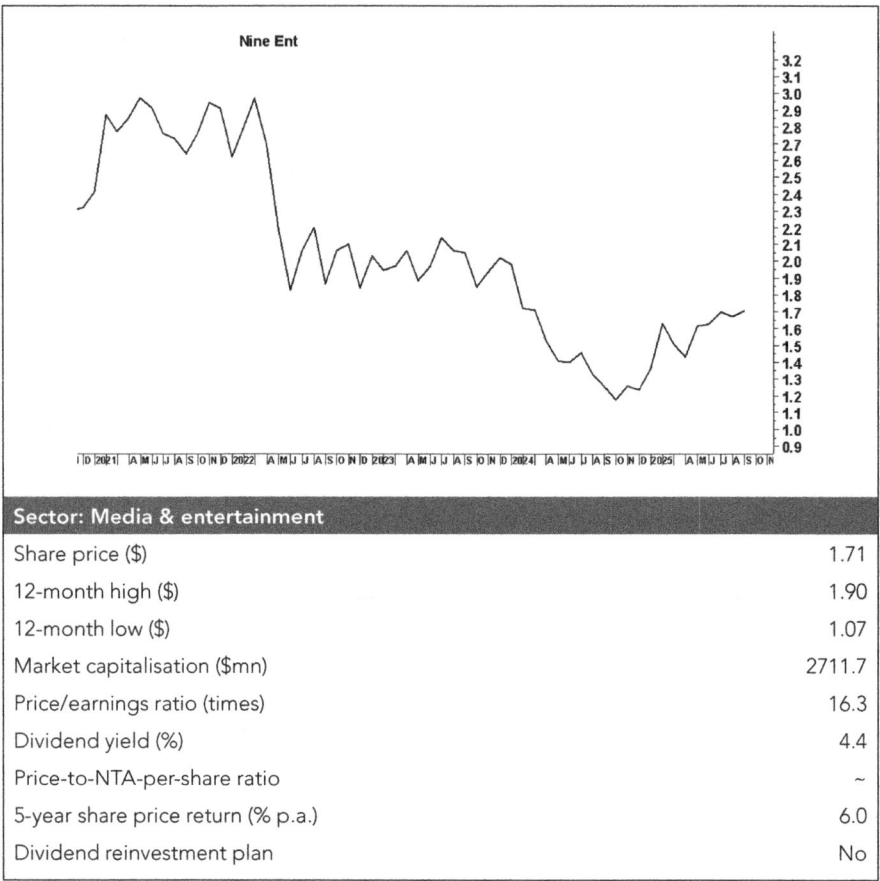

Sector: Media & entertainment	
Share price ($)	1.71
12-month high ($)	1.90
12-month low ($)	1.07
Market capitalisation ($mn)	2711.7
Price/earnings ratio (times)	16.3
Dividend yield (%)	4.4
Price-to-NTA-per-share ratio	~
5-year share price return (% p.a.)	6.0
Dividend reinvestment plan	No

With roots that stretch back to the first edition of the *Sydney Herald* in 1831 and the launch of channel TCN-9 in 1956, Sydney-based Nine Entertainment is today one of Australia's media giants. From August 2025 it divides its activities into three broad segments. The Broadcasting division incorporates its free-to-air television activities, its 9Now streaming video service and radio stations. Publishing comprises a portfolio of newspapers, including the *Sydney Morning Herald, The Age* and the *Australian Financial Review*, as well as magazines and online publications. The Stan division represents the Stan subscription video on demand service. In August 2025 Nine sold for $1.4 billion its 60 per cent interest in Domain Group, an ASX-listed real estate media business.

Latest business results (June 2025, full year)

Revenues rose but underlying profits fell for a third straight year, due especially to further weakness in the core broadcasting and publishing businesses. Revenues edged up for the Broadcasting division as audience numbers rose, boosted by Nine's coverage of the 2024 Olympics and the 2025 Australian Open tennis. However, the higher costs associated with those sporting events pushed profits down. Publishing revenues fell, with digital subscription revenue growth insufficient to offset a softer advertising environment and the end of payments from Facebook owner Meta, although profits were in line with the previous year. The best result came from Stan, with rising subscriber numbers boosting revenues by 10 per cent and profits by more than 30 per cent. Nevertheless, profit margins at Stan remained below those at the other divisions. Domain reported single-digit growth in revenues and profits.

Outlook

Nine Entertainment occupies a central position in Australia's media landscape. In the past it benefited from a robust economy and from its own restructuring efforts. The challenge now is to maintain this momentum as the economy slows and inflationary pressures grow. A key strategy is an acceleration of the shift to digital platforms for its content, along with the embedding of artificial intelligence technology into its operations. The company continues its efficiency drive, aiming for annualised cost savings of $150 million by June 2027. Its 9Now business continues to grow strongly and an increasing share of the company's radio audience is listening online or via apps. Stan remains on a growth trajectory, with 2.5 million subscribers, boosted by the deal with Optus to acquire the rights to English Premier League soccer. Nine plans targeted investment in content and technology in its Publishing division to support longer-term growth.

Year to 30 June	2024	2025
Revenues ($mn)	2629.8	2693.3
Broadcasting (%)	47	47
Publishing (%)	21	20
Stan (%)	17	18
Domain Group (%)	15	15
EBIT ($mn)	370.4	342.2
EBIT margin (%)	14.1	12.7
Profit before tax ($mn)	307.4	271.6
Profit after tax ($mn)	189.4	166.1
Earnings per share (c)	11.73	10.49
Cash flow per share (c)	21.40	20.47
Dividend (c)	8.5	7.5
Percentage franked	100	100
Net tangible assets per share ($)	~	~
Interest cover (times)	5.9	4.8
Return on equity (%)	11.6	10.5
Debt-to-equity ratio (%)	35.8	32.8
Current ratio	1.0	1.0

Northern Star Resources Limited

ASX code: NST　　　　　　　　　　　　　www.nsrltd.com

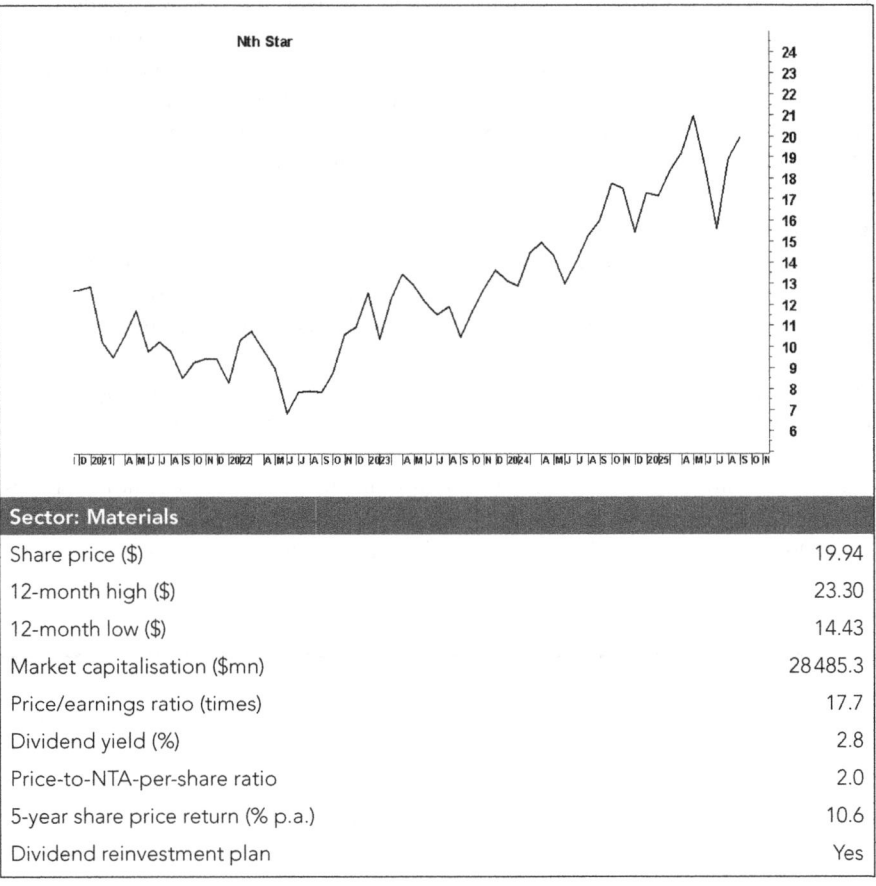

Sector: Materials	
Share price ($)	19.94
12-month high ($)	23.30
12-month low ($)	14.43
Market capitalisation ($mn)	28 485.3
Price/earnings ratio (times)	17.7
Dividend yield (%)	2.8
Price-to-NTA-per-share ratio	2.0
5-year share price return (% p.a.)	10.6
Dividend reinvestment plan	Yes

Perth-based Northern Star Resources, one of Australia's largest gold producers, was founded in 2000. Its key production site is the Kalgoorlie Consolidated Gold Mines (KCGM) operation in Western Australia, known as the Super Pit. Also in the state, it is mining at the Jundee, Carosue Dam, Thunderbox and Bronzewing operations. It is involved in the Pogo gold mine in Alaska, the eighth-largest gold mine in the US. In May 2025 it acquired De Grey Mining and its massive Hemi gold deposit. In July 2025 it sold its 50 per cent stake in the Central Tanami gold project in the Northern Territory.

Latest business results (June 2025, full year)

A surging gold price helped Northern Star to a big rise in revenues and profits. Gold sales of 1.63 million ounces were up 1 per cent from the previous year, less than earlier forecast, due especially to delays and inefficiencies at KCGM. The average price received of $3922 per ounce was up from $3031. Inflationary pressures pushed expenses up 11 per cent, with rising costs for labour, contractor rates, maintenance and energy.

Outlook

Northern Star is a low-cost producer by global standards and is actively working to boost its output, with a goal of eventual production of 2 million ounces per year. In particular, it is investing heavily in its KCGM site. It is spending $1.5 billion to expand milling operations there, with initial production expected early in the June 2027 year. It will spend a further $500 million to $550 million on mine development projects at KCGM and $315 million to $370 million on related infrastructure work, including a thermal power plant and an accommodation camp. It will also spend $220 million on development work at its Thunderbox site and US$70 million to US$80 million to increase mining volumes at the Pogo site. Its $5 billion acquisition of De Grey Mining gives Northern Star control of the Hemi Development Project in the Pilbara region, regarded as potentially one of the largest gold mines in Australia, holding more than 11 million ounces of gold. Northern Star is expected to spend some $1.3 billion to develop the mine, with eventual production of more than 500 000 ounces annually. Northern Star also maintains an active exploration program in Western Australia and Alaska. For the June 2026 year it forecasts total gold sales of 1.7 million to 1.85 million ounces, with an all-in sustaining cost of $2300 to $2700 per ounce, compared to $2163 in June 2025.

Year to 30 June	2024	2025
Revenues ($mn)	4921.2	6414.9
KCGM (%)	27	26
Pogo (%)	17	17
Jundee (%)	17	17
Carosue Dam (%)	15	15
Thunderbox & Bronzewing (%)	13	14
EBIT ($mn)	1041.7	2084.1
EBIT margin (%)	21.2	32.5
Gross margin (%)	24.3	35.4
Profit before tax ($mn)	927.4	1952.2
Profit after tax ($mn)	638.5	1339.7
Earnings per share (c)	55.61	112.64
Cash flow per share (c)	153.62	226.74
Dividend (c)	40	55
Percentage franked	0	55
Net tangible assets per share ($)	7.45	10.09
Interest cover (times)	9.1	15.8
Return on equity (%)	7.4	11.3
Debt-to-equity ratio (%)	0.7	~
Current ratio	2.6	1.8

NRW Holdings Limited

ASX code: NWH   www.nrw.com.au

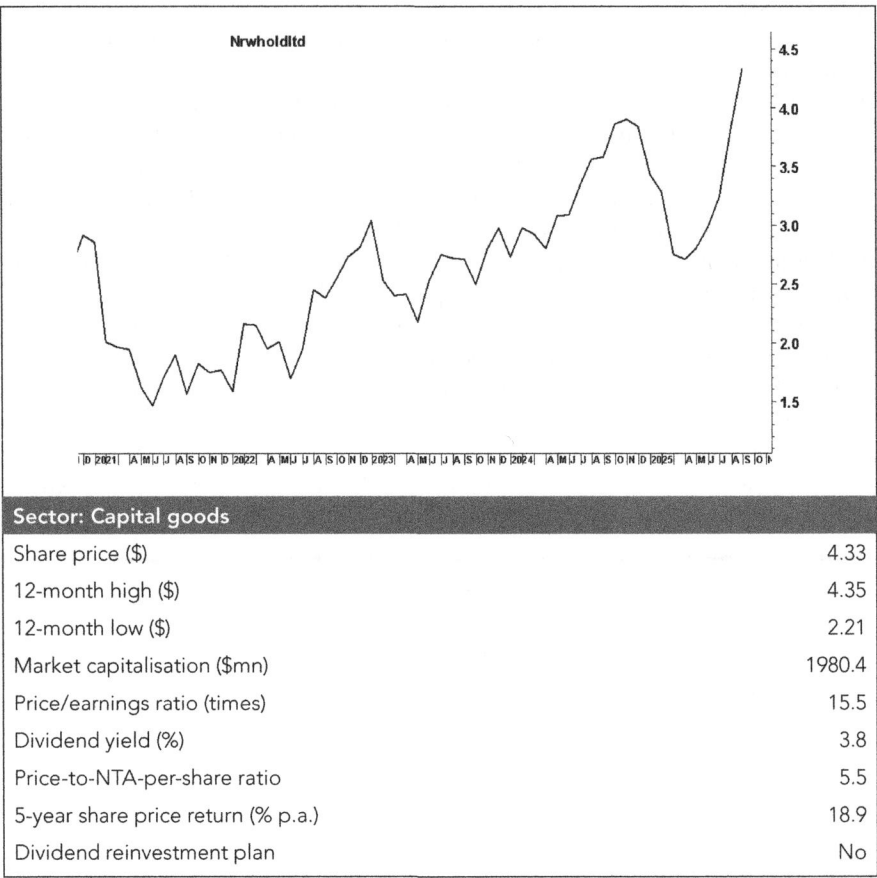

Sector: Capital goods	
Share price ($)	4.33
12-month high ($)	4.35
12-month low ($)	2.21
Market capitalisation ($mn)	1980.4
Price/earnings ratio (times)	15.5
Dividend yield (%)	3.8
Price-to-NTA-per-share ratio	5.5
5-year share price return (% p.a.)	18.9
Dividend reinvestment plan	No

Perth company NRW Holdings, a specialist provider of services to the mining and resources industries, was founded in 1994. It segments its operations into three divisions. The Mining division specialises in mine management, contract mining, drill and blast operations and maintenance services. The Civil division is involved in the delivery of a wide range of private and public civil infrastructure projects, including roads, bridges and renewable energy facilities. The Minerals, Energy and Technologies (MET) division incorporates mining equipment manufacturer RCR Mining Technologies, specialist metals and mining engineer DIAB Engineering, resources and energy construction specialist Primero and industrial electrical engineer OFI Group Holdings.

Latest business results (June 2025, full year)

Revenues and profits rose again. The successful completion of several major projects, including a haul road development for Rio Tinto and the 27-kilometre Wilman

Wadandi Highway in Western Australia, generated a 26 per cent rise in revenues for the Civil division, with underlying profits jumping 48 per cent. The MET division saw revenues up 18 per cent, with profits surging 50 per cent, and a strong contribution from all four of its businesses. By contrast, revenues for the Mining division just edged up, with profits down, affected by project delays caused by heavy rains in Queensland and the early termination of the Mt Cattlin lithium contract. Nevertheless, Mining division profit margins remained higher than for the other two divisions.

Outlook

NRW held an order book of $6.1 billion at June 2025, up from $5.5 billion a year earlier, with around $3 billion of this already secured for the June 2026 year. It also sees some $17.3 billion of potential projects coming up for tender, and it is optimistic about the long-term outlook. It expects mining profits to rebound, with new contracts that include the $1.6 billion, five-year Stanmore South Walker Creek coal project in Queensland and the $360 million Evolution Mining Mungari gold project in Western Australia. It sees major opportunities emerging for its Civil division in Western Australia and Queensland with a surge in new infrastructure developments. It also expects significant demand for new civil construction works from the iron ore sector. It views its $973 million contract from Northern Star Resources for the Fimiston gold development in Kalgoorlie as providing a possible launching pad for further major contracts in the gold sector for its MET division. For June 2026 NRW forecasts revenues of more than $3.4 billion and EBITA of $218 million to $228 million, compared to $208 million in June 2025.

Year to 30 June	2024	2025
Revenues ($mn)	2913.0	3267.7
Mining (%)	51	47
Minerals, energy & technologies (%)	27	28
Civil (%)	22	25
EBIT ($mn)	198.2	213.3
EBIT margin (%)	6.8	6.5
Profit before tax ($mn)	176.8	181.7
Profit after tax ($mn)	123.8	127.2
Earnings per share (c)	27.27	27.85
Cash flow per share (c)	59.34	69.58
Dividend (c)	15.5	16.5
Percentage franked	100	100
Net tangible assets per share ($)	0.89	0.78
Interest cover (times)	9.2	6.8
Return on equity (%)	19.6	20.1
Debt-to-equity ratio (%)	5.1	16.1
Current ratio	1.3	1.1

Objective Corporation Limited

ASX code: OCL   www.objective.com.au

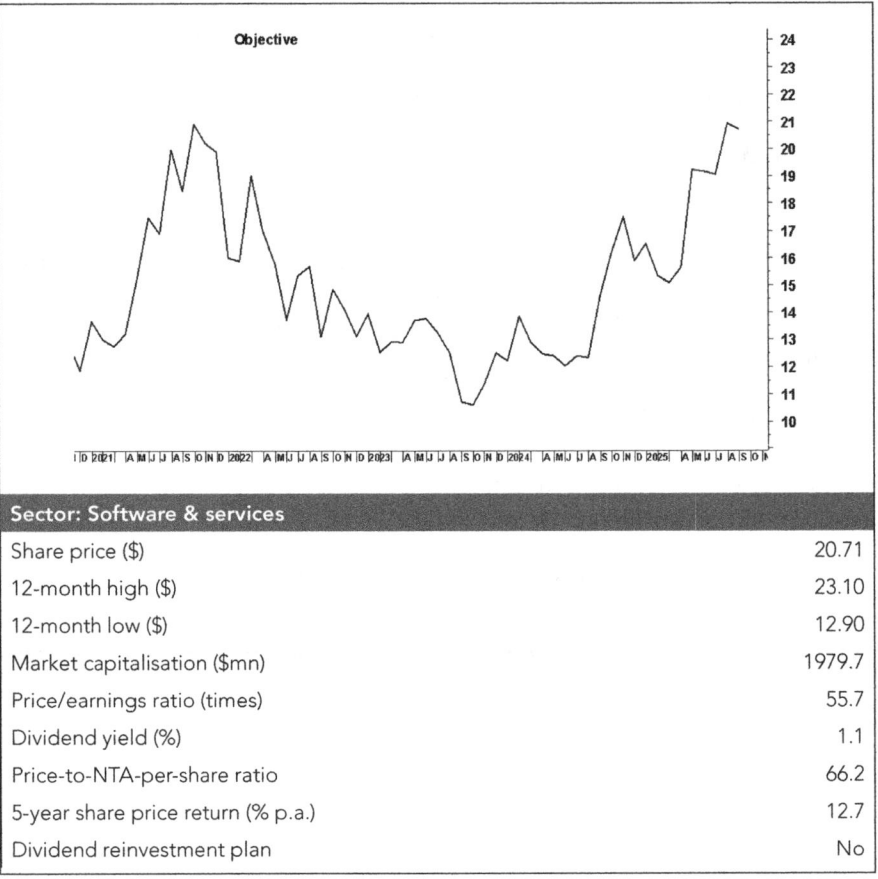

Sector: Software & services	
Share price ($)	20.71
12-month high ($)	23.10
12-month low ($)	12.90
Market capitalisation ($mn)	1979.7
Price/earnings ratio (times)	55.7
Dividend yield (%)	1.1
Price-to-NTA-per-share ratio	66.2
5-year share price return (% p.a.)	12.7
Dividend reinvestment plan	No

Sydney-based Objective, founded in 1987, provides information technology software and services. Its particular specialty is working with federal, state and local governments, as well as government agencies and regulated industries, and it has operations in Australia, New Zealand and the United Kingdom. It has grown substantially, organically and through acquisition, and now operates under numerous product categories.

Latest business results (June 2025, full year)

Revenues and profits both rose for a second straight year. For reporting purposes the company divides its businesses into three broad segments. Content Solutions, by far the largest segment, incorporates the company's core software products that allow customers to manage, process and publish information and collaborate with external organisations. It reported 4 per cent growth in revenues and achieved success in steadily moving major customers from on-premise service to the cloud. A second segment, Regulatory Solutions, comprising products that manage governmental safety and compliance regulatory processes, achieved 6 per cent growth in sales. The third segment, Planning and Building, digitally manages the development and construction planning consent process, and also recorded a 6 per cent increase in revenues. British sales, representing 11 per of total company income, rose 16 per cent. However, New Zealand, representing a further 10 per cent, saw sales down 9 per cent. During the year Objective spent a high $31.2 million on research and development work, up from $28.2 million in the previous year.

Outlook

Objective is a small company working in niche businesses but with a solid reputation and a high level of profitability. The company's particular goal is to help customers digitalise and streamline the processes of compliance, accountability and governance. It has succeeded in moving the majority of its contracts to a subscription model, and most income now is in the form of recurring revenue. It is steadily moving customers to its Objective Nexus next-generation software-as-a-service platform. It has launched its Objective Build product — which originated in New Zealand — to the Australian market, and believes this can transform the local council planning process, resulting in faster building approvals. It is working with customers to embed artificial intelligence technology into all its products. It is expanding its presence in the British market and is also working to build its presence in the US. In July 2025 it announced the acquisition of Isovist, a specialist provider of planning software for local governments. At June 2025 Objective had no debt and nearly $100 million in cash holdings, and it is seeking further acquisition opportunities.

Year to 30 June	2024	2025
Revenues ($mn)	117.5	123.5
Content solutions (%)	70	69
Regulatory solutions (%)	19	20
Planning & building (%)	11	11
EBIT ($mn)	39.0	42.0
EBIT margin (%)	33.2	34.0
Profit before tax ($mn)	38.4	41.4
Profit after tax ($mn)	31.3	35.4
Earnings per share (c)	32.92	37.17
Cash flow per share (c)	39.20	44.76
Dividend (c)	17	22
Percentage franked	47	0
Net tangible assets per share ($)	0.29	0.31
Interest cover (times)	59.4	72.1
Return on equity (%)	37.8	35.7
Debt-to-equity ratio (%)	~	~
Current ratio	1.6	1.6

Origin Energy Limited

ASX code: ORG   www.originenergy.com.au

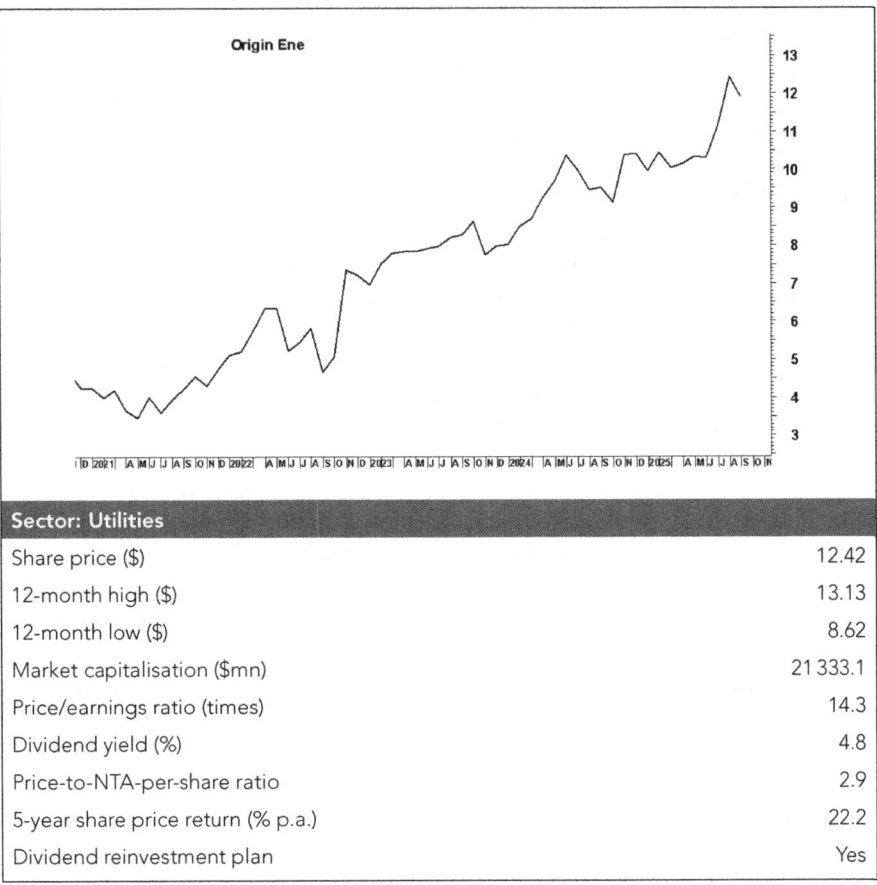

Sector: Utilities	
Share price ($)	12.42
12-month high ($)	13.13
12-month low ($)	8.62
Market capitalisation ($mn)	21 333.1
Price/earnings ratio (times)	14.3
Dividend yield (%)	4.8
Price-to-NTA-per-share ratio	2.9
5-year share price return (% p.a.)	22.2
Dividend reinvestment plan	Yes

Sydney-based Origin Energy, formerly the energy arm of the Boral group, was de-merged in 2000 and is today one of Australia's leading energy companies. It operates the Eraring coal-fired power station in New South Wales, Australia's largest power station, as well as gas-fired power stations in Queensland, New South Wales, Victoria and South Australia. It is also involved in a range of renewable energy projects throughout Australia. Through its joint venture Australia Pacific LNG (APLNG) it supplies 30 per cent of east coast gas demand and also exports LNG to customers in Asia. Its retailing arm supplies electricity, gas and broadband internet to residential and business customers. It owns 22.7 per cent of the fast-growing United Kingdom renewable energy retailer Octopus Energy.

Latest business results (June 2025, full year)

Revenues rose but profits were generally down. However, a substantially reduced tax bill meant that the after-tax profit and EPS figures rose. Most of Origin's revenues derive from its electricity and gas generation, wholesaling and retailing operations, and sales rose 7 per cent to $16.7 billion as the company boosted total customer accounts by 104 000 to 4.7 million. However, profits for these businesses fell, due especially to lower electricity retail tariffs and higher coal costs. More than half Origin's profits come from gas operations, notably its 27.5 per cent holding in APLNG. Thanks to successful LNG trading, gas operations realised higher profits, partially offset by lower production and lower commodity prices. Origin also receives dividends from APLNG that were previously only partially franked but are now fully franked, enabling Origin to reduce its own tax payments. The investment in Britain's Octopus Energy moved from profit to loss as Octopus spent heavily on growth initiatives.

Outlook

Origin expects underlying EBITDA of $1.4 billion to $1.7 billion in June 2026 for its core energy business — compared to $1.4 billion in June 2025 — as electricity and gas markets stabilise. For the longer term, it has a pipeline of renewable energy projects, in line with government plans to reduce carbon emissions. It manages a series of wind and solar energy developments, including the 1.5-gigawatt Yanco Delta Wind Farm in New South Wales. It is also involved in 1.7 gigawatts of battery projects for energy storage. It had intended to close its giant Eraring power station in 2025. However, to support the security of electricity supplies, it has agreed with the New South Wales government to delay this closure for at least two years.

Year to 30 June	2024	2025
Revenues ($mn)	16 138.0	17 224.0
Electricity (%)	56	54
Gas (%)	29	26
Pool revenue (%)	13	18
EBIT ($mn)	1 987.0	1 940.0
EBIT margin (%)	12.3	11.3
Gross margin (%)	20.5	19.7
Profit before tax ($mn)	1 818.0	1 765.0
Profit after tax ($mn)	1 183.0	1 490.0
Earnings per share (c)	68.69	86.75
Cash flow per share (c)	98.94	114.58
Dividend (c)	55	60
Percentage franked	100	100
Net tangible assets per share ($)	4.05	4.29
Interest cover (times)	11.8	11.1
Return on equity (%)	12.9	15.4
Debt-to-equity ratio (%)	29.0	47.2
Current ratio	1.1	1.2

Perpetual Limited

ASX code: PPT

www.perpetual.com.au

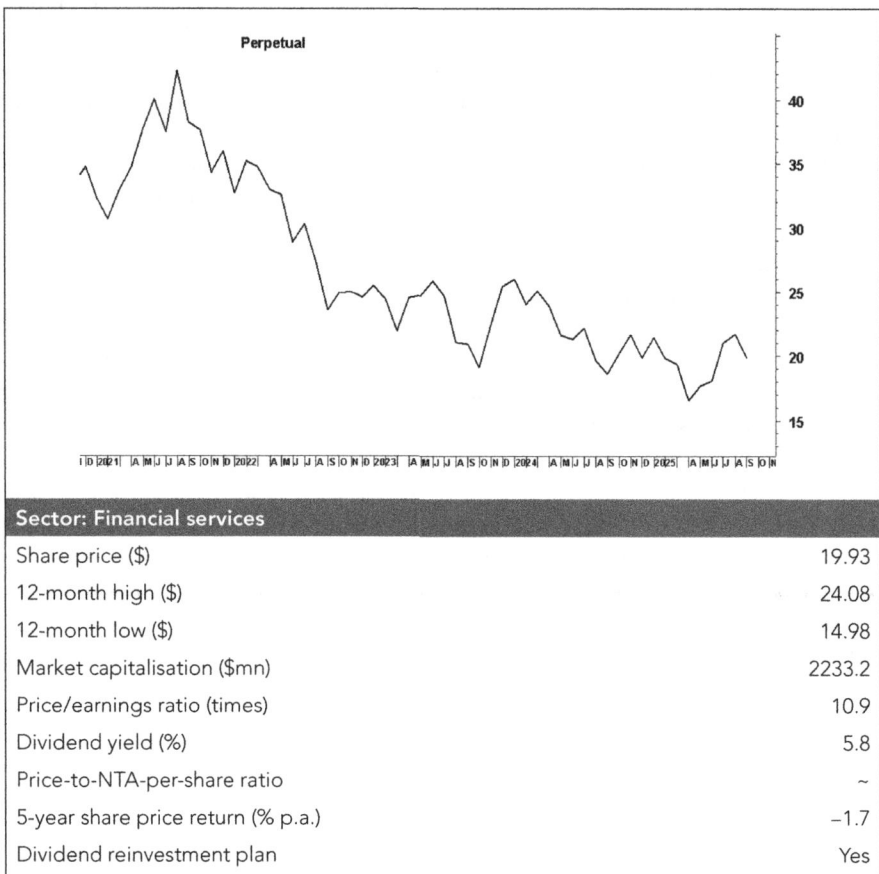

Share price ($)	19.93
12-month high ($)	24.08
12-month low ($)	14.98
Market capitalisation ($mn)	2233.2
Price/earnings ratio (times)	10.9
Dividend yield (%)	5.8
Price-to-NTA-per-share ratio	~
5-year share price return (% p.a.)	–1.7
Dividend reinvestment plan	Yes

Sydney-based financial services company Perpetual was established in 1886 as Perpetual Trustees. It divides its operations into three broad areas. Asset Management offers an extensive range of specialist investment capabilities on a global basis through seven brands. Wealth Management provides advisory and trustee services to individuals, families, companies and not-for-profit organisations. The Corporate Trust division is a prominent provider of fiduciary and digital services to the banking and financial services industry in Australia and Singapore. Nearly half of Perpetual's income derives from overseas operations.

Latest business results (June 2025, full year)

Revenues rose but underlying profits edged down. The core Asset Management division achieved slight gains in revenues and profits, despite net outflows from its funds of $16.2 billion, principally at its J O Hambro and Barrow Hanley brands. However, thanks to buoyant markets the division achieved a modest rise in funds under management, up 5.5 per cent to $226.8 billion. The Wealth Management division saw revenues up but rising staff and technology expenses sent profits down, with this division also adversely affected by uncertainty surrounding its ownership. The best result came from the Corporate Trust division, with solid growth in revenues and profits and strength across all business lines. In particular, a record year in securitisation, with both new and existing clients, provided a strong boost to the division's debt market services work. Perpetual also announced significant items of $262 million, including a large impairment of the value of J O Hambro and costs related to the aborted acquisition of parts of its business, and on a statutory basis the company reported another large loss.

Outlook

During the year the company worked on the internal separation of its three divisions in order to sell the Wealth Management and Corporate Trust divisions to global investment company Kohlberg Kravis Roberts for $2.175 billion. However, an independent expert concluded that the planned deal was not in the best interests of shareholders, and it did not proceed. Nevertheless, the company continues the internal separation of its three businesses, with a view to simplifying operations. It achieved annualised cost savings of $44 million in the June 2025 year and its target is $70 million to $80 million by June 2027. It also continues to work towards a sale of the Wealth Management division. Its Corporate Trust business continues to grow. Perpetual sees particular potential for this division's fast-growing digital and markets segment, which delivers software platforms that greatly simplify and make more secure a client's complex financial operations.

Year to 30 June	2024	2025
Revenues ($mn)	1357.5	1390.5
Asset management (%)	68	66
Wealth management (%)	17	17
Corporate trust (%)	14	15
EBIT ($mn)	353.9	350.2
EBIT margin (%)	26.1	25.2
Profit before tax ($mn)	283.6	279.2
Profit after tax ($mn)	206.1	204.1
Earnings per share (c)	183.66	182.84
Cash flow per share (c)	289.25	291.33
Dividend (c)	118	115
Percentage franked	42	0
Net tangible assets per share ($)	~	~
Interest cover (times)	5.0	4.9
Return on equity (%)	10.2	12.0
Debt-to-equity ratio (%)	35.4	38.4
Current ratio	0.5	1.4

Pinnacle Investment Management Group Limited

ASX code: PNI   www.pinnacleinvestment.com

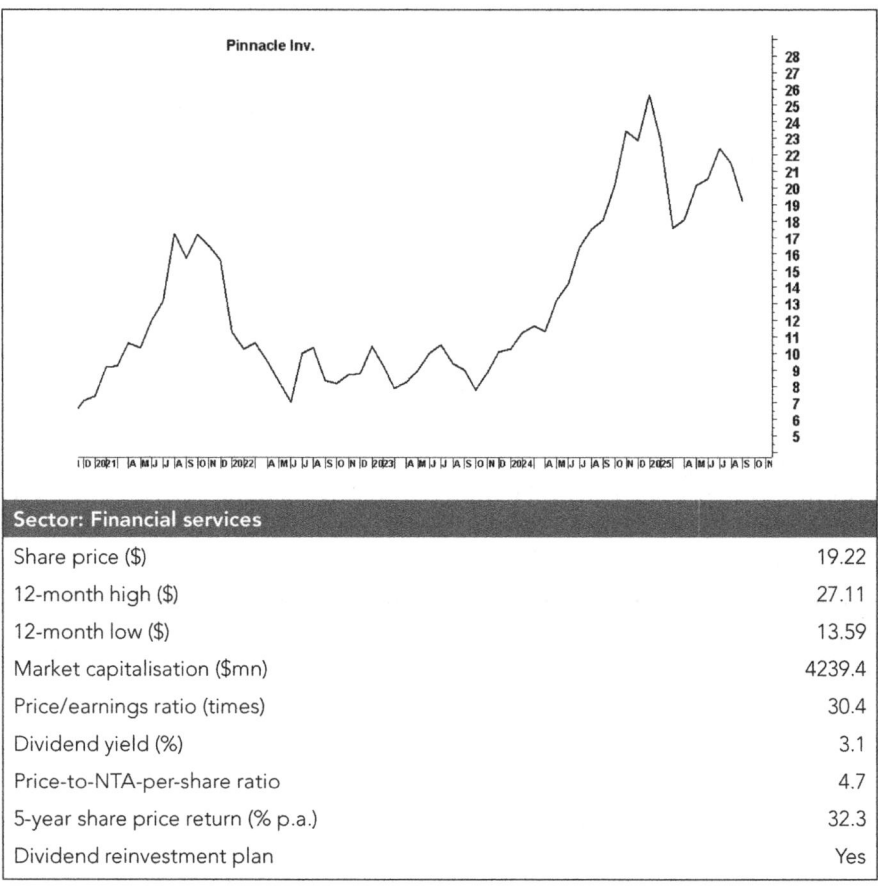

Sector: Financial services	
Share price ($)	19.22
12-month high ($)	27.11
12-month low ($)	13.59
Market capitalisation ($mn)	4239.4
Price/earnings ratio (times)	30.4
Dividend yield (%)	3.1
Price-to-NTA-per-share ratio	4.7
5-year share price return (% p.a.)	32.3
Dividend reinvestment plan	Yes

Sydney-based Pinnacle Investment Management started life in 2006 as a boutique funds management company that was majority-owned by Wilson HTM Investment Group. In 2016 it was fully acquired by Wilson Group, with Wilson Group changing its own name to Pinnacle. Today it is a prominent adviser to small funds management groups, providing them with distribution services, business support and responsible entity services, while also holding an equity stake in these companies.

Latest business results (June 2025, full year)

Profits rose strongly in another excellent year for Pinnacle. At June 2025 the company comprised 18 fund management affiliates — up from 15 a year earlier — collectively managing investments across a diverse range of asset classes. Pinnacle held shareholdings in these affiliates that ranged from 22.5 per cent to 49.9 per cent. Total revenues during the year for the 18 fund managers of $925 million was up from $663.4 million in the previous year, and this included $153.6 million in performance fees, up from $109.8 million. Total funds under management soared to $179.4 billion at June 2025, up from $110.1 billion a year earlier, thanks to market movements and a strong investment performance, together with net inflows during the year of $23.1 billion and the addition of new funds.

Outlook

Pinnacle's initial role is to provide its fund manager affiliates with equity, seed capital and working capital. It then allows its managers to focus on investment performance by providing them with marketing and other support services. Pinnacle's own revenues and profits derive from the revenues it receives from its affiliates for its services, together with its share of their profits, and performance is important. It has achieved significant success with the fund management companies it has chosen to join its group, reporting that 91 per cent of funds with a five-year track record had by June 2025 outperformed their relevant benchmarks during this period. The company is confident about its long-term evolution and has a variety of strategies for growth. These include investment in high-margin retail channels and moves into new asset classes, and it is seeking further acquisitions. It is also working to attract more investment from abroad, thanks to a growing international team, and funds under management sourced from non-Australian clients have risen sharply to represent nearly 29 per cent of total funds. Nevertheless, Pinnacle recognises that, at least in the short term, global economic conditions remain uncertain, with continuing geopolitical tensions exerting a significant impact on financial markets.

Year to 30 June	2024	2025
Revenues ($mn)	139.8	195.2
EBIT ($mn)	97.7	151.8
EBIT margin (%)	69.9	77.8
Profit before tax ($mn)	90.4	144.5
Profit after tax ($mn)	90.4	134.4
Earnings per share (c)	45.81	63.21
Cash flow per share (c)	45.87	63.29
Dividend (c)	42	60
Percentage franked	82	79
Net tangible assets per share ($)	2.25	4.11
Interest cover (times)	13.3	20.7
Return on equity (%)	20.6	19.6
Debt-to-equity ratio (%)	14.8	8.0
Current ratio	11.5	18.3

Premier Investments Limited

ASX code: PMV   www.premierinvestments.com.au

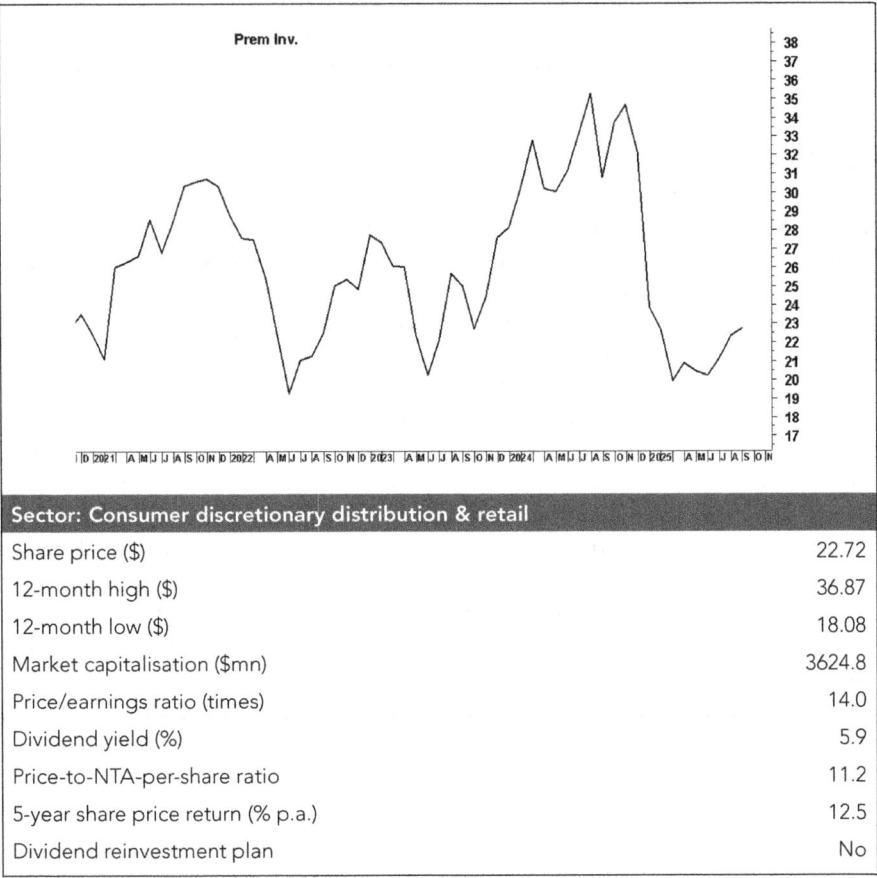

Sector: Consumer discretionary distribution & retail	
Share price ($)	22.72
12-month high ($)	36.87
12-month low ($)	18.08
Market capitalisation ($mn)	3624.8
Price/earnings ratio (times)	14.0
Dividend yield (%)	5.9
Price-to-NTA-per-share ratio	11.2
5-year share price return (% p.a.)	12.5
Dividend reinvestment plan	No

Melbourne-based Premier was founded in 1987 and operates as an investment company. Following the January 2025 sale of its Just Jeans, Jay Jays, Jacqui E, Portmans and Dotti apparel businesses, its main holdings now are the Peter Alexander sleepwear retailer and Smiggle, which specialises in colourful school stationery and other products for children. The company also holds a 25 per cent stake in home appliance specialist Breville Group. Premier's chairman Solomon Lew owns more than 40 per cent of the company's equity.

Latest business results (January 2025, half year)

With the sale of five of its brands right at the end of its January reporting period, Premier has treated these as discontinued businesses. So the January results were for continuing businesses Peter Alexander and Smiggle only. Revenues and profits were down, reflecting a 14.5 per cent decline in sales for Smiggle to $157.3 million as its global customer base became increasingly exposed to rising cost-of-living pressures. By contrast,

Peter Alexander saw sales up 6.6 per cent to $297.7 million, with solid growth across all product categories and a good result from both the retail store network and online channels. Four new stores opened during the reporting period helped boost business.

Outlook

In January 2025 Premier sold five apparel businesses to the department store chain Myer in exchange for more than 890 000 000 Myer shares. These shares were then distributed to Premier shareholders, along with other Myer shares already owned by Premier. The company sees strong potential for both its remaining brands. In November 2024 it launched Peter Alexander in the United Kingdom with three stores and a dedicated website. It also plans a continuing roll-out of new and expanded stores in both Australia and New Zealand. It is developing a new loyalty program that it believes will help drive sales. In January 2025 Premier operated 307 Smiggle stores in Australia, New Zealand, the United Kingdom, Ireland, Singapore and Malaysia, and plans at least 10 further stores in the near term. It is also developing wholesale partnerships to help it expand further, giving it a presence in more than 20 countries. It sees particular potential in Indonesia and the Middle East. In addition, the company has reported that it envisages future product collaborations with film studios and sporting codes. At January 2025 Premier's investment in Breville had a market value of $1.3 billion. The company also had net cash holdings of $268 million, and has expressed interest in growth through acquisition.

Year to 27 July*	2023	2024
Revenues ($mn)	1643.5	1595.3
EBIT ($mn)	398.7	384.3
EBIT margin (%)	24.3	24.1
Profit before tax ($mn)	382.1	354.1
Profit after tax ($mn)	271.1	257.9
Earnings per share (c)	170.31	161.78
Cash flow per share (c)	270.97	265.93
Dividend (c)	114	133
Percentage franked	100	100
Interest cover (times)	24.1	12.7
Return on equity (%)	15.9	14.6
Half year to 25 January**	2024	2025
Revenues ($mn)	463.2	457.4
Profit before tax ($mn)	169.9	142.1
Profit after tax ($mn)	124.1	101.3
Earnings per share (c)	77.88	63.47
Dividend (c)	63	0
Percentage franked	100	~
Net tangible assets per share ($)	3.88	2.02
Debt-to-equity ratio (%)	~	~
Current ratio	2.1	1.1

*29 July 2023
**27 January 2024

Pro Medicus Limited

ASX code: PME   www.promed.com.au

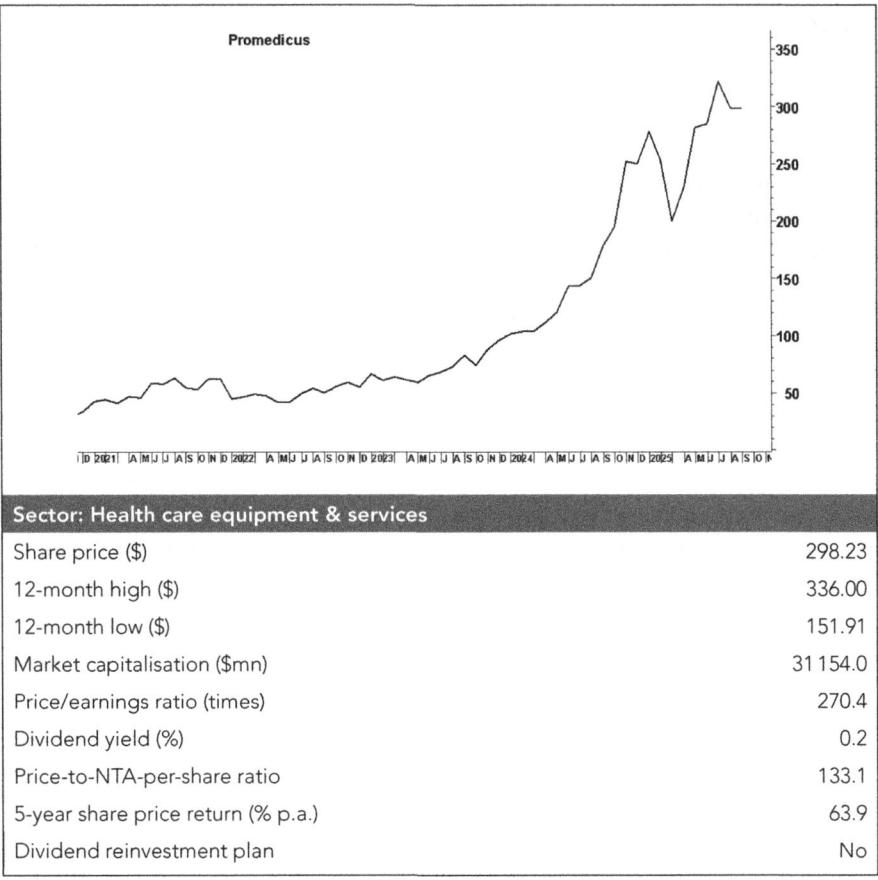

Sector: Health care equipment & services	
Share price ($)	298.23
12-month high ($)	336.00
12-month low ($)	151.91
Market capitalisation ($mn)	31 154.0
Price/earnings ratio (times)	270.4
Dividend yield (%)	0.2
Price-to-NTA-per-share ratio	133.1
5-year share price return (% p.a.)	63.9
Dividend reinvestment plan	No

Melbourne-based Pro Medicus, established in 1983, provides a range of medical imaging software and services to the medical profession. Its Visage 7 medical imaging software provides radiologists and clinicians with advanced visualisation capability for the rapid viewing of medical images. Its Radiology Information Systems (RIS) product provides proprietary medical software for practice management. In Australia it operates the Promedicus.net online network for doctors. It has extensive business operations throughout Australia, the US and Germany, with offices in Melbourne, San Diego and Berlin, and overseas sales represent around 90 per cent of total turnover.

Latest business results (June 2025, full year)

Pro Medicus enjoyed another successful year of strong double-digit revenue and profit growth. America is by far the company's largest market, accounting for more than 85 per cent of sales, and revenues there jumped 36 per cent with the signing of seven new contracts with a combined minimum total contract value of $520 million. These included its largest contract to date, with Trinity Health, worth $330 million over 10 years. Australian sales rose 5 per cent, with a further strong contribution from the company's contract with Healius, along with the renewal of another large contract and additional licence revenue from private radiology groups. The relatively small German operation marked time, though revenues actually rose 9 per cent thanks to currency gains.

Outlook

Pro Medicus continues to enjoy some outstanding success in America for its Visage 7 software, which has the speed, functionality and versatility to meet the requirements of many different kinds of users. The company is now a market leader in this business, and says that 11 of the 20 leading American hospitals are using its products. It now claims a market share of around 10 per cent in the US. A global shortage of radiologists is helping boost demand. It is making a substantial investment in research and development activities aimed at new products and enhancements to existing products, including artificial intelligence–based products. It is benefiting from moves to cloud-based systems. It has introduced a cardiology application to its existing imaging platform and is working on further extensions, with a pathology application to be released. It has developed a breast density algorithm based on artificial intelligence and has submitted this for official approval in the US. It has announced plans to work with Australian company 4DMedical on its lung imaging technology. With no debt and cash holdings of more than $107 million at June 2025 Pro Medicus is seeking out acquisition opportunities.

Year to 30 June	2024	2025
Revenues ($mn)	161.5	213.0
EBIT ($mn)	116.5	163.3
EBIT margin (%)	72.1	76.7
Profit before tax ($mn)	116.5	163.3
Profit after tax ($mn)	82.8	115.2
Earnings per share (c)	79.27	110.28
Cash flow per share (c)	87.42	117.21
Dividend (c)	40	55
Percentage franked	100	100
Net tangible assets per share ($)	1.59	2.24
Interest cover (times)	~	~
Return on equity (%)	50.7	51.8
Debt-to-equity ratio (%)	~	~
Current ratio	6.0	6.5

PWR Holdings Limited

ASX code: PWH   www.pwr.com.au

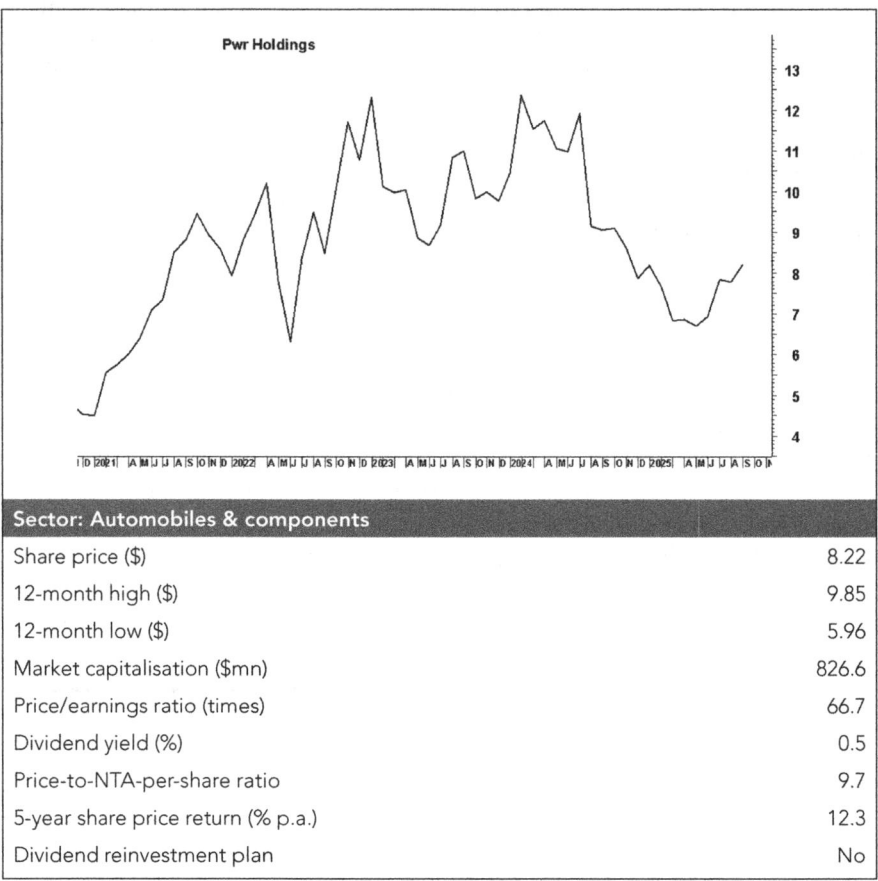

Sector: Automobiles & components	
Share price ($)	8.22
12-month high ($)	9.85
12-month low ($)	5.96
Market capitalisation ($mn)	826.6
Price/earnings ratio (times)	66.7
Dividend yield (%)	0.5
Price-to-NTA-per-share ratio	9.7
5-year share price return (% p.a.)	12.3
Dividend reinvestment plan	No

Based on the Gold Coast, automotive products company PWR got its start in 1987. It specialises in cooling systems, with a particular specialty in the supply of cooling systems to racing car teams. Other customers include the automotive original equipment manufacturing (OEM) sector and the automotive aftermarket sector, along with the aerospace, defence and renewable energy industries. It operates from manufacturing and distribution facilities in Australia, the United States and the United Kingdom. More than 90 per cent of company sales are to customers overseas, mainly in Europe and North America.

Latest business results (June 2025, full year)

Revenues were down and underlying profits fell sharply, as the company suffered a 44 per cent decline in its OEM sales. This resulted from the completion of two major OEM programs, along with delays and cancellations in several niche electric vehicle contracts. Automotive aftermarket sales also fell, down 17 per cent, due in part to price rises and reduced demand in Australia for some of the company's products. By contrast, the aerospace and defence sector achieved 28 per cent growth in revenues — following a doubling of sales in the previous year — despite delays in completing some orders as the company moved to new premises. Motorsports revenues were up 4 per cent. The company's research and development spending rose to $12.7 million, from $11 million in the previous year.

Outlook

PWR supplies its cooling systems to all Formula One racing teams, as well as to teams in other motor sports around the world, including Nascar and Indycar. It also supplies bespoke cooling systems to a range of high-performance automobile companies. It spends heavily on research and development in order to maintain its market-leading position, and it is working to move into other market areas with high growth prospects. With a strong order book it is optimistic about the outlook for its business. It sees aerospace and defence as offering particularly strong potential and is investing heavily in this business. It is working with several aircraft manufacturers, and with the completion of pre-production program certifications is progressing towards long-term production supply contracts. It is expanding its American manufacturing facility and has moved into new global headquarters at Stapylton, on Queensland's Gold Coast, more than doubling its Australian factory space. It sees particular potential in the advance of electric vehicles, and it is working with several electric car manufacturers for the supply of sophisticated cooling technology. Other applications include helicopters, drones and storage batteries for alternative energy systems.

Year to 30 June	2024	2025
Revenues ($mn)	139.4	130.1
Motorsports (%)	48	54
Aerospace & defence (%)	15	21
Automotive OEM (%)	20	12
Automotive aftermarket (%)	14	12
EBIT ($mn)	35.4	17.7
EBIT margin (%)	25.4	13.6
Profit before tax ($mn)	34.8	16.9
Profit after tax ($mn)	24.8	12.4
Earnings per share (c)	24.69	12.33
Cash flow per share (c)	34.78	24.26
Dividend (c)	14	4
Percentage franked	100	100
Net tangible assets per share ($)	0.84	0.84
Interest cover (times)	53.4	22.4
Return on equity (%)	26.3	12.3
Debt-to-equity ratio (%)	~	8.0
Current ratio	3.0	2.1

QBE Insurance Group Limited

ASX code: QBE   www.qbe.com/au

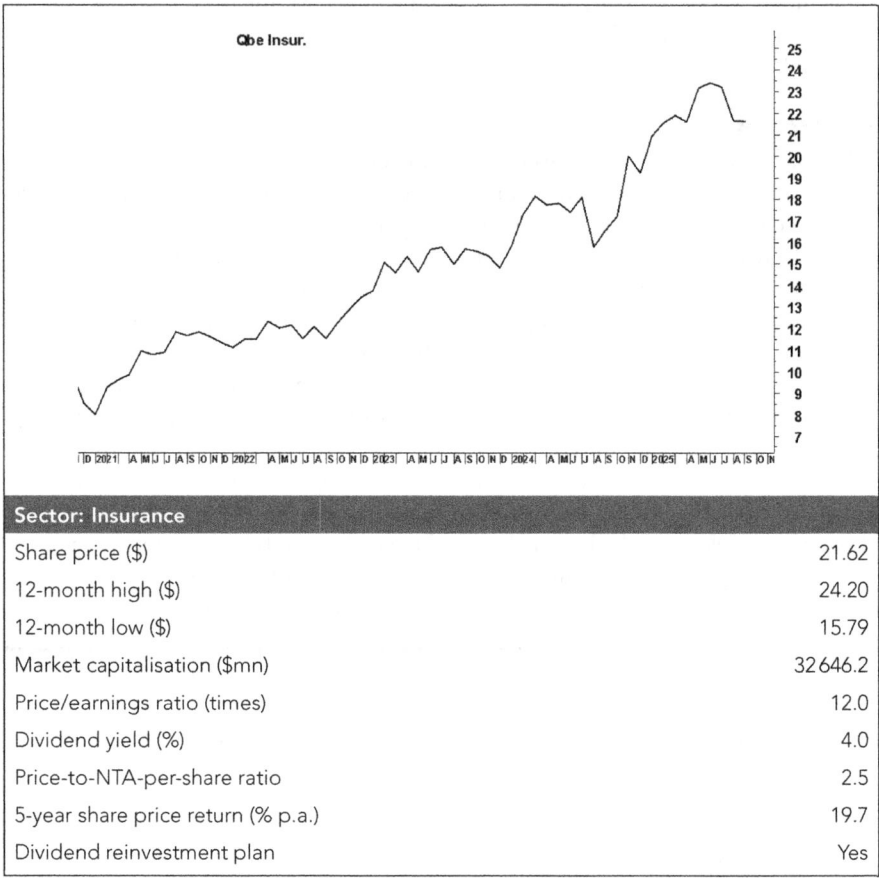

Sector: Insurance	
Share price ($)	21.62
12-month high ($)	24.20
12-month low ($)	15.79
Market capitalisation ($mn)	32 646.2
Price/earnings ratio (times)	12.0
Dividend yield (%)	4.0
Price-to-NTA-per-share ratio	2.5
5-year share price return (% p.a.)	19.7
Dividend reinvestment plan	Yes

Sydney-based QBE — founded as North Queensland Insurance Company in 1886 — is one of Australia's leading insurance companies, specialising in general insurance and reinsurance. Through a long series of acquisitions it has expanded globally to become a major international insurer and reinsurer, with operations in 26 countries. It operates through three broad divisions: International, which incorporates Europe and Asia; Australia Pacific; and North America. Over three-quarters of business comes from abroad, with particular strength in Europe and the US.

Latest business results (June 2025, half year)

Strong premium growth in international markets and a decline in claims combined to deliver a solid increase in profits for QBE. The result was also helped by reduced costs as the company exited some weaker-performing businesses. Gross written premiums of US$13.8 billion rose by nearly 6 per cent from the June 2024 half, thanks to volume growth and price rises, augmented by the company's targeted expansion into more profitable insurance classes in North America and Europe. The combined operating ratio — claims costs as a percentage of premium income — fell pleasingly from 93.8 per cent to 92.8 per cent. Net investment income of US$788 million rose from US$733 million. The company's catastrophe costs remained below their allowance, despite the devastating Los Angeles bushfires and some severe flooding during the period in Texas and Australia. The company paid US$479 million in catastrophe-related claims, down from US$527 million in the June 2024 period, and less than the allowance of US$549 million. Note that QBE reports its results in US dollars. The figures in this book are based on prevailing exchange rates.

Outlook

The insurance business is inherently risky, and QBE has been working for several years to restructure and simplify its operations, with moves into more profitable insurance lines, while discarding non-core businesses. A particular goal is to deliver a more predictable performance, together with sustainable long-term growth. It benefits from a range of factors — including geopolitical volatility, extreme weather events and some major cyber-crime cases — which combine to make customers more risk-averse and therefore desirous of insurance. It also benefits from an inflationary environment that helps it continue to raise prices. It views cyber-crime as a growth area for its business, and it is also boosting its North American health and accident insurance exposure. It is working to cross-sell more policies to existing corporate customers. QBE expects continuing gross written premium growth during 2025 with a combined operating ratio of around 92.5 per cent.

Year to 31 December	2023	2024
Revenues ($mn)	37 533.3	38 157.6
EBIT ($mn)	3 134.8	3 813.6
EBIT margin (%)	8.4	10.0
Profit before tax ($mn)	2 783.3	3 471.2
Profit after tax ($mn)	2 053.0	2 695.5
Earnings per share (c)	137.79	179.58
Cash flow per share (c)	152.53	194.21
Dividend (c)	62	87
Percentage franked	10	20
Interest cover (times)	8.9	11.1
Return on equity (%)	14.8	16.8
Half year to 30 June	2024	2025
Revenues ($mn)	18 565.2	20 031.7
Profit before tax ($mn)	1 592.4	2 117.5
Profit after tax ($mn)	1 215.2	1 622.2
Earnings per share (c)	78.64	104.92
Dividend (c)	24	31
Percentage franked	20	25
Net tangible assets per share ($)	7.96	8.62
Debt-to-equity ratio (%)	13.1	14.3

Ramelius Resources Limited

ASX code: RMS www.rameliusresources.com.au

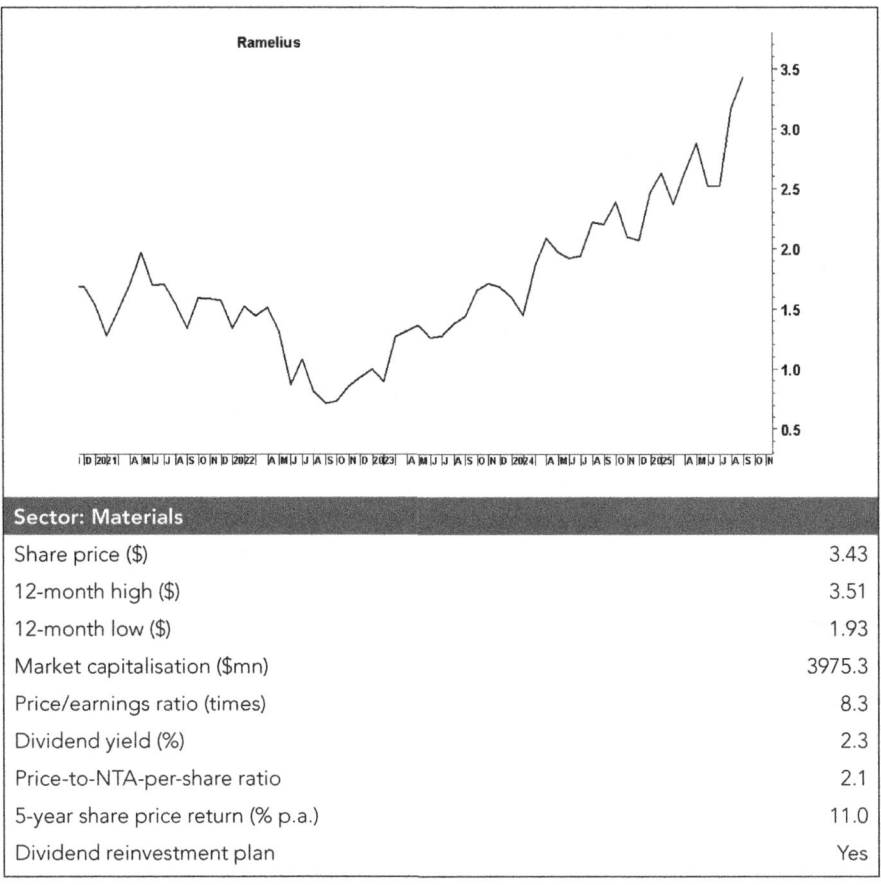

Sector: Materials

Share price ($)	3.43
12-month high ($)	3.51
12-month low ($)	1.93
Market capitalisation ($mn)	3975.3
Price/earnings ratio (times)	8.3
Dividend yield (%)	2.3
Price-to-NTA-per-share ratio	2.1
5-year share price return (% p.a.)	11.0
Dividend reinvestment plan	Yes

Perth gold miner Ramelius Resources was founded in 1979 and is involved in major gold mining projects around Western Australia. It owns mines and processing centres at Mt Magnet and Edna May. It maintains an active exploration program. In July 2025 it acquired Spartan Resources.

Latest business results (June 2025, full year)

The surging gold price, increased production and reduced costs again generated soaring revenues and profits for Ramelius, with 90 per cent of profit deriving from Mt Magnet. Production of 301 664 ounces was up from 293 033 ounces in the June 2024 year. Sales of 302 882 ounces rose from 293 966 ounces, with the average realised price of $3963 per ounce up from $2995. The average All-In Sustaining Cost (AISC) — the normal measure for evaluating the total cost of producing an ounce of gold — was $1551 per ounce, down from $1583 the previous year, which the company attributed in part to a higher-grade ore at Mt Magnet.

Outlook

The Mt Magnet Gold Project dates back to the discovery of gold in the region in 1891 and today incorporates numerous open-pit and underground mines, as well as exploration targets, over a wide area. At present the Mt Magnet production centre comprises open-pit mines at Mt Magnet and Cue and underground mines at Mt Magnet and Penny. Ore from Cue and Penny is hauled to the Mt Magnet mill for processing. Work on a $95 million upgrade to the Mt Magnet mill is expected to begin late in 2026. Ramelius maintains a major program of resource development and exploration at Mt Magnet in order to extend its life. Mining has ceased at the Edna May production centre, and operations during the June 2025 year involved processing the remaining stockpiles. In March 2025 the mine was placed into care and maintenance, and June 2025 profits for Edna May actually fell from the previous year. The $2.4 billion acquisition of Spartan Resources delivers to Ramelius the major Dalgaranga Gold Project, 65 kilometres from Mt Magnet. It gives Ramelius the potential for operational synergies and the opportunity of sharing processing facilities, along with an enhanced presence in Western Australia's gold-rich regions. Now holding a mineral resource estimated at some 12.1 million ounces of gold, Ramelius is preparing a five-year plan for the future of Mt Magnet and Dalgaranga. Its target is to be producing 500 000 ounces of gold annually by 2030. At June 2025 Ramelius had no debt and more than $780 million in cash holdings.

Year to 30 June	2024	2025
Revenues ($mn)	882.6	1203.4
Mt Magnet (%)	55	81
Edna May (%)	45	19
EBIT ($mn)	277.2	676.3
EBIT margin (%)	31.4	56.2
Gross margin (%)	35.5	57.8
Profit before tax ($mn)	271.9	670.5
Profit after tax ($mn)	200.3	474.2
Earnings per share (c)	18.06	41.12
Cash flow per share (c)	34.42	55.24
Dividend (c)	5	8
Percentage franked	100	100
Net tangible assets per share ($)	1.16	1.64
Interest cover (times)	51.9	117.1
Return on equity (%)	17.7	29.3
Debt-to-equity ratio (%)	~	~
Current ratio	3.4	4.1

REA Group Limited

ASX code: REA
www.rea-group.com

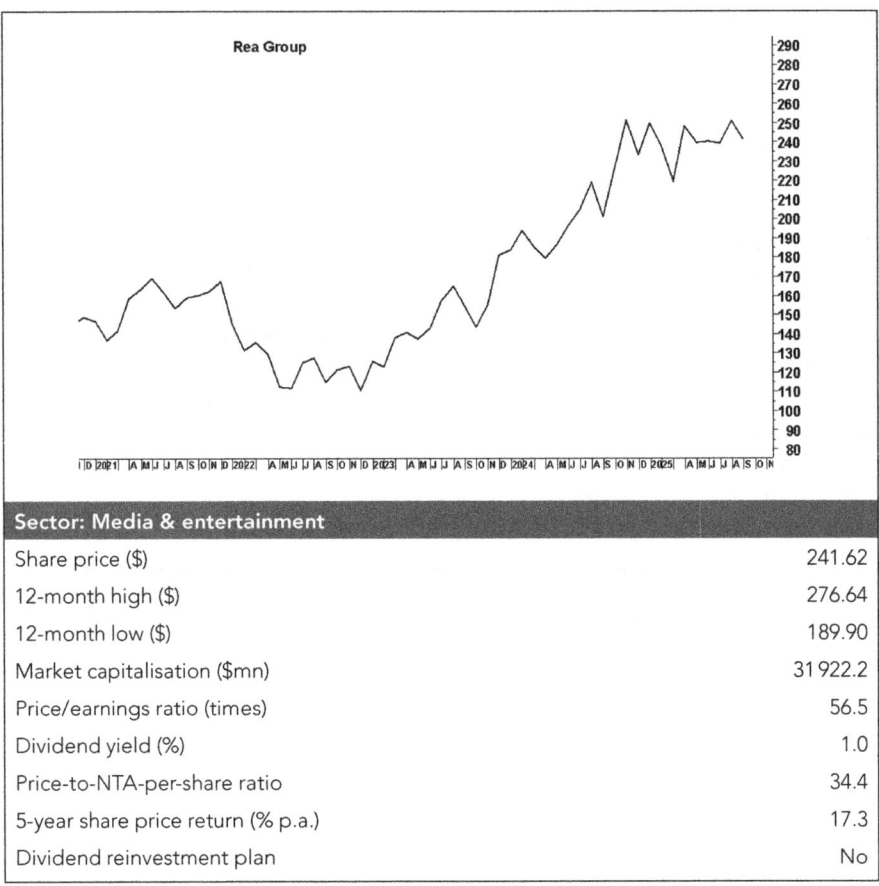

Sector: Media & entertainment	
Share price ($)	241.62
12-month high ($)	276.64
12-month low ($)	189.90
Market capitalisation ($mn)	31 922.2
Price/earnings ratio (times)	56.5
Dividend yield (%)	1.0
Price-to-NTA-per-share ratio	34.4
5-year share price return (% p.a.)	17.3
Dividend reinvestment plan	No

Melbourne-based REA was founded in 1995. Through its websites realestate.com.au and realcommercial.com.au it is the leader in the provision of online real estate advertising services in Australia. It also operates the share property website flatmates. com.au and the property research website property.com.au. In addition, it owns the mortgage broking franchise group Mortgage Choice, the property data company PropTrack, and the advertising and home preparation finance platform CampaignAgent. It has a 78 per cent controlling interest in REA India and holds a 20 per cent shareholding in the Move online property marketing company in the US. It has sold its 17.2 per cent equity stake in the South-East Asian real estate platform PropertyGuru. News Corp owns more than 60 per cent of REA's equity.

Latest business results (June 2025, full year)

Revenues and profits rose strongly for the second straight year, thanks especially to higher prices and moves by customers to premium products. Residential revenues rose

16 per cent to $1156 million, despite just a 1 per cent increase in national residential listings. Commercial and developer revenues were up 10 per cent to $218 million, driven by price rises and an increase in listings. Financial services revenues rose 10 per cent to $81 million as the company expanded its broker network. Other revenues rose 8 per cent to $89 million, with the CampaignAgent business especially strong, partially offset by a fall in sales for PropTrack. Indian business, representing nearly 8 per cent of total turnover, grew well, but remained in the red. American activities, represented by the 20 per cent shareholding in Move, were again hit by lower transaction volumes, and reported another loss.

Outlook

REA is heavily geared to trends in the domestic housing market, and it expects continuing growth, thanks to high levels of demand and generally rising property prices. Underlying fundamentals are also positive, with low unemployment, wages growth, increasing migration and the possibility of further interest rate cuts. It continues to invest heavily in product advances and has launched the REA Cyber City technology centre in India to drive innovation. It sees great potential in financial services, thanks to its Mortgage Choice business, and has augmented this with the acquisition of a 20 per cent equity stake in the digital non-bank lender Athena Home Loans. However, fears have been expressed that REA could face heightened competition following the sale of its main rival, Domain Holdings Australia, to CoStar Group of the US, with the possibility of a price war, potentially driving down profits.

Year to 30 June	2024	2025
Revenues ($mn)	1430.0	1640.8
EBIT ($mn)	697.1	817.6
EBIT margin (%)	48.7	49.8
Profit before tax ($mn)	670.8	806.9
Profit after tax ($mn)	460.5	564.4
Earnings per share (c)	348.70	427.42
Cash flow per share (c)	434.65	532.99
Dividend (c)	189	248
Percentage franked	100	100
Net tangible assets per share ($)	4.18	7.03
Interest cover (times)	26.5	76.4
Return on equity (%)	30.6	32.7
Debt-to-equity ratio (%)	4.9	~
Current ratio	1.5	2.1

Reliance Worldwide Corporation Limited

ASX code: RWC   www.rwc.com

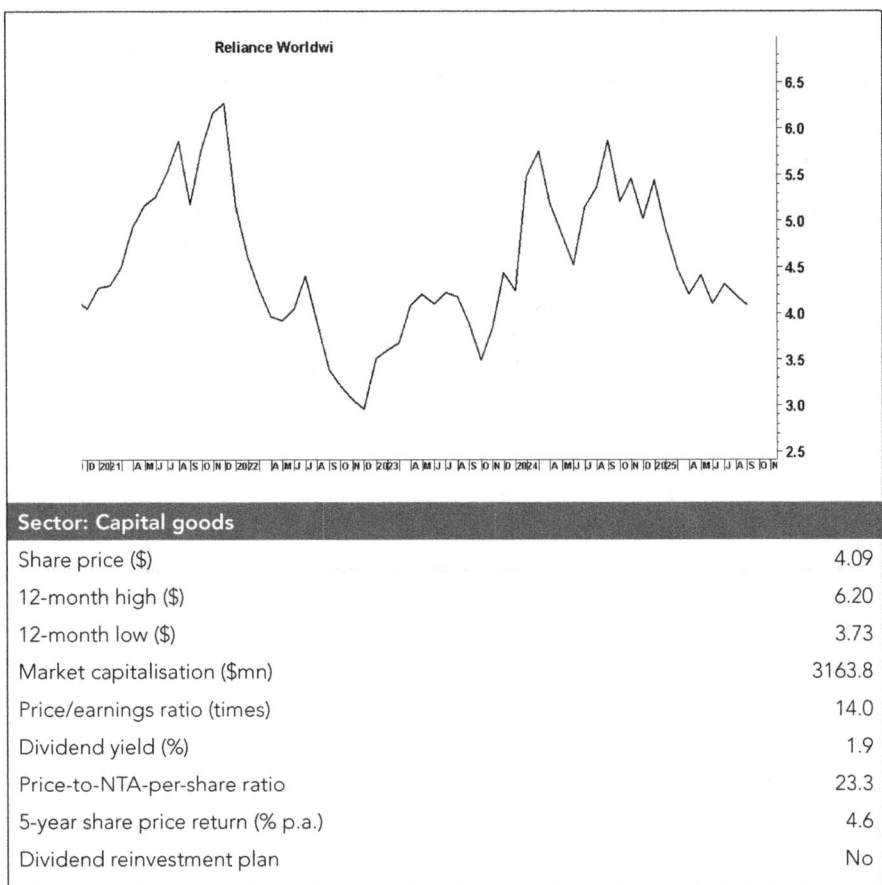

Sector: Capital goods	
Share price ($)	4.09
12-month high ($)	6.20
12-month low ($)	3.73
Market capitalisation ($mn)	3163.8
Price/earnings ratio (times)	14.0
Dividend yield (%)	1.9
Price-to-NTA-per-share ratio	23.3
5-year share price return (% p.a.)	4.6
Dividend reinvestment plan	No

Melbourne-based engineering firm Reliance dates back to 1949 and the establishment of a small tool shop in Brisbane. It is today a major global manufacturer and distributor of a range of products, particularly for the plumbing and heating industries. Its businesses and brands include SharkBite, Speedfit, HoldRite, MultiSafe, Reliance Valves and John Guest. In 2024 it acquired Australian plumbing supplies specialist Holman Industries.

Latest business results (June 2025, full year)

Revenues rose again and profits edged up after two years of decline. However, a full year's contribution from Holman, acquired in March 2024, lay behind much of the positive result. Excluding Holman, American and European operations were hit by weak construction and renovation markets, with sales down. Asia-Pacific benefited from organic growth in Australia, with sales—excluding Holman—up 2.4 per cent. Restructuring initiatives in the Europe/Middle East/Africa segment, together with other productivity benefits, helped boost profits. The company also benefited from US$2.3 million in Holman synergies that were realised during the year. Note that Reliance reports its results in US dollars. The figures in this book are based on prevailing exchange rates.

Outlook

Reliance has a significant exposure to housing markets in many countries, including both new house construction and renovation activity. Consequently, it is wary about the near-term outlook for its businesses, with economic conditions again expected to remain challenging across most of its markets. In particular, with up to half its US sales reliant on items sourced in China, it is being hurt by tariffs. It expects a US$25 million to US$30 million hit to profits for June 2026, and has declared that tariff mitigation has become its most urgent priority, with product sourcing being actively switched to countries that include Vietnam, Taiwan and South Korea. It is also concerned about weak housing activity in each of its key markets. Nevertheless, Reliance estimates that it operates in addressable markets worth a total of some US$25.3 billion, with significant long-term growth opportunities, and with few major rivals. It is especially optimistic about the long-term potential of the US$19.9 billion American market, where Reliance currently holds just a 4 per cent share. Thanks to significant levels of ageing housing stock, together with a long period of under-construction, the company believes that home-building activity will eventually rise strongly. Due to a strong capital investment program over several years, Reliance believes it has in place sufficient manufacturing capacity to meet surging demand for its products. It also continues to see many opportunities from its Holman acquisition.

Year to 30 June	2024	2025
Revenues ($mn)	1887.6	2022.6
Americas (%)	70	65
Asia Pacific (%)	12	18
Europe/Middle East/Africa (%)	18	17
EBIT ($mn)	326.0	324.6
EBIT margin (%)	17.3	16.0
Gross margin (%)	39.2	38.9
Profit before tax ($mn)	278.2	280.0
Profit after tax ($mn)	222.6	227.2
Earnings per share (c)	28.37	29.26
Cash flow per share (c)	39.96	42.89
Dividend (c)	7.24	7.8
Percentage franked	0	0
Net tangible assets per share ($)	0.01	0.18
Interest cover (times)	6.8	7.3
Return on equity (%)	11.8	11.3
Debt-to-equity ratio (%)	33.1	23.7
Current ratio	2.8	2.7

Ricegrowers Limited

ASX code: SGL   investors.sunrice.com.au

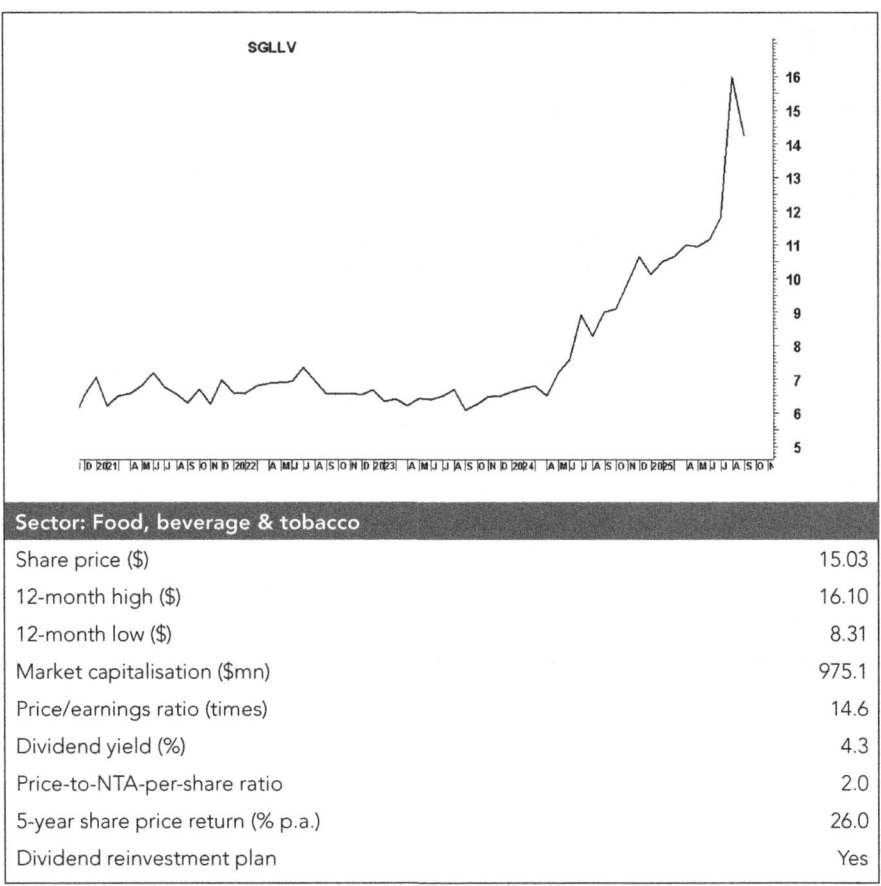

Sector: Food, beverage & tobacco	
Share price ($)	15.03
12-month high ($)	16.10
12-month low ($)	8.31
Market capitalisation ($mn)	975.1
Price/earnings ratio (times)	14.6
Dividend yield (%)	4.3
Price-to-NTA-per-share ratio	2.0
5-year share price return (% p.a.)	26.0
Dividend reinvestment plan	Yes

Ricegrowers Limited, based in Leeton in the Riverina region of NSW, is the official ASX name for the rice company SunRice. Founded in 1950, it is today one of Australia's largest foodstuffs companies, with operations in many countries. It divides its many businesses into five core divisions. International Rice manages the global processing, manufacturing, marketing and distribution of bulk or branded rice products. Rice Pool involves the receipt, storage, milling, marketing and distribution of Riverina rice. The CopRice division manufactures and distributes bulk stockfeed. Riviana Foods markets specialty gourmet food products. The Rice Food business handles rice-based products. Note that Ricegrowers has a dual-class share structure, with A class shares held by the company's ricegrower partners and B class shares held by outside investors.

Latest business results (April 2025, full year)

Sales edged down but profits were up, with particular strength in the company's portfolio of branded products, which were responsible for 70 per cent of total revenues.

The high-margin Rice Food division generated an excellent result, with the pre-tax profit jumping by 44 per cent, thanks to solid volume growth in rice cakes and rice flour, product innovation and operational efficiencies. Though just 7 per cent of company sales, this business contributed more than 17 per cent of pre-tax profit. The CopRice business continued its recovery, with profits up 55 per cent, having doubled in the previous year, and with particular strength in pet food. By contrast, the International Rice division, which in the previous year achieved double-digit growth in sales and profits, this time saw sales edge down with profits only marginally higher in an environment of intensified global competition and price volatility. Sales were up for the low-margin Riviana Foods business, but increased competition and cost-of-living pressures pushed profits down. Around 60 per cent of total company sales were generated overseas.

Outlook

Ricegrowers dominates the Australian rice industry, with a solid presence in around 50 overseas markets, and stands to benefit as global food demand grows. It has a particular focus on the development of a strong and popular portfolio of brands. In addition, it has initiated a review of its growth strategies with the aim of identifying new markets and product segments. It is also seeking strategic acquisitions that will deliver growth. Nevertheless, sales and profits for Ricegrowers can be buffeted by a multiplicity of influences, including weather patterns, droughts and floods, global rice prices, competition from low-cost foreign growers, exchange rates, inflationary pressures, supply chain issues and shipping disruptions.

Year to 30 April	2024	2025
Revenues ($mn)	1874.2	1844.6
International rice (%)	47	47
Rice pool (%)	21	20
CopRice (%)	14	14
Riviana (%)	12	12
Rice food (%)	6	7
EBIT ($mn)	105.7	116.5
EBIT margin (%)	5.6	6.3
Profit before tax ($mn)	86.7	97.6
Profit after tax ($mn)	63.1	68.4
Earnings per share (c)	97.50	102.92
Cash flow per share (c)	142.01	149.05
Dividend (c)	55	65
Percentage franked	100	100
Net tangible assets per share ($)	7.41	7.51
Interest cover (times)	5.6	6.2
Return on equity (%)	11.4	11.6
Debt-to-equity ratio (%)	34.0	31.3
Current ratio	1.5	1.5

Ridley Corporation Limited

ASX code: RIC   www.ridley.com.au

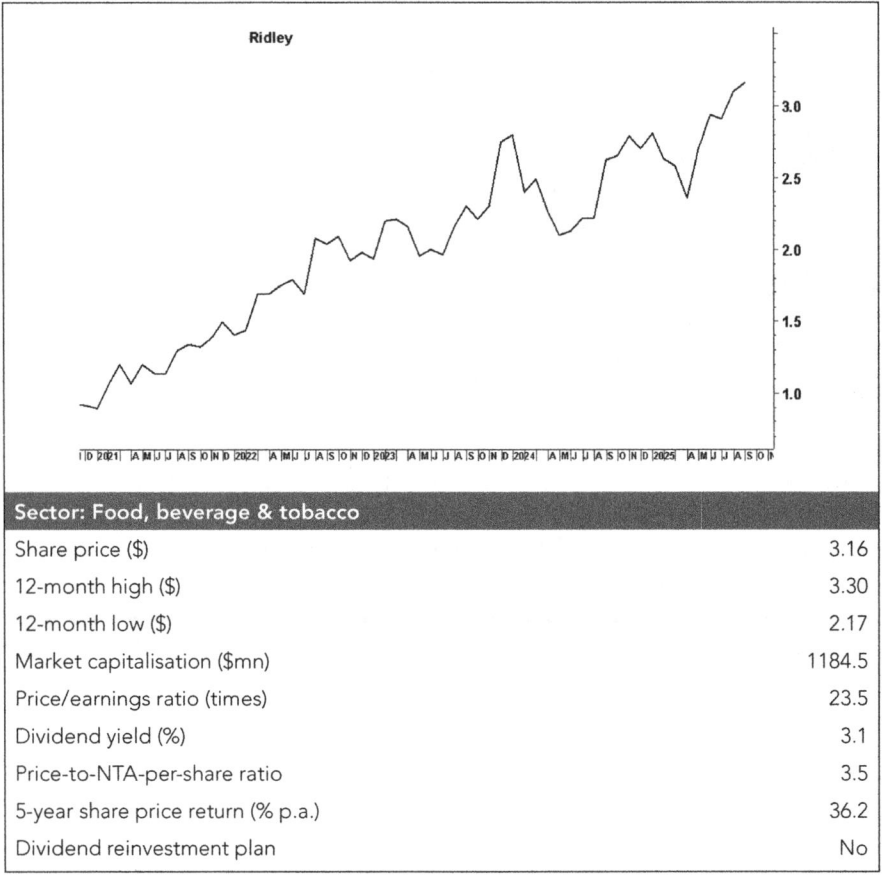

Sector: Food, beverage & tobacco	
Share price ($)	3.16
12-month high ($)	3.30
12-month low ($)	2.17
Market capitalisation ($mn)	1184.5
Price/earnings ratio (times)	23.5
Dividend yield (%)	3.1
Price-to-NTA-per-share ratio	3.5
5-year share price return (% p.a.)	36.2
Dividend reinvestment plan	No

Melbourne-based Ridley, founded in 1987, is a leading producer of animal feed. It operates from some 20 sites in Victoria, New South Wales, Queensland and South Australia, producing around two million tonnes annually of finished feeds and feed ingredients, based on locally grown cereal grains. It also owns an aquafeed manufacturing facility in Thailand. It classifies its production into two broad divisions. Bulk Stockfeeds comprises the company's animal nutrition feed that is delivered in bulk. Packaged Feeds and Ingredients represents animal nutrition feed and ingredients that are delivered in packaged form, ranging from three-kilogram bags to one-tonne containers. Ridley is acquiring the Incitec Pivot Fertilisers (IPF) Distribution business.

Latest business results (June 2025, full year)

Revenues and profits edged up again, with single-digit gains for both divisions. Bulk Stockfeeds was helped by 11 per cent volume growth for ruminant feed, as well as by rising demand for higher-margin supplementary feeds during dry conditions in the June 2025 second half. The Packaged Feeds and Ingredients division benefited from a full year's contribution from New Zealand pet food manufacturer Oceania Meat Processors (OMP), acquired in March 2024. This division also enjoyed stronger packaged dogfood sales. Though responsible for just 30 per cent of company revenues, the Packaged Feeds and Ingredients division contributed more than half of company profit.

Outlook

Ridley occupies a prominent place in the Australian agricultural sector as one of the leading producers of stockfeeds, nutritional blocks, mineral concentrates, supplements and other products for a wide range of animal species that include cattle, poultry, pigs, horses, sheep, working dogs, pets and fish. It has an extensive research and development program and strong partnerships with industry bodies, universities and key research organisations. It benefits as the Australian agricultural sector expands. It is set to be greatly changed by the $300 million acquisition of IPF Distribution from Dyno Nobel. IPF Distribution is Australia's largest fertiliser distributor, with 13 primary distribution centres and particular strength on the East Coast. Ridley regards the acquisition as delivering a new pillar for growth, boosting company EPS by some 25 per cent. It expects annual synergies from the acquisition of around $7 million, primarily from the consolidation of back office and support costs. Ridley also sees particular potential in the premium pet food market, and its NZ$57 million OMP acquisition is designed to boost this business. OMP has factories in Timaru, New Zealand, and in Melbourne, and is a leading supplier of premium meat to the global pet industry.

Year to 30 June	2024	2025
Revenues ($mn)	1262.9	1302.6
Bulk stockfeeds (%)	70	70
Packaged feeds & ingredients (%)	30	30
EBIT ($mn)	67.5	68.5
EBIT margin (%)	5.3	5.3
Gross margin (%)	9.2	9.3
Profit before tax ($mn)	58.9	57.8
Profit after tax ($mn)	42.3	43.3
Earnings per share (c)	13.39	13.46
Cash flow per share (c)	21.67	22.87
Dividend (c)	9.05	9.75
Percentage franked	100	100
Net tangible assets per share ($)	0.68	0.91
Interest cover (times)	7.8	6.4
Return on equity (%)	13.2	11.1
Debt-to-equity ratio (%)	19.8	~
Current ratio	1.1	1.3

Rio Tinto Limited

ASX code: RIO   www.riotinto.com

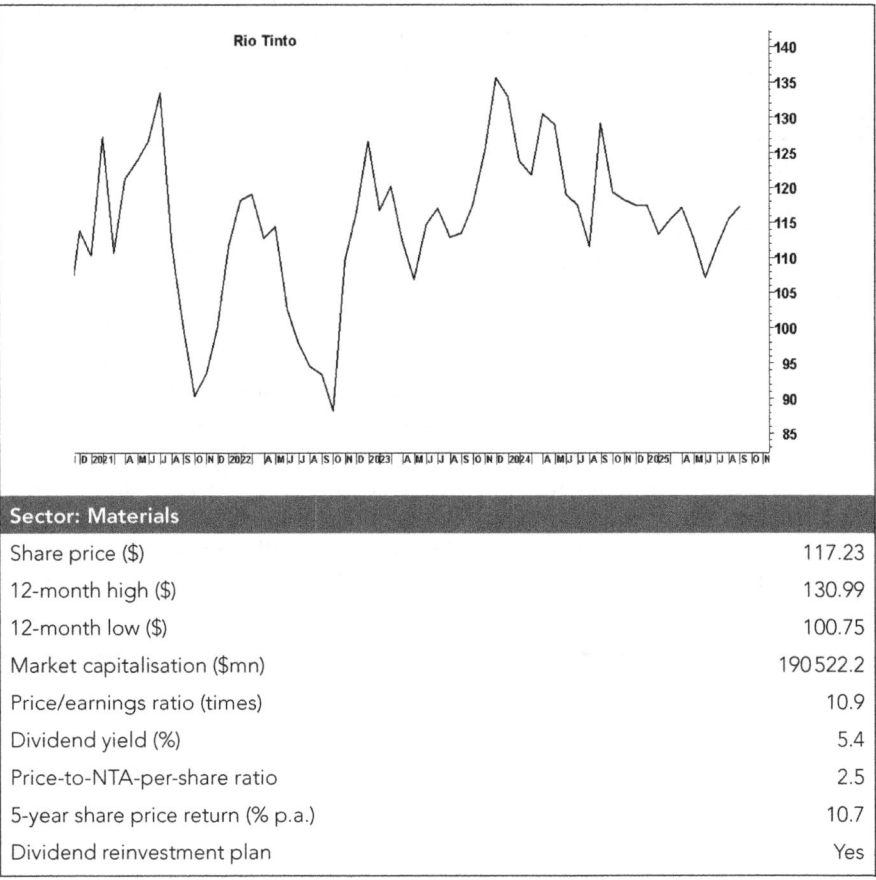

Sector: Materials	
Share price ($)	117.23
12-month high ($)	130.99
12-month low ($)	100.75
Market capitalisation ($mn)	190 522.2
Price/earnings ratio (times)	10.9
Dividend yield (%)	5.4
Price-to-NTA-per-share ratio	2.5
5-year share price return (% p.a.)	10.7
Dividend reinvestment plan	Yes

British-based Rio Tinto, one of the world's largest mining companies, was founded by European investors in 1873 in order to reopen some ancient copper mines at the Tinto River in Spain. It maintains an ASX presence in a dual-listing structure and continues to pay franked dividends to Australian shareholders. Its products include iron ore, copper, gold, lithium, industrial minerals, diamonds and aluminium.

Latest business results (June 2025, half year)

Profits fell, with a good performance from the company's aluminium and copper interests insufficient to offset a lower iron ore price. Iron ore represented 43 per cent of total company revenues — down from 57 per cent in the June 2024 half — and a 13 per cent fall in average prices sent profits down. This business was also disrupted by severe storm activity in Western Australia. Nevertheless, iron ore contributed more than half of total underlying earnings during the period. The aluminium business, representing 26 per cent of revenues, achieved another good result, thanks to higher production and rising prices, and underlying profits were up by nearly 50 per cent. Higher prices and an excellent performance from two of the company's key operations, Oyu Tolgoi in Mongolia and Escondida in Chile, boosted copper revenues by 41 per cent with profits jumping 69 per cent. The company's minerals business, incorporating iron ore pellets and concentrates, titanium dioxide, lithium, borates and diamonds, reported stable sales, but with profits sharply down, due especially to lower prices. Altogether, 55 per cent of total company sales were to China and a further 13 per cent to the rest of Asia. Note that Rio Tinto reports its results in US dollars. The figures in this book are based on prevailing exchange rates.

Outlook

Rio Tinto maintains a substantial portfolio of well-run assets across many countries, and with generally low operating costs. It continues to boost production at the major Oyu Tolgoi project, and copper is set to become a growing contributor to business operations. It expects to bring the giant Simandou iron ore project in Guinea into production during 2025 and it is also investing heavily to extend the life of its Pilbara iron ore operations. It is moving strongly into lithium developments, and has launched a new Rio Tinto Lithium business division. In March 2025 it completed the US$6.7 billion acquisition of Arcadium Lithium, which incorporates the Rincon lithium project in Argentina, and in May 2025 it announced a joint-venture lithium project in Chile.

Year to 31 December	2023	2024
Revenues ($mn)	81 880.3	81 300.0
EBIT ($mn)	22 351.5	24 815.2
EBIT margin (%)	27.3	30.5
Profit before tax ($mn)	20 886.4	23 659.1
Profit after tax ($mn)	15 239.4	17 503.0
Earnings per share (c)	939.89	1 078.37
Cash flow per share (c)	1 438.34	1 630.81
Dividend (c)	653.67	633.02
Percentage franked	100	100
Interest cover (times)	15.3	21.5
Return on equity (%)	19.7	20.7
Half year to 30 June	2024	2025
Revenues ($mn)	40 609.1	42 655.6
Profit before tax ($mn)	12 295.5	10 693.7
Profit after tax ($mn)	8 800.0	7 187.3
Earnings per share (c)	542.27	442.54
Dividend (c)	261.70	221.97
Percentage franked	100	100
Net tangible assets per share ($)	46.60	47.06
Debt-to-equity ratio (%)	6.3	21.0
Current ratio	1.7	1.5

Schaffer Corporation Limited

ASX code: SFC

schaffer.com.au

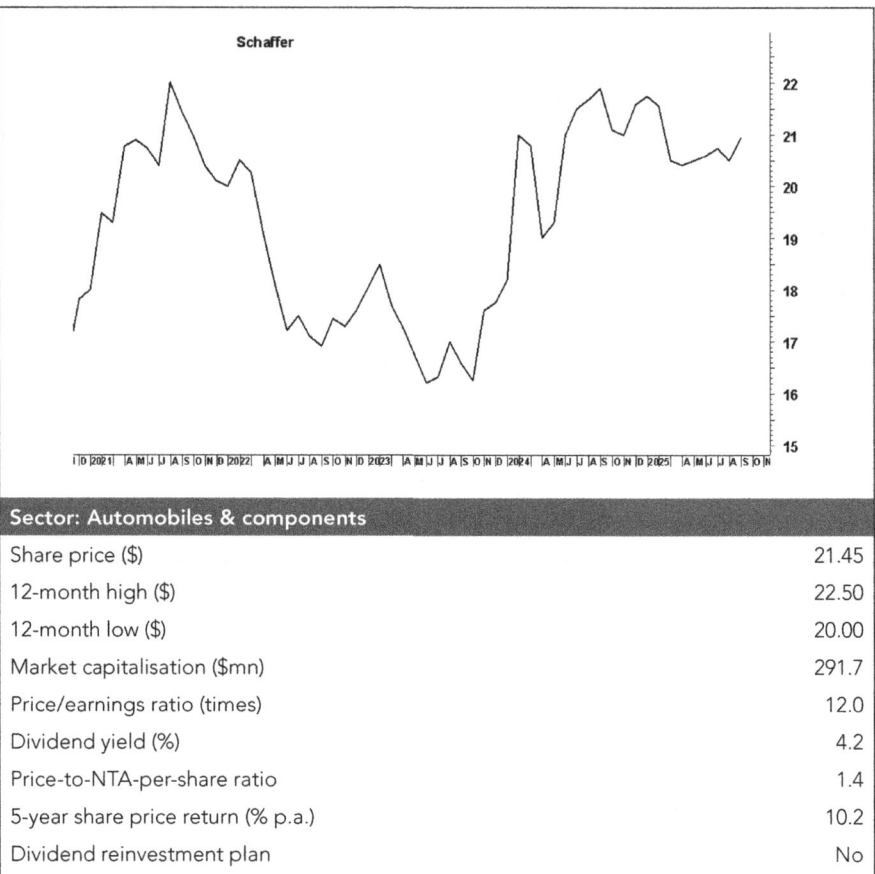

Sector: Automobiles & components	
Share price ($)	21.45
12-month high ($)	22.50
12-month low ($)	20.00
Market capitalisation ($mn)	291.7
Price/earnings ratio (times)	12.0
Dividend yield (%)	4.2
Price-to-NTA-per-share ratio	1.4
5-year share price return (% p.a.)	10.2
Dividend reinvestment plan	No

Perth company Schaffer was founded in 1955 to manufacture sand-lime bricks for the construction industry. Today its Delta Corporation subsidiary produces precast and prestressed concrete floors, beams and wall products, aimed mainly at the Western Australian construction market. However, its primary business now is the manufacture of leather goods, with a particular emphasis on products for the automotive industry, through its 83 per cent–owned subsidiary Automotive Leather. This business operates from facilities in Australia, China and Slovakia and supplies leading auto makers around the world. A third business for Schaffer is investments and property development, and it owns a portfolio of rental and development sites, mainly in Western Australia.

Latest business results (June 2025, full year)

Revenues and underlying profits rose, but a sharp reduction in unrealised revaluation gains meant the declared profit fell. The core Automotive Leather division achieved a

7 per cent boost to after-tax profit on a small increase in sales to $185.5 million. New Audi and Porsche business was behind much of the good result, partially offset by a reduction in Land Rover demand. Productivity gains and some currency rate benefits helped lift profit margins. The much smaller Building Materials division saw profits up 9 per cent on a modest rise in revenues to $31.5 million, thanks especially to a series of major infrastructure projects in Western Australia, bolstered by operational efficiencies. The company's investment portfolio contributed $3.3 million to after-tax profit, up from $1.9 million in the previous year. In addition, the company benefited from a $2.3 million unrealised revaluation gain on its major South Connect property holding at Jandakot. However, this was sharply down from $8.1 million in the previous year, and total company profit fell.

Outlook

Schaffer's core automotive leather goods business is highly dependent on trends in the global car-making sector, with a large part of demand coming from luxury automobile manufacturers. It expects increasing sales to Audi during the first half of the June 2026 year. However, the company notes that all its automotive customers are expressing their concerns about mounting economic challenges. This business is also affected by currency rate fluctuations. The company reports that its Building Materials division faces a more competitive operating environment as some significant large-scale construction projects reach completion. Schaffer valued its investment portfolio at $227.3 million — or $16.73 per share — at June 2025. It continues development work on its 34-hectare Jandakot Road land holding, 15 minutes from the Perth CBD, and is initially building a large logistics warehouse on the site.

Year to 30 June	2024	2025
Revenues ($mn)	216.2	218.8
EBIT ($mn)	46.5	43.1
EBIT margin (%)	21.5	19.7
Gross margin (%)	21.3	22.4
Profit before tax ($mn)	42.8	39.5
Profit after tax ($mn)	27.1	24.3
Earnings per share (c)	198.84	178.50
Cash flow per share (c)	260.84	247.12
Dividend (c)	90	90
Percentage franked	100	100
Net tangible assets per share ($)	14.15	15.28
Interest cover (times)	12.7	12.0
Return on equity (%)	12.4	10.5
Debt-to-equity ratio (%)	11.9	17.2
Current ratio	2.1	2.0

Servcorp Limited

ASX code: SRV   www.servcorp.com.au

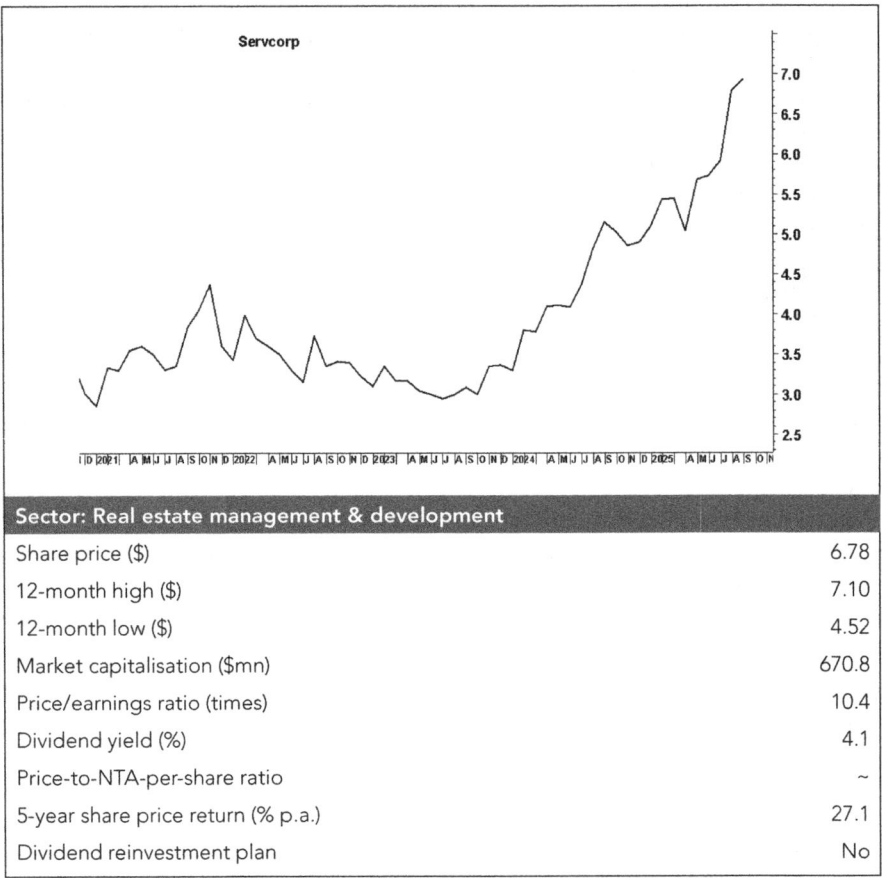

Sector: Real estate management & development	
Share price ($)	6.78
12-month high ($)	7.10
12-month low ($)	4.52
Market capitalisation ($mn)	670.8
Price/earnings ratio (times)	10.4
Dividend yield (%)	4.1
Price-to-NTA-per-share ratio	~
5-year share price return (% p.a.)	27.1
Dividend reinvestment plan	No

Sydney-based Servcorp was founded in 1978 to provide serviced office space to small businesses. It has expanded to provide advanced corporate infrastructure, including IT and telecommunications services and office support services. It also offers what it terms virtual offices, providing a prestigious address and a range of services for people or businesses not needing a physical office.

Latest business results (June 2025, full year)

Underlying profits posted a second consecutive double-digit rise, with strength in most regions. For a fourth consecutive year the Europe/Middle East segment showed strong growth, with double-digit rises in sales and profits, as five new operations were added to the portfolio. This segment is responsible for 42 per cent of company turnover but contributes about half of total profit. North Asia achieved a double-digit gain in profits on a 4 per cent rise in revenues, with strength in Japan offsetting

Chinese weakness. The third major operating segment, Australia/New Zealand/South East Asia, benefited from disciplined cost control, with 5 per cent growth in revenues leading to a double-digit gain in profits. The underperforming US market realised a small underlying profit. During the year Servcorp increased net capacity by 221 offices to 5547, and at June 2025 it was operating 136 floors of offices in 39 cities across 19 countries.

Outlook

Servcorp is a world leader in its business, with good market shares and a reputation for quality. It continues to invest heavily, both for new office space and for its major new IT platform, which it has developed with a goal of sustainable long-term growth. It is planning a full redesign of its client portal, aimed at simplifying access to core services, while also unlocking new revenue streams. It is working to integrate artificial intelligence technology into its operations and expects eventually to establish new AI-based service offerings. It is seeing a slow recovery in its American business, thanks to an emphasis on building volume growth and improving efficiency. Operating losses in China have begun to narrow. It expects to open six new operations during the June 2026 year, with a total of 452 new offices. At June 2025 it had no debt and more than $131 million in cash holdings. Its early forecast is for underlying profits to rise by around 7 per cent in the June 2026 year, with a full-year dividend payout of at least 30 cents per share. Nevertheless, with operations around the world, Servcorp is heavily exposed to geopolitical volatility as well as to currency rate fluctuations.

Year to 30 June	2024	2025
Revenues ($mn)	300.7	332.9
Europe/Middle East (%)	39	42
North Asia (%)	28	27
Australia/NZ/South East Asia (%)	25	24
USA (%)	6	7
EBIT ($mn)	70.3	83.1
EBIT margin (%)	23.4	25.0
Profit before tax ($mn)	56.3	69.1
Profit after tax ($mn)	51.2	64.4
Earnings per share (c)	52.32	65.28
Cash flow per share (c)	169.38	187.54
Dividend (c)	25	28
Percentage franked	20	10
Net tangible assets per share ($)	~	~
Interest cover (times)	5.0	5.9
Return on equity (%)	26.8	30.1
Debt-to-equity ratio (%)	~	~
Current ratio	0.8	0.9

Shaver Shop Group Limited

ASX code: SSG   investors.shavershop.com.au

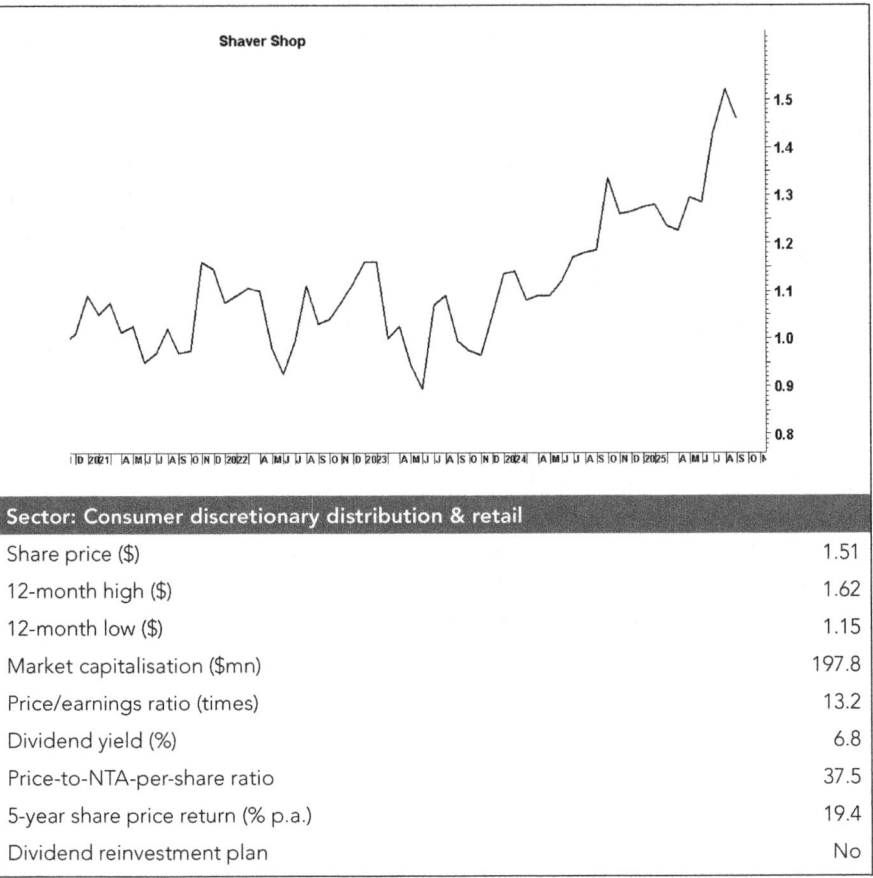

Sector: Consumer discretionary distribution & retail	
Share price ($)	1.51
12-month high ($)	1.62
12-month low ($)	1.15
Market capitalisation ($mn)	197.8
Price/earnings ratio (times)	13.2
Dividend yield (%)	6.8
Price-to-NTA-per-share ratio	37.5
5-year share price return (% p.a.)	19.4
Dividend reinvestment plan	No

Shaver Shop, with its headquarters in Melbourne, was established in 1986 as a service centre for men's electric shavers, providing repairs and spare parts. It has since grown steadily into a nationwide chain of stores offering a wide range of men's and women's personal grooming products. It expanded to New Zealand in 2014. It has an online presence, representing about 23 per cent of sales.

Latest business results (June 2025, full year)

Revenues and profits edged down as inflationary pressures and economic weakness adversely affected consumer sentiment. A 2.3 per cent drop in online sales to $49.7 million also hurt business. A pleasing increase in the gross profit margin was driven by the launch of the company's first private brand, Transform-U, and by securing exclusive distribution rights to the Skull Shaver range of products. During the year the company opened four new stores and closed three. At June 2025 it operated 124 stores throughout Australia and New Zealand.

Outlook

Shaver Shop is the only major specialty retailer focused solely on men's and women's personal grooming products across Australia and New Zealand, and it enjoys strong brand recognition and significant market shares. Thanks to these strengths, it is often able to secure from its global partners exclusive access to new and innovative products as they come to market. In addition, it works closely with manufacturers and suppliers to source products that cater to the emerging demands of consumers. It has achieved greater-than-expected success with its Transform-U range of private brand shaving and personal grooming products. Launched only in October 2024, it has realised sales of more than 120 000 units, representing 3.4 per cent of total company revenues in the June 2025 year, including 5.4 per cent of revenues in the June 2025 second half. The company has also achieved good results for its five-year agreement, from June 2024, for exclusive distribution rights to the popular Skull Shaver range of products. It is a beneficiary of moves by men to buy and use more grooming and beauty tools than previously, and it expects this trend to continue. Shaver Shop plans to open three new stores during the June 2026 year, two in New South Wales and one in New Zealand, and expects to be managing 130 to 135 stores within the coming three years. The company also maintains an active policy of upgrading existing stores. It is developing plans for a store of the future concept to showcase innovative and cutting-edge products.

Year to 30 June	2024	2025
Revenues ($mn)	219.4	218.6
EBIT ($mn)	21.9	22.5
EBIT margin (%)	10.0	10.3
Gross margin (%)	44.4	45.5
Profit before tax ($mn)	21.4	21.1
Profit after tax ($mn)	15.1	14.9
Earnings per share (c)	11.73	11.46
Cash flow per share (c)	24.31	24.44
Dividend (c)	10.2	10.3
Percentage franked	100	100
Net tangible assets per share ($)	0.10	0.04
Interest cover (times)	42.2	16.4
Return on equity (%)	17.6	16.9
Debt-to-equity ratio (%)	~	~
Current ratio	1.3	1.2

Smartgroup Corporation Limited

ASX code: SIQ   www.smartgroup.com.au

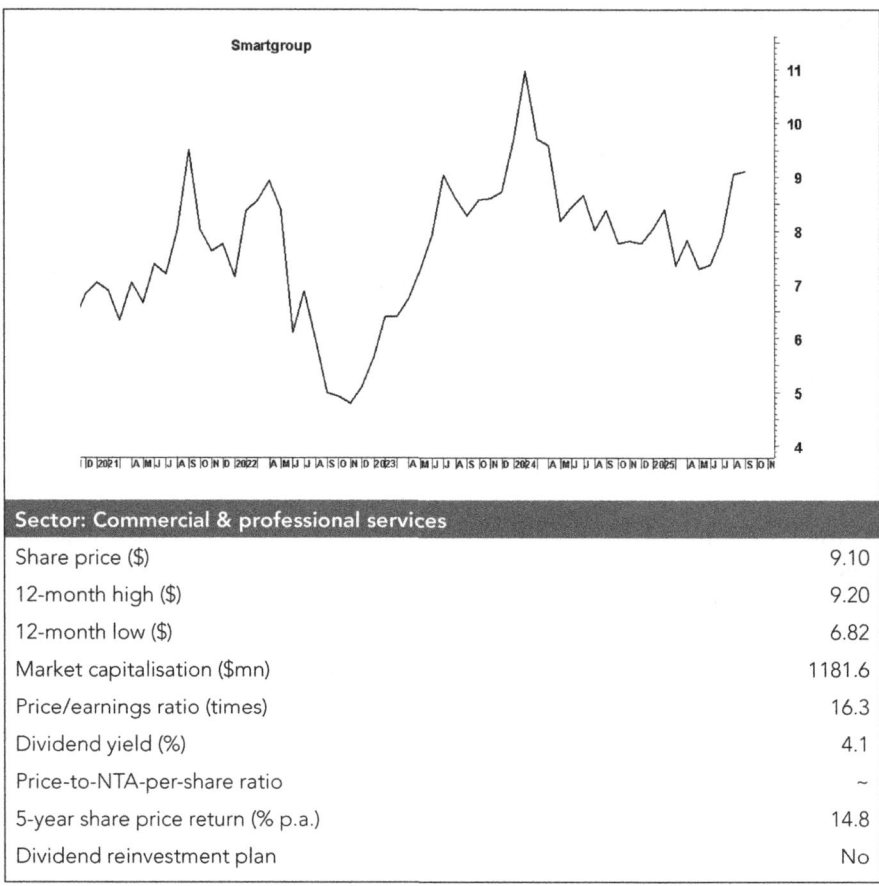

Sector: Commercial & professional services	
Share price ($)	9.10
12-month high ($)	9.20
12-month low ($)	6.82
Market capitalisation ($mn)	1181.6
Price/earnings ratio (times)	16.3
Dividend yield (%)	4.1
Price-to-NTA-per-share ratio	~
5-year share price return (% p.a.)	14.8
Dividend reinvestment plan	No

Sydney-based specialist employee management services provider Smartgroup got its start in 1999 as Smartsalary, a salary packaging specialist. It later branched into other businesses, and has grown significantly, both organically and through acquisition. It is now engaged in salary packaging services, vehicle novated leasing and fleet management.

Latest business results (June 2025, half year)

Continuing strong demand for the company's novated leases generated a solid increase in revenues and profits, but with strength also in other businesses. The number of leases under management grew 24 per cent from the June 2024 half to 80 000, thanks to both rising demand and improving vehicle supply. From April 2025 the government's Electric Car Discount Policy ceased being available to plug-in hybrid vehicles, so demand for these accelerated in the first quarter of 2025, then fell back in the second quarter. Salary packaging customer numbers of 484 000 were up from 402 000 a year earlier, thanks to new clients and organic growth from existing clients. The high-margin managed fleet vehicle business saw vehicle numbers rise 6 per cent to 32 400.

Outlook

Smartgroup is one of Australia's largest companies involved in the salary packaging and novated leasing businesses, with a high reputation for its work and good profit margins. Thanks to a large addressable market, it sees significant growth potential for its salary packaging operations. It notes that some 2.4 million wage earners are employed by Smartgroup clients, yet fewer than a quarter of these employees have salary packaging arrangements in place. The company believes this provides a great opportunity for new business, and it is working to increase its penetration of this existing client base. It is also actively seeking new clients. A new digital portal, aimed at simplifying the salary packaging process, has boosted business. As client numbers grow the company achieves economies of scale, and profit margins increase. The novated lease business involves taking advantage of complex legislation to provide tax deductions for employees, mainly those working in the non-profit or public sectors, and Smartgroup is one of the market leaders. It has become a particular beneficiary of government policies designed to stimulate demand for electric vehicles. This has helped make the company's customers more aware of the benefits of novated leasing, and electric vehicles represented 48 per cent of all new car novated lease orders in the June 2025 half, up from 42 per cent in June 2024. It has launched strategic partnerships with BMW Financial Services and Stratton Finance aimed at streamlining the novated leasing process.

Year to 31 December	2023	2024
Revenues ($mn)	251.6	305.8
EBIT ($mn)	91.1	109.4
EBIT margin (%)	36.2	35.8
Profit before tax ($mn)	88.1	104.0
Profit after tax ($mn)	63.2	72.4
Earnings per share (c)	48.73	55.80
Cash flow per share (c)	54.84	64.11
Dividend (c)	31.5	37.5
Percentage franked	100	100
Interest cover (times)	30.3	20.2
Return on equity (%)	26.1	28.8
Half year to 30 June	2024	2025
Revenues ($mn)	148.5	159.1
Profit before tax ($mn)	49.6	55.4
Profit after tax ($mn)	34.3	38.1
Earnings per share (c)	26.40	29.30
Dividend (c)	17.5	19.5
Percentage franked	100	100
Net tangible assets per share ($)	~	~
Debt-to-equity ratio (%)	23.0	16.9
Current ratio	1.0	1.1

Southern Cross Electrical Engineering Limited

ASX code: SXE   www.scee.com.au

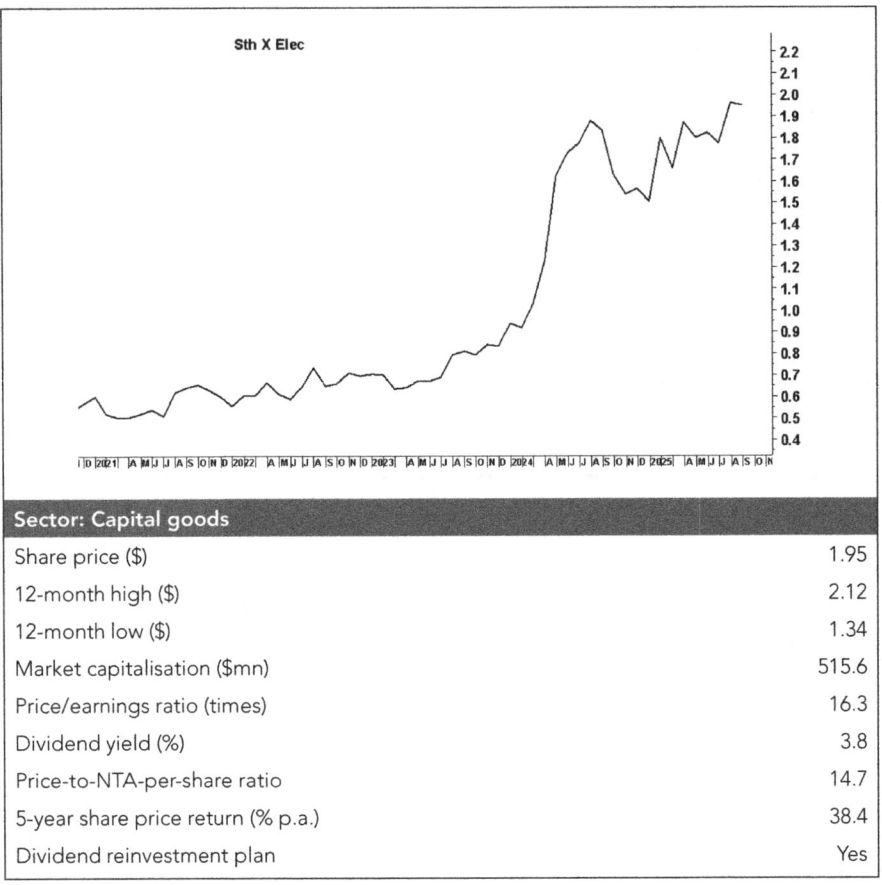

Sector: Capital goods	
Share price ($)	1.95
12-month high ($)	2.12
12-month low ($)	1.34
Market capitalisation ($mn)	515.6
Price/earnings ratio (times)	16.3
Dividend yield (%)	3.8
Price-to-NTA-per-share ratio	14.7
5-year share price return (% p.a.)	38.4
Dividend reinvestment plan	Yes

Perth-based Southern Cross Electrical Engineering (SCEE) was founded in 1978. A series of acquisitions has generated some strong expansion and the company is now a leading national provider of specialised electrical, instrumentation, maintenance and communication services, operating through a portfolio of eight dedicated businesses. In April 2025 it acquired fire safety contractor Force Fire.

Latest business results (June 2025, full year)

SCEE's fast-expanding strength in infrastructure work once again helped deliver substantial gains in revenues and profits. Infrastructure revenue of $511.6 million, was more than double the figure of the previous year, with notable contributions from Synergy's Collie Battery Energy Storage System (CBESS) project in Western Australia and from the Western Sydney International Airport project. However, the other two operating segments experienced relative weakness. Commercial division revenues fell

11 per cent to $152.5 million and Resources division revenues fell again, down 7 per cent to $137.4 million. The year-end order book of $685 million was down 5 per cent from the previous year.

Outlook

As a diversified national electrical contractor SCEE believes it is well-positioned to benefit from three structural trends. The first is growing demand for data centres, due to developments in cloud computing and artificial intelligence and the consequent growth in data storage requirements. Electrical work is the largest component of data centre construction costs. The company received revenues of $120 million from data centres in the June 2025 year, and it expects to tender for more than $500 million of data centre work over the coming two years. The second trend is the electrification and decarbonisation of the economy, requiring a huge investment in renewable energy. SCEE has already participated in many solar farm, wind farm and battery energy storage developments and is tendering for further work. A third trend is the growth of infrastructure projects in Australia. SCEE expects to tender for further work for the Western Sydney International Airport as well as for some major hospital projects in New South Wales and Canberra. It views its $53.5 million acquisition of Force Fire as offering an attractive platform for expansion in the fragmented fire safety sector. It also envisages attractive cross-selling opportunities, thanks to Force Fire's large client base. SCEE is actively pursuing further acquisition opportunities, particularly companies offering increased geographic diversification and new capabilities. Its early forecast is for June 2026 EBITDA growth of 18 per cent to 24 per cent. At June 2025 SCEE had no debt and cash holdings of more than $88 million.

Year to 30 June	2024	2025
Revenues ($mn)	551.9	801.5
Infrastructure (%)	42	64
Commercial (%)	31	19
Resources (%)	27	17
EBIT ($mn)	35.1	48.8
EBIT margin (%)	6.4	6.1
Gross margin (%)	15.0	13.2
Profit before tax ($mn)	31.7	45.6
Profit after tax ($mn)	21.9	31.7
Earnings per share (c)	8.34	11.99
Cash flow per share (c)	11.17	15.38
Dividend (c)	6	7.5
Percentage franked	100	100
Net tangible assets per share ($)	0.26	0.13
Interest cover (times)	10.2	15.2
Return on equity (%)	11.7	16.0
Debt-to-equity ratio (%)	~	~
Current ratio	1.4	1.1

Steadfast Group Limited

ASX code: SDF   www.steadfast.com.au

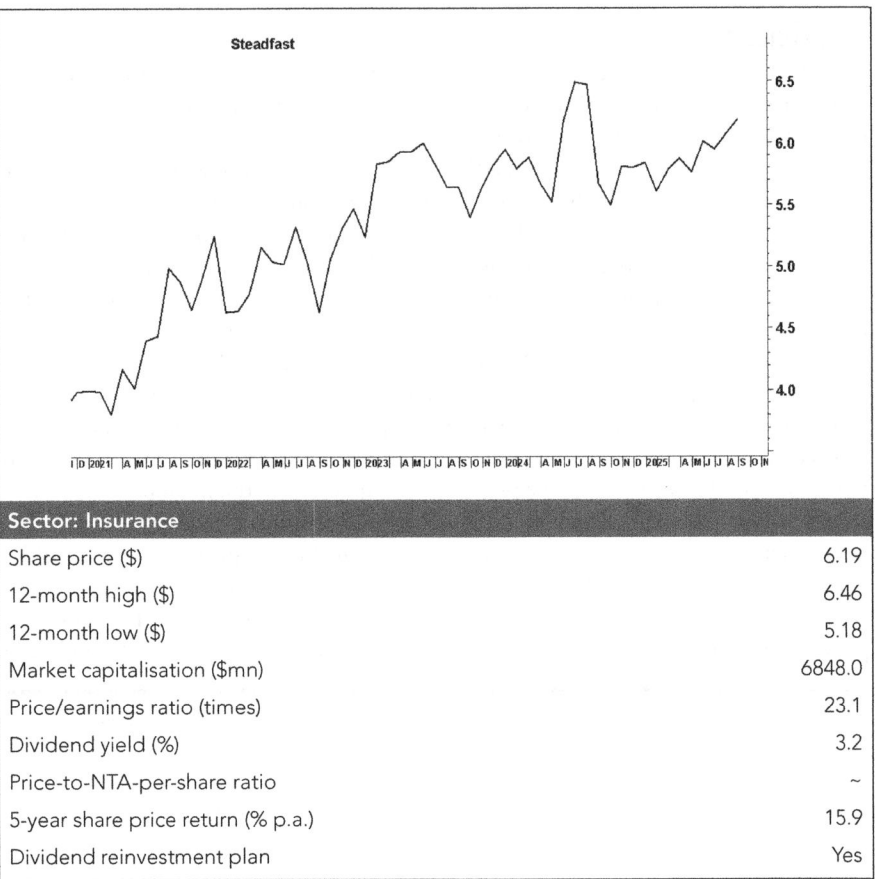

Sector: Insurance	
Share price ($)	6.19
12-month high ($)	6.46
12-month low ($)	5.18
Market capitalisation ($mn)	6848.0
Price/earnings ratio (times)	23.1
Dividend yield (%)	3.2
Price-to-NTA-per-share ratio	~
5-year share price return (% p.a.)	15.9
Dividend reinvestment plan	Yes

Melbourne-based insurance broking firm Steadfast launched in 1996 with the aim of boosting the buying power of a group of 43 small independent general insurance brokers in their dealings with insurers. It has since grown to become the largest insurance broker network and underwriting group in Australasia, with further operations abroad. It also manages a range of complementary businesses that include back-office services, risk services guidance, work health consultancy, reinsurance and legal advice. It owns the ISU Steadfast broking network in the US and has a 60 per cent stake in Hamburg-based UnisonSteadfast, one of the world's largest networks of general insurance brokers. In December 2024 it acquired the British insurance business H.W. Wood and in August 2025 it acquired a majority stake in the American specialty underwriting agency Novum Underwriting Partners.

Latest business results (June 2025, full year)

Revenues and underlying profits rose, with organic growth bolstered by the benefits of acquisitions. It was the company's 12th consecutive profit increase since its ASX listing in 2013. The core Steadfast Australasian Network broking business recorded gross written premium of $12.5 billion, with underlying profit growth of 10.6 per cent. At June 2025 Steadfast incorporated a network of 402 brokers, with nearly 1800 offices in Australia, New Zealand and Singapore. The Steadfast Underwriting Agencies business, comprising 30 specialist agencies offering over 100 specialised products, generated gross written premium of $2.5 billion, with underlying profits up 10 per cent. The ISU Steadfast network of independent agents in the US had 241 members located across 40 states.

Outlook

Steadfast continues its strong growth trajectory. It sees particular long-term potential in its moves overseas and continues to seek further acquisition opportunities. H.W. Wood, acquired for £23.5 million and now rebranded as HWS Specialty, is a London-based independent insurance broker providing wholesale, retail and reinsurance services, with specialties that include marine and cargo, property and fine art. It is also a Lloyd's broker, and Steadfast expects it to provide strong support for its Australian and American broking networks. Novum is a wholesale brokerage that specialises in the digital delivery of insurance products to agents with its proprietary technology platform NovumOnline. Steadfast expects Novum, through its specialist technology, to provide a range of broking services to ISU Steadfast members in the US and also support the launch to the US market of products from Steadfast Underwriting Agencies in Australia and HWS Specialty in the UK. Steadfast's early forecast is for June 2026 underlying after-tax profit of $315 million to $325 million.

Year to 30 June	2024	2025
Revenues ($mn)	1676.2	1825.7
EBIT ($mn)	478.7	543.3
EBIT margin (%)	28.6	29.8
Profit before tax ($mn)	425.0	486.1
Profit after tax ($mn)	252.2	295.5
Earnings per share (c)	23.45	26.79
Cash flow per share (c)	32.52	35.80
Dividend (c)	17.1	19.5
Percentage franked	100	100
Net tangible assets per share ($)	~	~
Interest cover (times)	8.9	9.5
Return on equity (%)	11.5	12.5
Debt-to-equity ratio (%)	41.2	49.9
Current ratio	1.5	1.4

Suncorp Group Limited

ASX code: SUN www.suncorp.com.au

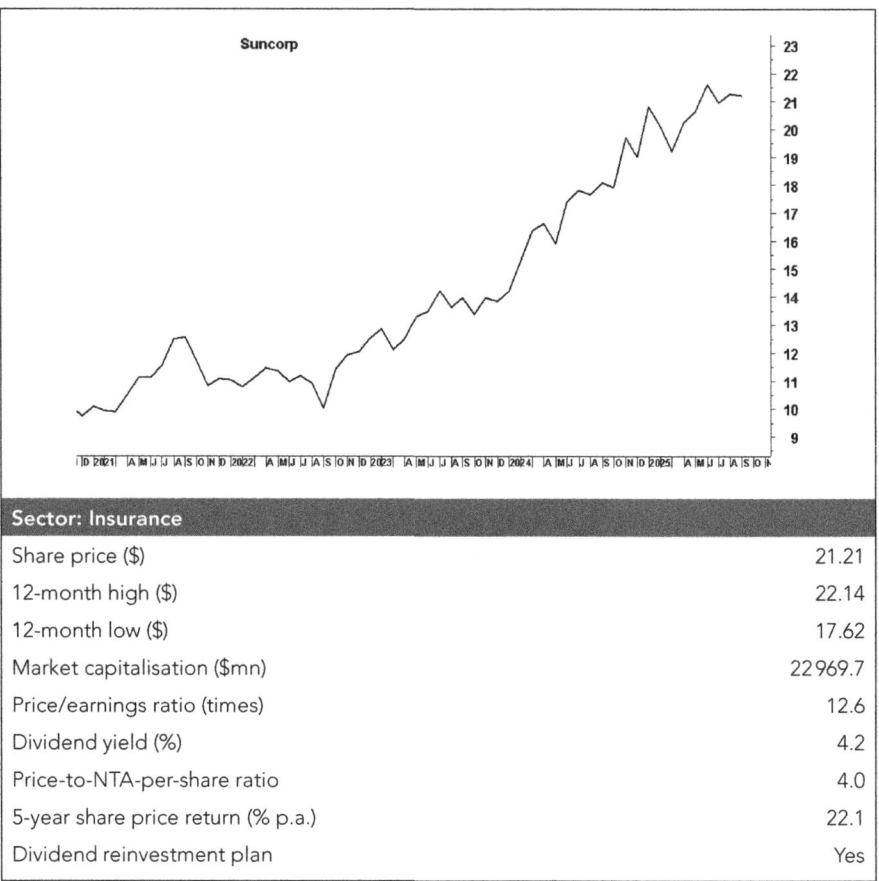

Sector: Insurance	
Share price ($)	21.21
12-month high ($)	22.14
12-month low ($)	17.62
Market capitalisation ($mn)	22 969.7
Price/earnings ratio (times)	12.6
Dividend yield (%)	4.2
Price-to-NTA-per-share ratio	4.0
5-year share price return (% p.a.)	22.1
Dividend reinvestment plan	Yes

Brisbane-based insurance company Suncorp has a heritage that dates back to the establishment of the Queensland Agricultural Bank in 1902. Following a long series of mergers and acquisitions it became a major force in banking and insurance throughout Australia, and with particular strength in Queensland. In 2024 it sold its banking operations to ANZ. It is now one of Australia's insurance leaders, with brands that include Suncorp, AAMI, GIO, Bingle, Apia, Shannons, Terri Scheer, CIL Insurance, Vero and Essentials by AAI. In New Zealand it operates under the AA Insurance and Vero brands.

Latest business results (June 2025, full year)

In a buoyant insurance environment, Suncorp reported a strong result, supported by higher premiums, growing investment returns and reduced natural hazard claims. Gross written premium of $15 billion was up from $14.1 billion in the previous year, although the company noted a second-half slowdown in growth as inflationary pressures eased and competitive activity increased. The consumer insurance business enjoyed a particularly strong year as the company boosted premiums for home and vehicle policies. The commercial and personal injury business was also solid, thanks to premium increases and positive investment returns. New Zealand saw just modest gross written premium growth, but profits were boosted by higher premiums, lower reinsurance costs and fewer natural hazard claims than expected. Net investment returns of $766 million were up from $661 million in the previous year. The reported profit figure included gains from the sale of Suncorp's bank to ANZ. The company said that on a cash earnings basis its after-tax profit rose from $1.37 billion in June 2024 to $1.49 billion.

Outlook

Now a pure-play general insurer, Suncorp continues working to restructure and simplify its operations. It sees premium price rises starting to moderate as inflationary pressures ease and reinsurance markets stabilise, and it forecasts gross written premium growth in the mid-single digits for the June 2026 year. It responded to 17 serious weather events during the June 2025 year, including severe flooding in Queensland and New South Wales, but costs were $205 million below its natural hazard allowance of $1.56 billion. Nevertheless, it believes the likelihood is high for further unpredictable weather events, and it is raising the natural hazard allowance to $1.77 billion for June 2026. It is working to introduce artificial intelligence technology to its operations to accelerate claims processing and boost customer service, and reports that AI systems have already delivered significant reductions in the time taken to process claims.

Year to 30 June	2024	2025
Revenues ($mn)	15 034.0	17 355.0
Consumer insurance (%)	41	50
Commercial & personal injury (%)	23	29
Suncorp New Zealand (%)	14	18
EBIT ($mn)	1 532.0	2 414.0
EBIT margin (%)	10.2	13.9
Profit before tax ($mn)	1 400.0	2 254.0
Profit after tax ($mn)	1 197.0	1 823.0
Earnings per share (c)	110.96	168.52
Cash flow per share (c)	132.84	183.40
Dividend (c)	78	90
Percentage franked	100	100
Net tangible assets per share ($)	6.95	5.27
Interest cover (times)	11.6	15.1
Return on equity (%)	8.8	14.9
Debt-to-equity ratio (%)	12.9	11.0

Super Retail Group Limited

ASX code: SUL   www.superretailgroup.com.au

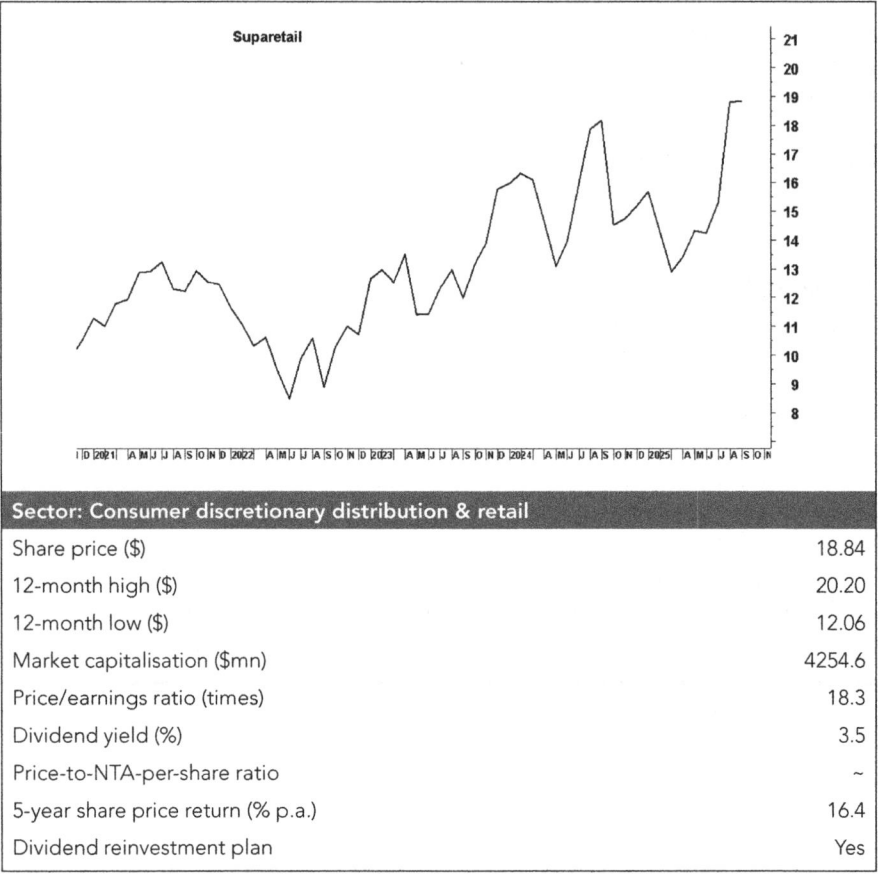

Sector: Consumer discretionary distribution & retail	
Share price ($)	18.84
12-month high ($)	20.20
12-month low ($)	12.06
Market capitalisation ($mn)	4254.6
Price/earnings ratio (times)	18.3
Dividend yield (%)	3.5
Price-to-NTA-per-share ratio	~
5-year share price return (% p.a.)	16.4
Dividend reinvestment plan	Yes

Specialist retail chain Super Retail Group was established as a mail-order business in 1972 and has its headquarters in Strathpine, Queensland. It now comprises four retail brands, with more than 780 stores throughout Australia and New Zealand. Supercheap Auto is a retailer of automotive spare parts and related products. Rebel is a prominent sporting goods chain. BCF is a retailer of boating, camping and fishing products. Macpac is an outdoor adventure and activity specialist retailer.

Latest business results (June 2025, full year)

Revenues rose but profits fell for a second consecutive year. The opening of a net 23 new stores contributed to a 4.5 per cent increase in sales, or 2.6 per cent on a like-for-like basis. Sales growth accelerated markedly in the second half, following a relatively weak first half. For a second year the best result came from BCF, with sales up 7.9 per cent, and with fishing-related products again much in demand. Among the four divisions only BCF enjoyed a rise in pre-tax profit, up 12 per cent. Rebel sales were up 4.8 per cent, with sporting equipment returning to growth after a post-Covid consolidation. The biggest division, Supercheap Auto, recorded a small increase in sales in a competitive environment. The small Macpac operation achieved modest growth in sales, and the company claimed an increase in market share in Australia. However, the pre-tax profit for Macpac plunged 45 per cent, which follows a 34 per cent decline in the previous year. Total group online sales of $524 million were up 8 per cent.

Outlook

Super Retail controls four prominent brands with strong positions in their respective markets. Nevertheless, it operates in a competitive retail environment at a time when inflationary pressures and economic weakness have been dampening consumer spending. With much of its product range imported, it is also vulnerable to currency fluctuations and supply chain disruptions. It plans a roll-out of 23 new stores during the June 2026 year. Its Supercheap Auto division generates the strongest profit margins of the four businesses, and the company expects solid sales as car numbers continue to grow in Australia and New Zealand. A particular focus is meeting growing demand for electric vehicle aftermarket products. It sees scope for leveraging its loyalty programs, with some 12.5 million active club members, one of the largest such schemes in Australia. Nearly 80 per cent of group sales come from club members. At June 2025 Super Retail had no debt and cash holdings of $63 million.

Year to 28 June*	2024	2025
Revenues ($mn)	3893.7	4070.1
Supercheap Auto (%)	38	38
Rebel (%)	33	33
BCF (%)	23	23
Macpac (%)	6	6
EBIT ($mn)	400.4	399.7
EBIT margin (%)	10.3	9.8
Gross margin (%)	46.1	45.6
Profit before tax ($mn)	342.6	329.4
Profit after tax ($mn)	242.1	232.4
Earnings per share (c)	107.21	102.91
Cash flow per share (c)	256.97	261.57
Dividend (c)	69	66
Percentage franked	100	100
Net tangible assets per share ($)	~	~
Interest cover (times)	6.9	5.7
Return on equity (%)	17.7	17.2
Debt-to-equity ratio (%)	~	~
Current ratio	1.2	1.1

*29 June 2024

Supply Network Limited

ASX code: SNL   www.supplynetwork.com.au

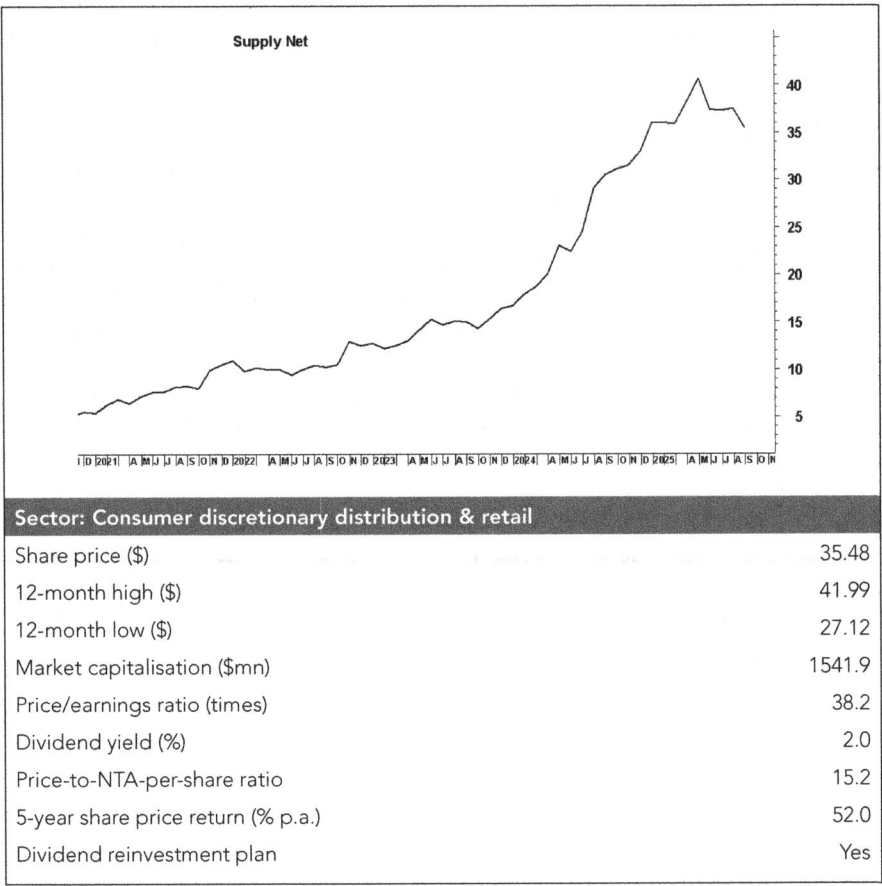

Sector: Consumer discretionary distribution & retail	
Share price ($)	35.48
12-month high ($)	41.99
12-month low ($)	27.12
Market capitalisation ($mn)	1541.9
Price/earnings ratio (times)	38.2
Dividend yield (%)	2.0
Price-to-NTA-per-share ratio	15.2
5-year share price return (% p.a.)	52.0
Dividend reinvestment plan	Yes

Sydney-based Supply Network is a supplier of truck and bus parts in the commercial vehicle aftermarket, operating under the brand name Multispares, which was established in 1976. It manages offices, distribution centres and workshops at 26 locations throughout Australia and New Zealand.

Latest business results (June 2025, full year)

Strong demand for its products and services generated another excellent result, although the company noted that, with inflation and GDP growth lower than over the previous two years, its own growth rate was also lower. With earnings rising at a faster pace than revenues, the company's profit margins expanded. Its growth came from all major customer segments, though skewed towards truck fleets and truck repairers. Sales in Australia were up 16 per cent, with profits rising 13 per cent.

New Zealand, representing 15 per cent of total income, saw revenues up 11 per cent but profits jumping 35 per cent. New Zealand profit margins are now in line with those in Australia.

Outlook

Supply Network is one of the leaders in the Australian market for the supply of truck and bus parts. It is a challenging and fragmented market. The huge distances travelled in Australia make it crucial that truck and bus operators have parts suppliers who are dependable and proficient. With a great diversity of vehicle makes and models, and with a considerable difference in requirements between various regions of the country, Supply Network has established a decentralised management structure with a strong regional focus. Its core activity has become the supply of truck components, representing more than 80 per cent of total income. Company fleets, the largest customer group, are sophisticated buyers of parts with a focus on costs, making this business highly competitive. The company is a beneficiary of the increasing complexity of trucks, which require an ever-growing range of expensive components. It also benefits from a slow rise in the average age of trucks in Australia. It continues to expand its network. In April 2025 it began trading at its new Wangara branch, servicing the north Perth growth corridor, and in June it opened a small parts store in Karratha, Western Australia, to service the Pilbara region. In July it started distribution from its building extension at Truganina, Victoria. It expects to begin trading in February 2026 at a new facility at Albany, in the north of Auckland, and it plans to expand branch capacity in Brisbane, Toowoomba and Perth. The company's June 2026 target is for revenues of around $400 million.

Year to 30 June	2024	2025
Revenues ($mn)	302.6	348.8
EBIT ($mn)	49.5	58.9
EBIT margin (%)	16.4	16.9
Profit before tax ($mn)	47.1	56.6
Profit after tax ($mn)	33.0	40.0
Earnings per share (c)	78.61	92.95
Cash flow per share (c)	100.24	116.92
Dividend (c)	56	70
Percentage franked	100	100
Net tangible assets per share ($)	1.56	2.33
Interest cover (times)	20.9	25.6
Return on equity (%)	36.5	33.2
Debt-to-equity ratio (%)	3.6	~
Current ratio	2.7	3.1

Technology One Limited

ASX code: TNE   www.technology1.com

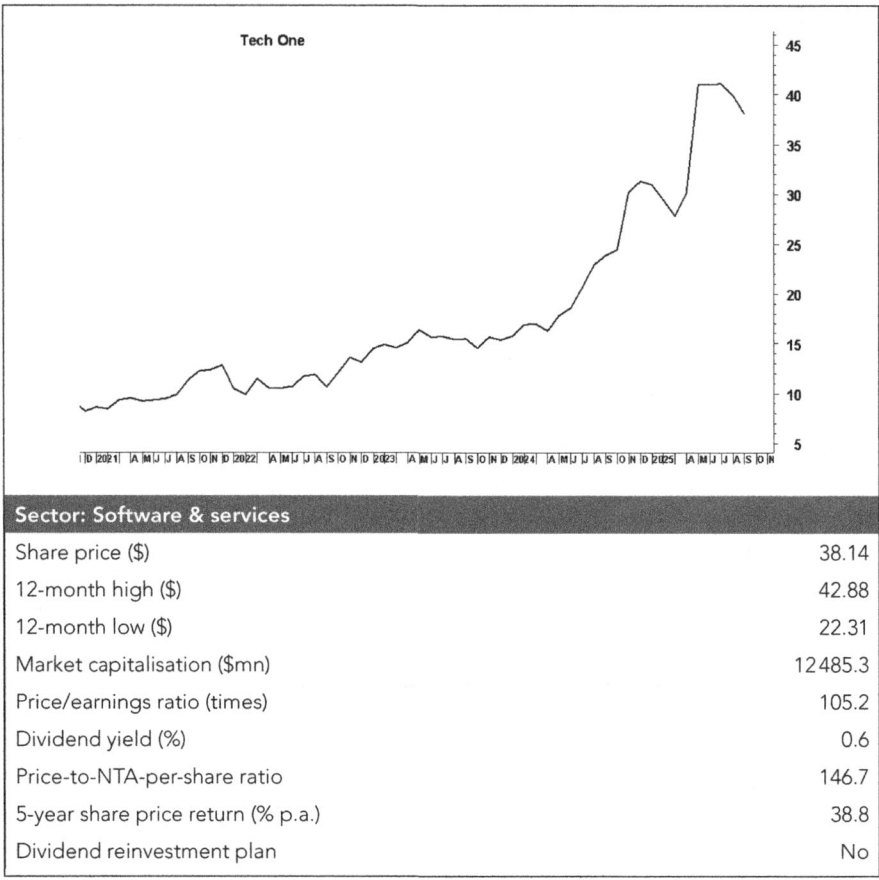

Sector: Software & services	
Share price ($)	38.14
12-month high ($)	42.88
12-month low ($)	22.31
Market capitalisation ($mn)	12 485.3
Price/earnings ratio (times)	105.2
Dividend yield (%)	0.6
Price-to-NTA-per-share ratio	146.7
5-year share price return (% p.a.)	38.8
Dividend reinvestment plan	No

Brisbane-based Technology One, founded in 1987, designs, develops, implements and supports a wide range of financial management, accounting and business software. It enjoys particular strength in local government. Its software is also used by educational institutions, including many Australian universities. Other key markets are financial services, central government and health and community services. It derives revenues not only from the supply of its products but also from annual licence fees. It operates from offices in Australia, New Zealand, Malaysia and the UK.

Latest business results (March 2025, half year)

Technology One posted another excellent result, with profits up for the 16th straight March half year, as once again it enjoyed success in moving its customers onto its Software as a Service (SaaS) cloud platforms. Total annual recurring revenue of $511 million was a 21 per cent jump from a year before. In the British market annual recurring revenue jumped 50 per cent to $43.1 million. Consulting services — essentially the business of implementing the company's software, and representing about 16 per cent of company turnover — saw sales rise but profits fall. The company maintained its high level of research and development spending, up 21 per cent to $68.8 million.

Outlook

Technology One has become a star among Australian high-tech companies, with growing profits and regular dividend increases. In large part this reflects a strong product line, a solid flow of recurring income and a heavy investment in new products and services, which it believes will enable it to double in size every five years. It has achieved great success with its SaaS offerings, which put software in the cloud, rather than on the customers' own computers, meaning the customers always have the latest software versions, and giving them greater flexibility than previously. A key measure of its success is annual recurring revenue, which by March 2025 exceeded $500 million for the first time, 18 months ahead of schedule, and representing some 90 per cent of total revenue. Its new goal is annual recurring revenue of $1 billion by September 2030 with expanded profit margins. It claims a total addressable market for its products of $13.5 billion and sees significant potential for growth. It is also seeking appropriate acquisitions, and in November 2024 acquired for $60 million software developer CourseLoop, a leading provider of curriculum management digital products to the higher education sector. At March 2025 Technology One had no debt and cash holdings of $68 million.

Year to 30 September	2023	2024
Revenues ($mn)	429.4	506.5
EBIT ($mn)	132.0	155.5
EBIT margin (%)	30.7	30.7
Profit before tax ($mn)	129.9	152.9
Profit after tax ($mn)	102.9	118.0
Earnings per share (c)	31.71	36.24
Cash flow per share (c)	48.20	57.36
Dividend (c)	16.52	22.45
Percentage franked	60	65
Interest cover (times)	61.9	58.8
Return on equity (%)	37.7	34.4
Half year to 31 March	2024	2025
Revenues ($mn)	240.8	285.7
Profit before tax ($mn)	61.5	81.9
Profit after tax ($mn)	48.0	63.0
Earnings per share (c)	14.75	19.26
Dividend (c)	5.08	6.6
Percentage franked	65	65
Net tangible assets per share ($)	0.21	0.26
Debt-to-equity ratio (%)	~	~
Current ratio	1.2	1.2

Universal Store Holdings Limited

ASX code: UNI   investors.universalstore.com

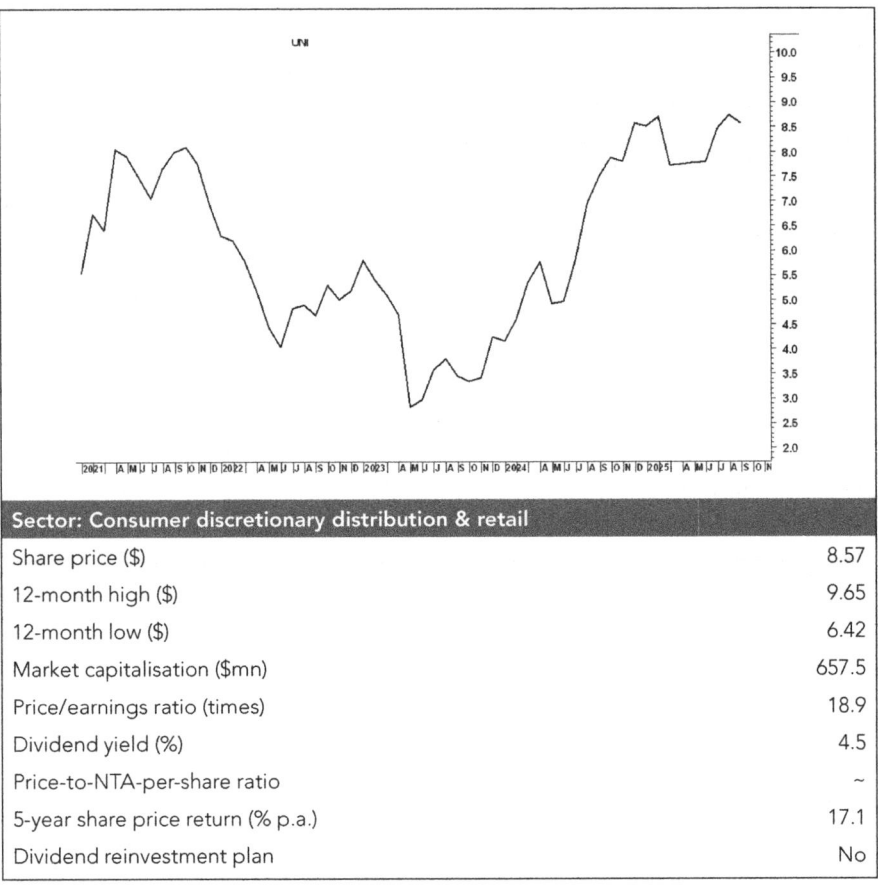

Sector: Consumer discretionary distribution & retail	
Share price ($)	8.57
12-month high ($)	9.65
12-month low ($)	6.42
Market capitalisation ($mn)	657.5
Price/earnings ratio (times)	18.9
Dividend yield (%)	4.5
Price-to-NTA-per-share ratio	~
5-year share price return (% p.a.)	17.1
Dividend reinvestment plan	No

Brisbane-based clothing retailer Universal was founded in 1999. Today it specialises in casual men's and women's fashion clothing, shoes, accessories and lifestyle products. Its CTC business manages the Thrills and Worship fashion brands. The company operates its stores under the Universal Store, Perfect Stranger and Thrills banners. It also manages wholesale and online businesses.

Latest business results (June 2025, full year)

Universal delivered a solid result, with double-digit increases in sales and profits. The core Universal Store business achieved sales of $280.9 million, up 15 per cent from the previous year, or 13 per cent on a like-for-like basis. This reflected both an increase in the number of sales transactions and a higher average transaction value. Five new stores opened during the period. The much smaller Perfect Stranger business achieved sales growth of 83.1 per cent to $25.5 million, or growth of 25.5 per cent on a like-for-like basis. Five new Perfect Stranger stores opened during the year. However, the CTC business, incorporating the Thrills and Worship brands, saw sales down 9.8 per cent, due mainly to declining wholesale demand for Thrills products. During the year the company recognised a $13.6 million goodwill impairment charge, based on poor wholesale business, and on a statutory basis its profits fell. At June 2025 the company operated 111 stores, comprising 84 Universal Store, 19 Perfect Stranger and 8 Thrills.

Outlook

Universal owns a portfolio of premium youth brands, aimed at 16- to 35-year-old fashion-focused consumers. It aims to build a large network of stores around Australia, with between 11 and 17 new stores expected to open during the June 2026 year. It is achieving success with a steady rise in the proportion of store sales that derive from its own brands, where margins are higher than for sales of third-party brands. Its Neovision brand has been notably successful, contributing 18 per cent of Universal Store sales in the June 2025 year, up from 11 per cent in the previous year. However, this is a competitive business, with numerous brands serving the youth apparel segment. Fashion apparel is also a discretionary purchase, and sales can suffer in times of economic weakness. The company is working to elevate its fast-growing Perfect Stranger brand as a premium line of products, with a focus on quality and refinement. It has brought in a new leadership team to reinvigorate the Thrills brand. The company's wholesale business represents less than 5 per cent of total turnover, and Universal expects it to remain challenging.

Year to 30 June	2024	2025
Revenues ($mn)	288.5	333.3
EBIT ($mn)	48.2	55.5
EBIT margin (%)	16.7	16.7
Profit before tax ($mn)	43.3	50.1
Profit after tax ($mn)	30.2	34.8
Earnings per share (c)	39.60	45.43
Cash flow per share (c)	85.32	96.02
Dividend (c)	35.5	38.5
Percentage franked	100	100
Net tangible assets per share ($)	~	~
Interest cover (times)	9.8	10.3
Return on equity (%)	20.9	23.4
Debt-to-equity ratio (%)	~	~
Current ratio	1.2	0.8

Wesfarmers Limited

ASX code: WES   www.wesfarmers.com.au

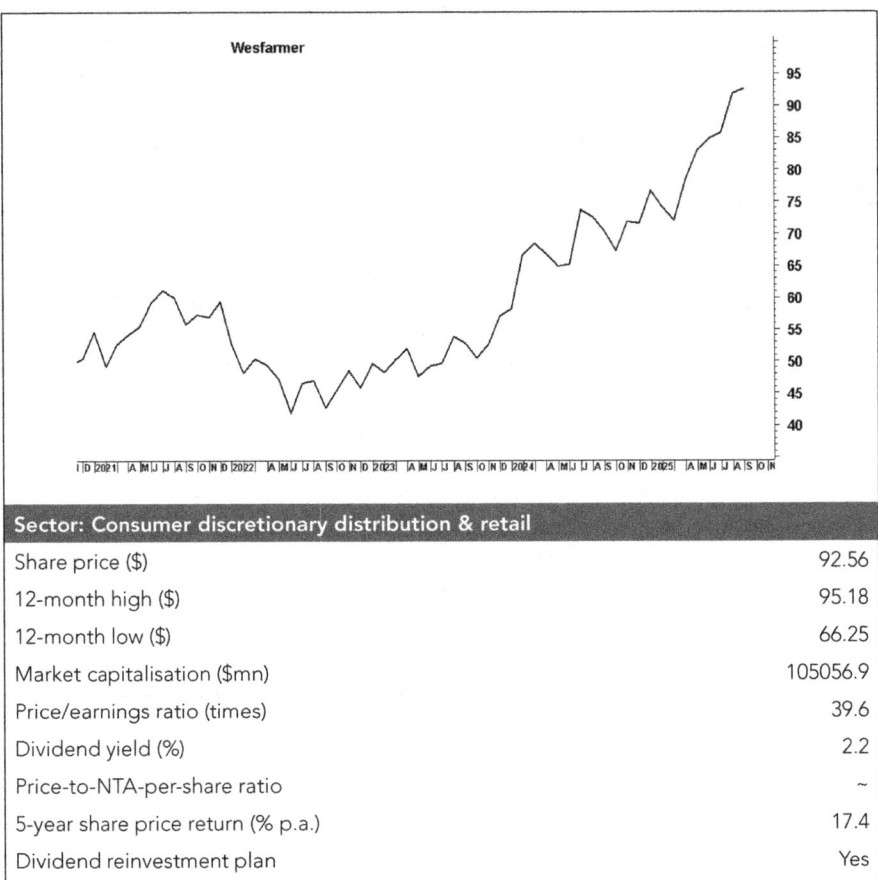

Sector: Consumer discretionary distribution & retail	
Share price ($)	92.56
12-month high ($)	95.18
12-month low ($)	66.25
Market capitalisation ($mn)	105056.9
Price/earnings ratio (times)	39.6
Dividend yield (%)	2.2
Price-to-NTA-per-share ratio	~
5-year share price return (% p.a.)	17.4
Dividend reinvestment plan	Yes

Perth-based Wesfarmers, founded in 1914 as a farmers' cooperative, is now a conglomerate with many areas of operation. Its primary business is the Bunnings network of hardware stores. Other retail businesses include the Kmart, Officeworks, Priceline Pharmacy, Soul Pattinson Chemist and Target chains. In addition, it produces fertilisers, chemicals and industrial safety products. It holds 50 per cent of the Flybuys loyalty card business, owns a 25 per cent interest in the ASX-listed BWP property trust — which owns many Bunnings warehouses — and holds half the equity in the financial services business Gresham Partners, the timber business Wespine Industries and the lithium producer Covalent Lithium. At June 2025 Wesfarmers operated 1971 stores across Australia and New Zealand.

Latest business results (June 2025, full year)

Sales and underlying profits again rose moderately, led by the company's largest divisions. The Bunnings business saw sales and profits edge up, thanks to solid consumer demand for home repair products, though demand from home builders remained weak. The Kmart division, which includes Target stores, achieved another good result, with sales up 3 per cent and profits rising 9 per cent. Officeworks also saw sales and profits rise modestly, thanks again to continuing growth in demand for technology equipment, partially offset by lower furniture sales. Further strong sales growth at Priceline helped deliver a double-digit rise in profits for the Health division. However, profit margins remained substantially lower than at the company's other divisions. The WesCEF division, which manages a portfolio of businesses in the chemicals, energy, fertilisers and lithium sectors, saw profits again fall, driven largely by lower global commodity prices.

Outlook

Wesfarmers depends on its retail businesses for more than 80 per cent of its income, and is highly exposed to trends in consumer sentiment as well as to the state of the economy. Its Kmart stores have achieved particular success with the Anko range of low-cost products, which have helped drive a significant recovery in this division. The company has initiated Anko sales abroad. A transformation program, including an expansion of the Priceline Pharmacy network, continues to boost profits for the Health division. The company's Covalent Lithium joint venture realised its initial output in July 2025 and will ramp up production during the July 2026 year, with the goal of producing 50 000 tonnes annually of lithium hydroxide for use in lithium batteries. Wesfarmers has sold its Coregas industrial gas business and is closing its loss-making Catch online marketplace. It plans to launch its own retail media network at its stores.

Year to 30 June	2024	2025
Revenues ($mn)	44 189.0	45 700.0
Bunnings Group (%)	43	43
Kmart Group (%)	25	25
Health (%)	13	13
Officeworks (%)	8	8
WesCEF (%)	6	6
EBIT ($mn)	3 989.0	4 186.0
EBIT margin (%)	9.0	9.2
Profit before tax ($mn)	3 587.0	3 774.0
Profit after tax ($mn)	2 557.0	2 653.0
Earnings per share (c)	225.68	233.95
Cash flow per share (c)	384.55	395.59
Dividend (c)	198	206
Percentage franked	100	100
Net tangible assets per share ($)	~	~
Interest cover (times)	9.9	10.2
Return on equity (%)	30.3	29.9
Debt-to-equity ratio (%)	45.7	44.4
Current ratio	1.1	1.2

Westpac Banking Corporation

ASX code: WBC   www.westpac.com.au

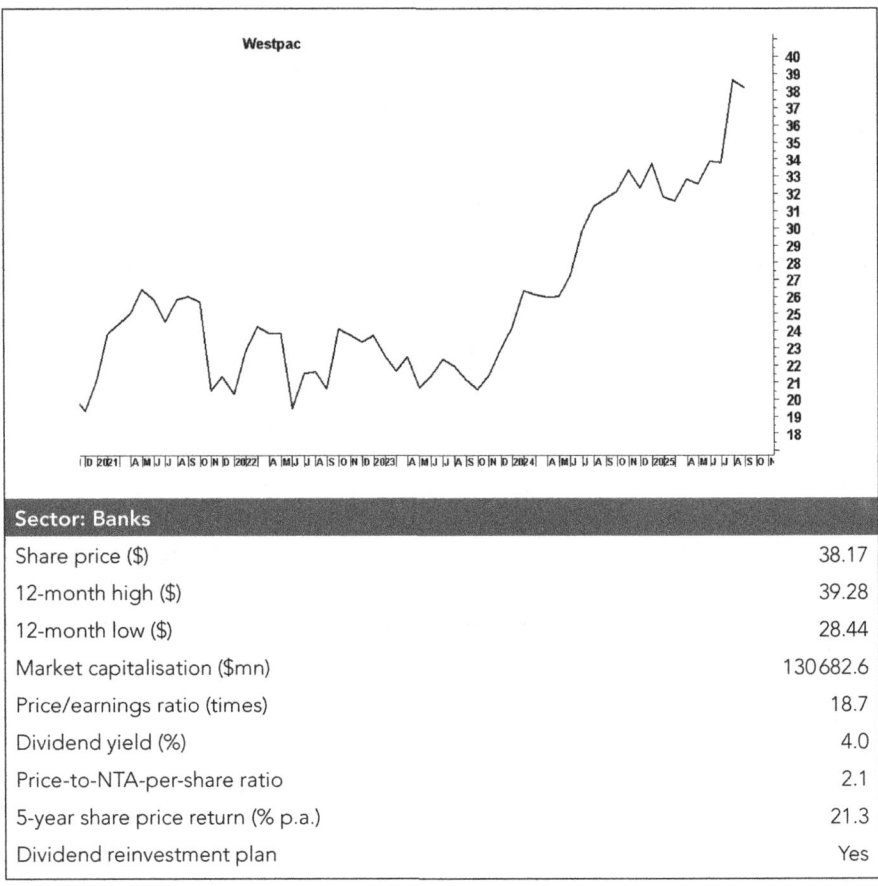

Sector: Banks	
Share price ($)	38.17
12-month high ($)	39.28
12-month low ($)	28.44
Market capitalisation ($mn)	130 682.6
Price/earnings ratio (times)	18.7
Dividend yield (%)	4.0
Price-to-NTA-per-share ratio	2.1
5-year share price return (% p.a.)	21.3
Dividend reinvestment plan	Yes

Sydney-based Westpac, which began trading in 1817 as the Bank of New South Wales, is one of Australia's big four banks, with interests in most areas of financial services. It is also one of New Zealand's leading banks and has some smaller businesses in the Pacific region. It owns St George Bank, BankSA and Bank of Melbourne. Its wealth management arm is BT and it also operates the Asgard investment advisory service and the RAMS home loans business.

Latest business results (March 2025, half year)

Profits edged down as rising operating costs more than offset growth in home, business and institutional lending volumes. Continuing strong competition in the home loans market drove down the bank's net interest margin by one basis point to 1.88 per cent. Loans increased by 5 per cent from the March 2024 half to $825 billion, with particular strength in business lending. Customer deposits rose 7 per cent to $697 billion. Of the four key divisions, the Westpac Institutional Bank business recorded higher earnings, thanks to increased underwriting activity, a larger loan book and higher sales and risk management income. However, both the Consumer and the Business and Wealth divisions saw profits down, with New Zealand also weak.

Outlook

Westpac has expressed concern that global trade patterns and supply chains that have been formed across decades are now facing significant disruption. It expects the Australian economy to continue to grow, but worries that escalating trade and geopolitical tensions could harm business confidence and consumer spending. Nevertheless, it forecasts continuing increases in demand for housing and business credit. In particular, it sees a growing population, the energy transition and rising demand for technology and innovation as providing a backdrop for further business investment. It is strengthening its business and institutional banking businesses, with the aim of boosting both market share and margins, and is working to cross-sell more products to its existing customer base. Its new BizEdge platform delivers faster and simpler loan decisions, and the bank is also piloting its new Business Lending Virtual Assistant powered by artificial intelligence. Its Westpac One technology for institutional clients brings together real-time treasury management, foreign exchange, trade and lending, along with powerful data insights. However, operating expenses continue to rise, due especially to the bank's $2 billion Unite program, which runs until 2028. This scheme aims to streamline Westpac's operating structure and reduce the number of its technology platforms and systems through the introduction of some 60 strategic initiatives.

Year to 30 September	2023	2024
Operating income ($mn)	21 645.0	21 588.0
Net interest income ($mn)	18 317.0	18 753.0
Operating expenses ($mn)	10 692.0	10 944.0
Profit before tax ($mn)	10 662.0	10 282.0
Profit after tax ($mn)	7 368.0	7 113.0
Earnings per share (c)	210.39	204.63
Dividend (c)	142	151
Percentage franked	100	100
Non-interest income to total income (%)	15.4	13.1
Cost-to-income ratio (%)	49.4	50.7
Return on equity (%)	10.3	10.0
Return on assets (%)	0.7	0.7
Half year to 31 March	2024	2025
Operating income ($mn)	10 816.0	10 993.0
Profit before tax ($mn)	5 059.0	5 045.0
Profit after tax ($mn)	3 506.0	3 457.0
Earnings per share (c)	100.30	100.80
Dividend (c)	75	76
Percentage franked	100	100
Net tangible assets per share ($)	17.79	17.94

WiseTech Global Limited

ASX code: WTC   www.wisetechglobal.com

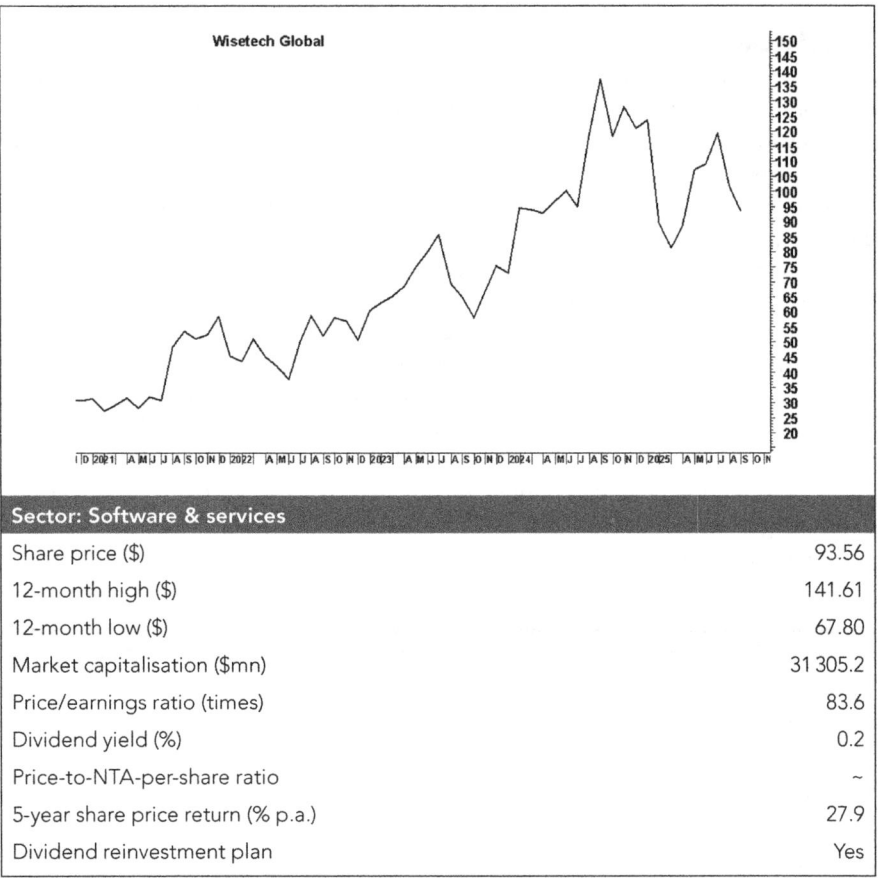

Sector: Software & services	
Share price ($)	93.56
12-month high ($)	141.61
12-month low ($)	67.80
Market capitalisation ($mn)	31 305.2
Price/earnings ratio (times)	83.6
Dividend yield (%)	0.2
Price-to-NTA-per-share ratio	~
5-year share price return (% p.a.)	27.9
Dividend reinvestment plan	Yes

Sydney-based logistics software specialist WiseTech was founded in 1994 to supply code for local freight forwarders. Today it is a global leader in international logistics software, with customers that include most of the world's largest global third-party logistics providers and global freight forwarders. It has more than 50 offices worldwide and 40 product development centres. Its flagship product CargoWise is sold in 193 countries, with more than 17 000 customers. It has become the largest technology stock on the ASX. In August 2025 it acquired trade and transportation software specialist E2open Parent Holdings.

Latest business results (June 2025, full year)

Revenues and underlying profits continued to rise strongly, with new customers and increased usage by existing customers both contributing to the good result. Acquisitions over two years added revenues of $14.9 million. Price increases designed to offset the impact of inflation also helped boost revenues and profits. Recurring revenues edged up from 97 per cent to 98 per cent of total income. The customer attrition rate remained below 1 per cent. A company-wide cost efficiency program achieved US$40 million in annual savings. The research and development expense rose 9 per cent to US$263.8 million, with the product design and development budget up 10 per cent to US$185.3 million. Note that WiseTech now reports its results in US dollars. The Australian dollar figures in this book have been converted at prevailing exchange rates.

Outlook

WiseTech's strategy is to target the 25 leading global freight forwarders and the 200 leading global logistics providers, and it benefits as these companies consolidate and increasingly dominate their industries. It says its focus is on growth through six key development priorities — landside container haulage logistics, warehousing, Neo (the company's global integrated platform for consumers of logistics services), digital documents, customs and compliance, and international eCommerce. It expects that embedding artificial intelligence technology at the core of its CargoWise software will substantially streamline usability. It continues to seek out new markets. WiseTech is set to be radically changed by its $3.2 billion acquisition of US company E2open, by far its largest-ever acquisition. E2open sells logistics software to manufacturers, retailers and distributors. This makes it complementary to WiseTech, which specialises in software sales to freight companies, and the company expects it to deliver annual synergies of some US$50 million. Thanks to the acquisition, WiseTech's early June 2026 forecast is for revenue growth of 79 per cent to 85 per cent, with EBITDA growth of 44 per cent to 53 per cent.

Year to 30 June	2024	2025
Revenues ($mn)	1035.9	1198.0
EBIT ($mn)	408.8	527.8
EBIT margin (%)	39.5	44.1
Profit before tax ($mn)	392.0	516.6
Profit after tax ($mn)	281.7	372.0
Earnings per share (c)	85.10	111.98
Cash flow per share (c)	119.81	154.40
Dividend (c)	16.9	22.15
Percentage franked	100	100
Net tangible assets per share ($)	~	~
Interest cover (times)	24.3	47.0
Return on equity (%)	13.7	15.5
Debt-to-equity ratio (%)	~	~
Current ratio	1.0	1.2

XRF Scientific Limited

ASX code: XRF — www.xrfscientific.com

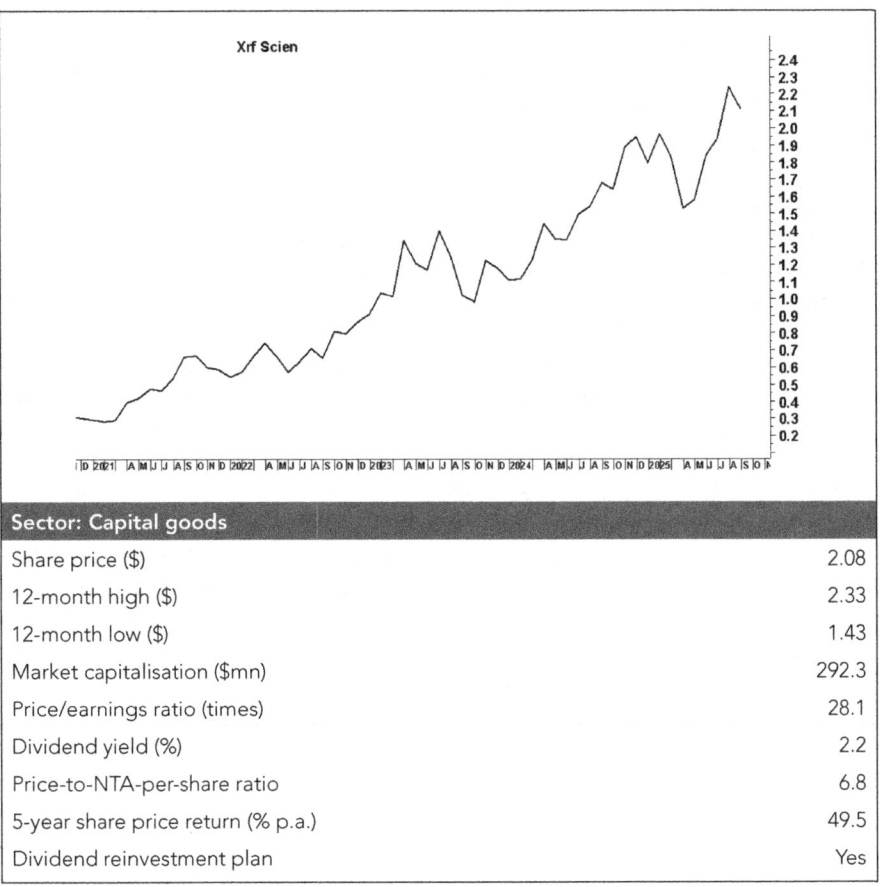

Xrf Scien

Sector: Capital goods	
Share price ($)	2.08
12-month high ($)	2.33
12-month low ($)	1.43
Market capitalisation ($mn)	292.3
Price/earnings ratio (times)	28.1
Dividend yield (%)	2.2
Price-to-NTA-per-share ratio	6.8
5-year share price return (% p.a.)	49.5
Dividend reinvestment plan	Yes

Perth company XRF Scientific has roots that extend back to 1972, when the founding director began producing flux materials for XRF (X-ray fluorescence) analysis. It has since grown into a prominent global supplier of precision scientific testing equipment and chemicals for the purpose of preparing samples for analysis. The company has manufacturing, sales and support facilities in Australia, Canada, Belgium and Germany, and a global network of distributors.

Latest business results (June 2025, full year)

Revenues marked time but profits rose, driven by a strong performance from the company's consumables activities, along with a focus on cost control and productivity improvements. The Consumables division, responsible for the manufacture of chemicals and other supplies essential for analytical laboratories, was a beneficiary of continuing demand from the mining sector, with sales up just 2 per cent but pre-tax profit jumping 26 per cent. The Capital Equipment division, which is involved in the design and manufacture of automated fusion equipment, high-temperature test and production furnaces and general laboratory equipment, saw sales generally flat for the year, and with profits down. The Precious Metals division makes products for laboratory and platinum alloy markets, catering especially to the needs of analytical laboratories. It saw sales down but with profits largely in line with the previous year, thanks in part to a recovery in the German office. About 30 per cent of total sales were abroad.

Outlook

XRF Scientific is a leader in XRF-fusion technology for measuring the composition and purity of materials. This is applied mainly in industrial quality control applications and for manufacturing processes in industries such as metals and mining, construction materials, chemicals and petrochemicals. Through this technology, businesses can improve product quality, increase productivity and yield, and reduce downtime and waste. Customers include many large multinationals, such as BHP, Rio Tinto, Glencore, Alcoa and ArcelorMittal, and XRF enjoys solid demand for its products and high profit margins. Thanks to a growing installed base of equipment, it is seeing an increasing amount of recurring revenue in the form of consumable sales. It is also achieving success in its cross-selling strategy, with customers increasingly purchasing numerous products across its range. In July 2024 XRF acquired full ownership of Orbis Mining, a manufacturer of specialised mining equipment, and this business is growing solidly, thanks especially to demand from the gold sector. XRF has many new machines in advanced stages of product development for release during the June 2026 year. It is also working to diversify into new markets overseas.

Year to 30 June	2024	2025
Revenues ($mn)	59.8	59.2
Capital equipment (%)	34	35
Consumables (%)	32	33
Precious metals (%)	34	32
EBIT ($mn)	13.8	14.8
EBIT margin (%)	23.0	25.1
Gross margin (%)	42.4	46.9
Profit before tax ($mn)	13.5	14.6
Profit after tax ($mn)	8.9	10.4
Earnings per share (c)	6.45	7.41
Cash flow per share (c)	7.59	8.62
Dividend (c)	3.9	4.5
Percentage franked	100	100
Net tangible assets per share ($)	0.28	0.31
Interest cover (times)	47.9	57.8
Return on equity (%)	17.1	18.0
Debt-to-equity ratio (%)	~	~
Current ratio	3.8	4.4

PART II
THE TABLES

Table A

Market capitalisation

A company's market capitalisation is determined by multiplying the share price by the number of shares. To be included in this book, a company must be in the All Ordinaries Index, which comprises the 500 largest companies by market capitalisation.

	$mn
Commonwealth Bank	281 103.5
BHP	211 182.8
Rio Tinto	190 522.2
National Australia Bank	131 879.2
Westpac Banking	130 682.6
Wesfarmers	105 056.9
CSL	101 321.4
Macquarie Group	84 937.3
Fortescue	58 017.2
Aristocrat Leisure	43 590.2
Brambles Industries	36 307.4
QBE Insurance	32 646.2
Coles	32 137.5
REA Group	31 922.2
WiseTech Global	31 305.2
Pro Medicus	31 154.0
Northern Star Resources	28 485.3
Suncorp	22 969.7
Computershare	21 666.4
Origin Energy	21 333.1
Insurance Australia	20 551.9
Cochlear	19 523.0
Evolution Mining	18 141.5
CAR Group	14 910.3
Medibank Private	13 990.3
JB Hi-Fi	12 682.7
Technology One	12 485.3
ASX	11 943.6
Harvey Norman	9 245.4
HUB24	8 309.6
Netwealth	7 715.7
Steadfast	6 848.0
Codan	5 586.9
AGL Energy	5 536.7
Downer EDI	4 674.2
Lovisa	4 599.1
Breville	4 548.6
Metcash	4 537.1
Super Retail	4 254.6
Pinnacle Investment	4 239.4
AUB Group	4 130.7
Ramelius Resources	3 975.3
New Hope	3 770.2
Premier Investments	3 624.8
NIB Holdings	3 589.3
ARB	3 288.3
Reliance Worldwide	3 163.8
Beach Energy	2 760.4

Nine Entertainment	2 711.7
Iluka Resources	2 711.2
Perpetual	2 233.2
Monadelphous	2 085.4
Nick Scali	2 063.0
NRW Holdings	1 980.4
Objective Corp.	1 979.7
Magellan Financial	1 776.5
Mader	1 707.9
Helia	1 570.0
Supply Network	1 541.9
IDP Education	1 536.4
Data#3	1 420.5
Amotiv	1 330.9
Collins Foods	1 223.6
Ridley Corp.	1 184.5
Smartgroup	1 181.6
Hansen Technologies	1 169.4
IPH	1 149.0
Credit Corp	1 116.3
Ricegrowers	975.1
Macmahon	938.6
GenusPlus	933.4
PWR Holdings	826.6
Accent Group	823.6
Australian Ethical Investment	807.5
Beacon Lighting	770.6
Jumbo Interactive	703.3
GR Engineering	691.2
GWA	686.9
Servcorp	670.8
Universal Store	657.5
Cedar Woods Properties	627.1
Clinuvel Pharmaceuticals	565.4
Southern Cross Electrical	515.6
Lycopodium	476.3
Adairs	459.5
Ive Group	437.9
Duratec	431.6
Fiducian	394.0
Horizon Oil	357.6
XRF Scientific	292.3
Schaffer	291.7
Monash IVF	272.7
Bisalloy Steel	261.6
Lindsay Australia	215.7
Shaver Shop	197.8
Capral	175.0
Cosol	112.8

Table B

Revenues

This list ranks the companies in the book according to their most recent full-year revenues figures (operating income for the banks). The figures include revenues from sales and services, but other revenues — such as interest receipts and investment income — are not generally included.

	$mn
Rio Tinto	81 300.0
BHP	78 864.6
Wesfarmers	45 700.0
Coles	44 352.0
QBE Insurance	38 157.6
Commonwealth Bank	28 290.0
CSL	23 935.4
Fortescue	23 909.2
Westpac Banking	21 588.0
National Australia Bank	20 646.0
Suncorp	17 355.0
Metcash	17 323.0
Origin Energy	17 224.0
Insurance Australia	17 221.0
Macquarie Group	17 208.0
AGL Energy	14 393.0
JB Hi-Fi	10 554.8
Downer EDI	10 481.5
Brambles Industries	10 261.1
Medibank Private	8 604.0
Aristocrat Leisure	6 603.6
Northern Star Resources	6 414.9
Computershare	4 715.7
Harvey Norman	4 465.3
Evolution Mining	4 351.5
Super Retail	4 070.1
NIB Holdings	3 631.3
NRW Holdings	3 267.7
Nine Entertainment	2 693.3
Macmahon	2 427.5
Cochlear	2 343.1
Monadelphous	2 162.6
Beach Energy	2 106.0
Reliance Worldwide	2 022.6
Ricegrowers	1 844.6
Steadfast	1 825.7
New Hope	1 802.2
Breville	1 696.6
REA Group	1 640.8
Premier Investments	1 595.3
Collins Foods	1 519.5
Accent Group	1 476.3
Perpetual	1 390.5
Ridley Corp.	1 302.6
Ramelius Resources	1 203.4
WiseTech Global	1 198.0
CAR Group	1 183.9
Iluka Resources	1 170.3

AUB Group	1 111.6
ASX	1 107.2
Amotiv	997.4
Ive Group	959.2
IDP Education	882.2
Mader	872.2
Data#3	852.7
Lindsay Australia	849.8
Southern Cross Electrical	801.5
Lovisa	798.1
GenusPlus	751.3
ARB	729.9
IPH	706.2
Codan	674.2
Capral	649.7
Adairs	618.1
Duratec	573.0
Credit Corp	545.6
Helia	532.7
Technology One	506.5
Nick Scali	495.3
GR Engineering	479.0
Cedar Woods Properties	465.9
GWA	418.5
HUB24	400.4
Hansen Technologies	392.5
Supply Network	348.8
Lycopodium	333.9
Universal Store	333.3
Servcorp	332.9
Beacon Lighting	328.9
Netwealth	316.4
Smartgroup	305.8
Monash IVF	271.9
Magellan Financial	247.3
Schaffer	218.8
Shaver Shop	218.6
Pro Medicus	213.0
Pinnacle Investment	195.2
Horizon Oil	162.0
Bisalloy Steel	152.8
Jumbo Interactive	145.3
PWR Holdings	130.1
Objective Corp.	123.5
Australian Ethical Investment	119.4
Cosol	116.8
Clinuvel Pharmaceuticals	95.0
Fiducian	87.6
XRF Scientific	59.2

Table C

Year-on-year revenues growth

Companies generally strive for growth, though profit growth is usually of more significance than a boost in revenues. In fact, it is possible for a company to increase its revenues by all kinds of means — including cutting profit margins or acquiring other companies — and year-on-year revenues growth is of little relevance if other ratios are not also improving. The figures used for this calculation are the latest full-year figures.

	%
Southern Cross Electrical	45.2
Pinnacle Investment	39.6
Ramelius Resources	36.3
GenusPlus	36.3
Evolution Mining	35.3
Pro Medicus	31.9
Northern Star Resources	30.4
Netwealth	26.8
HUB24	23.8
Codan	22.5
Smartgroup	21.6
Cedar Woods Properties	20.6
Macmahon	19.5
Australian Ethical Investment	18.8
Technology One	18.0
IPH	16.6
WiseTech Global	15.6
Universal Store	15.5
Suncorp	15.4
Supply Network	15.3
REA Group	14.7
Cosol	14.6
Lovisa	14.2
Beach Energy	13.3
GR Engineering	13.0
Mader	12.6
NRW Holdings	12.2
Hansen Technologies	11.2
Breville	10.9
Servcorp	10.7
Fiducian	10.5
AUB Group	10.1
JB Hi-Fi	10.0
Steadfast	8.9
Metcash	8.9
Harvey Norman	8.6
NIB Holdings	7.8
Clinuvel Pharmaceuticals	7.8
CAR Group	7.7
Monadelphous	7.3
Reliance Worldwide	7.2
ASX	7.0
Insurance Australia	6.8
CSL	6.7
Origin Energy	6.7
Computershare	6.7
Monash IVF	6.7
AGL Energy	6.0

Data#3	5.8
Nick Scali	5.8
Lindsay Australia	5.6
ARB	5.3
Medibank Private	5.2
Objective Corp.	5.1
Commonwealth Bank	5.1
Credit Corp	5.0
Aristocrat Leisure	4.9
Cochlear	4.8
Super Retail	4.5
Adairs	4.0
Brambles Industries	3.5
Wesfarmers	3.4
Ridley Corp.	3.1
Duratec	3.1
Perpetual	2.4
Nine Entertainment	2.4
Collins Foods	2.1
Accent Group	1.9
Macquarie Group	1.9
Beacon Lighting	1.8
Coles	1.8
QBE Insurance	1.7
Schaffer	1.2
GWA	1.2
Amotiv	1.0
Bisalloy Steel	0.0
National Australia Bank	0.0
Westpac Banking	−0.3
Shaver Shop	−0.4
Rio Tinto	−0.7
XRF Scientific	−1.1
Capral	−1.1
Ive Group	−1.4
Ricegrowers	−1.6
Premier Investments	−2.9
Lycopodium	−3.1
Horizon Oil	−4.1
Downer EDI	−4.5
BHP	−6.5
PWR Holdings	−6.7
Jumbo Interactive	−8.8
Iluka Resources	−9.3
Magellan Financial	−11.1
Helia	−11.3
Fortescue	−13.4
IDP Education	−14.9
New Hope	−34.6

Table D
EBIT margin

A company's earnings before interest and taxation (EBIT) is sometimes regarded as a better measure of its profitability than the straight pre-tax or post-tax profit figure. EBIT is derived by adding interest payments to the pre-tax profit. Different companies choose different methods of financing their operations; by adding back interest payments to their profits we can help minimise these differences and make comparisons between companies more valid.

The EBIT margin is the EBIT figure as a percentage of annual sales. Clearly a high figure is to be desired, though of course this can be achieved artificially by inflating borrowings (and hence interest payments). And it is noteworthy that efficient companies with strong cashflow like some of the retailers can operate most satisfactorily on low margins.

The EBIT margin figure has little relevance for banks, and they have been excluded.

	%
Magellan Financial	88.4
Pinnacle Investment	77.8
Pro Medicus	76.7
ASX	67.0
Helia	65.4
Ramelius Resources	56.2
Clinuvel Pharmaceuticals	54.3
Netwealth	49.8
REA Group	49.8
CAR Group	48.5
WiseTech Global	44.1
BHP	41.7
Jumbo Interactive	39.8
New Hope	39.4
Smartgroup	35.8
Fortescue	34.5
Evolution Mining	34.1
Objective Corp.	34.0
AUB Group	33.8
Fiducian	33.1
Beach Energy	32.9
Northern Star Resources	32.5
HUB24	32.2
Credit Corp	31.1
Technology One	30.7
Rio Tinto	30.5
Steadfast	29.8
Computershare	29.6
Australian Ethical Investment	28.8
Aristocrat Leisure	28.6

Iluka Resources	28.6
CSL	26.8
Perpetual	25.2
XRF Scientific	25.1
Servcorp	25.0
Premier Investments	24.1
Cochlear	22.6
Nick Scali	22.1
Codan	21.7
Horizon Oil	21.5
Brambles Industries	20.6
Schaffer	19.7
IPH	19.6
Harvey Norman	19.5
Bisalloy Steel	18.8
ARB	18.8
Lycopodium	18.5
GWA	18.2
Cedar Woods Properties	18.0
Lovisa	17.4
Amotiv	17.1
Supply Network	16.9
Universal Store	16.7
Monash IVF	16.6
Reliance Worldwide	16.0
Beacon Lighting	15.5
Hansen Technologies	14.1
Insurance Australia	14.0
Suncorp	13.9
IDP Education	13.8
PWR Holdings	13.6
Nine Entertainment	12.7

Breville	12.2
Origin Energy	11.3
Cosol	11.0
GR Engineering	11.0
Adairs	10.8
Shaver Shop	10.3
QBE Insurance	10.0
Super Retail	9.8
Ive Group	9.8
Mader	9.6
Wesfarmers	9.2
Medibank Private	8.6
AGL Energy	8.5
Data#3	8.2
NIB Holdings	7.7
Accent Group	7.6
Collins Foods	7.5
GenusPlus	7.3
Macmahon	7.2
JB Hi-Fi	6.7
NRW Holdings	6.5
Ricegrowers	6.3
Southern Cross Electrical	6.1
Duratec	5.7
Monadelphous	5.7
Lindsay Australia	5.5
Capral	5.3
Ridley Corp.	5.3
Coles	4.9
Downer EDI	4.5
Metcash	2.9

Table E
Year-on-year EBIT margin growth

The EBIT (earnings before interest and taxation) margin is one of the measures of a company's efficiency. A rising margin is much to be desired, as it suggests that a company is achieving success in cutting its costs. This table does not include banks.

	%
Ramelius Resources	78.9
Northern Star Resources	53.5
Suncorp	36.5
GenusPlus	35.9
Insurance Australia	34.4
Downer EDI	33.4
Evolution Mining	28.3
Hansen Technologies	23.5
Harvey Norman	22.8
Bisalloy Steel	21.1
Monadelphous	19.7
QBE Insurance	19.7
Ive Group	17.1
Magellan Financial	16.0
Beach Energy	15.5
HUB24	15.0
Credit Corp	13.8
Ricegrowers	11.9
Rio Tinto	11.8
WiseTech Global	11.7
Pinnacle Investment	11.3
Australian Ethical Investment	10.1
XRF Scientific	9.2
Fiducian	8.8
Servcorp	6.8
Brambles Industries	6.5
Pro Medicus	6.3
Data#3	4.9
Codan	4.7
Steadfast	4.2
Computershare	4.1
GWA	3.5
Supply Network	3.3
CSL	3.1
Shaver Shop	2.8
Netwealth	2.8
Macmahon	2.4
Cochlear	2.3
Objective Corp.	2.3
Cedar Woods Properties	2.2
REA Group	2.2
CAR Group	1.6
Wesfarmers	1.5
Coles	0.5
Duratec	0.4
Amotiv	0.3

ASX	−0.1
Technology One	−0.1
Mader	−0.2
AUB Group	−0.3
Universal Store	−0.4
GR Engineering	−0.5
Premier Investments	−0.7
Breville	−1.1
Jumbo Interactive	−1.1
Aristocrat Leisure	−1.2
Smartgroup	−1.2
Ridley Corp.	−1.5
Medibank Private	−2.0
Accent Group	−2.1
Monash IVF	−2.2
JB Hi-Fi	−2.6
Beacon Lighting	−3.3
Perpetual	−3.4
NRW Holdings	−4.1
Adairs	−4.2
Southern Cross Electrical	−4.2
Super Retail	−4.5
Helia	−4.7
Lovisa	−5.2
Clinuvel Pharmaceuticals	−5.6
Metcash	−5.7
BHP	−6.7
NIB Holdings	−6.8
Reliance Worldwide	−7.1
Collins Foods	−8.2
Schaffer	−8.5
Origin Energy	−8.5
ARB	−8.9
Capral	−9.6
Lycopodium	−9.7
Nine Entertainment	−9.8
IPH	−13.0
Cosol	−16.7
AGL Energy	−21.7
Nick Scali	−22.1
Iluka Resources	−22.9
Lindsay Australia	−24.1
Fortescue	−27.6
New Hope	−30.4
IDP Education	−41.0
Horizon Oil	−43.1
PWR Holdings	−46.5

Table F
After-tax profit

This table ranks all the companies according to their most recent full-year after-tax profit.

	$mn
Rio Tinto	17 503.0
BHP	15 626.2
Commonwealth Bank	10 252.0
Westpac Banking	7 113.0
National Australia Bank	7 102.0
Fortescue	5 189.2
CSL	4 618.5
Macquarie Group	3 715.0
QBE Insurance	2 695.5
Wesfarmers	2 653.0
Suncorp	1 823.0
Origin Energy	1 490.0
Insurance Australia	1 359.0
Northern Star Resources	1 339.7
Brambles Industries	1 329.5
Aristocrat Leisure	1 303.4
Coles	1 181.0
Evolution Mining	958.2
Computershare	931.7
AGL Energy	640.0
REA Group	564.4
Harvey Norman	518.0
ASX	510.0
Medibank Private	500.8
New Hope	475.9
Ramelius Resources	474.2
JB Hi-Fi	462.4
Beach Energy	450.5
Cochlear	388.9
CAR Group	377.0
WiseTech Global	372.0
Steadfast	295.5
Metcash	275.5
Downer EDI	264.7
Premier Investments	257.9
Super Retail	232.4
Iluka Resources	231.3
Reliance Worldwide	227.2
Helia	220.9
Perpetual	204.1
AUB Group	200.2
NIB Holdings	194.3
Nine Entertainment	166.1
Magellan Financial	159.7
Breville	135.9
Pinnacle Investment	134.4
NRW Holdings	127.2
Technology One	118.0

Netwealth	116.5
Pro Medicus	115.2
Codan	103.5
Amotiv	103.4
Macmahon	102.4
HUB24	97.8
ARB	97.5
Credit Corp	94.1
Lovisa	86.3
Monadelphous	83.7
IPH	82.0
Smartgroup	72.4
Ricegrowers	68.4
IDP Education	64.7
Servcorp	64.4
Nick Scali	62.0
Accent Group	57.7
Mader	57.1
Ive Group	52.1
Collins Foods	51.1
Data#3	48.2
Cedar Woods Properties	48.1
GWA	46.5
Ridley Corp.	43.3
Lycopodium	42.2
Jumbo Interactive	40.2
Supply Network	40.0
Hansen Technologies	39.6
Clinuvel Pharmaceuticals	36.2
Objective Corp.	35.4
GenusPlus	35.4
Universal Store	34.8
GR Engineering	34.2
Adairs	34.0
Capral	32.5
Southern Cross Electrical	31.7
Beacon Lighting	29.4
Monash IVF	26.7
Schaffer	24.3
Australian Ethical Investment	23.8
Duratec	22.8
Lindsay Australia	22.3
Fiducian	21.0
Bisalloy Steel	19.6
Horizon Oil	18.8
Shaver Shop	14.9
PWR Holdings	12.4
XRF Scientific	10.4
Cosol	7.9

Table G
Year-on-year earnings per share growth

The earnings per share (EPS) figure is a crucial one. It tells you — the shareholder — what your part is of the company's profits, for each of your shares. So investors invariably look for EPS growth in a stock. The year-on-year EPS growth figure is often one of the first ratios that investors look to when evaluating a stock. The figures used for this calculation are the latest full-year figures.

	%
Ramelius Resources	127.7
Northern Star Resources	102.6
Evolution Mining	91.5
GenusPlus	82.2
Insurance Australia	54.1
Hansen Technologies	52.0
Suncorp	51.9
Harvey Norman	47.0
HUB24	44.5
Southern Cross Electrical	43.8
Netwealth	39.4
Pro Medicus	39.1
Pinnacle Investment	38.0
Downer EDI	36.4
Monadelphous	32.7
Beach Energy	32.0
WiseTech Global	31.6
QBE Insurance	30.3
Australian Ethical Investment	29.0
Computershare	27.2
Codan	27.0
Origin Energy	26.3
Servcorp	24.8
Bisalloy Steel	23.8
REA Group	22.6
Ive Group	20.5
Cedar Woods Properties	18.7
Fiducian	18.6
Supply Network	18.2
Credit Corp	15.9
CSL	15.1
XRF Scientific	14.9
Rio Tinto	14.7
Universal Store	14.7
Smartgroup	14.5
Technology One	14.3
Steadfast	14.2
Breville	14.2
Brambles Industries	14.0
Objective Corp.	12.9
Mader	12.5
Data#3	11.1
Macmahon	10.3
NIB Holdings	9.7
AUB Group	9.5
CAR Group	9.4
Cochlear	9.2
GR Engineering	8.2
ASX	7.4
Magellan Financial	7.3
Macquarie Group	6.5
Capral	5.9
Ricegrowers	5.6
JB Hi-Fi	5.4
Duratec	5.0
Amotiv	4.9
Commonwealth Bank	4.3
Wesfarmers	3.7
Lovisa	3.6
Reliance Worldwide	3.1
NRW Holdings	2.1
GWA	1.9
Medibank Private	1.7
Clinuvel Pharmaceuticals	1.0
Ridley Corp.	0.5
Helia	−0.1
Perpetual	−0.4
Shaver Shop	−2.3
Coles	−2.5
Westpac Banking	−2.7
Beacon Lighting	−3.3
Super Retail	−4.0
IPH	−4.1
Accent Group	−4.7
Premier Investments	−5.0
Adairs	−5.5
ARB	−5.7
Jumbo Interactive	−6.8
National Australia Bank	−7.0
Aristocrat Leisure	−8.0
Collins Foods	−8.4
Schaffer	−10.2
Nine Entertainment	−10.6
Monash IVF	−10.6
Metcash	−11.2
Cosol	−11.9
Lycopodium	−16.8
AGL Energy	−21.2
BHP	−24.6
Lindsay Australia	−27.3
Nick Scali	−27.7
Iluka Resources	−32.7
Fortescue	−39.7
PWR Holdings	−50.1
Horizon Oil	−52.3
New Hope	−55.3
IDP Education	−58.1

Table H
Return on equity

Shareholders' equity is the company's assets minus its liabilities. It is, in theory, the amount owned by the shareholders of the company. Return on equity is the after-tax profit expressed as a percentage of that equity. Thus, it is the amount of profit that the company managers made for you — the shareholder — from your assets. For many investors it is one of the most important gauges of how well a company is doing. It is one of the requirements for inclusion in this book that all companies have a return on equity of at least 10 per cent in their latest financial year.

	%
Lovisa	108.7
Netwealth	67.8
Australian Ethical Investment	67.4
Data#3	60.6
Pro Medicus	51.8
GR Engineering	50.6
Fiducian	36.6
Objective Corp.	35.7
Technology One	34.4
Duratec	34.2
Jumbo Interactive	33.9
Supply Network	33.2
REA Group	32.7
Coles	31.8
Mader	30.7
Lycopodium	30.2
Servcorp	30.1
Computershare	30.0
Wesfarmers	29.9
Ramelius Resources	29.3
JB Hi-Fi	29.1
Smartgroup	28.8
Brambles Industries	26.7
Ive Group	25.6
Bisalloy Steel	25.5
GenusPlus	25.2
Nick Scali	23.6
Universal Store	23.4
BHP	22.3
Medibank Private	21.6
Codan	21.3
Evolution Mining	21.1

Rio Tinto	20.7
Cochlear	20.5
NRW Holdings	20.1
Aristocrat Leisure	20.0
Helia	19.9
Pinnacle Investment	19.6
Insurance Australia	19.4
New Hope	18.8
HUB24	18.6
NIB Holdings	18.3
XRF Scientific	18.0
Metcash	17.5
Monadelphous	17.4
Fortescue	17.3
Super Retail	17.2
Shaver Shop	16.9
Beacon Lighting	16.9
QBE Insurance	16.8
Horizon Oil	16.7
CSL	16.6
Clinuvel Pharmaceuticals	16.3
Southern Cross Electrical	16.0
Magellan Financial	15.8
WiseTech Global	15.5
Macmahon	15.4
Origin Energy	15.4
GWA	15.3
Adairs	15.2
Capral	15.1
Suncorp	14.9
Breville	14.9
Lindsay Australia	14.6
Premier Investments	14.6

Beach Energy	13.9
ARB	13.8
Commonwealth Bank	13.5
ASX	13.4
Accent Group	12.9
CAR Group	12.9
Downer EDI	12.8
Steadfast	12.5
AUB Group	12.5
Amotiv	12.5
AGL Energy	12.4
PWR Holdings	12.3
IPH	12.3
Collins Foods	12.3
IDP Education	12.3
Perpetual	12.0
National Australia Bank	11.6
Ricegrowers	11.6
Northern Star Resources	11.3
Reliance Worldwide	11.3
Harvey Norman	11.1
Ridley Corp.	11.1
Hansen Technologies	11.0
Credit Corp	11.0
Monash IVF	11.0
Cosol	10.8
Macquarie Group	10.8
Nine Entertainment	10.5
Schaffer	10.5
Iluka Resources	10.2
Cedar Woods Properties	10.1
Westpac Banking	10.0

Table I

Year-on-year return on equity growth

Company managers have a variety of strategies they can use to boost profits. It is much harder to lift the return on equity (ROE). Find a company with a high ROE figure, and one that is growing year by year, and it is possible that you have found a real growth stock. This figure is simply the percentage change in the ROE figure from the previous year to the latest year.

	%
Suncorp	69.3
Ramelius Resources	66.1
Evolution Mining	62.8
Northern Star Resources	52.9
GenusPlus	47.8
Beach Energy	46.6
Insurance Australia	44.0
Hansen Technologies	43.6
HUB24	41.6
Harvey Norman	41.1
Downer EDI	38.1
Southern Cross Electrical	36.3
Monadelphous	26.2
Computershare	24.3
Origin Energy	19.3
Perpetual	18.6
Ive Group	15.5
Bisalloy Steel	13.9
Amotiv	13.9
QBE Insurance	13.8
WiseTech Global	12.9
Servcorp	12.3
Codan	11.8
Universal Store	11.8
Cedar Woods Properties	11.6
CAR Group	11.3
Smartgroup	10.5
Credit Corp	9.7
Fiducian	9.0
Netwealth	8.8
Steadfast	8.4
REA Group	6.7
XRF Scientific	5.8
Lovisa	5.7
Brambles Industries	5.1
Rio Tinto	4.9
Macmahon	4.4
CSL	4.3
ASX	4.3
NIB Holdings	4.1
Australian Ethical Investment	4.0
Magellan Financial	3.3
Cochlear	3.2
NRW Holdings	2.8
GR Engineering	2.3
GWA	2.3
Pro Medicus	2.2
Macquarie Group	2.1

AUB Group	2.0
Breville	1.8
Ricegrowers	1.6
Data#3	0.2
Medibank Private	−0.3
Commonwealth Bank	−0.7
JB Hi-Fi	−1.2
Wesfarmers	−1.5
Super Retail	−2.4
Westpac Banking	−3.0
Shaver Shop	−3.9
Reliance Worldwide	−4.0
IPH	−4.4
Pinnacle Investment	−4.9
Objective Corp.	−5.5
Monash IVF	−5.7
Helia	−5.8
Capral	−6.4
Accent Group	−6.8
Premier Investments	−8.0
Coles	−8.3
Technology One	−8.7
Adairs	−9.1
Supply Network	−9.1
Nine Entertainment	−9.2
National Australia Bank	−10.0
Collins Foods	−10.5
Beacon Lighting	−11.8
Aristocrat Leisure	−12.1
Mader	−14.8
ARB	−15.0
Schaffer	−15.8
Jumbo Interactive	−15.8
Clinuvel Pharmaceuticals	−15.9
Duratec	−16.0
Ridley Corp.	−16.3
AGL Energy	−19.2
Metcash	−19.6
BHP	−27.1
Lycopodium	−27.8
Cosol	−29.0
Lindsay Australia	−33.3
Nick Scali	−36.9
Iluka Resources	−39.4
Horizon Oil	−42.1
Fortescue	−42.8
PWR Holdings	−53.1
New Hope	−58.2
IDP Education	−58.7

Table J

Debt-to-equity ratio

A company's borrowings as a percentage of its shareholders' equity is one of the most common measures of corporate debt. Many investors will be wary of a company with a ratio that is too high. However, a company with a steady business and a regular income flow — such as an electric power company or a large supermarket chain — is generally considered relatively safe with a high level of debt, whereas a small company in a new business field might be thought at risk with even moderate debt levels. Much depends on surrounding circumstances, including the prevailing interest rates. Of course, it is often from borrowing that a company grows, and some investors are not happy buying shares in a company with little or no debt.

There are various ways to calculate the ratio, but for this book the net debt position is used. That is, a company's cash has been deducted from its borrowings. For inclusion in this book no company was allowed a debt-to-equity ratio of more than 70 per cent. Some of the companies had no net debt — their cash position was greater than the amount of their borrowings, or they had no borrowings at all — and so have been assigned a zero figure in this table. The ratio has no relevance for banks, and they have been excluded.

	%
ARB	0.0
ASX	0.0
Australian Ethical Investment	0.0
Beacon Lighting	0.0
Bisalloy Steel	0.0
Breville	0.0
Capral	0.0
Clinuvel Pharmaceuticals	0.0
Cochlear	0.0
Data#3	0.0
Duratec	0.0
Fiducian	0.0
GenusPlus	0.0
GR Engineering	0.0
Helia	0.0
Horizon Oil	0.0
HUB24	0.0
JB Hi-Fi	0.0
Jumbo Interactive	0.0
Lycopodium	0.0
Magellan Financial	0.0
Medibank Private	0.0
Monadelphous	0.0
Netwealth	0.0
New Hope	0.0
Nick Scali	0.0
Northern Star Resources	0.0
Objective Corp.	0.0
Premier Investments	0.0
Pro Medicus	0.0

Ramelius Resources	0.0
REA Group	0.0
Ridley Corp.	0.0
Servcorp	0.0
Shaver Shop	0.0
Southern Cross Electrical	0.0
Super Retail	0.0
Supply Network	0.0
Technology One	0.0
Universal Store	0.0
WiseTech Global	0.0
XRF Scientific	0.0
Lindsay Australia	3.2
Mader	3.9
NIB Holdings	4.3
Hansen Technologies	4.5
Fortescue	5.6
Aristocrat Leisure	5.9
PWR Holdings	8.0
Pinnacle Investment	8.0
Suncorp	11.0
Downer EDI	11.2
Beach Energy	11.6
Harvey Norman	13.6
QBE Insurance	14.3
Codan	14.9
NRW Holdings	16.1
Smartgroup	16.9
Schaffer	17.2
Evolution Mining	19.4
Iluka Resources	20.5

Rio Tinto	21.0
Accent Group	21.1
Macmahon	23.5
Reliance Worldwide	23.7
Insurance Australia	23.8
BHP	24.1
Computershare	24.5
Cedar Woods Properties	25.7
Cosol	25.7
GWA	27.7
AUB Group	28.6
Adairs	30.0
IDP Education	30.9
Ricegrowers	31.3
Nine Entertainment	32.8
Coles	33.6
Collins Foods	34.1
Metcash	35.3
CAR Group	35.4
Monash IVF	35.6
Perpetual	38.4
Credit Corp	38.7
CSL	43.6
Lovisa	43.8
Wesfarmers	44.4
Origin Energy	47.2
Steadfast	49.9
Brambles Industries	50.3
IPH	50.7
Ive Group	51.7
Amotiv	52.8
AGL Energy	61.5

Table K
Current ratio

The current ratio is simply the company's current assets divided by its current liabilities. Current assets are cash or assets that can, in theory, be converted quickly into cash. Current liabilities are normally those payable within a year. The current ratio helps measure the ability of a company to repay in a hurry its short-term debt, should the need arise. Banks and insurance companies are not included.

Pinnacle Investment	18.3	Objective Corp.	1.6
Clinuvel Pharmaceuticals	9.7	Evolution Mining	1.5
Credit Corp	6.9	Rio Tinto	1.5
Pro Medicus	6.5	Cosol	1.5
Netwealth	4.8	Ricegrowers	1.5
XRF Scientific	4.4	BHP	1.5
ARB	4.1	Perpetual	1.4
Ramelius Resources	4.1	Steadfast	1.4
Iluka Resources	3.8	IDP Education	1.4
Fiducian	3.2	Harvey Norman	1.4
Supply Network	3.1	Ive Group	1.4
Magellan Financial	3.0	Ridley Corp.	1.3
Reliance Worldwide	2.7	Technology One	1.2
IPH	2.7	Duratec	1.2
Lycopodium	2.6	Shaver Shop	1.2
CSL	2.5	GR Engineering	1.2
Fortescue	2.4	Wesfarmers	1.2
Jumbo Interactive	2.4	GenusPlus	1.2
Cochlear	2.4	WiseTech Global	1.2
Amotiv	2.3	JB Hi-Fi	1.2
Horizon Oil	2.3	Macmahon	1.2
New Hope	2.3	Origin Energy	1.2
Bisalloy Steel	2.2	Southern Cross Electrical	1.1
NIB Holdings	2.2	AUB Group	1.1
Computershare	2.2	ASX	1.1
Breville	2.2	NRW Holdings	1.1
PWR Holdings	2.1	Accent Group	1.1
REA Group	2.1	Data#3	1.1
Schaffer	2.0	Smartgroup	1.1
Australian Ethical Investment	2.0	Super Retail	1.1
HUB24	1.9	Premier Investments	1.1
Medibank Private	1.9	Metcash	1.0
Capral	1.9	Nick Scali	1.0
Mader	1.9	Nine Entertainment	1.0
Northern Star Resources	1.8	AGL Energy	0.9
Aristocrat Leisure	1.8	Downer EDI	0.9
CAR Group	1.8	Servcorp	0.9
Beacon Lighting	1.7	Adairs	0.8
Codan	1.7	Lovisa	0.8
Cedar Woods Properties	1.6	Universal Store	0.8
Hansen Technologies	1.6	Beach Energy	0.7
Monadelphous	1.6	Monash IVF	0.7
GWA	1.6	Brambles Industries	0.7
Lindsay Australia	1.6	Collins Foods	0.6
		Coles	0.6

Table L

Price/earnings ratio

The price/earnings ratio (PER) — the current share price divided by the earnings per share figure — is one of the best known of all sharemarket ratios. Essentially it expresses the amount of money investors are ready to pay for each cent or dollar of a company's profits, and it allows you to compare the share prices of different companies of varying sizes and with widely different profits. A high PER suggests the market has a high regard for the company and its growth prospects; a low one may mean that investors are disdainful of the stock. The figures in this table are based on share prices as of 5 September 2025.

Company	PER	Company	PER	Company	PER
Capral	5.6	Ricegrowers	14.6	Collins Foods	23.9
Beach Energy	6.1	GWA	14.8	Monadelphous	24.8
Helia	7.5	Insurance Australia	15.1	Beacon Lighting	26.1
New Hope	7.9	NRW Holdings	15.5	GenusPlus	26.2
Ramelius Resources	8.3	Clinuvel Pharmaceuticals	15.6	Coles	27.1
Ive Group	8.4			JB Hi-Fi	27.4
AGL Energy	8.7	Southern Cross Electrical	16.3	Commonwealth Bank	27.4
Macmahon	9.1	Nine Entertainment	16.3	Brambles Industries	27.6
Lindsay Australia	9.6	Smartgroup	16.3	Medibank Private	27.9
Monash IVF	10.2	Metcash	16.4	XRF Scientific	28.1
Servcorp	10.4	Jumbo Interactive	17.6	Data#3	29.5
Rio Tinto	10.9	Downer EDI	17.6	Hansen Technologies	29.6
Perpetual	10.9	Northern Star Resources	17.7	Mader	29.8
Fortescue	11.2			Pinnacle Investment	30.4
Magellan Financial	11.5	Harvey Norman	17.8	Nick Scali	33.2
Lycopodium	11.5	Super Retail	18.3	Australian Ethical Investment	33.4
Iluka Resources	11.7	NIB Holdings	18.4		
Credit Corp	11.9	Westpac Banking	18.7	Breville	33.5
Schaffer	12.0	Fiducian	18.7	ARB	33.6
QBE Insurance	12.0	Duratec	18.8	Aristocrat Leisure	34.0
Suncorp	12.6	Evolution Mining	18.8	Supply Network	38.2
Cedar Woods Properties	13.0	National Australia Bank	18.8	CAR Group	39.5
Shaver Shop	13.2	Universal Store	18.9	Wesfarmers	39.6
Amotiv	13.2	Horizon Oil	19.0	Cochlear	50.2
Bisalloy Steel	13.3	GR Engineering	20.2	Lovisa	53.2
Adairs	13.4	AUB Group	20.6	Codan	53.9
BHP	13.5	Macquarie Group	21.8	Objective Corp.	55.7
Accent Group	13.5	CSL	21.9	REA Group	56.5
Reliance Worldwide	14.0	Steadfast	23.1	Netwealth	66.1
Premier Investments	14.0	ASX	23.4	PWR Holdings	66.7
Cosol	14.1	Ridley Corp.	23.5	WiseTech Global	83.6
IPH	14.3	Computershare	23.6	HUB24	85.2
Origin Energy	14.3	IDP Education	23.7	Technology One	105.2
				Pro Medicus	270.4

Table M
Price-to-NTA-per-share ratio

The NTA-per-share figure expresses the worth of a company's net tangible assets — that is, its assets minus its liabilities and intangible assets — for each share of the company. Intangible assets, such as goodwill or the value of newspaper mastheads, are excluded because it is deemed difficult to place a value on them (though this proposition is debatable), and also because they might not have much worth if separated from the company. The price-to-NTA-per-share ratio relates this figure to the share price.

A ratio of one means that the company is valued exactly according to the value of its assets. A ratio below one suggests that the shares are a bargain, though usually there is a good reason for this. Profits are more important than assets.

In some respects, this is an 'old economy' ratio. For many high-tech companies in the 'new economy' the most important assets are human ones whose worth does not appear on the balance sheet.

Companies with a negative NTA-per-share figure, as a result of having intangible assets valued at more than their net assets, have been omitted from this table.

Company	Ratio	Company	Ratio
Beach Energy	0.9	NRW Holdings	5.5
Capral	1.0	NIB Holdings	6.0
Iluka Resources	1.1	Insurance Australia	6.6
Cedar Woods Properties	1.3	XRF Scientific	6.8
Credit Corp	1.3	Medibank Private	7.6
Schaffer	1.4	Mader	8.3
New Hope	1.5	Duratec	9.0
Macmahon	1.5	Breville	9.7
Helia	1.6	PWR Holdings	9.7
Fortescue	2.0	ASX	10.5
Northern Star Resources	2.0	Brambles Industries	10.5
Magellan Financial	2.0	Premier Investments	11.2
Ricegrowers	2.0	Fiducian	12.6
Ramelius Resources	2.1	Southern Cross Electrical	14.7
Westpac Banking	2.1	Supply Network	15.2
National Australia Bank	2.3	Cochlear	15.7
Clinuvel Pharmaceuticals	2.4	Jumbo Interactive	17.3
Rio Tinto	2.5	GenusPlus	17.5
QBE Insurance	2.5	Beacon Lighting	20.6
Macquarie Group	2.6	GR Engineering	21.4
Harvey Norman	2.7	Reliance Worldwide	23.3
Origin Energy	2.9	Aristocrat Leisure	24.8
BHP	3.0	Australian Ethical Investment	25.4
Bisalloy Steel	3.2	Data#3	25.7
Ridley Corp.	3.5	REA Group	34.4
Lycopodium	3.6	Codan	36.9
Horizon Oil	3.6	Shaver Shop	37.5
Evolution Mining	3.7	CSL	39.7
AGL Energy	3.7	Netwealth	47.9
Commonwealth Bank	4.0	Objective Corp.	66.2
Suncorp	4.0	HUB24	114.5
Monadelphous	4.3	Pro Medicus	133.1
Pinnacle Investment	4.7	Technology One	146.7
ARB	5.0		

Table N
Dividend yield

Many investors buy shares for income, rather than for capital growth. They look for companies that offer a high dividend yield (the dividend expressed as a percentage of the share price). Table N ranks the companies in this book according to their historic dividend yields. Note that the franking credits available from most companies in this book can make the dividend yield substantially higher. The dividend yield changes with the share price. The figures in this table are based on share prices as of 5 September 2025.

	%
Horizon Oil	13.6
New Hope	8.7
IPH	8.3
Beach Energy	7.4
Shaver Shop	6.8
Ive Group	6.3
GWA	6.0
Premier Investments	5.9
AGL Energy	5.8
Fortescue	5.8
Perpetual	5.8
Lindsay Australia	5.6
Rio Tinto	5.4
Helia	5.4
GR Engineering	5.3
Accent Group	5.1
Magellan Financial	5.1
Jumbo Interactive	4.8
Origin Energy	4.8
Universal Store	4.5
Bisalloy Steel	4.5
Metcash	4.4
Nine Entertainment	4.4
Ricegrowers	4.3
Suncorp	4.2
Schaffer	4.2
Credit Corp	4.1
Amotiv	4.1
Servcorp	4.1
Smartgroup	4.1
BHP	4.1
Adairs	4.0
QBE Insurance	4.0
Westpac Banking	4.0
NIB Holdings	3.9
National Australia Bank	3.9
Southern Cross Electrical	3.8
Cedar Woods Properties	3.8
NRW Holdings	3.8
Capral	3.8
Fiducian	3.7
Monash IVF	3.7
ASX	3.6
Downer EDI	3.6
Harvey Norman	3.6
Insurance Australia	3.6
Medibank Private	3.5
Super Retail	3.5
Cosol	3.5
Monadelphous	3.4
Macmahon	3.4
Steadfast	3.2
Pinnacle Investment	3.1
Ridley Corp.	3.1
Data#3	3.1
Macquarie Group	2.9
Commonwealth Bank	2.9
Coles	2.9
Lycopodium	2.9
Northern Star Resources	2.8
Nick Scali	2.6
AUB Group	2.6
IDP Education	2.5
Collins Foods	2.5
Duratec	2.5
Computershare	2.5
Beacon Lighting	2.4
JB Hi-Fi	2.4
Brambles Industries	2.3
Ramelius Resources	2.3
Wesfarmers	2.2
Evolution Mining	2.2
XRF Scientific	2.2
CSL	2.2
CAR Group	2.0
Supply Network	2.0
Australian Ethical Investment	2.0
Reliance Worldwide	1.9
Lovisa	1.9
ARB	1.7
Hansen Technologies	1.7
Cochlear	1.4
Iluka Resources	1.3
Netwealth	1.2
Breville	1.2
Aristocrat Leisure	1.1
Objective Corp.	1.1
Mader	1.0
REA Group	1.0
Codan	0.9
GenusPlus	0.7
Technology One	0.6
HUB24	0.5
PWR Holdings	0.5
Clinuvel Pharmaceuticals	0.4
WiseTech Global	0.2
Pro Medicus	0.2

Table O
Year-on-year dividend growth

Most investors hope for a rising dividend, and this table tells how much each company raised or lowered its dividend in its latest financial year.

	%
Evolution Mining	185.7
Beach Energy	125.0
Credit Corp	78.9
Ramelius Resources	60.0
Australian Ethical Investment	55.6
HUB24	47.4
Downer EDI	46.5
GenusPlus	44.0
Pinnacle Investment	42.9
Macmahon	42.9
QBE Insurance	40.3
Netwealth	37.5
Northern Star Resources	37.5
Pro Medicus	37.5
Technology One	35.9
REA Group	31.2
WiseTech Global	31.1
Objective Corp.	29.4
Codan	26.7
Bisalloy Steel	25.6
Southern Cross Electrical	25.0
Supply Network	25.0
Monadelphous	24.1
Aristocrat Leisure	21.9
Harvey Norman	20.5
Brambles Industries	19.7
Smartgroup	19.0
Fiducian	18.6
Ricegrowers	18.2
Premier Investments	16.7
Cedar Woods Properties	16.0
GR Engineering	15.8
XRF Scientific	15.4
Suncorp	15.4
AUB Group	15.2
Insurance Australia	14.8
Iluka Resources	14.3
Steadfast	14.0
CSL	13.8
Computershare	13.4
Mader	12.8
Breville	12.1
Servcorp	12.0
Data#3	10.2
CAR Group	9.6
Origin Energy	9.1
Universal Store	8.5
Medibank Private	8.4
Reliance Worldwide	7.7
Ridley Corp.	7.7
ASX	7.4
Helia	6.9
NRW Holdings	6.5
Westpac Banking	6.3
Duratec	6.3
JB Hi-Fi	5.4
Cochlear	4.9
Commonwealth Bank	4.3
IPH	4.3
Wesfarmers	4.0
GWA	3.3
Macquarie Group	1.6
Coles	1.5
Beacon Lighting	1.3
National Australia Bank	1.2
Shaver Shop	1.0
Amotiv	0.0
ARB	0.0
Clinuvel Pharmaceuticals	0.0
Hansen Technologies	0.0
Horizon Oil	0.0
Ive Group	0.0
Jumbo Interactive	0.0
NIB Holdings	0.0
Schaffer	0.0
Perpetual	−2.5
Rio Tinto	−3.2
Super Retail	−4.3
Collins Foods	−7.1
Nick Scali	−7.4
Metcash	−7.7
Cosol	−9.3
Lovisa	−11.5
Nine Entertainment	−11.8
Adairs	−12.5
Magellan Financial	−19.7
AGL Energy	−21.3
BHP	−22.1
Lindsay Australia	−22.4
New Hope	−23.5
Capral	−27.3
Fortescue	−44.2
Accent Group	−46.2
Monash IVF	−48.0
Lycopodium	−54.5
IDP Education	−58.8
PWR Holdings	−71.4

Table P

Five-year share price return

The five-year share price return is a single percentage figure that shows how much an investor has earned from a stock over the five years to September 2025. It includes both the change in the share price and all dividends received, and expresses the result as a compounded annual rate of return.

	% p.a.
Pro Medicus	63.9
Mader	59.3
Supply Network	52.0
XRF Scientific	49.5
Horizon Oil	46.0
Bisalloy Steel	43.5
HUB24	43.5
Lovisa	43.4
New Hope	43.1
Helia	40.8
GR Engineering	40.3
GenusPlus	39.9
Technology One	38.8
Southern Cross Electrical	38.4
Ridley Corp.	36.2
Ive Group	35.1
Pinnacle Investment	32.3
Lycopodium	28.2
Capral	27.9
WiseTech Global	27.9
Servcorp	27.1
Nick Scali	26.6
Computershare	26.5
Beacon Lighting	26.4
Ricegrowers	26.0
Duratec	25.7
Codan	24.9
National Australia Bank	23.8
Commonwealth Bank	23.2
Origin Energy	22.2
Suncorp	22.1
JB Hi-Fi	21.6
Brambles Industries	21.3
Westpac Banking	21.3
Lindsay Australia	20.8
Aristocrat Leisure	20.2
Fiducian	19.9
AUB Group	19.8
QBE Insurance	19.7
Shaver Shop	19.4
NRW Holdings	18.9
Netwealth	18.2
Medibank Private	17.7
Wesfarmers	17.4
REA Group	17.3
Universal Store	17.1
Monadelphous	17.0
CAR Group	16.7

Super Retail	16.4
Steadfast	15.9
Harvey Norman	15.5
Insurance Australia	15.4
Macquarie Group	14.9
Smartgroup	14.8
NIB Holdings	14.5
Downer EDI	13.3
Macmahon	13.3
Objective Corp.	12.7
Premier Investments	12.5
PWR Holdings	12.3
Metcash	11.8
Evolution Mining	11.6
BHP	11.2
Cedar Woods Properties	11.2
Ramelius Resources	11.0
Data#3	10.9
Fortescue	10.9
Rio Tinto	10.7
Northern Star Resources	10.6
ARB	10.5
Cochlear	10.5
Australian Ethical Investment	10.3
Hansen Technologies	10.3
Schaffer	10.2
Coles	9.7
Monash IVF	6.8
Nine Entertainment	6.0
GWA	5.2
Accent Group	4.6
Iluka Resources	4.6
Reliance Worldwide	4.6
Breville	3.8
Collins Foods	2.6
Amotiv	1.8
Cosol	1.0
Credit Corp	0.7
Jumbo Interactive	0.1
Adairs	−0.1
Beach Energy	−0.1
Perpetual	−1.7
IPH	−2.1
ASX	−2.9
CSL	−4.0
AGL Energy	−6.6
Clinuvel Pharmaceuticals	−10.5
IDP Education	−19.1
Magellan Financial	−22.1

Best-selling author Alan Hull presents the complete sharemarket solution for novices to experts. Whether you're managing your portfolio, trading tactically on the sharemarket or investing in blue chip shares, Alan Hull explains the ins and outs of investing and trading in easy-to-understand and engaging language.

Available in print and e-book formats

Printed and bound by CPI Group (UK) Ltd, Croydon, CR0 4YY

22/10/2025

14749192-0001